Growing up with Tok Pisin

Contact, creolization, and change in Papua New Guinea's national language

by

Geoff P Smith

2002
Battlebridge Publications

Published by: Battlebridge Publications,
37 Store Street, London WC1E 7QF, United Kingdom
(+44) (0)20 7278 1246
fax (+44) (0)20 7636 5550
<battlebridge@talk21.com>
<www.battlebridge.com>

Copyright: Geoff P Smith, January 2002
<gpssmith@hkusua.hku.hk>

All rights reserved.

ISBN 1 903292 06 9

All photographs on the cover and within this book were taken by Geoff P Smith and are his copyright. The front cover colour photographs (top to bottom) are from Madang, Morobe, and New Ireland, respectively.
The back cover colour photographs (top to bottom) are respectively from Madang, Daru, and West New Britain.

All the maps in this book were designed by Ken Burrage.

Cover design by Philip Baker and Jeehoon Kim.

Printed by Hobbs the Printers Ltd, Brunel Road, Totton, Hampshire, SO40 3WX, UK.

Contents

Acknowledgements — vi
    Photographs: *Canoes at Aramot* and *Papuan hornbill* — viii
    Photographs: *Fishing* and *A wallaby for dinner* — ix
    Photograph: *Play continues despite stormy weather* — x
    Photographs: *Portraits of four Papua New Guineans* — xi

Prologue — 1

1 **Pidgins, Creoles, and Tok Pisin** — 3
  1.1 The rise of Pidgin and Creole studies — 3
  1.2 Studies of Melanesian Pidgin and Tok Pisin — 4
  1.3 The Papua New Guinea language scene — 7
    1.3.1 Languages of Melanesia — 7
      Map 1 *The Southwest Pacific* — 7
      Map 2 *Austronesian and Papuan languages of Papua New Guinea* — 9
    1.3.2 Language contact and change in Papua New Guinea — 9
      Map 3 *Papua New Guinea* — 10
      Language contact in traditional Melanesian society — 10
      Mission lingua francas — 11
      Map 4 *Mission lingua francas in Papua New Guinea* — 11
      Colonial languages — 12
      Map 5 *Papua New Guinea - colonial history* — 12
  1.4 The origins of Tok Pisin — 12
    1.4.1 Early contact languages in the Pacific — 13
    1.4.2 Melanesian Pidgin English — 14
      Map 6 *Melanesian Pidgins and related varieties* — 15
  1.5 Development within Papua New Guinea — 17
    1.5.1 Establishment as a lingua franca — 17
    1.5.2 The sources of the lexicon — 17
      English as the major lexifier language — 17
      German influence — 18
      Languages of New Britain and New Ireland — 18
      The influence of other languages — 19
    1.5.3 Stabilization and expansion — 19
    1.5.4 Creolization — 19
    1.5.5 Variation — 20
    1.5.6 The influence of language policy and planning — 21
  1.6 The current linguistic situation in Papua New Guinea — 21
  1.7 The aims of the present research — 22

2 **Research design and procedure** — 23
  2.1 Theoretical orientation — 23
  2.2 Research design and procedure — 28
    2.2.1 Aims of the present research — 28
    2.2.2 Location and selection of informants — 29
      Map 7 *Papua New Guinea - Location of informants* — 30
      The Momase region — 31
      Photograph: *Wampit schoolchildren* — 32
      The Highlands region — 32
      Photograph: *Camp fire at Enga* — 33
      The Islands region — 34
      Photograph: *Kokopo schoolchildren* — 34
    2.2.3 Elicitation and recording of data — 35

	2.3 Data analysis	37
	2.3.1 Transcription	37
	2.3.2 Organizing the corpus	39
	The major corpus	39
	Regional sub-corpora	39
	2.3.3 Computer assisted analysis	40
3	**Phonology**	43
	3.1 The phoneme inventory	43
	3.2 Phonological variants in the lexicon	48
	3.3 Prosodic and suprasegmental features	53
	3.4 Phonological reduction	54
	3.5 Regional variation	56
4	**Morphology**	59
	4.1 The transitive marker *-im*	59
	4.2 The adjectival *-pela* suffix	62
	4.3 Plural marking on nouns	65
	4.3.1 The pluralizing particle *ol*	65
	4.3.2 The pluralizing suffix *-s*	71
	4.4 The pronoun system	76
	4.4.1 The standard pronoun paradigm	76
	4.4.2 Number distinctions: dual, trial, paucal and plural	76
	Dual pronouns	76
	Trial pronouns	80
	Plural pronouns	81
	4.4.3 The inclusive/exclusive distinction	81
	4.4.4 *Em* and *en*	82
	4.4.5 Other pronoun forms	83
	4.5 Cliticization	84
	4.6 Other suffixes	87
	4.6.1 The *-ing* suffix	87
	4.6.2 The *-ed* suffix	89
	4.6.3 Phrasal elements in verbs	90
5	**Lexicon**	93
	5.1 Identifying new lexis	93
	5.2 Established new words	95
	5.3 Borrowed items of lower frequency	98
	5.4 Regional variation in word frequency	100
	5.5 Semantic changes	103
	5.6 New words formed by internal productive processes	105
	5.6.1 Compounding, multifunctionality and reduplication	105
	5.6.2 Idiomatic language	109
	Photograph: *Masta mak at work*	109
	Photograph: *Watching the Mendi show for free* (I)	113
6	**Syntax**	115
	6.1. Word order	115
	6.2 The particle *i*	115
	6.2.1 Separation of subject and predicate	117
	6.2.2 Collocations of *i* with other words	119
	6.2.3 Use of *i* with post-verbal aspect markers	122
	6.2.4 The role of *i* in discourse	123
	6.3 The verb phrase: marking tense, mood and aspect	124
	6.3.1 The scope of tense, mood and aspect (TMA)	124
	6.3.2 The particle *bai*	125
	6.3.3 The particle *laik*	128
	6.3.4 *Bin* - past time reference	129

Chapter 6 continued

6.3.5 *Pinis* - completed action	130
6.3.6 More aspect distinctions: *save, wok long (i) stap, (i) go and (i) kam*	132
Save	132
Wok long	133
Stap	134
The particles *(i) go* and *(i) kam*	134
6.3.7 Modal particles	135
Mas	136
Ken and *inap*	137
6.3.8 Other TMA markers	137
Kirap	138
Bek	139
6.3.9 TMA particles in combination	140
6.4 Verb serialization	142
6.5 The noun phrase	147
6.6 Relativization	150
6.6.1 Standard relativizing structures	150
6.6.2 Relative pronouns: *husat* and *we*	150
Husat	151
We	153
6.6.3 The particle *ia* in relative clause delimitation	154
6.6.4 The use of *longen/long em* in relativization	156
6.7 Complementation	158
6.7.1 *Olsem*	158
6.7.2 *Se*	159
6.7.3 *We*	161
6.7.4 Other complementizers	161
6.8 Focus and topicalization	161
6.8.1 Existing studies of focus and topicalization in Tok Pisin	162
6.8.2 Word order	163
6.8.3 Wh- question forms	163
6.8.4 The role of *em*	166
6.8.5 The particle *yet*	167
6.8.6 Other focusing devices	171
7 Discourse Processes	**173**
7.1 Cohesion	174
7.1.1 Reference	174
Personal deixis: pronominal reference	174
Possessive pronouns	177
Demonstrative pronouns	177
Anaphoric reference with *ia*	178
Spatial deixis	179
Temporal deixis	179
7.1.2 Substitution and ellipsis	181
Substitution	181
Ellipsis	182
7.1.3 Lexical cohesion	183
7.1.4 Conjunction	185
Additive conjunctions	186
Adversative relations	187
Causative relations	188
Other conjunctions: *Nogat* and *Yes*	188
7.2 Maintaining coherence in spoken discourse	190
7.2.1 Beginning a narrative	191
7.2.2 Temporal sequence	192
7.2.3 Reporting speech	195

8	**Discussion of findings**	199
	8.1 Superstrate, substrate and universals	199
	8.1.1 Superstrate influence	199
	8.1.2 Substrate influences on Tok Pisin	199
	8.1.3 Evidence for universals in Tok Pisin's development	201
	8.2 The relationship between Tok Pisin and English	202
	8.2.1 Borrowing and code-switching	202
	Where Tok Pisin begins and ends	202
	Matrix and embedded languages	204
	Language mixing	205
	8.2.2 The post-Creole continuum	209
	8.3 Conclusion and recommendations	211
	8.3.1 Uniformity and variation	211
	Factors promoting uniformity	211
	Factors promoting variation	212
	8.3.2 Suggestions for further research	213
	Photographs: *Dancers at Manus* and *Saveman placing a marila*	216
Appendix - Samples of speech from different regions		217
	1. Momase	217
	2. Highlands	218
	3. Islands	220
	Photographs: *Tubuans* (ancestor figures)	222
References		223
	Photographs: *Watching the Mendi show for free* (II) and *Mount Hagen show*	237
	Photographs: *Participants at a singsing*	238
Index		239
	Photographs: *Faces of singsing participants* and *Tree dancers*	244

Acknowledgements

From the time I arrived in PNG in the early 1970s, I was continually fascinated by the vitality of Tok Pisin and how it was used by its speakers. Not convinced by some of the more uninformed opinions about the language still held by many expatriates, I was fortunate to come across works by Mihalic and Mühlhäusler, which gave the impetus for more serious study. During the 22 years I lived and worked in the country I gradually became aware of some of the more subtle aspects of the language in use, and this book represents the fruits of the insights into Tok Pisin gained during those years.

My thanks for assistance with various aspects of this project go to a number of people, foremost among whom are the citizens of Papua New Guinea whose language is being described here. I am most grateful for the cheerful assistance of the young informants who provided speech samples, and teachers and administrators in various provinces who facilitated the research in one way or another. Among these I am particularly grateful for the assistance of James Pokris, Rose Bolgy, Jack Fenton, Br. Bernard Cooper, and Maran Nataleo. For help with the daunting task of transcribing taped material, as well as introducing me to young informants in Goroka, I am indebted to Jill Kaack, formerly a secretary in the Department of Language and Communication Studies.

At the Papua New Guinea University of Technology ("Unitech"), I was encouraged by a number of people to embark on a PhD programme, and the thesis based on speech samples from this project was completed in 1999.

I greatly appreciate the material assistance given by the Research Committee of Unitech between 1988 and 1993. The grants provided enabled me to travel to inaccessible parts of the country in search of data, which would otherwise not have been possible.

I am also grateful to Kevin Ford of the University of Papua New Guinea, who agreed to act as Principal Supervisor at short notice, thus allowing my candidacy to continue. Andrew Taylor was a local supervisor in Hong Kong during the latter part of the writing process, and made many helpful comments on earlier drafts.

I also benefited greatly from discussion of various areas related to this work with Jim Moody, Steve Matthews, Justin Kehatsin, Malcolm Ross, John Lynch, Jill Tuno, Patricia Iha, Ana Kila, Shem Yarupawa, John Hamau and Suzanne Holzknecht. Jeff Siegel was particularly helpful and encouraging in reading earlier drafts and commenting on issues related to this research. Thesis examiners Terry Crowley and Suzanne Romaine also provided very detailed feedback on various aspects of the work for which I am grateful.

For the design of all the maps which appear in this book, I am indebted to Ken Burrage of the National Mapping Bureau.

I would also like to place on record my thanks to my family for their forbearance during the long and time-consuming process of conducting and writing up this research, and of revising this for publication.

Finally, I greatly appreciate the help of Philip Baker, Jeehoon Kim, and John Ladhams in preparing the text and illustrations for publication.

Canoes at Aramot, Siassi Islands (Morobe)

Kokomo
The Papuan hornbill (*Aceros plicatus*)

Coastal fishing scene

A wallaby for dinner (Pahoturi River, Western Province)

Play continues despite stormy weather at Aramot
in the Siassi Islands (Morobe)

Portraits of four Papua New Guineans
Above left: Girl from Popondetta, Oro. Above right: Man from Buang, near Lae, Morobe.
Below left: Young man from East Sepik.   Below right: Young woman from Mendi,
Southern Highlands.

Prologue

Mi laik stori long taim mi liklik yet na mi bin statim Tok Pisin. Papa bin stap long bus, em bin tich lo bus na mi bin gro lo bus. Mi bin liklik yet, long eich long abaut faif, na mi bin statim Tok Pisin. Papa wantem mama save tok ples, tasol mipla no sawe kechim tok ples blo ol, mipla sa Tok Pisin tasol, i kam i kam, mi bikpla. Nau mi stil mi sawe long harim tok ples, tasol mi no sawe tok - osem tok ples long bekim disla tok ples. Mi sawe harim tasol inap mi bikpla. Seim osem lo ogeta femli blo mipla, taim ol bin stap liklik, go bikpla mipla ogeta save tokple... - Tok Pisin. Nogat wanpla save tok ples, long - papa wantem mama, tupla sawe tok ples na mipla ogeta femili, mipla save tok pisin tasol. So Tok Pisin em osem fes lenggwidj blo mipla, lo mipla ol femili.

I'd like to tell you about the time I was still small and I started (to speak) Tok Pisin. Dad lived in the bush, he taught in the bush and I grew up in the bush. I was still small, at the age of about five, when I started to speak Tok Pisin. My father and mother knew the local language, but we couldn't catch their language, we only learned Tok Pisin right up to the time we were big. Now I still can understand the local language but I don't know how to talk - don't know the language to reply. I could merely hear it right up to the time I was big. It's like that with all my family, from the time they were small until they were big we all (just) knew Tok Pisin. No one of us knows the local language. Our parents know the local language and all the family only speak Tok Pisin. So Tok Pisin is like the first language of our family.

Peter, aged 16, from Vanimo, West Sepik Province

Peter's story is typical of an increasing number of young people growing up in Papua New Guinea today, not only in the urban centres, but throughout those areas of the country where Tok Pisin is widely used as a lingua franca to communicate across linguistic boundaries. The form of his language is also revealing of some of the changes taking place in it: a fluency, speed and confidence typical of first language speakers, phonological streamlining and lexical and semantic innovation, including extensive borrowing from English.

In the following chapters, the characteristics of the first language speech of a sample of young people in Papua New Guinea in the late 1980s and early 1990s will be documented. Young people aged from about 10 to late adolescence who spoke Tok Pisin as a first language were sought out in remote corners of the country when the opportunity for travel presented itself. Their recorded stories not only provided a linguistic data base from a wide range of geographical locations, but gave a unique glimpse of contemporary life in Papua New Guinea as seen through young people's eyes. It is hoped that the profile of first language speech described here will provide insights into some current areas of linguistic interest, such as the development and nativization of Pidgin languages and language contact scenarios. The data may also be of interest to linguists, language planners and others concerned with the implementation of language and education policy in Papua New Guinea.

1

Pidgins, Creoles, and Tok Pisin

This book is concerned with Tok Pisin, the variety of Melanesian Pidgin English spoken in Papua New Guinea. To understand what is happening to Tok Pisin, it is necessary to look at Pidgin and Creole languages in general, and this chapter begins with a brief account of how interest in these languages has grown over the last few decades and how the area of study has become increasingly significant for mainstream linguistics (§ 1.1). Then a brief account of the work of major investigators in the field of Melanesian Pidgin English and Tok Pisin is given (§ 1.2), before taking a more detailed look at the origin and development of the language (§ 1.3 - § 1.6). The aims and scope of the present study are then outlined in terms of gaps in our current knowledge (§ 1.7).

1.1 The rise of Pidgin and Creole studies

For many years, the study of Pidgin and Creole languages was widely regarded as marginal, esoteric or even frivolous, but recently there has been great interest in these languages as legitimate areas of study. The number of publications dealing with studies of individual Pidgins and Creoles has increased dramatically since the 1960s, and several books devoted to the whole field of Pidgin and Creole linguistics have been published.[1] The *Carrier Pidgin* newsletter was launched in the early 70s and the specialized *Journal of Pidgin and Creole Studies* began publication in 1986. There are also newsletters and journals serving this field in French, Portuguese and Spanish. More recently *CreoLIST*, an e-mail forum for debate and exchange of information, was established.[2]

A Pidgin can be roughly defined as a language which develops to meet a specific communication need among groups of people who lack a common language. It is not normally the native language of its speakers, and is not mutually intelligible with any of the languages from which it derives (Thomason & Kaufman 1988:167). Although it may arise partly as a result of the simplification of existing languages, and it may have a fairly basic grammar and restricted lexicon, it is not merely the product of ad hoc simplification, and it is subject to conventional rules like any other language. Many different Pidgins, arising in trading or other contact situations and used in a restricted range of contexts, have been reported from around the world. Some examples from widely separated areas and language groups are Russenorsk from the Russia-Norway border, Chinook Jargon of the American Pacific Northwest, and West African Pidgin English.

A Pidgin may remain a marginal second language for a considerable time, but in certain circumstances, usually involving major social upheaval, it may become the native language of a new generation of speakers. The language which develops in this way is often referred to as a Creole. Creoles, roughly defined as the descendants of Pidgins which have become nativized, are now well established in many areas, notably the Caribbean, West Africa and the Pacific. It should be noted that the definition of Pidgin and Creole languages is by no means universally agreed, and some of the problems of definition will be discussed in the appropriate sections below.

Pidgins and Creoles have not merely been studied for their own sake. Research has also been motivated by an increasing realization that they represent phenomena which have a crucial bearing on many current linguistic issues. The relevance of pidginization and creolization to such concerns as language contact and change, historical linguistics, language learning, first and second language acquisition, psycholinguistics and language universals is now generally acknowledged.

Atlantic Creoles, defined as those spoken in the Caribbean and West African coastal regions, have received the most attention, and many in-depth studies of these languages have appeared.[3] Parallel with these studies, there has been considerable refinement of the theoretical issues in

---

[1] These include Arends, Muysken & Smith 1995, Holm 1988, 1989a, Hymes 1971, Mühlhäusler 1986b, Romaine 1988a, Todd 1984, 1990, Valdman 1977.

[2] Visit <www.ling@su.se/Creole/> for details.

[3] A small sample of a burgeoning body of descriptive work includes Cassidy (1971), DeGraff (1993), Robertson (1990), Spears (1990) Valdman (1991), and Winford (1993).

Pidgin and Creole linguistics.[4] Prominent among the issues discussed have been questions of origins, especially the role of African languages in the formation of New World contact varieties.

A number of interesting accounts of Indian Ocean Creoles such as those of Mauritius and Réunion have also been produced, for example, Baker & Corne (1986). Of particular interest are accounts of Pidgins and Creoles which have not been based on European languages, including those of central and southern Africa (Mufwene 1990b), the north-west Pacific coast (Thomason 1983) and an improbable Pidgin based on Basque and Amerindian languages (Bakker 1989). Pidgins in the Pacific with languages other than English as the lexifier are discussed in a later section. In the northern Pacific, Bickerton's research on Hawaiian Creole led to the formation of the controversial Bioprogram Hypothesis (Bickerton 1981).

1.2 Studies of Melanesian Pidgin and Tok Pisin

In the southwest Pacific, several varieties of Melanesian Pidgin English have developed. This study deals with the variety which is now widely spoken in the independent nation of Papua New Guinea. It is often referred to simply as Pidgin or New Guinea Pidgin, and although the name Neo-Melanesian was promoted by a small number of European observers, today it is usually referred to as Tok Pisin, the name adopted by the majority of its speakers. Tok Pisin has caught the attention of outside observers for several decades, but many early references were mainly concerned with the humorous effect of what was perceived as a quaint, curious or plain stupid way of speaking English. Much of the credit for establishing the study of Pidgin languages as a respectable area of linguistics goes to the American linguist Robert A Hall, whose seminal *Hands off Pidgin English!* (1955) argued passionately for a reversal of the current attitudes of ridicule and hostility towards Melanesian Pidgin English. Since then, Tok Pisin has become one of the world's best documented Pidgin languages, having attracted the attention of many eminent linguists over the past 40 years or so. Publications dealing with origins, linguistic description and pedagogy have multiplied, and a brief review of some of the major work on Tok Pisin is presented in the following paragraphs. Details cannot be given here of every relevant work, but a comprehensive account of the history of the study of Tok Pisin up to 1984 can be found in Mühlhäusler (1985c).

The question of the origin of Tok Pisin from English-based jargons of the Pacific has been the subject of some detailed historical analyses. Mühlhäusler (1976) first proposed the 19th century origin of the language from plantation Pidgins of the central Pacific. Further work by Clark (1979) filled in many of the details of early forms of Pidgin English in the Pacific during this period. Refinements by later scholars have helped to clarify the picture.[5] However, there is still considerable disagreement, particularly about the precise date of the crystallization of Tok Pisin as a distinct language. The main opposing views are represented by Mühlhäusler, who considers that Tok Pisin's principal features arose around the late 1880s in New Guinea, and Keesing, who considered that many of these developments took place much earlier in the Central Pacific. Mosel's work (1979, 1980) relates to the influence of Tolai on Tok Pisin after the return of labourers from the Central Pacific to New Britain and New Guinea. The influence of returning labourers from Queensland is discussed by Dutton (1980) and Dutton & Mühlhäusler (1984). Many details of these processes are still incomplete, and further historical research will no doubt shed more light on the origin of Melanesian Pidgins. However, due to the long time which has elapsed since their initial formation, and the nature of early contacts, much crucial information needed for a complete account necessarily remains inaccessible.

Much of the original linguistic description of Tok Pisin was carried out by mission personnel. In particular, Father Francis Mihalic of the Society of the Divine Word has devoted much of his life to producing material in Tok Pisin. He was the first to produce a detailed grammar and dictionary (1957), and the revised edition (1971) has remained the uncontested standard dictionary. Mihalic's standard also provided the basis for the style sheet of Word Publishing (Mihalic 1982). This is a national publishing company based in Port Moresby which is responsible for a wide variety of religious and secular material. The most notable publication is the Tok Pisin-language weekly *Wantok Niuspepa*, one of the few newspapers in the world to be published in a Pidgin language. Father Mihalic himself translated the Papua New Guinea constitution into Tok Pisin based on this standard (1986).

---

[4] For example, Byrne (1991), Hancock (1977), Holm (1992), Mufwene (1990a), Muysken (1995) and Singler (1990b).

[5] For example, Baker (1993) Crowley (1990a), Goulden (1990b), Keesing (1988), Ross (1992), Siegel (1987a, b), Troy (1990, 1994) and Walsh (1978).

The Bible Society's work in translating the bible into Tok Pisin has also provided many insights into the language. The New Testament translation remains a valuable source of Tok Pisin written material and has become a standard of its own (Bible Society 1966, Verhaar 1996). In spite of early work around Rabaul on the Gazelle Peninsula of East New Britain, both the Word Publishing and New Testament standards are based on the language spoken around the Madang area of north-east New Guinea, but the extent to which this is acceptable in other regions has not been fully explored. The Summer Institute of Linguistics (SIL) has also contributed a good deal to our knowledge of Tok Pisin. SIL started work in Papua New Guinea in 1957, and has had teams working in over 100 languages, producing religious and vernacular literacy material in addition to linguistic descriptive works (Siegel 1996). Several important publications on Tok Pisin have appeared.[6]

A number of courses and commentaries appeared in the 60s and early 70s. Pedagogic material by Murphy was produced as early as 1943, although the best-known revision is dated 1966. Several other courses followed,[7] while Bell (1971) discusses the role of Tok Pisin in the armed forces. Salisbury (1967) argues for more acceptance of Tok Pisin as a legitimate language, while Wolfers (1971) provides further remarks about the status of the language during the 1960s.

Work on Tok Pisin by a number of linguists based at the Australian National University (ANU) began in the 1960s and is still continuing. Wurm's enormous contribution to our knowledge of the linguistic scene in Papua New Guinea included a course based on the Highlands variety of Tok Pisin (1971) and numerous co-authored articles and edited works. The last part of his monumental three-volume work *New Guinea Area Languages and Language Study* (1977) is devoted to socio-cultural aspects of language use, and contains much useful material on Tok Pisin. Laycock (1970) produced a course along similar lines to Wurm's Highlands Pidgin course, but featuring the 'coastal and lowlands' variety, based on the Sepik and Madang regions. He also produced several commentaries on various aspects of language description and planning (1979, 1982, 1985). Dutton's *Conversational New Guinea Pidgin* (1973), accompanied by tapes containing teaching drills and exercises, was a landmark in the production of stimulating instructional materials, and greatly facilitated the provision of Tok Pisin courses to expatriate workers in Papua New Guinea. It was later revised as Dutton & Thomas (1985).

The scholar who has probably made the greatest contribution to our knowledge of Tok Pisin is Mühlhäusler, whose doctoral thesis was presented at ANU in 1976. This material was the basis for the major work *Growth and Structure of the Lexicon of New Guinea Pidgin* (1979), a comprehensive account of the sources of lexical items in Tok Pisin and word formation processes. Since then, he has produced dozens of works dealing with various aspects of Tok Pisin's origin, use and linguistic properties, many of which are referred to in this book. Mühlhäusler's painstaking research of historical sources, including German language material, has filled in many details of the early development of the language. Wurm & Mühlhäusler's important reference work *Handbook of Tok Pisin* (1985) firmly established Tok Pisin as one of the best known and most exhaustively researched Pidgin languages in the world.

Another linguist who has made a significant contribution to the study of Tok Pisin is Romaine, whose field work in Morobe and Madang provinces in the 1980s produced a sizeable corpus of transcriptions of the spoken language controlled for age, education, urban versus rural life style and other factors. The size of the corpus and the detailed quantitative treatment of various phonological and syntactic variables was particularly noteworthy. Several of Romaine's articles have made use of the data in the corpus, mostly summarized in *Language, Education and Development* (1992a). The successful marketing of this text has served to make Tok Pisin widely known to many readers whose primary area of study is not Pidgin and Creole languages.

A number of other linguists have dealt with various aspects of Tok Pisin. Aitchison used data from field work in Lae in a widely read text on language change (1981). Holm's exhaustive review of Pidgin and Creole languages (1988, 1989) is supplemented by his own investigations of the Tok Pisin of Southern Highlands (Holm & Kepiou 1993), while Chowning's field work in West New Britain, although primarily anthropological, has provided many unique insights into the language (1983, 1986). Woolford's descriptions of Tok Pisin grammar (1979a, b; 1981) were also based on extensive field work. Long acquaintance with the country and language have led to illuminating

---

[6] Conrad (1990), Franklin (1975, 1980, 1990), Hooley (1962), Litteral (1969, 1975) and McElhanon (1975, 1978) are particularly worthy of mention.

[7] For example, those by Litteral (1969), Sadler (1973), Scorza & Franklin (1989) and Steinbauer (1969).

observations by a number of linguists.[8] Todd's extensive work at Leeds on Pidgins and Creoles is well known (1978, 1984, 1985, 1990), and one of the few accounts of cohesion in Tok Pisin appears in a dissertation in her department (Lomax, 1983). The present writer has written a number of articles on various aspects of the description, use and teaching of Tok Pisin.[9]

Some studies with a sociolinguistic perspective have involved Tok Pisin, notably those of Sankoff (summarized in Sankoff 1986), which have had considerable influence, especially in North America. Sankoff's work[10] has provided a major stimulus to new theoretical perspectives on the language, especially with respect to creolization and grammaticalization. Sankoff's themes have been taken up by such well-known figures in the field as Hymes (1971) and Labov (1990), and further analysis of some of her data was carried out by Smeall (1975). A sociolinguistic study which includes a detailed consideration of code-switching between Tok Pisin and the Sepik language Gapun is described in Kulick (1992) and Kulick & Stroud (1990). A monumental two-volume collection of PNG folktales in Tok Pisin has been published by Slone (2001). This collection comprises over 1000 stories from all provinces of the country which originally appeared in a regular column in *Wantok Niuspepa*.

While not directly on the subject of Tok Pisin, some recent work on other languages has considerable relevance. In particular, detailed studies of sister dialects of Melanesian Pidgin have provided useful parallels to the development of Tok Pisin. These include work on Solomons Pijin by Jourdan, on Bislama by Crowley and Tryon, and on Torres Strait Broken by Shnukal.[11]

As the earlier negative attitudes towards Tok Pisin gave way to a more serious appreciation of the language, more attention was paid to a possible role in education and national development. Early statements on language policy and planning issues include those by Olewale (1977) on Tok Pisin in education and McDonald (1976) on Tok Pisin and national development. Swan & Lewis (1987, 1990) discuss the use of Tok Pisin in tertiary institutions, while an overview of language planning issues appears in Kale (1990). Siegel has contributed much useful discussion of Tok Pisin's use in the media and role in education as well as a stimulating discussion of more general theoretical issues.[12] Other writers have looked at the relationship between Tok Pisin and emerging varieties of English.[13]

The issue of identifying Tok Pisin vocabulary and distinguishing it from items borrowed from English was taken up by Healey (1975). Vocabulary development was also considered by Bálint (1969, 1973), although the adequacy of the resulting work has been seriously questioned (Mühlhäusler 1985f:647). Others who have tackled practical issues of language development include those authors who have produced written material in Tok Pisin involving the use of new terminology, such as Bergmann (1982), the Bible Society (1966) and Mihalic (1977, 1982, 1986).

One encouraging aspect of the study of Tok Pisin has been the contribution in recent years of Papua New Guinean linguists who speak the language themselves and are familiar with its socio-cultural setting. Dicks Thomas in particular has been active in promoting the teaching of the language (1990a). He is currently working on a monolingual dictionary and successfully completed the first Masters' thesis to be written in Tok Pisin (1996). Other articles that have been produced include Ahai (1987, 1989), Nekitel (1984, 1990, 1994) and Sumbuk (1987, 1993).

Tok Pisin is somewhat unusual among the Pidgins of the world in its gradual development over several generations as a second language before any extensive creolization took place. This is a major difference from some other Pidgins, such as Hawaiian Pidgin English, whose allegedly abrupt transition to a Creole followed a relatively short period of use as a Pidgin. The question thus arises as to how far Tok Pisin is relevant to the general discussion of issues in Pidgin and Creole linguistics, such as the role of universals in creolization. Bickerton (1981) has specifically excluded Tok Pisin from the debate by redefining Creoles as arising from Pidgins which exist for no more than a single generation. However, as Mühlhäusler (1990c) has pointed out, use as a

---

[8] For example, Bee (1971), Brash (1971, 1975), Faraclas (1989, 1990), Lynch (1975a, b; 1979a, b; 1990, 1993), Reesink (1990), and Verhaar (1991a, b, c; 1996).

[9] For example, G Smith 1986a, b; 1987, 1988, 1989, 1990a, b; 1991, 1994a, b; 1995a, b; 1997; 1998a, b; G Smith & Matthews 1996.

[10] Sankoff 1968, 1976, 1977a, b, c; 1984, 1991, 1993, 1994; Sankoff & Brown 1976; Sankoff & Laberge 1973; Sankoff & Mazzie 1991.

[11] See, for example, Jourdan 1985a, b; 1989, 1990; Crowley 1989b, c; 1990 a, b, c; 1991; Tryon 1987, 1991, Shnukal 1988, 1991.

[12] On Tok Pisin in the media and education see Siegel 1981, 1983, 1985a, b; 1992a, 1993, 1996; and on general theoretical issues Siegel 1990, 1997a, b, c, d; 1998, 1999.

[13] For example, Barron (1986), A-M Smith (1978, 1984, 1987, 1988) and Yarupawa (1986).

second language does not mean that universal tendencies are no longer in operation. In a situation where such a varied array of languages is spoken, there may still be universals involved in the making of certain choices rather than others (Aitchison 1989).

As Mühlhäusler also notes (1990c), Tok Pisin has a number of advantages as a source of data informing the debate, as it is one of the best documented contact languages. Nevertheless, one should beware of over-generalization of what may be unique features to Pidgin and Creole languages in general.

1.3 The Papua New Guinea language scene

This section gives some linguistic background to the development of Tok Pisin in Papua New Guinea. A brief account of the number and types of indigenous languages in Melanesia is first given. Traditional strategies to deal with communication difficulties caused by the extreme multilingualism in the area are then described, and the effects of intrusive languages of wider communication, such as those of colonial powers or evangelizing missions, are reviewed.

1.3.1 Languages of Melanesia

This overview of language in Melanesia refers extensively to G Smith (1995a) and Polinsky & G Smith (1996). Melanesia is an area in the south-west Pacific, so named because early European explorers to the region were impressed by the dark skins of the inhabitants. Since the definition of Melanesia is based on fundamentally racial criteria, its boundaries are somewhat arbitrary, but it is generally considered to include the independent states of Papua New Guinea, Solomon Islands and Vanuatu; the Indonesian province of Irian Jaya; and the French overseas territory of New Caledonia (see Map 1).

Map 1

The Southwest Pacific

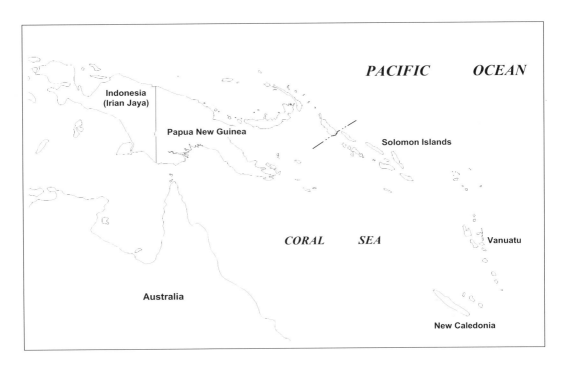

Although Fijians are 'Melanesian' in appearance, Fiji is culturally more similar to the Polynesian societies to the east. Some Torres Strait Islanders appear to be Melanesian physically, and have linguistic and cultural affinities with Papuan groups to the north, but as Australians, their political history has been somewhat different, and they may not share that perception themselves. Further west in Southeast Asia, what might be called a Melanesian component can be found in the ethnically diverse population.

The table below shows the population and approximate number of languages in the major Melanesian areas, according to the latest estimates from a number of sources (e.g. *ITN* 1990).

Melanesian languages and populations (approximate)

Country/Territory	Population	Languages	Average number of speakers
Papua New Guinea	3,800,000	862	4500
Solomon Islands	300,000	86	3500
Vanuatu	150,000	105	1500
Irian Jaya	1,500,000	250+	6000
New Caledonia	150,000	27	5500

The numbers are only approximate; exact figures are notoriously difficult to establish, as knowledge of many of the languages is still sketchy. Although Melanesia contains only about 0.1% of the world's population, approximately 20% of all the world's languages are spoken there. The latest estimate from the Summer Institute of Linguistics indicates a figure of 862 languages for Papua New Guinea alone <www.ethnologue.com>. This large number of languages spoken in such a restricted area is remarkable, and the reason for such diversity is not exactly known. Although it may popularly be thought that the rugged terrain is responsible for isolating small cultural groups, this cannot be the whole explanation, as the largest indigenous language community in Papua New Guinea, Enga, with approximately 160,000 speakers, occupies some of the most rugged terrain on earth. Geographical isolation may, however, be an important contributing factor, together with other factors such as a pride in and emphasis on cultural and linguistic differences, and word taboos, which may have led to the speciation of a large number of languages over the 30,000 or so years that human beings have been in Melanesia (Foley 1986). In addition to the factors mentioned above, some conditions favouring the formation of large linguistic units, such as centralized political control and writing systems, were not present in Melanesia (Laycock 1982).

The languages of Melanesia can be classified into two major divisions, Austronesian and non-Austronesian or Papuan. Austronesian languages of Melanesia are part of the huge group stretching from Madagascar in the west to Polynesia in the east and Taiwan in the north. It is thought that Austronesian speakers moved through the southwestern Pacific some 3,000 years ago, although the details of these migrations are still being debated by linguists, archaeologists and pre-historians (Bellwood et al. 1995).

What we can say with a good degree of certainty is that many of the Austronesian languages of the area have been in close contact with non-Austronesian languages for a very long time, and have been quite extensively influenced by them. As a result, many of them are rather untypical of Austronesian languages as a whole. Indeed, in the case of some languages such as Maisin of the north-eastern Papuan coast, it is difficult to say whether it is Austronesian or not, and it is sometimes described as a 'mixed language' (Capell 1969, Dutton 1994).

The late arrival of the Austronesian languages in Melanesia is reflected in their distribution. Most are spoken by groups living in coastal or island locations, although there has been a considerable penetration inland in north-east New Guinea (see Map 2). Further east, the Austronesian-speaking voyagers colonized uninhabited islands, and so the whole of Polynesia is an Austronesian-speaking area.

villages near the capital Port Moresby. Hiri Motu arose due to the adoption and use of a simplified Motu by the British colonial administration in Papua, especially the police, which gave it its earlier name 'Police Motu' (Dutton 1985). Thus, while Hiri Motu is a pidginized form of an indigenous language, it is not exactly an indigenous Pidgin. However, such Pidgins did exist in this area. The name 'Hiri Motu' arose from an erroneous belief that it was derived from languages used on trading expeditions known as *hiri* to the Eleman-speaking people of the Gulf of Papua. These have since been shown to have been based on languages of the Gulf region (Dutton & Kakare 1977). A more detailed description of the Pidgin languages used on *hiri* expeditions, an Eleman variety and a Koriki variety, appears in Dutton (1983a).

Other Pidgins based on indigenous languages have been described by Foley (1988) and Williams (1993). These are mainly accounts of simplified trading languages of the middle Sepik area centring on Yimas, where Foley has carried out intensive field work. There is some doubt about whether some of these languages would satisfy all the normal criteria for 'true' Pidgins, for example, that they are not mutually intelligible with any of the source languages, or that more than two languages were involved in their genesis (Thomason & Kaufman, 1988). It may be that they would be better considered as simplified trading registers involving some incorporation of lexis from the language of the trading partners. Nevertheless, these languages are of considerable interest as pidginized or simplified forms which are not based on European languages. They have some features not often encountered elsewhere, such as relatively complex morphologies, although still simplified compared with Yimas.

Other references to indigenous Pidgins include Harding's mention of a pidginized form of Siassi languages used on trading expeditions in the Huon Gulf between New Britain and the New Guinea mainland (1967). Unfortunately, no details of the language are given. The urban variety of Kiwai known as Daru Kiwai, described by Wurm (1973:235) has a considerably reduced morphology which suggests it has been simplified and possibly pidginized. Some pidginization may also have been involved in the use of vernaculars as languages of wider communication by missions, as described in the following section.

Mission lingua francas

Missionaries arrived in the area comprising what is now Papua New Guinea during the 19th century. A number of denominations were represented from a variety of countries. Since missions were intimately concerned with communicating with native people, the language adopted for such contact was important. Many missions made an effort to investigate the indigenous languages with a view to learning them for the purpose of evangelism (Renck 1977a, b). A number of local vernaculars such as Kiwai, Suau, Gogodala, Kuanua, Yabêm, Kâte, Dobu and Motu were adopted as languages of wider communication for evangelizing and other mission-related activities. The geographical areas over which they were so used cannot easily be established but their approximate locations are indicated on Map 4.

Map 4 - Mission lingua francas in Papua New Guinea

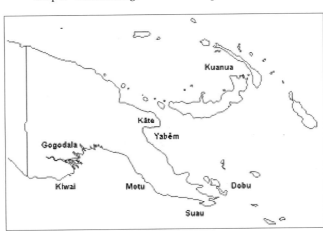

Although several mission lingua francas lasted for quite a long time, they were rather restricted in range. Some still have a useful role; for example, Kâte is still used in many parts of the Huon Peninsula in Morobe Province. Today, however, most of these languages appear to be in terminal decline as lingua francas, as English and Tok Pisin continue to expand into more domains of life.

Colonial languages

Like many other parts of the world, the southwest Pacific was involved in the European scramble for power and sovereignty over distant territories in the 19th century. The history of first colonial occupation is illustrated in Map 5.

Map 5 - Papua New Guinea - colonial history

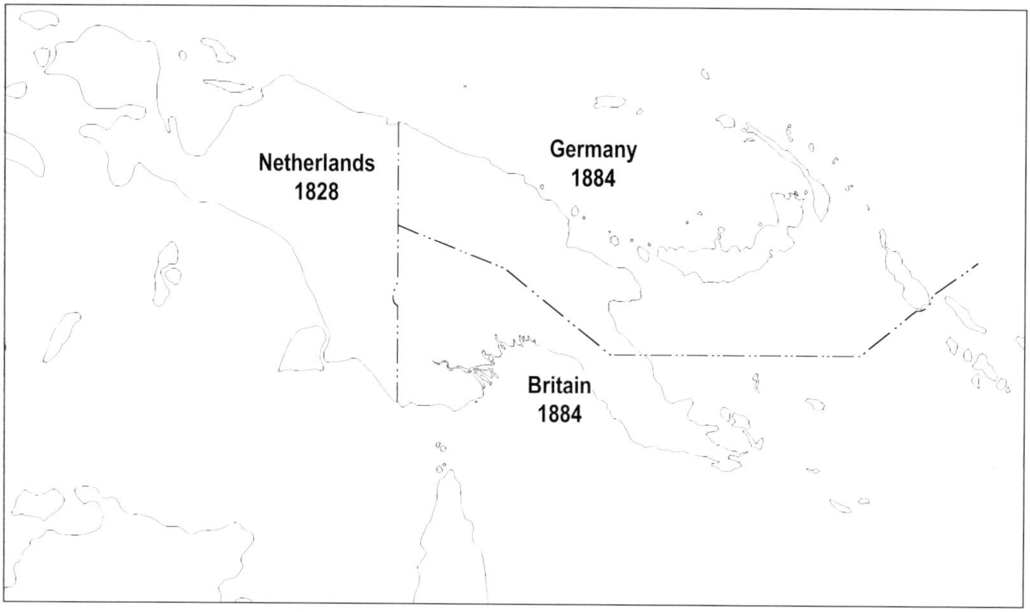

[Map showing: Netherlands 1828, Germany 1884, Britain 1884]

The western half of the island of New Guinea was colonized by the Dutch in 1828, while Britain and Germany occupied the remainder of the island and the Bismarck Archipelago in 1884. Britain occupied the southern half of the mainland, known as British New Guinea and later Papua. Germany took control of the northern half of the mainland and the islands of New Britain, New Ireland and Bougainville. The Solomon Islands eventually became a protectorate of Britain, long after the Spanish, who originally claimed the discovery of the fabled 'Isles of Solomon', failed to rediscover the location of their prize. Following the defeat of Germany in World War I, the whole of the eastern part of New Guinea and adjacent islands came under Australian administration in the second decade of the twentieth century, while Dutch New Guinea became the Indonesian province of Irian Jaya in 1963 after an 'act of free choice' by selected members of the resident population. The New Hebrides became a unique Anglo-French condominium under the joint administration of Britain and France, while in 1853, the French annexed New Caledonia, which remains a French overseas territory today. Thus English, French, German and Dutch and more recently Bahasa Indonesia came to be spoken in the region. Papua New Guinea became independent in 1975, the Solomon Islands in 1978 and Vanuatu in 1980. In addition to the languages of colonial powers, some of the Western New Guinea area came under limited influence from Malay (Seiler 1985) and there is also possible influence from some other languages in the region (Mühlhäusler 1985a).

1.4 The origins of Tok Pisin

This account of Tok Pisin's early development is not divided into discrete chronological periods, but broad developmental stages are reviewed. The emergence of a Pacific Pidgin English from early trading contacts is briefly traced and then developments within the Melanesian area are outlined.

1.4.1 Early contact languages in the Pacific

The appearance of the antecedents of Tok Pisin must be seen against this backdrop of extreme indigenous linguistic diversity and colonial expansion into the Pacific, together with the increased mobility of indigenous inhabitants. The need for a language of wider communication was clearly present and, with accelerating social and political changes, became more acute. The situation was thus one in which a language such as Tok Pisin could easily flourish. It was the movement of Melanesian labourers in the latter half of the 19th century which provided the stimulus for the formation of an English lexifier Pidgin on which later developments were based.

The question of the origin of Tok Pisin and other varieties of Melanesian Pidgin has generated considerable interest in recent years. Careful historical research in the past two decades, as well as evidence from the distribution of linguistic features in present-day Melanesian Pidgin varieties, has greatly increased our knowledge of Tok Pisin's roots. Since the main focus of this book is a synchronic study of contemporary Tok Pisin, a full discussion of the validity of the various historical reconstructions is not possible here. However, as has repeatedly been shown by Mühlhäusler (e.g. 1985e, 1986a) and others, synchronic forms are the product of diachronic forces, and the history of the language is of considerable relevance when attempting to explain why the present-day language is as it is. Thus, reference will sometimes be made to the historical origin of various lexical items or structural features, and a brief review of the origin and development of Tok Pisin is in order to provide the context for evaluating Tok Pisin's current status.[14] Some other accounts of various aspects of Tok Pisin whose focus is not primarily historical nevertheless include an overview of the history of Tok Pisin, for example Romaine (1992a).

The precise age of Tok Pisin is difficult to determine, and depends to some extent on the arbitrary delineation of this variety from a complex of English-based Pidgins which emerged in the context of the European exploration of the Pacific. Even the earliest contact languages of the Pacific may have had features of a generic maritime trading language carried over from earlier times. What we can say with certainty is that by far the greater part of Tok Pisin's history belongs to the last 150 years.

Nevertheless, the search for the origins of Tok Pisin has led further and further back in history. Items of vocabulary or grammar once seemingly pinned down to a definite origin have repeatedly been shown to have been attested in earlier periods (Baker 1993). This section begins with the search for the earliest widely used contact languages in the area which could have had an influence on the formation of Tok Pisin. The search inevitably leads to the maritime voyages of the early European explorers, whose quest for knowledge and economic advantage was spurred by advances in technology from the time of the Renaissance onwards.

One of the most significant technological advances of the Renaissance was the production of ships and navigation equipment which allowed Europeans for the first time to make extended voyages to distant shores. Early maritime traders discovered unprecedented trading opportunities, and the conditions favouring the establishment of a world-wide trading language were established. A contact language variety known as Lingua Franca had already emerged in the context of trade in the Mediterranean and the Near East as early as the 13th century. It has been suggested that relexification of Lingua Franca could have been significant in the formation of the first Portuguese-based Pidgins (Whinnom 1977b:4), and hence later contact jargons based on European languages. Whatever the status of this 'monogenesis' theory of Pidgin origins, varieties of European-based trading language spread out over the oceans from the 17th century onwards.

Among the early European powers, the Spanish and Portuguese were perhaps the most accomplished and energetic maritime explorers of exotic parts of the globe. Mendaña's exploration of the southwest Pacific in the 16th century, which led to the naming of the 'Isles of Solomon', was one of the earliest documented incursions into this area. Words from Portuguese and Spanish are also found in Tok Pisin. Such words as *pikinini* (Portuguese 'pequeno', small), *save* (Portuguese 'sabe', to know) came via English foreigner talk while *kalabus* (Spanish 'calabozo', prison) seems to have travelled via overseas French. Later expeditions in the late 18th century, including English, French and Dutch explorers, were led by such famous names as Cook, Bligh,

---

[14] Detailed historical accounts of early developments can be found in a number of sources, especially Baker (1993), Clark (1979), Crowley (1990a), Dutton (1980), Keesing (1988), Mühlhäusler (1978b), Siegel (1987a) and Troy (1990, 1994).

Bougainville, Huon, La Perouse, van Diemen and D'Entrecasteaux. These expeditions signified increasing competitive interest by European powers in establishing spheres of influence and trading opportunities in remote corners of the globe, and while the early expeditions themselves may have had little linguistic impact, they set the scene for the kind of intercultural contact where trade languages emerge.

European settlement in Australia began in the 1780s. Troy (1990, 1994) investigates language contact between Aboriginals and English-speaking immigrants in New South Wales from the start of European settlement, while Baker (1993) traces many of the features of Melanesian Pidgin English (MPE) to early contact varieties in Australia. The social circumstances surrounding the emergence of jargons and Pidgins in Australia were quite different from those in the Pacific, with European settlers and Aboriginal landowners co-existing on the same land and using the language for a much broader range of functions. It is also interesting to note that many of the well-known features of MPE, such as *-im* transitive marking and lexical items such as *gammon* 'lie, to deceive' were attested in New South Wales from the earliest periods of settlement (Baker 1993).

In the Pacific area, a number of commodities of economic importance motivated exploration from Australia and other parts of the world. Whaling vessels based in New South Wales visited the Pacific from the late 18th century, while the early decades of the 19th century saw successive interest in sandalwood and trepang or 'sea slugs', which were keenly sought to trade in the Far East (Crowley 1990a:51). The linguistic significance of these voyages was the need to establish contact and communication for the purposes of effective trade. A number of the trading vessels were engaged in extensive contact with trading partners, including extended periods on shore, while ship's crews were recruited from various parts of the Pacific. Thus, the conditions necessary for the development of a widespread common medium of communication in the Pacific were established.

The possibility of a world-wide maritime register or simplified trading language has already been mentioned. In spite of the multi-national nature of European trading in the Pacific, the use of predominantly English words as the basis of the contact languages was soon established (Siegel 1987a:35). In addition to this, there is evidence that explorers and traders adopted words and phrases from local languages for the purposes of trade (Crowley 1990a:56). The result was a highly variable language with elements of English and various languages of the South and Central Pacific. Details of such 'nautical jargon' can be found in Keesing (1988), and it is likely that this was the source of the jargons on which later developments were based.

Later, in the 19th century, from the 1860s onwards, plantations producing sugar, cotton and copra were established in various parts of the region. This had profound significance for language contact, as the establishment of these labour-intensive plantations stimulated large-scale movements of people to work there. Melanesians were mostly recruited for the cane fields of Queensland and plantations in Fiji and Samoa. Now Europeans for the first time lived and worked among native Melanesian populations for extensive periods, thereby creating the conditions favouring the stabilization of contact languages. It is thus on the trading vessels and in the plantation environment that the early forms of Pacific Pidgin English are likely to have emerged.

Different contact scenarios developed in different situations. Siegel's painstaking historical research (1987a) has shown that on the plantations of Fiji, a pidginized form of Fijian was the dominant language. In many other parts of the Pacific, on the other hand, English was the language from which contact varieties drew most of their initial lexicon.

1.4.2 Melanesian Pidgin English

Our understanding of the origin of a distinctly Melanesian variety of Pidgin English has become much clearer in the past few years with the appearance of several in-depth historical accounts. The delineation of an exact beginning of Melanesian Pidgin English from Pacific Pidgin English is somewhat arbitrary, as, by its nature, the latter was used across a wide geographical area. Language development in the Melanesian region has been traced by a number of notable studies of the three major varieties of Melanesian Pidgin English currently identified: Pijin in the Solomon Islands, Bislama in Vanuatu and Tok Pisin in Papua New Guinea, as well as varieties with connections to these languages in Queensland, Torres Strait and northern Australia (see Map 6).

Map 6

Melanesian Pidgins and related varieties

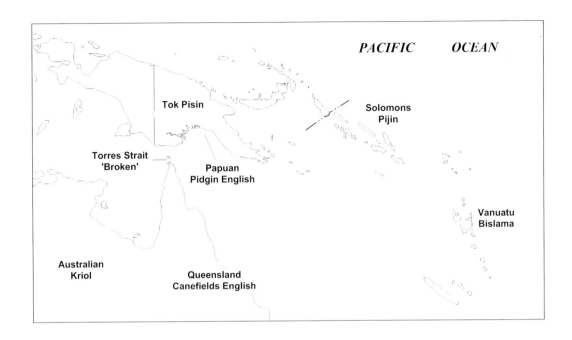

Keesing's ground-breaking *Melanesian Pidgin and the Oceanic Substrate* (1988) traces the development of Solomon Islands Pijin from early Pacific contact languages. Keesing's focus is by no means confined to Solomon Islands Pijin, and he looked at the earliest developments of contact languages in the area. His work demonstrates parallels suggesting the Oceanic Austronesian languages of the Central Pacific as the source of early grammatical influences on Pacific Pidgin English during its formative period in nautical contexts. Keesing's assertion that in later development, extensive calquing of Eastern Solomonic languages is responsible for much of the present character of Pijin is somewhat controversial, and some doubts about the data and time frame have been raised (e.g. Crowley 1989b, Mühlhäusler 1990b, Siegel 1990). Also currently unresolved is the degree to which various grammatical features had stabilized prior to the independent development of the different strands of Melanesian Pidgin English in the late 1880s.

A comprehensive account of the development of Bislama in Vanuatu was written by Crowley (1990a), supplementing earlier work by Camden (1977), Charpentier (1979) and Tryon (1987). Crowley's careful historical reconstruction gives a number of new insights into the early years of Pidgin formation in the Pacific. Much of the remainder of the work is concerned with the emergence of the grammar of the modern language and structural features which distinguish Bislama from other varieties of Melanesian Pidgin. Crowley is somewhat more cautious than Keesing about the role of substrate languages in Bislama's development, but demonstrates a number of parallel structures which could be implicated, without ruling out alternative explanations.

Mühlhäusler's many investigations have filled in innumerable gaps in our knowledge of Tok Pisin. With regard to origins, his seminal article (1978b) provided evidence for an early precursor of Tok Pisin on the plantations of Samoa, where large numbers of labourers from the New Guinea Islands were employed by German companies. Until this time, the dominant view of the origin of Tok Pisin was that it developed on sugar cane plantations in Queensland. Mühlhäusler's work was important in that it provided strong historical evidence for the primacy of Samoan Plantation Pidgin in the genesis of Tok Pisin. It appears that very few New Guinea Islanders were employed in Queensland compared with those from the New Hebrides or Solomon Islands (Mühlhäusler

1978b:69), but there is still the possibility of mutual influence on different varieties due to the complex labour movements of the late 19th century.

In a careful comparison of grammatical structures, Mühlhäusler shows that Samoan Plantation Pidgin, among all the Pacific varieties, had the closest relationship to New Guinea Pidgin. Samoan Plantation Pidgin was spoken on the German-owned plantations in the latter decades of the 19th century, but fell out of use in the monolingual Samoan society when Melanesian labourers were no longer recruited. The distinctive character of Samoan Plantation Pidgin emerged from the common features of Pacific jargons due to the large number of labourers from the Bismarck Archipelago being isolated from other Pacific labour movements. This was as a result of the special relationship between New Guinea and Samoa under German administration. Labourers from the Samoan plantations were extensively used in later contracts on the plantations of mainland New Guinea, and Mühlhäusler considers that speakers of Samoan Plantation Pidgin and other varieties of Pidgin English in German New Guinea constituted a single speech community until as late as 1914 (1978b:109).

Apart from the three current varieties of Melanesian Pidgin outlined above, some other contact languages have been linked to Melanesian Pidgin English, although in some cases their exact status is not clear. These are Papuan Pidgin English; Torres Strait Creole, sometimes known as 'Broken' in the islands of the Torres Strait in Far North Queensland; Queensland Canefield English; and the Northern Australian English-based Creole known as Kriol.

Papuan Pidgin English was formerly spoken along the Papuan coast (Dutton & Mühlhäusler 1979). The Finnish anthropologist Landtmann (1927) also includes a glossary of this Pidgin compiled during his field work among the Kiwai of western Papua in 1910-12. The relationship with other Melanesian Pidgins is still open to question, although it appears that the language was effectively isolated from contact with the New Guinea variety after the beginning of the 20th century, and eventually died out as Hiri Motu was adopted as the lingua franca of the territory (Mühlhäusler 1978a, Dutton & Mühlhäusler 1979).

Queensland was one of the major destinations for Melanesian labourers, especially from the Southern New Hebrides, in the 19th century, and the pidginized variety known as Queensland Canefield English (Dutton 1980) or Queensland Kanaka English (Dutton & Mühlhäusler 1984; Mühlhäusler 1991a) was spoken here. There are still many gaps in our knowledge of this language, although it is clear that there were links to the emerging Melanesian Pidgins of the south-west Pacific and probably to Australian Creoles as well. Labour recruiting was abolished in Queensland in 1904, and most Melanesian labourers returned home in the first few years of the twentieth century (Mühlhäusler 1991a:174), so the influence of this variety on subsequent developments in Melanesia, especially on Bislama and Solomons Pijin, is likely to have been considerable.

Torres Strait Creole or Broken shares many of the features of Tok Pisin and other dialects of Melanesian Pidgins, as seen by Lee's comparison of features (1995). Details of Broken's history and linguistic features can be found in Shnukal (1988). It is seen that the influence from Tok Pisin has not been direct, and that a Pidgin influenced by the prevailing Pacific Pidgin English was established in the Torres Strait area during the 1840s in association with marine industries based on bêche-de-mer, pearl shell and trochus. A great variety of outsiders lived and worked on Thursday Island and other parts of Torres Strait, including both Melanesian and Polynesian 'South Sea Islanders'. Shnukal notes (1988:5) that the Pidgin had a high status among Torres Strait Islanders in the early years due to its use by Pacific Islanders, who were seen as having access to the Europeans' world of economic privilege. Also notable is the fact that until the Second World War, many Torres Strait Islanders believed that they were actually speaking English when speaking Broken. Broken creolized relatively early, and children on Erub, an island in the north-eastern Torres Strait, were already speaking it as a first language in the late 1890s.

The Australian Aboriginal Creole known as Kriol, widely spoken by Aboriginal Australians in the north of Northern Territory and adjacent regions (Harris 1991:195) also has possible links to Melanesian Pidgin English. As with Broken, common features probably date back to a very early Pacific contact variety at the time the north coast of Australia was first being colonized by Europeans. It should be noted that a contact language based on Macassan (from Sulawesi in Indonesia) was already spoken at the time of first European contact (Harris 1991:196). As Troy has demonstrated (1990), some characteristic features of Melanesian Pidgin English appeared in New South Wales in the early decades of the 19th century, and there may have been more contact between Australian colonists and Pacific traders than has formerly been thought.

Thus it can be seen that inter-relationships between the various Pacific jargons, Pidgins and Creoles are extremely complex. The inadequacy of the 'family tree' type of model has been discussed by Mühlhäusler (1985i), and the challenge is to produce a model which takes into account the hybrid relationship of unrelated languages and development through time.

1.5 Development of Tok Pisin in Papua New Guinea

This section is concerned with the development of the distinct Papua New Guinean variety of Melanesian Pidgin now known as Tok Pisin. It traces the isolation of New Guinea Pidgin from other Pacific varieties, its early establishment as a lingua franca, and linguistic influences on the stabilizing language. Functional and structural expansion are described up to the current situation where a creolized form coexists with second language varieties. Although isolated from English and other Pidgin varieties during the German era, there has recently been intensive contact with English and more frequent exchanges between speakers of the different Melanesian Pidgins. This situation is one in which decreolization has emerged in other cultures, and the current situation in Papua New Guinea is examined.

1.5.1 Establishment as a lingua franca

It was shown in §1.4.2 how a distinctive variety of Pidgin emerged from the plantations of Samoa, and this was transplanted to the New Guinea area via New Britain by returning labourers. Unlike other areas of the Pacific such as Samoa or Fiji, the highly multilingual societies of Melanesia had immediate use for a language such as Melanesian Pidgin English. In New Guinea and the Bismarck Archipelago, colonization, plantation labour schemes and mission activity had brought new opportunities for mobility and a pressing need for a language of wider communication. Since many labourers on the plantations of the Pacific had already experienced the unifying influence of a relatively easily acquired Pidgin, its survival and spread were not surprising.

Tok Pisin as a distinct language can, for practical purposes, be dated to the return of Melanesian indentured labourers to their homes in New Britain and New Guinea in the late 19th century. Mühlhäusler is somewhat more specific, and gives 1884 as the significant date marking the beginning of Tok Pisin's independent development (1985i:44). This coincided with the beginning of effective German colonization of the area and the virtual cutting off of Tok Pisin from wider contact, as labour movements from German New Guinea ceased outside the sphere of German influence. Thus, from the widespread but variable Melanesian Pidgin English spoken throughout the Central and South-western Pacific, Tok Pisin developed along its own course as it came under the influence of the languages of the labourers' home areas, as well as German as a source of additional vocabulary.

1.5.2 The sources of the lexicon

The lexicon of Tok Pisin was shaped by a number of influences, including the languages of successive European colonizing powers English and German as well as languages of the central and south-west Pacific, New Britain, New Ireland and a number of other sources. This section looks in somewhat more detail into the relative influence of these sources.

English as the major lexifier language

As the former name Melanesian Pidgin English suggests, the main lexifier language is English, i.e. most of the vocabulary items are ultimately derived from English. There are problems with classifying Pidgins in this way, as it tends to suggest that Melanesian Pidgin English is basically a variety of English, and under-emphasizes the role that other languages may have played in its development, especially of features other than the lexicon.

As noted above, the precursors of Tok Pisin arose in the context of the use of English as a lingua franca by sailors and traders from about the 18th century onwards in many areas of the world including the Pacific. Accounts such as Clark (1979), Crowley (1990a), Keesing (1988) and Mühlhäusler (1978b) describe some of the lexical items in common use in the early days of European trade in the Pacific. Some of these reflect changes in the lexifier language itself, for example, the word *giaman*, still current in Tok Pisin is derived from the English word 'gammon', meaning 'deceit, a lie', which was common in 19th century slang but now obsolete.

German influence

As noted above, Tok Pisin became effectively isolated from other dialects of Melanesian Pidgin English around 1884 when German occupation of New Guinea commenced, and labour recruiting from New Guinea and the Bismarck Archipelago to parts of the Pacific not controlled by Germany ceased (Mühlhäusler 1985i:44). The German language, as the language of the colonizing power, naturally contributed words to the lexicon during Germany's period of colonization. German influence was especially prevalent in some semantic fields such as workshop tools, school room terms, and agricultural implements. This continued beyond the hand-over to an English-speaking Australian administration after the First World War, as many German missionaries continued to reside in New Guinea until the Second World War or well beyond (Mühlhäusler 1985a:200). The influence of German on the language declined steadily thereafter, and although a considerable inventory of Tok Pisin words of German origin appear in Mühlhäusler (1985a:201), only a few of these appear to be in regular use today (Mihalic 1990). The most common is probably *rausim* from the German *heraus,* although an alternative etymology from the English 'rouse' is also possible here. However, it is worth mentioning, as Mühlhäusler notes (1985a:182), that the etymology of many items in Tok Pisin could equally well be from German as from English (for example, *haus* 'house'). Apart from the influence of the German lexicon, probably the most significant linguistic consequence of the German occupation was the fact that English was no longer available as a model, thus stimulating Tok Pisin's independent development (Mühlhäusler 1985i:48).

Languages of New Britain and New Ireland

Most contract labourers from New Guinea and the Bismarck Archipelago, who had worked in the Pacific in the late decades of the 19th century, were returned to an area centred on the Gazelle Peninsula of New Britain in the late 1880s. The Duke of York Islands, a group of islands between New Britain and New Ireland, was the site of a German trading station at Mioko, which became a transit point for many labourers before returning to their homes (Mühlhäusler 1978b:82). Later, the German administrative centre of Rabaul was more important (Ross 1992:383).

It is therefore not surprising that languages of this area have been suggested as a major source of influence on the development of Tok Pisin in the early years of its independent development. The influence of the Tolai language in particular has been suspected for a long time. Mihalic's (1971) dictionary gives the etymology of many of the entries, and he notes (1971:56) that "almost 15 per cent" of the items listed come from around the Gazelle Peninsula, although he does acknowledge that many of the words are similar in Tolai and related languages of New Ireland. Other estimates such as those of Salisbury (1967:46) and Laycock (1970:115) are somewhat smaller, with both giving the figures of about 11% from Tolai (Mühlhäusler 1985a:179).

While these percentages are interesting, as Mühlhäusler notes (1985a:179), they do not really tell us a great deal. They merely show what percentage of the total inventory of lexemes recorded can be traced as cognates of the various languages, without indicating anything about use in different genres, or relative frequency, especially at different stages of the language's development. For example, a large proportion of the words of Melanesian origin appearing in Mihalic's dictionary are names for various living organisms, although they may be quite infrequently used, or even unknown to many speakers. A more detailed study of the relationship between Tok Pisin and the Tolai language was carried out by Mosel (1980), where many structural similarities were demonstrated. Goulden (1989, 1990b) looks at a wider range of languages of the area and shows that a significant number of syntactic features have parallels in Melanesian languages, but says little about the lexicon.

There are, however, problems with attributing a Tolai origin to many structures and lexical items. Mühlhäusler (1986a) has pointed out the pitfalls of comparing synchronic data in his analysis of adjective position, and demonstrated that some apparent similarities are shown to be coincidental if the historical development of the language is taken into consideration. Similarly, some of the lexical items which have been attributed to Tolai possess phonemes not present in the language, making this derivation most unlikely. In addition, many words which do show similarities may be cognate with items in a number of related Austronesian languages of northeast New Britain or southern New Ireland (Mühlhäusler 1985a:212). Recently some of this confusion has been clarified by Ross (1992), who made a thorough analysis of Austronesian influence on the lexis of Tok Pisin. The probable sources of a number of items were identified, and it was indeed the Tolai and Ramoaaina (Duke of York) languages which were shown to be the predominant sources.

The influence of other languages

Mühlhäusler (1985a) gives details of a number of other languages which have contributed to the Tok Pisin lexicon, including Fijian, Malay, other languages of New Guinea, Spanish and Portuguese, Chinese and even possibly African languages. The etymology of an item cannot always be traced unequivocally to a single source, and it appears that multiple etymologies may have been involved in a number of cases. Also, what Mühlhäusler refers to as 'multi-level syncretism' (1985a:181) may be involved, where a word's phonetic, syntactic and semantic properties are derived from different sources. This would accord with the nature of Pidgin formation, where similarities in two or more different languages might contribute to the choice of a particular form and meaning. One example is the possible conflation of the Tolai word *atip* for 'thatched roof' and the English *on top* in the formation of the Tok Pisin **antap** 'on top, roof', although the presence of *antap* in Bislama, where there is no vernacular reinforcement, challenges this interpretation. Some other examples of possible lexical conflation can be found in Mühlhäusler (1985a:184). Both the Tolai word *ikilik* 'small' and English *little* may have been involved in the formation of Tok Pisin *liklik* 'small'. Similarly, Tolai *lok* 'push through' and English *lock* could have contributed to Tok Pisin *lokim* 'to lock' while Tolai *tun* 'to cook' together with two English words, *turn* and *done*, may be related to Tok Pisin *tanim* 'to turn or cook food'. A number of similar items in the current corpus will be discussed in Chapter 5.

It is well known that words from sources such as English adopt quite different semantic ranges when they become part of Tok Pisin, often in accord with substrate patterns. Thus the English word 'die' does not have the same range of meanings as the Tok Pisin *dai* 'to die, cease, be unconscious', while the latter is semantically closer to many languages of Papua New Guinea. The underlying semantics in different areas may well be analogous to those of substrate languages, but as Mühlhäusler notes (1985a:187), this area has been neglected, and a word's meaning as determined by dictionary makers may not be the same as the meaning to speakers of the language in various localities.

1.5.3 Stabilization and expansion

After the beginning of the independent development of Tok Pisin in New Guinea, there was a considerable period of use as a second language by successive generations of adults. Its use as a lingua franca continued throughout the New Guinea islands and north coastal region, although the use of Hiri Motu in Papua limited Tok Pisin's spread there. Stabilization is an on-going process, and was proceeding from the 1860s onwards. However, by 1900 the language appears to have stabilized to a considerable degree, and the process of expansion proceeded. As Tok Pisin was used in an increasing number of functional domains, corresponding structural expansion resulted. Expansion of the lexicon has been exhaustively documented by Mühlhäusler (1979), and development of grammatical structures by Goulden (1989), Mühlhäusler (1985h), Sankoff (1984, 1993) and others. Descriptive accounts and text samples from various stages of Tok Pisin's development are available to document this process. What has emerged is an unusually complex Pidgin, one that is extensively used in a wide range of functional contexts, and one which in some respects more closely resembles Creoles than typical Pidgins.

Tok Pisin is continuing to expand its geographical range into more remote areas, thus recapitulating the diachronic development of the language. The possibility that the expanded language will re-pidginize in these remote areas has been raised, and this was investigated by Holm & Kepiou (1993) in the Southern Highlands. They conclude that there may have been some initial Pidgin-like forms in adult learners due to incomplete acquisition, but reject the idea of the formation of a stable re-pidginized variety. They also consider that the influence of Australians in the formation of Highlands Tok Pisin has been overstated (Mühlhäusler 1985i:61) and that contact with coastal Tok Pisin speakers has been the crucial factor.

The process of expansion, begun in the late 19th century, is still continuing today. As the language spreads further into all parts of Papua New Guinea, the influence of local languages via second language speakers is also likely to be felt. In addition, the creolization of the language by communities of first language speakers is having an effect in various parts of the country, as described in the following section.

1.5.4 Creolization

Pidgins by definition are predominantly second languages, reserved for a restricted range of secondary functions. If children grow up in circumstances where the primary linguistic input is a

Pidgin, the language is acquired as a first language. A typical situation where such conditions prevail is one where the parents are speakers of different languages and use a Pidgin in the home. If a community of children grows up speaking this as a first language, it is said to be nativized or creolized. Since a first language typically has a considerably wider range of functions to perform than a Pidgin, in fact all the linguistic functions necessary for a normal life, modification of the input language is inevitable. As children are the agents of this change, creolization will have a distinctive character associated with their capabilities. It is widely believed that children below a certain critical age have a greatly enhanced facility to acquire languages compared with adults (see e.g. Andersen 1983), and it is thus quite probable that the unique psycholinguistic abilities of children will influence the development of creolized languages in distinctive ways.

This psycholinguistic facility is the basis of Bickerton's postulated bioprogram (1981), which he considers crucial in the formation of distinctive Creole features. However, he worked mainly on so-called 'abrupt' or 'radical' Creoles, which are described as forming within a single generation from highly impoverished input. Tok Pisin is clearly not in the same category. The Pidgin has stabilized and expanded over several generations, and has a sophisticated range of linguistic resources to deal with a variety of functions. Nevertheless, the process of creolization is relevant to development and change in Tok Pisin, and a number of studies have appeared, notably those of Sankoff among the Buang of north-east New Guinea (1977a, 1986). She has shown that children do indeed take the lead in a number of innovations, but that these tendencies are already present in the developing language as used by fluent second language speakers (Sankoff & Laberge 1973). Moreover, unlike in the situation described by Bickerton, any drastic innovations produced by children are likely to be neutralized by currently existing norms.

Romaine's studies have also shed considerable light on the effects of creolization among young people in Morobe and Madang. She has shown that certain grammatical tendencies, such as the movement of the future marker *bai* into preverbal position, appear to be influenced by creolization. Mühlhäusler's studies of creolization (1977a, 1985e) have also produced some interesting observations, including a description of some creolized rural varieties. In the rural community of Malabang (Manus), for example, a reduplicated verbal form was described as agreeing with number in the subject. Whether such innovations will survive normative pressures from more standard varieties is not known. A review of some of the factors affecting variation and uniformity in creolized varieties appears in Smith (1990a), while a detailed study of creolization of a related dialect of Solomon Islands Pijin, is described by Jourdan (1985a, b).

Following creolization, a possible outcome in a situation of sustained contact with the lexifier language is a post-Creole or post-Pidgin continuum. Such a situation may thus be emerging with respect to contemporary Tok Pisin and English. This will be further discussed in relation to research design in Chapter 2.

1.5.5 Variation

Pidgins are typically subject to a great deal of variation along various dimensions. Regional varieties can be expected to occur under the influence of the first language of the speakers. Social differentiation is also to be expected, and Mühlhäusler's classic account of four sociolects of Tok Pisin (1975) illustrates this well. In addition, Tok Pisin is at different developmental stages in different areas of the country, from first tentative acquisition on the borders of its range to second or even third generation creolization. At the level of the individual speaker, idiolects feature a number of variant forms, alternating according to a number of factors including social setting, domain and degree of formality. However, some synchronic accounts of Tok Pisin have under-emphasized this variation. As noted by Mühlhäusler, very little is known about the geographical distribution of lexical items (1985n:259), or syntactic features such as the predicate marker (1985h:373). It is thus apparent that the lack of studies of regional variation precludes drawing more than provisional conclusions about linguistic features which may be described as characteristic of the language as a whole.

A number of writers have produced material referring to regional varieties of Tok Pisin (Laycock 1970, Wurm 1971), although the nature and extent of differences from other varieties has not always been made clear. Mühlhäusler (1985n) reviews the extent of regional variation in Tok Pisin, noting that many speakers claim to be able to identify the origin of a speaker from the way they speak. He notes the lack of previous studies, and identifies a number of dimensions of variation which can be investigated.

Mühlhäusler's classification of the social varieties of Tok Pisin (1975) has been widely quoted. The 'normal' variety as spoken in the majority of rural areas of the country is referred to as rural

Pidgin. Towards the fringes of its use, where the language is being newly acquired, interlanguage varieties heavily influenced by the phonology and syntax of the learners' first languages are referred to as 'Bush Pidgin'. Another unstable variety is referred to as 'Tok Masta'. It is allegedly typical of some Europeans attempting to communicate in Tok Pisin, but in reality producing an ad hoc simplified register of English together with a few inconsistently applied features of Tok Pisin. The final sociolect, 'urban Pidgin', is said to borrow heavily from English, and be typically associated with an urban setting. While these distinctions are extremely useful, in Chapter 7 it will be argued that the urban-rural distinction in Papua New Guinea may be becoming less critical, and that bilingual capacity in English and Tok Pisin may now be the crucial variable in producing anglicized forms of Tok Pisin.

Extensive stylistic variation is not typical of early unexpanded Pidgins, as the resources, conventions and range of functions are not likely to be adequate for successful communication of these features. However, the processes of stabilization, expansion and creolization of Tok Pisin have led to increasing resources for stylistic expression. Smith (1990b) reviews work on idioms and style, for example, Brash (1971), McElhanon (1978) and Todd & Mühlhäusler (1978), and documents a range of idiomatic expressions in current use. Crowley (1988) describes a similar inventory of currently fashionable idiomatic expressions in Bislama.

1.5.6 The influence of language policy and planning

Tok Pisin's importance to Papua New Guinea was acknowledged when national language status was bestowed on it at independence, but it continued to be perceived as inadequate and inferior in many quarters (McDonald 1976). It is only recently that Tok Pisin's role in education has been seriously considered (Siegel 1992a, 1996, 1997d; Swan & Lewis 1990).

The predominant attitude of successive governments in independent Papua New Guinea to the development of Tok Pisin has been one of *laissez-faire*. Official government communications in Tok Pisin are notorious for their variable and non-standard form (Franklin 1990), and no institution such as a national language planning institute is currently on the horizon. The mission standards previously mentioned are likely to be more influential in standardizing the language in the absence of official policy decisions. Suggestions about the development of the language have come mainly from expatriate academics (e.g. Dutton 1976, Lynch 1975a, 1990; McDonald 1976). There are occasional complaints in letters to *Wantok Niuspepa* about alleged misuse of particular language forms, but in general, a high degree of variability is tolerated by Papua New Guineans. Some discussion of the implications of the findings of the present research to national language policy can be found in Chapter 8.

1.6 The current linguistic situation in Papua New Guinea

In Papua New Guinea today, the constitution recognizes three 'national' languages, English, Tok Pisin and Hiri Motu, which are in fact the medium for most inter-group communication within the country. The inclusion of Hiri Motu, with a rather smaller number of speakers and more restricted range than the other national languages, was no doubt a conciliatory move at the time of independence in the face of political pressures for Papua to become a separate nation. English is still widely regarded as the key to social and economic opportunity and continues to be the language of most government education, from the earliest stages of primary schooling through tertiary institutions, although the amount of Tok Pisin used in practice may be more than is commonly imagined (Swan & Lewis 1987). Tok Pisin appears to be gaining ground as the preferred national language in an increasing number of geographical areas and social domains (Siegel 1992b). The weekly newspaper *Wantok Niuspepa* continues to flourish, while some programmes offering primary education in Tok Pisin have appeared (Siegel 1992a, 1993, 1996). Hiri Motu, formerly widespread in the Papuan region, appears to be losing ground, both to English and Tok Pisin (Ahai 1989).

In spite of the rise of Tok Pisin, the diversity of indigenous languages in Papua New Guinea appears to be as great today as ever. In fact, estimates of the number of languages in the country are continually being modified upwards, as more research is carried out, and new groups identified (Grimes 1992). However, some languages with a very small number of speakers appear to be in acute danger of extinction. Dutton (1992) documents some case studies, while Laycock (1979) identifies some of the warning signs indicating potential obsolescence. A longitudinal study of the use of a language in Morobe Province by Smith (1992b) shows that the number of speakers can decline dramatically in certain demographic conditions, such as universal bilingualism, minority status and the existence of exogamy rules resulting in frequent inter-marriage with speakers of other languages.

One of the factors potentially threatening the survival of minority languages is the spread of Tok Pisin into an increasing number of social domains. Sumbuk (1993) documents the effect of Tok Pisin on the Sare language in the East Sepik Province, while the incipient shift from another Sepik language, Gapun, to Tok Pisin is described by Kulick & Stroud (1990). At a time when many accounts around the world are indicating a gloomy prognosis for indigenous languages, it is not surprising that the viability of many of Papua New Guinea's languages has been questioned.[15] Mühlhäusler's (1996) Doomsday scenario is perhaps the gloomiest of all, predicting that all the indigenous languages of Papua New Guinea will ultimately be replaced by Tok Pisin which will in turn be replaced by English. However, Crowley (1994) is somewhat more sanguine, and considers that predictions of wholesale extinction may have been overstated.

1.7 The aims of the present research

In spite of the work already carried out, there are still significant gaps in our current knowledge of a number of aspects of Tok Pisin. Much of the literature is concerned with the historical development of the language and the description of its linguistic properties, and a great deal of careful analysis has been carried out. However, especially in some of the earlier accounts, it is not always clear just how representative the features described are, and to which speech communities they apply. Judgements by authors about what is acceptable and what is not acceptable Tok Pisin often do not specify whose norms or opinions they are based on. A corpus-based analysis avoids some of these pitfalls, and more corpora, especially of spoken language, are badly needed to improve the factual basis for specifying more precise parameters of language use. Romaine (1992a) has made a significant contribution in one area of the country, and it is to be hoped that further studies of this kind will eventually be carried out in other areas.

During most of its development, Tok Pisin has been a second language for the great majority of its speakers. Recently, however, a new generation has grown up speaking Tok Pisin as a mother tongue, and an interesting area of study is the effect that this process of creolization has on the language. Although a number of studies have addressed the question of nativization, especially the work of Romaine and of Sankoff, there remains much to be known about the characteristics of Tok Pisin as spoken as a first language in modern Papua New Guinea. In particular, an area which has been neglected is the degree to which regional variation has become established in different parts of Papua New Guinea.

This study aims to contribute in a small way to the filling in of some of these gaps by investigating the linguistic characteristics of the spoken Tok Pisin of first language speakers in a variety of geographical locations. A corpus-based approach is adopted, drawing data from samples of recorded speech obtained from young, mainly adolescent, first-language speakers. The study as originally conceived had two broad aims. The first was to provide an accurate account of the lexical, morphosyntactic and discourse features of the language as currently spoken by this sample of first-language speakers in the major Tok Pisin-speaking areas of Papua New Guinea. The second was to investigate the degree to which regional variation could be observed in the speech of first language speakers. In the course of the investigation, a number of related findings emerged, and the implications of these are also discussed as they relate to the contemporary social setting of Papua New Guinea. In particular, the relationship between Tok Pisin and the other major language of wider communication in current use, English, proved to be of primary importance, and is explored further.

In the following chapters, details of the research design and procedure are provided, along with linguistic findings based on an analysis of the corpus. Details of observations of interest relating to the phonology, morphology, syntax, lexicon and discourse processes are discussed, and numerous extracts from the corpus are provided for illustration. The degree to which features vary in different regions is explored where appropriate. The implications of the findings are considered in the final chapter. Discussion focuses especially on a number of theoretical issues, such as the influence of substrata and universals, code-switching, and the development of post-Creole continua.

---

[15] For example, Dutton 1994, Polinsky & Smith 1996, Smith 1992a, Yarupawa 1996.

2

Research design and procedure

In this chapter, the theoretical orientation of the current study is reviewed (§ 2.1), followed by an account of the research design and methodology, including practical aspects of locating and recording the speech of suitable informants (§ 2.2). Some of the limitations imposed by the data gathering method are discussed, and the method of assembling and analyzing the resulting corpus is then described (§ 2.3).

2.1 Theoretical orientation

The broad aims of this research are to give an account of the lexical, morphosyntactic and discourse features of contemporary first language Tok Pisin speech, and to obtain a preliminary indication of the degree of regional variation which currently exists within it. This task is basically descriptive, and its principal outcome is the database of contemporary spoken forms assembled, but a number of theoretical issues have a bearing on the approach taken to the investigation and the analysis of the data

Firstly, the question of which grammatical model to adopt has to be considered. Earlier grammatical descriptions have come under some criticism. For example, Mühlhäusler (1985c) takes issue with some structuralist models adopted, while Bickerton (1979:311) objects to the tendency to describe grammars exclusively in terms of categories taken from Indo-European languages. More recent descriptions of Tok Pisin, and Creole languages in general, have on the whole avoided these problems. They have attempted to deal with features of the languages in their own terms, by describing the functions of various components of the system as they operate within that system, rather than trying to squeeze the data into preconceived Procrustean grammatical moulds. For example, Bickerton's characterization of "typical" Creole structures (1980, 1981) was an important stimulus encouraging a consideration of the grammars of Pidgins and Creoles in a new light, especially with regard to the marking of tense, mood and aspect. Nevertheless, many studies naturally favour one theoretical school or another, and some collections of papers reflect this, for example, the generative studies in Muysken (1981).

The aim of the present work is to produce a description which is synchronic, being based on a corpus of data from one distinct period of time. It does not adhere to any particular grammatical school or approach, but aims to achieve a descriptive account of the structure of the language as far as possible on its own terms, with reference to other recent accounts and theoretical problems in the field of Pidgin and Creole linguistics where appropriate. Historical developments, based on earlier published descriptions, will be referred to where relevant when analyzing and discussing the features encountered. A major concern is locating and discussing features which have not been found or discussed in detail in previous descriptions of the language.

It is necessary to remember that this is a description of a spoken language, which may differ significantly from written standards. Classical descriptions of languages such as English have generally referred to written norms rather than vernacular speech, and it is indeed only recently that grammars of spoken English have been attempted (e.g. Knowles, Williams & Taylor 1996). Prescriptive grammars have thus been very influential in moulding perceptions of what is grammatical in the English language. This is, of course, very different from the case of most Papua New Guinean languages, which are predominantly oral, and where grammars are generally descriptive, compiled (usually by outsiders) from recordings of oral samples and elicitation of speech. Tok Pisin does not have a very long tradition of literacy, but written standards have nevertheless had a considerable influence on the language, and the most recent reference grammar (Verhaar 1996) relies almost exclusively on written sources, mainly translations, for exemplification. The present study, by contrast, relies on a different type of database, firmly rooted in actual spoken usage, and it aims to avoid some of the shortcomings which might arise from an over-reliance on written sources.

In addition, it should be borne in mind that all languages are dynamic, and those such as Tok Pisin have been subject to particularly rapid change. Indeed, the notion of a rather radical metamorphosis is implicit in the model of 'life cycle' which has been applied to Pidgins and

Creoles since the term was introduced by Hall (1966). One point repeatedly made by Mühlhäusler (e.g. 1986b:134) is that static models are inappropriate for languages such as Tok Pisin, and a historical, or at least a developmental perspective, is essential for the understanding of many features. This inherent tendency to variability and change is kept in mind in the present study. Variation along a geographical axis is one of the aims of the study, and change is considered especially with reference to the continuing debate over the effects of superstrate and substrate languages or universal tendencies, and the present dynamics of contact with English, as outlined below.

The names "superstrate" and "substrate" imply a vertical stratification of languages which can be roughly equated with social status. Hence, the languages described as superstrates have typically been the relatively prestigious and widespread European languages of trade and colonization such as English, French, Dutch, Spanish and Portuguese. Substrates have included a huge variety of other languages, often typologically remote from Western European languages, that have been the mother tongues of people who have ventured or been forced into contact with speakers of these superstrates. Consistent with this metaphor of vertical elevation, the term "adstrate" has been used to refer to a language of more or less equal prestige which has an effect on another language. It should be remembered that this metaphor has its limitations, as status and prestige are notoriously difficult to measure, and may be perceived differently by different parties.

Using criteria that are more specifically linguistic in nature, the superstrate is generally conceived of as the language which provides most of the words of an emerging contact variety, and it is sometimes termed the principal lexifier or just lexifier language. Theories assigning primacy to the superstrate or lexifier usually indicate that Pidgins and Creoles were derived from them by a process of simplification. The fact that the various Pidgins are often named after their main lexifier language, e.g. West African Pidgin English or Pidgin French indicates that this school of thought has been pervasive. This, however, is not without problems, as it betrays a view attributing greater importance to the lexicon than other grammatical features. It may also have given rise to the misconception that the language so named is no more than a corrupted or deviant form of the lexifier language.

A good deal of evidence is available to support the idea that simplification, including such phenomena as 'foreigner talk' (Naro 1978) or 'baby talk' (Koeford 1979) do play a role in Pidgin genesis. Also related to these superstrate theories are those monogenetic theories of origin suggesting relexification of early Portuguese-based Pidgins (D Taylor 1961) and theories attributing Creole characteristics to dialectal forms of the lexifier language (Turner 1974). During Tok Pisin's early history, it has been suggested that simplified forms of English were spoken by both first- and second-language English-speakers, which may have contributed to the character of the language. Although the question of ultimate origins is somewhat remote from the present study, possible influence from simplified registers of English in the continuing development of Tok Pisin will be kept in mind.

The search for the influence of substrate languages in both Atlantic and Pacific Creoles has been spurred on by repeated discoveries that various features in the Creoles correspond to similar structures in African or Pacific languages. It would seem to be little more than common sense to assume that there could be a causal link between them. Extreme positions characterize such Creoles as consisting, for example, of English lexis but grammar taken wholesale from another language. However, proving such a relationship is not so easy, and assuming substrate origins without rigorous proof has led to claims that the influence of the alleged substrates has been grossly exaggerated or even that it does not operate at all. The main nemesis of the substrate theorists has been Bickerton, whose dismissive labels 'substratophile' or the more provocative 'substratomaniac' have sharpened the debate. The over-zealous attribution of Creole features to a range of supposed substrates has also been dismissively termed the 'cafeteria principle'.[16] Although sometimes characterized by critics as dogmatic and uncompromising, Bickerton has forced many substratists to adopt more rigorous standards of analysis, which has been of considerable service to the field as a whole.

In particular, basic historical prerequisites, such as establishing that speakers of the languages in question were "in the right place at the right time" (Bickerton 1984), can no longer be ignored. Even if parallels can be demonstrated with other languages spoken, this does not by itself prove a

---

[16] The analogy is to casually selecting diverse food items from the range of things on offer. Interestingly, Dillard (1970), who coined this term, originally used it to characterize superstratists who were inclined to attribute all non-standard features of Black English to dialectal forms recorded anywhere in the British Isles. How this term subsequently became applied primarily to overzealous substratists remains to be investigated.

causal relationship or have much predictive value (Bickerton 1981, Mühlhäusler 1986b). A practical example illustrates this dilemma. Dutton & Bourke (1990) investigate the position of the conjunction *taim* in the Tok Pisin spoken on the Nembi Plateau of Southern Highlands, and note that its unusual clause-final pattern is exactly paralleled by structures in the language of the area (p 257). However, identical structures also exist in languages of adjacent areas, but are not reflected in the Tok Pisin spoken there. Thus, its presence on the Nembi Plateau demands further explanation. Dutton & Bourke suggest that its use may be related to identity, i.e. the desire for a distinctive speech style. However, they acknowledge that no concrete evidence exists. Data from the present corpus has shown that clause-final *taim* is in fact somewhat more widely distributed than Dutton & Bourke originally suggest (as these authors also confirm in a footnote). However, their reiteration of Bickerton's point (1986) that the presence of a feature does not prove a causal relationship is well taken.

It is important to separate the questions of the influence of the various substrate factors operating on Pidgin and Creole *genesis* from those on Pidgin and Creole *development*. Much of the discussion of Tok Pisin has been concerned with origins, i.e. how Tok Pisin arose from the garbled communicative resources available to inhabitants and visitors in the 19th century Pacific. Evidence of substrate influence on the early Pidgin English spoken in the Pacific can be found in a number of sources, especially Crowley (1990a) and Keesing (1988), while Baker (1993) shows that such substrate influence may merely have reinforced features already present in Australian PE. Studies referring to the early stages of development include Mosel's (1980) account of the relationship between Tolai and Tok Pisin. Goulden (1990b) also investigates possible influence from West New Britain languages, and the more general influence of the syntactic patterns of Melanesian languages (1989, 1990a).

While the genesis of Tok Pisin is now widely recognized to have been strongly influenced by Austronesian, probably Eastern Oceanic languages, the majority of Tok Pisin speakers today also speak Papuan languages, typologically unrelated to Austronesian languages. Thus, as Tok Pisin spread to the Madang and Sepik areas, and more recently to the Highlands, substrate influence from these sources would be expected. In an area of extreme multilingualism like Papua New Guinea, an obvious obstacle to the evaluation of substratum influence is inadequate knowledge of all the languages which may have had an effect. Nevertheless, as more studies of the grammars of indigenous languages appear, some attempts have been made to relate these to the Tok Pisin spoken in various areas. A detailed study of the transfer of Usurufa phonological features by Bee (1971) has shown that such influence tends to be greater when the use of Tok Pisin is marginal. Further discussion of substrate influence on phonology can be found in Laycock (1985), while a study of the mutual influence between local languages and Tok Pisin in West New Britain can be found in Chowning (1983).

In a seldom-quoted paper which deserves wider recognition, Reesink (1990) investigates the correlation between the presence of certain features in a number of Papua New Guinean languages of diverse typology and the Tok Pisin of second language speakers. Although the speech samples were quite small, and taken from a single speaker in each area, significant substrate parallels could be demonstrated in various aspects of discourse structure, such as switch reference, subordination, head-tail linkage and reporting speech. Reesink points out that inadequate knowledge of substrate languages may have led to an underestimation of substrate influences on regional varieties. While many of these studies have dealt with single or a small selection of languages, Siegel (1999) has attempted to deal with general principles of transfer from substrates to Tok Pisin, especially establishing possible routes by which individual features can be transferred and showing that the historical conditions were appropriate.

In the present investigation a good deal of indirect influence is expected from substrate languages. The subjects may well all be 'first language' speakers, but many are quite competent in some other languages, and even those who are not will be influenced by the language of those around them who speak Tok Pisin as a second language. This is likely to be relevant when comparing speakers for example, from the Highlands Region, where Papuan languages are spoken and the New Guinea Islands Region, where mostly Austronesian languages are spoken.

The search for universals in linguistics proceeded apace in the late 20th century, and has taken a number of forms. The most straightforward, perhaps, is work such as that of Comrie (1981) and Greenberg (1963), who examined the burgeoning linguistic data which had become available in order to search out universal or near-universal features in grammar, and to propose implicational restrictions and relations to typology. The work of Chomsky (e.g. 1968) has also had far-reaching influence. His generative model, further developed in the government and binding school, postulates a 'universal grammar' (UG) as the source of various structures and tendencies. Chomsky's models treat language as an abstract system, removed from many sociolinguistic factors. This is the main limitation as far as investigators of Pidgins and Creoles are concerned, as many of these factors have been shown to be crucial.

Bickerton's alternative (1980) to the substrate theories he dismisses is a 'bioprogram', somewhat akin to Chomsky's universal grammar in many ways. It is described as a species-specific faculty in the human brain which comes into play during first and second language acquisition and provides the source of innovation in Creoles. In the absence of adequate linguistic input, children are said to fall back on the default options of the bioprogram to set grammatical parameters. This was the scenario described in his accounts of Hawaiian Creole English, an abrupt Creole formed from a varied and supposedly impoverished input (Bickerton 1981). There is still considerable debate about the exact circumstances surrounding the formation of Hawaiian Creole (Goodman 1994, Roberts 1995), for example whether there was a stable English-based Pidgin preceding it, the role of a Hawaiian-based Pidgin, and whether the input available to children was really as impoverished as sometimes claimed.[17]

With regard to universal tendencies, the abrupt changes evident in incipient Creoles evolving from unstable Pidgins are not relevant for the purposes of this study, and those of most concern are phenomena such as grammaticalization, which have been described for many languages as well as evolving Pidgins and Creoles. The gradual change from lexical words to function words, or from particles to clitics or affixes makes a fascinating study, and in the course of this work, evidence for the existence of these processes was continually sought. Other universal tendencies such as phonological assimilation are somewhat beyond the scope of this study, and are referred to only in passing.

Some recent writing has questioned whether primacy should really be attributed only to either substrate language or universals (or to other theories of origin such as simplification of the superstrate), and a more balanced approach has been offered. Mufwene (1986) attempted to reconcile opposing camps by suggesting that the substratist and universalist positions are not mutually exclusive, but complementary. This notion will be kept in mind when analyzing the data. Another useful approach was suggested by Baker (1994), who adopts a 'creativist' position, stressing the creative capacity of language users, rather than implying a deficit model due to incomplete acquisition of a target. This concept, too, will be considered when evaluating the data, although it is perhaps more applicable to the genesis of Creoles than later stages.

A particularly significant advance in the theoretical treatment of Pidgins and Creoles, and contact-induced language change in general, was the work of Thomason & Kaufman, especially the seminal *Language contact, creolization and genetic linguistics* (1988). Thomason & Kaufman's contribution is not so much a new direction in theoretical modelling as a synthesis of ideas that have been in existence for some time, coupled with detailed case studies to support their assertions. Central to their ideas are the primacy of social over linguistic factors in determining the direction and extent of contact-induced change, and a clear distinction between borrowing and interference through shift, a distinction which has not always been made consistently in the literature.

In the case of borrowing, a community continues to use its first language, but some features from languages with which the community is in contact are added to the linguistic repertoire. Even monolingual speakers may do a fair amount of borrowing. Typically, lexical items are the first to be borrowed, but Thomason & Kaufman clearly demonstrate what had been considered by some to be impossible, namely that structural borrowing at any level can take place. This is typically only possible when there has been a long period of bilingualism between the borrowing and source languages by a significant section of the population.

Interference through shift involves whole populations abandoning their native language and adopting another language. In this situation, various features of the language *from* which they shifted (the 'substrate') will be retained in their version of the language *to* which they have shifted (the 'target'). This may range from a few lexical items to heavy structural interference, depending on the exact circumstances of the shift. For example, if the target language was imperfectly acquired at the time of shift, and there is little access to standard norms, there is likely to be major syntactic and phonological interference from the original language.

---

[17] For example, Bickerton (1981) failed to make it clear that the children in question attended English-medium schools.

One notable feature of Thomason & Kaufman's work is the assertion that it is possible to formulate a predictive model of language change, and that the factors affecting the direction and extent of change are primarily social, not linguistic. The significance for Pidgin and Creole linguistics is that the genesis of a Pidgin closely resembles the process of interference through shift, although it is not identical with it in that several substrate languages may contribute to the linguistic make-up of the Pidgin, the existing language(s) may not be abandoned and the lexical source language may not constitute a target. Since normal processes of transmission are not operating, the usual models of historical linguistics are not considered to apply.

In the case of contemporary Tok Pisin, there is considerable influence from the multifarious indigenous languages spoken in the country, and the main language of education, English. The influence of most local languages can be considered as substrate influence. This is mostly from other primary languages spoken, but there is some evidence that a number of small language groups are being abandoned in favour of Tok Pisin (Kulick 1992, Smith 1992a, b), a situation where interference through shift would apply. It does not appear that many people are abandoning their languages in favour of English, which remains a second language for the great majority of its speakers. However, there does appear to be a significant minority of bilingual speakers, and massive borrowing is currently taking place from English to Tok Pisin. This borrowing has a number of effects, and two areas in particular which will be explored are code-switching and the possible existence of a post-Creole continuum.

Code-switching did not receive much attention in the past as it was considered to be difficult to deal with or even irrelevant in studies focusing on a single language. However, work by Myers-Scotton (1992, 1993a, b, c, 1995) and other studies such as those of Poplack (1980, 1987, 1993) have highlighted the importance of the phenomenon for sociolinguistics.

The relationship between code-switching and code mixing and other language contact phenomena has been discussed by Myers-Scotton (1997), and the phenomenon is of clear relevance to the present study. There are a number of cases where utterances appear to contain a mixture of Tok Pisin and English, ranging from fully integrated new words to awkward stumbling between phrases in the two languages. Some way of sorting out the resulting language is needed. Myers-Scotton's matrix language frame model is a useful beginning here. According to this theory, one language provides the morpho-syntactic framework or matrix of an utterance, and there is only one matrix language operating at one time. Thus the matrix language is the point of reference for determining the well-formedness or grammaticality of, for example, word order and inflections. Although the theory has been criticised for failing to take account of all cases of language contact, the idea of a basic matrix into which code-switches are placed is a useful one. More recently, the theory has been extended to include 'composite' matrix languages, in which complex lexical structure may be derived from more than one language. In the present corpus, Tok Pisin can be seen as the matrix in the overwhelming majority of cases. In only a few isolated instances can real mixed utterances be found, and code-switching for stylistic effect is virtually absent. This will be discussed further in Chapter 8.

According to the 'life cycle' model of Pidgin and Creole development (Hall 1966), one possible scenario is a re-integration of a Creole with the lexifier or standard language. Typically, such a situation is likely to occur where there is extensive contact between the lexifier language and the Creole and a high degree of bilingualism in the two. Such post-Creole continua have been described for Jamaica (DeCamp 1971), Belize (Escure 1993) and Guyana (Bickerton 1975b), where a spectrum of variants or 'lects' ranges from a 'basilect', consisting of the Creole, to an 'acrolect' which approaches the standard language. Between the two extremes, various 'mesolects' merge into one another.

The post-Creole continua referred to above are based on Atlantic Creoles. A similar situation, which could be called a post-Pidgin continuum, obtains when an expanded Pidgin undergoes a similar process, and such continua have been described in some parts of West Africa (Todd 1982). The degree to which post-Pidgin continua are developing in Melanesia is open to question. In the Solomon Islands, Jourdan (1989) describes code-switching between Pijin and English in urban areas, but concludes that the structure of Pijin has not been significantly affected. Siegel (1997c) deals at some length with the question of whether such continua can be found in Melanesia, looking at Pijin in the Solomon Islands and Bislama in Vanuatu as well as Tok Pisin in Papua New Guinea. He critically examines the claims by a number of writers indicating that the development of a continuum is likely to happen, (Bickerton 1975a, Sankoff 1976); is in the process of happening (Aitchison 1981, Kale 1990); or has already happened (O'Donnell & Todd 1980, Romaine 1992a). Based on a close scrutiny of the data supporting these views, he concludes that the evidence currently available does not justify the claim that such continua exist. A study of Manus Tok Pisin by Smith (1994a, 1998b) based on the present data shows considerable influence from English, but does not find evidence of an established continuum, although an examination of more naturalistic data might not necessarily draw the same conclusions.

The theoretical construct of the post-Creole continuum or post-Pidgin continuum clearly has considerable relevance to the present data, recorded from a situation where a creolizing English-lexifier Pidgin is in contact with the original lexifier language. The extent of the changes in progress as revealed by the present data will be examined in detail in chapter eight, bearing in mind that the corpus is somewhat limited in its stylistic range. Finally, the role of creolization in the changes which take place if a Pidgin develops into a Creole has been the topic of considerable debate, and some suggestions regarding its role will be offered. However, as this is a study of first-language speakers only, the lack of comparative data from second language speakers will limit the scope of the discussion somewhat.

2.2 Research design and procedure

2.2.1 Aims of the present research

Research into the speech of first language Tok Pisin speakers by the present writer began in 1985 with an investigation of some pre-school children in Lae and Goroka (Smith 1986a). This research was extended to include some adolescent speakers, and follow-up samples of speech from the same group of children in Lae were recorded over the next few years. This initial investigation was essentially exploratory, and aimed to find out what changes were taking place in Tok Pisin as spoken by young people who were growing up speaking it as a first language.

In 1989, a research project supported by the Papua New Guinea University of Technology was initiated to collect data from adolescent first language speakers in different geographical locations. It had already been observed that there were some differences between the speech of children in Lae and Goroka. The larger investigation had as its specific aim an assessment of the degree of regional variation in first language speech. This project was the starting point of the present research.

Three regions of Papua New Guinea were selected for investigation, the Northern region (Morobe, Madang, East Sepik and West Sepik provinces); the Highlands region (Eastern, Western and Southern Highlands, Enga and Simbu provinces); and the Islands region (Manus, East and West New Britain, New Ireland and North Solomons provinces). The Northern region is often referred to as *Momase*, after the first two letters of the names Morobe, Madang and Sepik, and the region will hereafter be referred to in this work as Momase. The three regions selected for study are the regions of Papua New Guinea where Tok Pisin has been the preferred lingua franca over the last few decades.

Field work was not carried out in Western, Gulf, Central, Oro or Milne Bay Provinces, in what used to be known as Papua, and is now referred to as the Southern region. This was partly because of limitations of time and money, but also because of the fact that these have not been areas where Tok Pisin was widely spoken in the past. However, this appears to be changing (Ahai 1989), and the present status of Tok Pisin in these provinces relative to the established lingua franca, Hiri Motu, would make an interesting area of study.

Port Moresby in the National Capital District was also left out of the study, as the size of the investigation that would be involved was considered to be beyond the scope of the resources available. However, casual observation of language use in the National Capital indicates that the use of Tok Pisin is increasing rapidly, and Ahai's (1989) survey of language use confirms this. An in-depth study of Tok Pisin use in the National Capital would make another interesting and worthwhile project.

Although the stated objective of the original research project was an assessment of the degree of regional variation, this was modified as the research progressed. Since I was in full-time employment during the whole period of the research, data was collected wherever and whenever possible, usually in conjunction with travel for other official purposes. Visits, for example, to National High School Governing Council meetings provided opportunities to travel to different regions. On brief visits to various centres, the location and selection of ideal informants was not always possible, making a study properly controlled for a number of variables somewhat difficult. However, the assembly of an increasingly large corpus of recorded speech from young people speaking Tok Pisin as a first language presented an opportunity for a more general study. Thus, the primary aim of this research came to be providing a descriptive account of the linguistic characteristics of the contemporary spoken language of adolescent first language speakers in Papua New Guinea, especially in so far as it differs from the standard descriptions of Tok Pisin in the literature. The secondary aim of investigating regional variability is retained, bearing in mind the limitations of the data available.

2.2.2 Location and selection of informants

In the regions selected for study, a sample of first language speakers large enough to give an indication of regional differences was sought. Inevitably, due to the somewhat opportunistic nature of data collection outlined above, choice of informants was a compromise between what was theoretically desirable and what was practically possible. However, every effort was made to ensure that the informants chosen were first language speakers who had lived for a significant length of time in their area of residence. This posed some practical difficulties, such as determining what the first language was, what the primary place of residence was, and what should be considered a 'significant' length of time. Educational establishments proved invaluable in assisting with the location of suitable informants.

The question of what constitutes a first language is by no means clear-cut in a multilingual society such as Papua New Guinea. Information provided by informants about themselves, although essential, can be misleading, as there is considerable confusion surrounding certain terms. 'First language' may be interpreted by informants as 'first language learned', which may not be the current primary vehicle of communication. The term 'mother tongue' is also frequently confused with the language the mother speaks. Even simple questions designed to avoid such terminological confusion, such as 'which language do you use most of the time?' may not have a straightforward answer; many people use different languages in different situations, and 'most of the time' may be interpreted differently by different informants. Jourdan noted similar problems of definition in her studies of Solomon Pijin, commenting that urban children may have native-like fluency in two or three languages (1990:180) and that adults for whom Pijin is definitely a second language nevertheless tend to use it most of the time in a wide range of functions in urban contexts.

Thus the question of locating first language informants was not as straightforward as it seemed. Notwithstanding these problems, an operational definition of 'first language speaker' was adopted to include those who had used Tok Pisin in a wide range of circumstances for most or all of their lives. Those claiming to have Tok Pisin as their first language were generally accepted as informants, provided that follow-up indications such as fluency of speech confirmed with a reasonable degree of confidence that their claim to have used Tok Pisin as their primary language for most of their life was a credible one. The cooperation of teachers was also sought to determine the status of certain individuals.

Reliance on school populations limited the age range of informants somewhat. Data collected indicated that most were between the ages of 12 and 18, and this was initially chosen as the target population. In the final corpus, all suitable informants in the age range 10 to 19 were included. Some data had already been collected from rather younger pre-school children down to the age of six, but this was not included in the present corpus because of the more pronounced developmental differences at such a young age which would no doubt affect the various features investigated. In practice, not everyone contacted was sure of an exact date of birth, and some informants may have given what was a best estimate of their age.

The degree to which an informant in one area is typical of that area is similarly not always easy to determine without in-depth knowledge of the local population. There is now considerable opportunity to travel to different parts of the country, and improved road networks and coastal shipping links, combined with a curiosity about the development of the nation, have led many people to visit parts of the country which would formerly have been out of reach. Employment, too, has motivated many to move from their place of origin. Many employees in government service, such as teachers and police personnel, are posted to various centres as a routine part of their career. The search for jobs in the private sector also attracts many workers to urban centres, mining operations or forestry projects. A number of resettlement schemes, notably the oil palm blocks of West New Britain, have drawn people from all over the country to live as a mixed community. In addition, the number of marriages involving partners from other provinces appears to be increasing. Thus many communities, both urban and rural, contain significant numbers of people from outside the region.

There are, of course, many possible factors which could be relevant to language variation as well as the geographical area in which the speaker resides. These include social background, age, educational level, languages spoken by self, parents and peers, rural versus urban living environment, and the amount of schooling completed in English or other languages. To take only one variable, the number of different possible combinations of parental languages spoken is enormous, and attempting a study controlled for parents' language, for example, to investigate substratum influence, would be extremely difficult. It was assumed for the purposes of the study that roughly the same range of variables is operating in each region, and that as a result, broad differences might be attributed to regional factors. So rather than attempting, and almost certainly failing, to control for these variables, it was hoped that, within the limitations of the design, broad regional characteristics could be identified. Criteria for an operational definition of regional samples appear below in § 2.3.2.

Visits were made and data collected in all the provinces in the three regions selected for study (see Map 7). Centres visited were, in Momase: 1. Vanimo, 2. Aitape, 3. Wewak, 4. Madang, 5. Musom, 6. Lae; in the Highlands: 7. Kainantu, 8. Henganofi, 9. Goroka, 10. Mount Hagen, 11. Kundiawa, 12. Kondiu, 13. Mendi, 14. Wabag; and in the Islands: 15. Lorengau, 16. Kavieng, 17. Kimbe, 18. Keravat, 19. Rabaul, 20. Buka, 21. Arawa. Data was collected during the period from 1985 to 1993, the majority between 1990 and 1992.

Map 7 - Papua New Guinea - Location of informants

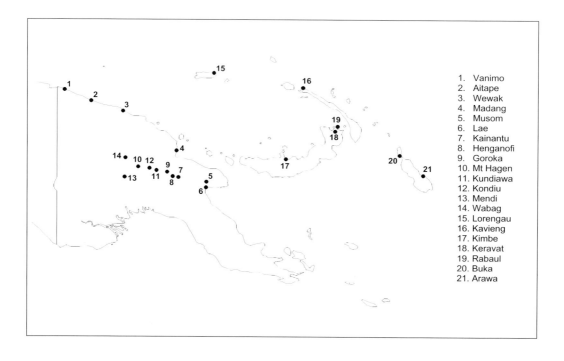

As noted, the aim of the visits was to locate and record adolescent first language speakers who had lived in the area for most or all of their lives. One of the most convenient ways of locating suitable informants without an intimate knowledge of the place or people was by enlisting the help of educational institutions, especially provincial high schools and primary schools. The majority of informants were provincial high school students aged 12-16, as secondary school administrations proved to be particularly helpful in assisting the research. Provincial high schools were selected, as they draw their students mainly from the local area, unlike the National High Schools, offering grades 11 and 12, where a significant percentage of students are drawn from other regions with the aim of creating a 'national' social environment.

A number of primary schools were also visited, and attention was concentrated on the final year classes. Grade 6 students proved to be very good informants, as they were generally secure in their senior social position in the schools and full of confidence and self-assurance. In addition, a number of young people were encountered casually or through friends, without the involvement of the education system, in Rabaul, Buka, Kundiawa, Kimbe, Goroka and Lae.

One consequence of the reliance on educational institutions for providing informants is the fact that most of these subjects were in a situation where the language of instruction is English. In theory, English is also spoken as the lingua franca by students in the playground and dormitories of government schools, and in some cases students are punished if caught speaking Tok Pisin, even in informal settings. In practice, however, it was evident that a good deal of Tok Pisin was spoken in most schools outside the formal lesson situation. This accords with Jourdan's experience (1990:169), and led to her distinguishing the 'domain of the classroom' from the 'domain of the school'. Nevertheless, that fact that the majority of the informants in these samples were used to speaking and listening to English must be taken into consideration, and it cannot be assumed that informants outside the educational system would provide comparable data.

The samples obtained from some provinces were much more satisfactory than those from others. The size of the sample was one factor. In East New Britain, for example, a much larger sample was recorded over several visits than that from a single visit to New Ireland. Accessibility was another factor. There was a severe problem obtaining access to Bougainville due to civil unrest and military action there, and the North Solomons sample is not as large as would have been desirable. However, this sample is supplemented with data from young people who had spent most of their life on Bougainville, but who had recently been evacuated to other centres. Access was also occasionally a problem in parts of the Highlands due to civil disturbances.

The quality of data also varies. When interviewing students in educational institutions, an effort was made to obtain cooperation from teachers to identify suitable informants who were first language Tok Pisin speakers and who had lived for most of their life in the province. Nevertheless, some of the demographic information provided can at best be regarded as an approximation. The need for caution is graphically illustrated by the case of a 17 year old girl, originally from Manus Province, who claimed to have lived in West Sepik for 24 years. In some institutions, the teacher charged with organizing the arrangements for data collection insisted (with the best of intentions) on choosing students who were inappropriate according to the criteria established, i.e. long residence in the area in question. In some such cases, data collected was useful for a consideration of the changes taking place in Tok Pisin in general but said little about the characteristics of the particular area visited. Generally, however, at most schools, in particular the Catholic boarding schools, staff members were effective in locating suitable informants. A detailed account of the location of informants interviewed in the different regions and the size of the samples is given below and summarized in the table on page 34.

Momase region

Altogether a total of nine and a half hours of recording were made from eight informants in Morobe Province. Informants in Lae included some of the youngest in the whole corpus, and extensive recordings were made of a group of children from the age of about seven over several years. Others were in their teens. Some members of this group were also used by Romaine in her major study of Tok Pisin in Morobe and Madang (1990a). For the purposes of the present study, data from informants aged less than eleven were not included. The data from this province is thus somewhat different from that of other provinces in that some of the informants gave substantial samples, and got to know the researcher very well. A full analysis of the longitudinal development of the children recorded is beyond the scope of the present study, but will hopefully form the basis of a subsequent analysis.

In Madang Province, 19 students at the Tusbab High School and Sagalau Community School in Madang provided a total of about one hour of recordings. In East Sepik Province, 63 students at the St Xavier's High School, Kairiru; Bishop Leo High School, Wewak; and St Mary's Community School, Wewak, provided about four hours of recordings. In West Sepik Province, approximately five hours of recordings were made from 88 students at the St Ignatius', Vanimo, and Aitape High Schools, Vanimo Community School, and St Anna's Community School, Aitape.

Schoolchildren at Wampit, Morobe Province

Highlands region

The most extensive samples were obtained from Eastern Highlands and Simbu Provinces. In Eastern Highlands, a total of 52 informants were recorded at the East Goroka Community School and Goroka, Kabiufa, Henganofi and Kainantu Provincial High Schools. This provided approximately five hours of recordings. In Simbu, 38 informants at the Rosary High School, Kondiu, provided about four and a half hours of recordings. This Catholic boarding high school takes students from all over the Simbu Province, and so provided good representation from different districts. Some other informants were contacted through friends.

Smaller samples were taken from the three more remote Highlands provinces, but they were large enough to provide some interesting insights. In Western Highlands, approximately one and a half hours of recordings were taken from 22 informants at the Mount Hagen and Hagen Park Provincial High Schools. In Southern Highlands, approximately one hour of recordings was made from a total of 18 informants at Mendi High School during a single visit in December 1990. In Enga, six students at Wabag Community School provided about one hour of recordings, and a single student at Wabag High School was recorded. Investigation during visits to Mendi and Wabag was also hampered due to civil unrest in the area at the time. In addition, location of suitable informants in Enga was more difficult, as here, unlike many parts of the country, there is an unusually large degree of linguistic uniformity, and fewer informants who claimed to speak Tok Pisin as a first language could be found. Most of the high school students interviewed appeared to speak Enga to one another and were unable to provide adequate Tok Pisin samples.

Group at Laiagam in Enga Province
(Highlands region)

Islands region

This region is probably the most coherent culturally and politically. There is a certain regional identity with which many inhabitants wish to be identified, and throughout the region there was evidence of an undercurrent of secessionist feeling at the time of my visits. The regional sample consists of extensive recordings from Manus and East New Britain, and smaller samples from New Ireland, West New Britain and North Solomons.

The East New Britain recordings were the most comprehensive, obtained on several visits to Rabaul and Keravat from 1985 to 1991. A total of 94 students at the Keravat and Waiau Ahnon Community Schools, Malabunga, Kokopo and Rabaul Provincial High Schools, Keravat National High School and Vunakanau Teachers' College were recorded. In addition, recordings were made of youths waiting to caddie at the golf course and contacts made through friends. The total East New Britain sample recorded amounted to approximately nine and a half hours.

Manus was visited during November 1991. Interviews were conducted with students at Manus, Ecom and Papitalai High Schools, and the Pombrut Community School in Lorengau. A total of approximately 4 hours of speech samples were recorded from 74 informants. The sample from West New Britain is quite small; seven informants from the Kimbe High School and community school provided just less than one hour of recordings. However, the quality was good, and all the informants had lived all their lives in West New Britain. The sample from New Ireland was collected on a single visit to the province in July 1990. A total of approximately one and a half hours of speech was recorded from 25 students at the Utu Provincial High School and Carteret Community School in Kavieng.

Schoolchildren at Kokopo, East New Britain

North Solomons is something of a special case due to the recent history of conflict in the province. Approximately one hour of speech was recorded in 1986 at Arawa and Buka Passage. This comprised speech from 16 young people. It has been extremely difficult to travel to North Solomons in recent years, and no attempt has been made to return to the province. However, a number of informants were encountered in different parts of Papua New Guinea who had very recently returned from the province, and they appeared to be effectively comparable to the informants located in North Solomons.

Samples by Province

Region	Province	Number of informants	Approximate recording time (in minutes)	Approximate number of words
Momase				
	Morobe	8	370	60,000
	Madang	19	60	14,000
	East Sepik	63	240	33,000
	West Sepik	88	300	50,000
Highlands				
	Eastern Highlands	52	300	38,000
	Simbu	38	285	41,000
	Western Highlands	22	90	11,000
	Southern Highlands	18	45	7,000
	Enga	12	60	13,000
Islands				
	Manus	74	250	39,000
	West New Britain	7	30	4,000
	East New Britain	94	480	53,000
	New Ireland	25	110	14,000
	North Solomons	16	60	6,000
Total		536	2940	383,000

The corpus is still limited, and less controlled than Romaine's larger corpus of speech from 482 informants in Madang (413,000 words) and Morobe (292,000 words), and extremely small by the standards of some present day corpora of languages such as English. It is nevertheless a significant resource for Tok Pisin, as it is larger, more up-to-date and more geographically diverse than many other studies of the spoken language.

2.2.3 Elicitation and recording of data

When suitable informants were located, the aim of the investigation was explained, and each was asked to provide a sample of recorded speech. This was done through the medium of Tok Pisin. Romaine & Wright (1986:13), following Labov (1972a) and Milroy (1980) used single-sex pairs of informants when working with children, to improve the quality of information elicited. They found that peer group influence tends to ensure that typical norms are adhered to, whereas with single students, the tendency to move towards the interviewer's register is more likely. Romaine was dealing with younger children, but I found this technique to be useful with older children as well. Pairs, or occasionally groups of three or four, were used wherever possible. Informants were usually rewarded with a small gift such as chewing gum or sweets.

In educational institutions, I was normally introduced as a visitor from the Papua New Guinea University of Technology, which usually generated a good deal of interest. The Papua New Guinea University of Technology has considerable prestige among school children, and I frequently gave general information about "Unitech", as it is widely known, to students, covering such topics as entry requirements, courses offered and career opportunities. If giving the talk in a formal context to a large group, I would use English, but to individuals asking specific questions in a less formal setting, I would use Tok Pisin. In all institutions visited, I found a positive and cooperative attitude from students.

Because of the rules concerning language use found in many schools, it was often necessary to ask an authority figure to explain that the use of Tok Pisin for the purposes of my research was acceptable and would not lead to punishment. I usually introduced the aims of the research with a small talk in Tok Pisin, and continued to use Tok Pisin throughout the sessions. Once the propriety of using Tok Pisin had been established, I did not encounter any inhibition from the students. The possibility was also considered that students in an English-medium educational establishment might have difficulty readjusting to a Tok Pisin-speaking task. However, I found this not to be so in the vast majority of cases. However, it is clearly possible that the students might adjust the type of language they used to a visitor from a high prestige English-speaking tertiary institution, and this is a factor which must be borne in mind when considering the nature of the corpus, as discussed further below.

After giving a few personal and demographic details, informants were asked to speak into the tape recorder to provide a sample of speech.[18] This request was usually framed in terms of 'telling a story', with further explanation that it could be a traditional story, something that happened recently, a memorable personal event or a funny story. The individual instructions, like the general introduction, were given in Tok Pisin. My request was generally framed roughly as follows:

> *Inap yu tokim mi wanpela stori na bai mi katim long tep rikoda? Yu ken tokim mi wanpela samting yu yet bin lukim long ai bilong yu, o wanpela fani stori, o tumbuna stori, kain kain stori olsem. Wanem kain stori yu laikim yu ken tokim mi. Yu tingting pastaim na stori.*
>
> Can you tell me a story and I'll record it on the tape recorder? You can tell me about something you have seen yourself, or a funny story, or a traditional story, any kind of story. Whatever kind of thing you want you can talk about. Think about it first then tell me.

The procedure was generally understood without difficulty, and some informants wished to ask further questions about the purpose of the research. Others needed to be reassured that they were

---

[18] Recordings were made using a portable cassette tape recorder. In most cases, this was a Sony TCS-430 stereo recorder, which has built-in microphones and is small enough to fit easily into the hand, but produces recordings of good quality. Informants were given the recorder to hold a short distance from their mouths. The optimum distance was demonstrated as the distance from thumb tip to little finger tip on an outstretched hand held close to the mouth. This worked well for the great majority of informants, although occasionally the quality of the recordings suffered if the recorder was held too far away from or too close to the lips. The informants generally felt happier and had more fun holding the portable machine themselves than when a more formal and apparently intimidating set-up was arranged, with a tape recorder placed on the table with microphones set up in front of it.

not being tested or assessed. Little difficulty was experienced obtaining a story from most informants, although one or two found themselves tongue-tied and with little to say or required further suggestions or prompting. Thus, although this was an interview situation, the verbal contribution from the interviewer during the recording was minimal, and usually confined to nods, laughter, or other responses appropriate when listening to a story. Occasionally informants required further prompting if the story was very short, or I intervened to ask for clarification of various details.

Early in the research, an attempt was made to elicit future constructions by asking specific questions about what informants wished to do in the future. However, as it became clear that most responses tended to be very brief and of little linguistic interest, this was soon abandoned. The most popular themes for the pupils' stories were recent newsworthy events and traditional stories. In some sessions, stories were dominated by particular recently occurring events, such as the dramatic thunderstorm which had caused the cancellation of the graduation at Mendi High School the previous day, or the recent riot by armed soldiers in Lorengau. The term 'traditional story' was interpreted rather loosely by some informants, and the genre appeared to include fairy stories, presumably heard as part of school lessons. For example, some of the offerings presented as *stori bilong tumbuna* (traditional stories) bore a remarkable resemblance to Western fairy tales such as Cinderella, Hansel and Gretel or Jack and the Beanstalk. The data obtained would in most cases be classified as 'unscripted monologue' or 'unscripted narrative'. It should be noted that traditional stories may have their own narrative conventions, as further discussed in the analysis of discourse processes in Chapter 7.

The corpus assembled in this way thus has certain limitations. The presence of the observer might affect the speech style, as might the particular genres elicited. How then, can we know how far the speech recorded was typical of that person's normal language? This question, of course, has occupied sociolinguists since Labov (1972b) drew attention to such methodological problems as the Observer's Paradox. Minimally monitored speech is most likely to give access to the vernacular style, which the researcher requires, but the presence of the observer may shift the style to a more formal register. A number of studies have illustrated ways of dealing with this problem, for example, the participant observation approach of Cheshire (1982) and Milroy (1980). These studies support Burton's observation (1978:169) that even when those being recorded knew what the observer's intention was, they could not be aware of the fact all the time, and tended to revert to minimally monitored speech. In the present study, participant observation was not an option as informants were usually encountered once only and for a brief period. Only in the case of the informants located in Lae who gave recordings over a long period was a close relationship built up. Thus, it has to be acknowledged that a large proportion of the data in the present corpus may have been influenced by the presence of the observer to some extent.

However, the degree to which the presence of the observer has influenced speech styles here is not exactly clear. In English, much more is known about the stylistic range influenced by variables such as socio-economic class, education, formality of situation, and so on. People learn grammatical rules of the standard written variety in schools, and non-standard varieties are stigmatized as uneducated or incorrect. Thus in formal situations, speakers of English may be expected to make a conscious effort to conform to the norms of educated or standard varieties.

In Tok Pisin, the situation is somewhat different. Grammatical rules for Tok Pisin are not taught in school, and there is no nationally promoted standard variety in education, although the written standards of religious works such as *Nupela Testamen* may be influential to some degree. Nevertheless, there is a general tolerance of a variety of styles. Mühlhäusler's description of four sociolects has given some indication of the range of varieties in existence, and some work on stylistic variation has been done as discussed in Chapter 6. However, we still know little about style shifting in Tok Pisin. From observation of the contemporary situation in Papua New Guinea, the most likely dimension for shifts of style to occur would be that from educated to 'bush' Tok Pisin. The speech of politicians and others has been observed to include many English borrowings, presumably in an attempt to impress (Nekitel 1990), while bush varieties of Tok Pisin are mercilessly lampooned in the "Kanage" column of *Wantok Niuspepa*. In the interview situation outlined above, the students might be expected to introduce more English words into their speech. This might be as a demonstration of mastery of a prestigious variant to a visiting English-speaker, or simply because of a shared knowledge of concepts expressed through the medium of English.

Another source of constraint might be the elimination of potentially obscene material. Expatriates in Papua New Guinea have a history of objecting to allegedly obscene words (Mühlhäusler 1985b:280), even if this may frequently have been due to misunderstanding or prejudice on the part of the visitors (Wurm 1985b:69). In the school culture, students might be expected to avoid certain taboo subjects, such as sex and swear words, but in fact one or two of the samples provided were quite uninhibited in this respect, as the following extract from a 12-year old boy in Kavieng demonstrates:

> *wanpla manggi bin toknogutim wanpla manggi na i tok,* "you fucking you" *em bin tok osem na manggi ia i go arim. Arim nau i go tok long - tokim mama blong em osem,* "*wonem em - wonem em* 'fucking you'?" *Em tok, "em narapla wed long susuim ol beibi"*
>
> A boy swore at another boy and said "you fucking you", he said this and the boy heard it. He heard it and asked his mother "what does 'fucking you' mean?" She said "it's another word for feeding babies."

Nevertheless, this taboo term only occurred in six extracts, and it can still be assumed that the majority of informants were inclined to present speech which was not considered too risqué or offensive to the interviewer.

The corpus is thus subject to a number of limitations resulting from the opportunistic nature of informant selection and the situation in which data was collected. It should also be noted that although this is an investigation of first-language speakers, and it can be fairly confidently stated that nearly all the informants use Tok Pisin as a primary vehicle of communication, it has not been contrasted with data from second language speakers. A further study would be needed, then, to confirm which features are attributable to nativization and which are not.

The main value of the corpus assembled here is considered to be as a database to exemplify current trends in the modern spoken Tok Pisin of adolescent first language speakers. With the current interest in Pidgin and Creole linguistics, Tok Pisin is frequently used in exemplification by scholars not intimately acquainted with the language, who thus have to rely on secondary sources. The data of Mühlhäusler and Sankoff are now somewhat dated, and Romaine's corpus, although recent and impressive in its size and the quality of its data analysis, is restricted in geographical range. Scholars within Papua New Guinea do not currently appear to be initiating large-scale studies of the language, and it is increasingly difficult for overseas researchers to obtain data in Papua New Guinea. The present data represents a sizeable corpus of the spoken language by present standards, and the inclusion of speakers from a wide variety of locations is also a feature not shared by many existing corpora. Thus the data may provide useful supplementary material for the continuing evaluation of trends in the evolution of Tok Pisin. It is the author's intention that the full corpus will be made available to other researchers in due course.

2.3 Data analysis

Recordings made were labelled, with details where possible of the speakers' name, sex, age, place of origin, educational level, parents' place of origin and language, the language(s) used in the home, and places of residence over the past ten years. Each tape was filed according to the province where the data was collected.

2.3.1 Transcription

Transcription of the tapes represented an enormous amount of work. It was not unusual for an hour of tape-recorded speech to require 20 hours of transcription time, and in some cases, especially recordings of children with extremely rapid speech, it could be considerably more. Some of the recordings were transcribed by myself, others initially by Jill Kaack, formerly a secretary in the Department of Language and Communication Studies at the University of Technology. Jill Kaack's transcription was of a high standard, but all transcriptions were nevertheless carefully checked by myself against the original recordings to ensure accuracy of content and standardization of transcription conventions. Transcripts were word-processed and stored in computer files using Microsoft Word.

Transcription followed a broad phonemic approach. It was beyond the scope of the present study to present a detailed phonetic transcript of the recordings. Nevertheless, some phonological distinctions which would have been obscured by standard spelling were preserved in the transcription. This was done where it was considered that (a) they were too obvious to ignore; (b) they might have morphological implications; and (c) even if not used in the present study, these phonological distinctions might be useful if the transcripts were to be used later for other purposes.

The Roman letters of the standard English alphabet were used throughout, as they could be used in word-processing search-and-replace operations which were essential to the analysis. The compounds 'dh' and 'th' were used in place of [ð] and [θ] to represent voiced and voiceless interdental fricatives; 'j' and 'dj' were used for voiced palato-alveolar fricatives and affricates, respectively, in place of [ʒ] and [dʒ]; 'sh' and 'ch' were used for voiceless palato-alveolar fricatives and affricates [ʃ] and [tʃ]; 'ng' was used for a velar nasal [ŋ] and 'ngg' [ŋg] to indicate a prenasalized voiced velar stop. Although a broad phonetic system was employed, it was not possible to determine the phonemic inventory of each individual speaker. There was thus considerable variation in the rendition of some words, even as produced by a single speaker.

The question of whether some items should appear as single compound words or separate words was frequently difficult to resolve, as has often been observed by those who compile dictionaries. For example, should compounds such as *haus kaikai* 'eating house, café' and reduplications such as *waswas* 'wash' be separated or joined? Again some of the choices were arbitrary, although if a regular productive word-formation process was employed, the tendency was to use a single word. Thus *wailpig* 'wild pig' is written as a single word, as the process is used to form a number of other lexical items by a regular process. Where an English phrasal verb or similar expression was adopted unanalyzed as a single item, it was represented as a single word e.g. *brekenenta* 'break and enter'.

Punctuation was considered important; commas were used to indicate pauses in a continuing sequence, and full stops were used to correspond roughly to sentence-level breaks. The distinction was usually decided on whether the pause was accompanied by rising or falling intonation, but in the absence of a more precise criterion, some of the choices are somewhat arbitrary. Direct quotations were enclosed in quotation marks ("quote"). False starts or sudden changes of topic were signalled by a dash (-) while uncompleted words in the middle of a change of topic were marked with a series of three periods (...). Italics were used to distinguish *Tok Pisin* from English. A single apostrophe indicates that part of a word normally present has been left out, for example *kisi'* for *kisim* 'to get'. In some samples used for exemplification in this thesis, missing letters have been replaced in brackets for clarity, so, for example, *kisi'* is presented as *kisi(m)* where appropriate. Question marks were used to indicate inaudible or incomprehensible items. The use of symbols is summarized in the following table.

Symbols used in transcription

Symbol	Meaning
?, ??	Speech was inaudible or incomprehensible. Where ? is attached to the front of a word, this indicates that the best guess at the shape of the item has been given. Where the ?? occurs alone, no attempt at a transcription of this word or words was attempted.
-	This indicates a false start or change of direction, where the speaker has started to say one thing and changed to a different course.
... -	This indicates that the change of direction occurred in the middle of a word. The part of the word preceding ... was heard before the change.
'	This indicates that a letter or letters normally present in the standard spelling have been omitted, e.g. *puti'* for *putim*. The apostrophe is also used when a word is reduced to less than a syllable, as in *bl' em*.

The following short samples illustrate these transcription conventions:

> *disla maleo ia i tokim manggi ia osem, "tapos bik moning turu, kakar... - nambawan kakaruk i no karai yet, yutupla kisi' ol bombom, laitim na yutupla go anta lo maunten na sidaun." Em nau mang... - manggi ia i kam bek lo aus.*
>
> the eel said to the boy, "if it is very early morning, the cocks have yet to crow, you two get burning flares, light them and go up the mountain and sit down." So the boy came back to the house. [East New Britain, M, 12.]
>
> *S(ap)os em kam antap ?to ?? maunten nabaut kam, aus blen ia em bai guria. Em kam nau, em brukim paiawud na kisim ?kam lo bilum kam, puti' lo dowe na em kam insaid*
>
> If she came to ?? mountain, her house would shake. She came and broke firewood and put it in her bilum, put it in the doorway and came inside. [Simbu, F, 16]

2.3.2 Organizing the corpus

The major corpus

The major corpus on which this thesis is based consists of the sum total of recorded data of first language speakers aged 10-19 obtained from the locations described above. It comprises transcriptions of approximately 50 hours of speech from just over 500 individuals. General observations about the morphosyntax, lexicosyntax and discourse structure of first language speech in contemporary Papua New Guinea are all drawn from actual occurrences in this corpus. There is no reliance on personal insights of what is acceptable or unacceptable, or recourse to written registers, except in discussion of features exhibited by samples from the corpus. This has the advantage that the analysis is based on actual language as used by contemporary informants, rather than what is considered to be correct according to perceived norms.

Since there are a large number of illustrative extracts, some of them quite long, they are accompanied by a free English translation unless a morpheme-by-morpheme breakdown is considered necessary to explain the point being made. Each sample is identified by the province where it was recorded, and the sex and age of the speaker, e.g. [East New Britain, F, 16]. This does not necessarily mean that the speaker is considered typical of that region or province, merely that this was the location of the recording. Details of the frequency of occurrence of linguistic features in the whole corpus are given wherever possible, but it should be remembered that the sample is somewhat heterogeneous and conclusions about overall frequency within Papua New Guinea should only be drawn with caution. A more stringent classification of informants was undertaken in the compilation of the regional sub-corpora used for comparative purposes as discussed below.

Such a corpus-based approach to language analysis has come to prominence in recent years, for example the COBUILD project at Birmingham University (Sinclair 1987), where an enormous corpus of English (200 million words at the latest count) is used as the basis of dictionaries and grammars of 'real' English. Using a corpus as the basis of an investigation has advantages and disadvantages. On the positive side, it is certain that the examples represent actual occurrences of language in use, and not the insights or impressions of a single person, which could possibly be idiosyncratic or distorted, especially when the investigator is not a native speaker. One limitation of some descriptions of Tok Pisin has been a failure to make clear whether what is being presented is an actual attestation and or an intuitive judgment. In more recent corpus-based approaches such as Romaine 1992a, it is certain that all examples are real.

However, this reliance on a corpus as an index of authenticity would be more convincing if the corpus were of the order of several millions or tens of millions of words like the COBUILD corpus, rather than the 400,000 or so presented here. Really large corpora are needed to have a realistic idea of the frequency of use of less common lexical items. Written corpora are somewhat easier to assemble than corpora of transcribed speech, and the present account of oral language is still significant for a language such as Tok Pisin. Grammatical analysis can proceed with confidence on a much smaller corpus than that required for investigating lexical frequencies, and it is hoped that the analysis presented here will provide some useful details of the grammatical features of contemporary spoken Tok Pisin.

Regional sub-corpora

Where regional variation appeared to be significant, this was explored further. The question thus arises of the selection of data considered to be representative of the region in question. Dividing the corpus into three parts on the basis of where it was recorded would be unacceptable, as there were many informants who had moved their place of residence, and thus might not show speech patterns typical of the region they were now living in. Thus these individuals were not considered when compiling the more selected regional samples, and only those informants who had spent the majority of their lives in the region were included.

This approach, of course, has its limitations. There are problems determining exactly what 'most of one's life' should be, and how much time out of the region is considered significant. For the purposes of this study, short visits, such as holidays, to other regions were discounted, as were the first four years of life. Also, residence within the region may not be a sufficient criterion to ensure that an individual is a typical speaker of a regional variety. The language of the parents, the home and the peer group are all likely to have an influence. However, as noted earlier, these variables are so numerous and diverse that, instead of trying to control for them, the analysis proceeded on the basis that any conclusions drawn will be subject to these limitations. Due to the paucity of data on regional variation, even such limited information is likely to be of value.

As noted above, an exception to the residence rule was made in the case of a number of students who had very recently returned from Bougainville due to civil unrest there, usually referred to as 'the crisis'. For example, at Henganofi High School in the Eastern Highlands Province, a group of these students who had lived all or most of their lives on Bougainville had all returned to the mainland only a few weeks previously, and formed a social group within their school. Considering the difficulty encountered obtaining data from the North Solomons, these informants were included with the North Solomons group. Details of other similar recent evacuees located in other provinces are included in the table below.

Thus, more selected sets of data were assembled for three broad regions corresponding to the main divisions generally used to refer to the different parts of Papua New Guinea. These divisions were used as being the most convenient, while it is recognized that they are somewhat artificial in nature, and may have significant internal heterogeneity. The three regional sub-corpora are the Momase, Highlands and Islands regional samples. The Momase sub-corpus consists of recordings by 155 speakers, a total of 94,000 words. The Islands sub-corpus consists recordings by 163 speakers, a total of 67,000 words. The Highlands sub-corpus consists of recordings by 115 speakers, and also contains about 67,000 words. These sub-corpora were used as the basis for quantitative regional comparisons. Sample texts from each of the three regional sub-corpora appear as an appendix.

It is quite possible that there are differences from one province to another within a region. For this reason, more selected provincial sub-corpora were also isolated according to the same criteria: having spent all or most of one's life residing in the province. However, as the provincial samples are in some cases rather small, and because provincial boundaries do not form natural social or geographical boundaries in the same way that the regional boundaries do, a detailed analysis of variation by province with respect to all features was not attempted. Comparison was restricted to any particularly notable features confined to a single province, which are commented on as appropriate. Certain ways of beginning stories in Manus, for example, or aspectual features only found in Enga, or phonological forms only found in Eastern Highlands are discussed below. The numbers of informants from each province included in the regional and provincial sub-corpora are summarized in the table which follows.

Number of informants in provincial and regional sub-corpora

Region	Province	Number of informants	Momase sub-corpus	Highlands sub-corpus	Islands sub-corpus
Momase					
	Morobe	8	8		
	Madang	19	11		
	East Sepik	63	53		
	West Sepik	88	82		
Highlands					
	Eastern Highlands	52		39	4
	Simbu	38		30	
	Western Highlands	22		18	
	Southern Highlands	18		15	
	Enga	12		12	
Islands					
	Manus	74			47
	West New Britain	7			7
	East New Britain	94	1	1	74
	New Ireland	25			16
	North Solomons	16			15
	Total	536	155	115	163

Thus, it can be seen that, as a result of adherence to the above criteria, the samples on which the regional comparisons are based are considerably smaller than the major corpus, and conclusions about regional variation based on these limited data are necessarily tentative and would bear comparison with other studies.

2.3.3 *Computer assisted analysis*

Analysis of the written transcripts was carried out in conjunction with intensive listening to the recordings. In addition, a computer was also used to assist in the analysis of transcribed texts in a rather basic way. The use of the Longman Mini Concordancer (version 1.01) and Oxford MicroConcord programmes was extremely helpful in locating words in context or assembling relative frequency tables of lexical items. Both these programmes basically produce concordances of specified search words, that is, they identify all occurrences of the search word and display the line of text in which these words occur to show the context. Each line can be expanded to a larger context sample if desired. The Oxford programme is useful for analysing extremely large amounts of text, and can simultaneously search through up to 500 different files from over 900 directories. However, it is limited to displaying a maximum of about 1600 concordance lines, the exact number depending on other computer software used.

The concordance lines can be arranged according to alphabetical listing of the word immediately to the right or left of the search word, or two or three places from it. Searches can be conducted for groups of alternate words, which is useful when dealing with transcripts which contain various renderings of the same word, such as *dispela* or *disla*. Searches can also be limited to collocations with other context words at a specified distance or 'horizon' from the search word. Wild card characters can also be specified, for example *sa** would include *sa*, *save* and any other word beginning with 'sa'. Appropriate use of wild cards can make data analysis somewhat less arduous.

The Longman Mini-concordancer can in addition produce word frequency lists, which can not be produced by MicroConcord. It can also produce larger numbers of samples than the 1600 limit of MicroConcord, which is occasionally useful in examining the contexts of frequently occurring items such as *i*. However, the size of the files that the Longman Mini-concordancer can handle is limited to about 50,000 words. The word frequency lists assembled in Chapter 5 were produced using Longman Mini-concordancer. Unfortunately, the more powerful concordancer *Wordsmith* was not available at the time of analysis. A more detailed description of the use of concordancers for analyzing word frequency can be found in Smith (1998a)

In addition, the standard word-processing search-and-replace facility was extensively used, both on its own, and as the basis for a number of custom-designed 'macros' or word-processing programmes. For example, one macro was used to restore the standard spelling of phonological variants to make various quantitative operations easier. Similarly, in the absence of a spelling checker for Tok Pisin, a macro to eliminate the words present in Mihalic's dictionary was devised and found to be useful for examining the 'residue', i.e. to see which lexical items not in the dictionary were present in the texts.

3

Phonology

Although the main focus of the study is on morphosyntax, lexis and discourse processes, a number of interesting phonological features became apparent in the course of the investigation, which seem worthy of at least a mention here. The following brief account is intended as an indication of some of the phonological changes taking place, and a pointer to potential areas for further study. Two areas stood out as particularly significant: the expansion of the phoneme inventory and phonological reduction.

3.1 The phoneme inventory

Tok Pisin is usually described as having around 25 phonemes. There is necessarily some variation because of Tok Pisin's status as a second language for many individuals. Second language speakers are very likely to be influenced in varying degrees by the phonology of their first language.

Mihalic (1971:4) lists an inventory of 26 phonemes, including three diphthongs. He notes certain phonotactic constraints, for example, that many speakers may split up consonant clusters with epenthetic vowels. He also acknowledges that the inventory is somewhat tentative, as for example, /p/ and /f/ may be merged as a bilabial fricative by some speakers. Laycock (1985:297) lists 24 basic phonemes, but observes that the four fricatives may be used contrastively only in heavily Anglicized speech. He describes the effect on what he identifies as core Tok Pisin phonology of widely occurring phonological characteristics of Papua New Guinean substrate languages. For example, intervocalic prenasalization of voiced stops is described as widespread in the languages of the Sepik and Madang areas, and this feature may appear in the Tok Pisin spoken there. Similarly, unvoiced stops may be realized medially as fricatives in many Highlands languages, and this too may carry over into Tok Pisin. While these features serve to give particular characteristics to speakers of various first languages, Laycock notes that there is such diversity in all provinces that distinct regional accents are not likely to emerge (1985:304). Although such variation generally does not adversely affect comprehensibility, he notes that the lack of a distinction between /t/ and /s/, carried over into Tok Pisin from many languages in New Ireland, New Britain, the Highlands and South Bougainville is actually "disturbing to communication" (ibid. p. 302). It is also worthy of note that the deliberate use of this feature was used for humorous effect by fluent speakers at the University of Papua New Guinea (Mühlhäusler 1985n:261). More generally, peculiarities of pronunciation provide the basis for many jokes at the expense of less fluent Tok Pisin speakers, for example the humorous stories featured in the 'Kanage' column of *Wantok Niuspepa*. This ridiculing of non-standard features is cited by Laycock (1985:304) as another reason why distinct regional accents are unlikely to emerge.[19]

Instances of more or less extensive substrate influence on the phonology of second language speakers no doubt occur widely throughout Papua New Guinea. The most detailed account of phonological interference affecting Tok Pisin is the study of a speaker of the Eastern Highlands language Usarufa by Bee (1971). She shows how phonological rules of Usarufa, such as complementary distribution of phones, were frequently applied to Tok Pisin, leading to numerous cases of ambiguity or misrepresentation. It should be noted that Bee describes the Usarufa people at the time of her study as having "about 20 years of marginal exposure" to Tok Pisin (Bee 1971:69). Thus the variety of the language is probably equivalent to what Mühlhäusler refers to as "bush pidgin", i.e. less completely acquired than standard rural pidgin and spoken in a more restricted range of contexts with considerable interference from first language phonological and syntactic patterns.

The above studies deal with second language speakers of various degrees of competence. The phonology of first language speakers has received less attention. Romaine (1990) looks at the variation between /p/ and /f/ in initial position by young people in Morobe and Madang

---

[19] Laycock (1985) states that the most comprehensive account of Tok Pisin phonological systems is an unpublished paper by Litteral (1970) of which, regrettably, I have been unable to obtain a copy.

provinces, including first language speakers. Greater consistency in the correspondence between initial /f/ in Tok Pisin and their English equivalents is shown to be related to such factors as urban or rural status. In rural areas, such as Indagen, there was greater variation, and some interesting observations are made, including instances of hypercorrection where initial /f/ was used on words derived from English words beginning with /p/.

In another study on a single phoneme pair, Romaine (1995a) discusses discrimination of the phonemes /r/ and /l/ in the same corpus of speech from Morobe and Madang Provinces. She again relates the use of this distinction to urban and rural status, but does report that first language urban speakers are more consistent in distinguishing /r/ from /l/, even though there is considerable variation. Among the rural speakers, those in Waritsian village were most likely to confuse the phonemes, which could be due to substrate influence, as the Adzera language does not distinguish these two sounds.

Looking at the present corpus, it is apparent that a number of phonemes outside the standard core phonology are present. The main source of innovations appears to be borrowing from English, which is continuing in all areas investigated. Newly incorporated words may adapt to Tok Pisin phonology or maintain features present in English. This situation corresponds to Thomason & Kaufman's (1988) classification of "slight structural borrowing" between languages in contact, where new phonemes are generally restricted to borrowed words and may or may not be used contrastively (p 74).

A number of examples from the corpus will make this clear, but first an explanation of some of the conventions appearing in the transcript samples should be given. In transcribing from recordings, the following core phonemes were used:

Consonants::   d, b, g, t, p, k, n, m, ng, s, f, h, l, r, w, v, y
Vowels and diphthongs: a, e, i, o, u, ai, au, ia, iu, oi

Mihalic (1971) was used as the standard for comparison because this remains the standard dictionary, but it should be borne in mind that the entries in Mihalic may not represent the most common spoken form. Reduction in rapid speech is indicated in the illustrative examples by inserting missing parts in brackets. For example if the standard *olgeta* is reduced to *ota*, this is written *o(lge)ta*. Words reduced to less than a single syllable are accompanied by an apostrophe, for example *bl' ol (bilong ol)*. Some reductions are so common that they have not been marked. These are *-pela* to *-pla*, *dispela* to *disla* or *sla*, *olsem* to *sem* or *se*, *save* to *sa*, *long* to *lo* or *l'* and *bilong* to *blo* or *bl'*. Indeed, although *-pela* is widely used in written forms, its occurrence in spoken Tok Pisin appears to be limited to formal domains or slow, deliberate speech, and it could be argued that *-pla* is in fact the standard spoken form.

As Laycock has noted (1985:295), speakers of Tok Pisin who also speak English well have potentially the whole phonology of English at their disposal. In the present corpus, words were considered to be Tok Pisin words only if they were morphologically and syntactically integrated, for example by adopting transitive marking or typical Tok Pisin word order. This was not always easy to determine, and there were inevitably borderline cases. However, where it appeared that extended English borrowings were being used, this is indicated as a code switch in the transcriptions by underlining and use of a non-italic font:

Okei, taim tupla i wokim pinis - taim tumbuna bl' ol dai ol wokim pinis, <u>some weeks later</u> *ston i bin kamap*

when the two had done it, when their grandfather had died they did it, <u>some weeks later</u> the stone appeared. [West Sepik, M, 16]

na taim mipla go, ol si ia wok lo kam osem <u>**one after the other**</u> *na mipla poret*

and when we went, the waves came <u>one after the other</u> and we were afraid [Manus, F, 16]

mi ting osem Kevieng i se wanpla intresting ples <u>**that's why**</u> *dedi blo mi i tok bai mipla stap hia osem* <u>**four to five years**</u>

I think that Kavieng is an interesting place, <u>that's why</u> my father says we'll stay here for <u>four to five years</u>. [New Ireland, F, 14]

Okei lo Mande moning <u>**the following day**</u> *mipela i go lo gaden*

Then on Monday morning, <u>the following day</u> we went to the garden [Western Highlands, M, 15]

As noted in an earlier discussion, it is possible that the recording situation may have encouraged speakers to use more English phonemes than usual, considering that the investigator was an English-speaker and the setting in an English-medium educational establishment may have been perceived as rather formal. A fuller investigation of the phonology of speech in more naturalistic settings would be needed to indicate how well established these are in Tok Pisin. The consonants shown in the table below, together with the Romanized equivalents used in the transcription of this corpus, were regularly attested:

Introduced phonemes

Phoneme	Representation in corpus	Phoneme	Representation in corpus
θ	th	ð	dh
ʃ	sh	z	z
ʒ	j	tʃ	ch
dʒ	dj		

An example illustrating the use of additional phonemes is seen in the following extract from the speech of an 11-year old girl from Eastern Highlands, recorded at Goroka.

> *Wanpla taim lo wanpla li(k)lik vilidj, olgeta man sa go lo gaden olge(t)a taim lo traipla moning. Na wanpla man ia, wanpla taim em giaman sik nau em stap lo haus nau, olge(t)a taim lo - ol fish ia ol sa kam antap lo bich bl' ol disla lain ia na, ol sa dens. Ol sa rausim skin bl' ol na puti(m) lo taro lif na ol sa dens. ... em swipim haus nau, em - em laik go draim ol kloudhz antap lo kapa blo haus bl' ol ia ... Nau, wanpla taim nau, meri ia em tichim - em tichim beibi bl' em ... tupla cheinj nau ...*

> Once in a small village, all the men always went to the garden very early in the morning. One man, once he pretended to be sick and stayed in the house. Always, the fish came up to the beach and danced. They took their skin off and put it on a taro leaf and danced. He swept the house, he was going to dry his clothes on the roof of their house. One time, the woman taught her baby, the two of them changed... [Eastern Highlands, F, 11]

Consonants outside the core phonology which occur in the above extract are seen in the table below:

English phonological influence

Standard pronunciation	Gloss	Current pronunciation	Introduced phoneme
vilis	village	vilidj	/dʒ/
pis	fish	fish	/f/, /ʃ/
lip	leaf	lif	/f/
klos	clothes	kloudhz	/ð/
tisim	teach	tichim	/tʃ/
senis	change	cheinj	/ʒ/

English sounds have clearly influenced the pronunciation both of new introductions, such as *kloudhz* and long-established items such as *pis* 'fish' and *tisim* 'teach'. It is not clear, however, whether all the above examples can be regarded as distinct phonemes of the language. To establish this, it would be necessary to demonstrate minimal pairs of words showing contrasts with the core phonemes. Otherwise they may best be considered as *ad hoc* borrowings of exotic phonemes along with borrowed lexical forms. With small samples from each speaker, minimal pairs are difficult to find. The question of phonological convergence between Tok Pisin and English will be further discussed in considering the question of a post-Pidgin continuum in Chapter 8.

Although not present in the previous sample, the phoneme /θ/, transcribed as *th* in the corpus, is now also sometimes used where rural Tok Pisin usually has /t/:

> *Ol tok olsem "ol soljes sta(p) lo polis steshen, na ol okei lo sut <u>nathing</u> lo gan" so, ol tokim mipla lo tanim go bek ken*
>
> they said "the soldiers are in the police station, and they are allowed to shoot <u>at will (=nothing)</u>" so they told us to turn back. [Manus, F, 16]
>
> *mi ka(m) woki(m) greid seven lo Vanimo Aiskul, greid seven, greid eit na nau greid nain lo tem <u>thri</u>*
>
> I came and did grade 7 at Vanimo High School, grade 7, grade 8, and now grade 9 in term <u>three</u>. [West Sepik, M, 15]

However, it often co-occurs with other cases where /th/ is not used, as in *tri* 'three' in the following example, suggesting it is a case of borrowing:

> *Fest taim blo mi lo kam lo aiskul mi bin fil boring liglig, i go inap tri <u>manths</u> nau mi painim ol poroman blo mi*
>
> First time for me to come to high school I felt a bit bored, after three <u>months</u> I found my friends [Western Highlands, M, 16]

Generally, however, the number of introduced phonemes was small compared with the standard equivalents. For example, there were 132 cases of θ in the corpus, including use in borrowed fragments from English such as the following:

> *Ol bikman osem osem midel eidj we ol i bin ekspiriensim <u>through marriage</u> ol ba kisim ol bois ia kam insait lo haus*
>
> Middle aged men who had experience of marriage would take the boys into the house. [Eastern Highlands, M, 17]

The frequency of use of θ compared with standard alternatives is illustrated by the word *tri/thri* (three). There are 128 occurrences of *tri*, only 8 of *thri*. The ratio is even more marked in the case of *mauth/maus* 'mouth'. There are 79 occurrences of *maus*, only one of *mauth*, and even this was followed by an immediate self-correction:

> *em rausim ol samting osem ol liklik ol spia o samting lo - a insait long - long <u>mauth blong - maus blong</u> manggi ia.*
>
> he took the things like little arrows inside - er from the boy's mouth. [West Sepik, F, 17]

The situation is similar for the phoneme /ð/, represented in the corpus as /dh/. There are 106 occurrences of /ð/, mainly in the words *bradha* 'brother', *fedha* 'feather and *kloudhz* 'clothes'. The term *bradha* occurs 41 times, the equivalent *brata/barata* 857 times, and an intermediate form *brada* 373 times. Again with /ʃ/ (sh), figures show that the standard alternative is much more frequent than the borrowed form, for example, *bus* 'bush, forest' occurs 704 times, while the alternative *bush* only 40 times. For a more recently introduced item, *lans/lansh* 'lunch', however, the contrast is not as great (*lans* 15, *lansh* 17), suggesting that those terms more recently borrowed from English are more likely to retain their phonology without modification.

In the case of *bus* and *bush*, there are also some regional differences here shown by the more restricted samples from the regional sub-corpora:

bus and *bush* in regional samples

	bus	*bush*	ratio of *bus* to *bush*
Momase	258	4	64.5
Highlands	174	24	7.3
Islands	148	6	24.7

The alternation between /p/ and /f/ also shows some regional variation, illustrated here by the word *pis(h)/fis(h)* 'fish'.

pis(h) and fis(h) in regional samples

	pis/pish	fis/fish	ratio of pis/pish to fis/fish
Momase	64	133	0.5
Highlands	35	24	1.5
Islands	69	64	1.1

Although it is difficult to draw conclusions from these figures, a number of factors might be at work, such as substrate phonology, exposure to English schooling and how recently Tok Pisin was introduced to the area in relation to English.

However, the situation is somewhat different with respect to /ch/, which seems to have become the standard in certain words in all regions. Comparing *tich* and *ticha* with the more usually cited standard forms *tis* and *tisa*, the figures from the whole corpus are quite dramatic:

	Whole corpus	Regional sub-corpora		
		Momase	Highlands	Islands
tis	0	0	0	0
tisa	1	0	1	0
tisas	0	0	0	0
tich	24	11	3	5
ticha	92	49	9	27
tichas	37	14	8	13

The /ch/ form is clearly the overwhelming choice for this particular word among this particular population. The plural form *tichas* appears 37 times in the main corpus. This might appear to be a code-switch, but the form can be fully integrated into the Tok Pisin utterance, and it appears that this particular form can now be regarded as a Tok Pisin word which frequently adopts the -s plural suffix:

> *mi to, "mi les," nau <u>ol tichas</u> kam na to sem, "yupla olgeta yupla no ken pilai, san hot na yupla sidaun isi."*
>
> I said "I'm tired" and the teachers came and said "All of you shouldn't play, the sun is hot so sit down and rest." [Morobe, F, 11]

Other uses of /ch/ do appear to depend on regional factors. For example, pronunciation of the word *pisin* 'bird' as *pichin* occurred 23 times in the Islands regional sample, exclusively from the North Solomons Province, but not at all from elsewhere.

On some occasions, informants appeared to be conscious of the conflicting phonological systems, and self-correction occurred to replace a phone with one from standard Tok Pisin, or replace a reduction with a fuller form. Since the researcher had a declared interest in Tok Pisin, rather than English forms, this may have had some influence too:

> *em rausim ol samting osem ol liklik ol spia o samting lo - a insait long - long <u>mauth</u> blong - <u>maus</u> blong manggi ia*
>
> he took out the things like little spears from inside the boy's <u>mouth</u>. [West Sepik, F, 17]

> *sapos osem <u>ol pigs</u> la go bai i no inap - <u>ol pik</u> no inap go insait long gaden na distroyim ol gaden.*
>
> if <u>the pigs</u> were about to go they couldn't - <u>the pigs</u> couldn't go into the garden and destroy them. [Manus, F, 14]

> *Nau wanpla taim wanpla liklik manggi em go na, em go antap lo <u>disla - displa</u> laulau.*
>
> One time a small boy went and climbed <u>this</u> laulau tree. [West Sepik, F, 13]

> *Em sa meki(m) gaden <u>bl' em - blong em</u> na - am - em sa planim ol kaikai blong em*
>
> She made <u>her</u> gardens and planted food (for herself). [Manus, F, 14]

In the second example, the self-correction included not only the standard phonology but the more standard plural marking as well. Such self-repairs are discussed further when considering the relationship between Tok Pisin and English in Chapter 8.

In addition to the introduction of the above exotic consonantal phonemes, other features such as consonant clusters or diphthongs not normally found in Tok Pisin were found in borrowed items. Laycock (1985:297) lists the following phonemic consonant clusters in Tok Pisin: *mp, nt, ngk, mb, nd, ngg*. In addition, the following initial combinations are found in Mihalic:

bl	*blak,*	br	*brata*	dr	*dring*	fr	*Fraide*	gl	*glas*	gr	*gras*	kl	*klia*
kr	*kros*	kw	*kwila*	pl	*planim*	pr	*pret*	skr	*skru*	sl	*slek*	sm	*smok*
sn	*snek*	sp	*spes*	sr	*srang*	st	*sting*	str	*stret*	tr	*traim*		

The table below lists some occurrences of words containing other consonant clusters which appear to have become established, together with the pronunciation which would be expected in standard Tok Pisin. The numbers in brackets are the number of attestations in the major corpus.

Sample non-standard consonant clusters

Meaning	Expected form	Non-standard form
house post	*pos* (6)	*post* (9)
next	*neks* (149)	*nekst* (15)
outside	*ausait/ausaid* (46)	*autsait/autsaid* (331)
get	*kisim* (2310)	*ksim* (522)
wild	*wel/wail* (51)	*waild* (1)
gold	*gol* (9)	*gold* (3)

Some of these clusters do occur regularly in other positions, for example, *st-* occurs in initial position in standard Tok Pisin but is normally rendered as *-s* in final position. Nevertheless, there is considerable variation, and many clusters may be separated by epenthetic vowels. As Pawley (1975) also observed, this appears to be related to speed of delivery in some cases. Many of the clusters here appear to be due to English influence, but as noted in §3.4, reduction due to rapid speech may also be a factor.

Vowels are also variable. Laycock lists 12 basic vowels which may be used in the core phonology (1985:302). However, it was apparent that some words with a single vowel in standard pronunciation were pronounced with diphthongs in the corpus, often apparently influenced by the corresponding English pronunciation. It was often difficult to decide whether vowels were diphthongized or not, and only very clear diphthongs were recorded as such in the corpus. Some were frequently attested, others only rarely, as illustrated by the figures below:

Sample non-standard diphthongs

Meaning	Expected form	Attested form
hole	*hul* (48)	*houl* (5)
road	*rot/rod* (283)	*roud* (1)
tail	*tel* (34)	*teil* (21)
wild	*wel* (36)	*wail(d)* (21)
sew up	*samapim* (15)	*soumapim* (2)

3.2 Phonological variants in the lexicon

As noted above, phonological changes have led to new distinctions and new pronunciations of words which have been present in Tok Pisin for some time. A number of alternative pronunciations appear to be well established. These include phonetic distinctions not normally associated with the standard Tok Pisin inventory (e.g. Mihalic 1971, Laycock 1985), but the degree to which they are phonemicized or are merely allophonic variations is still not clear. They include the use of some forms already well known as allophonic alternatives in Tok Pisin, such as [f] and [v], but which appear to be increasingly used on a more regular basis. Some examples from the corpus can be seen in the following table. They include phonological variants of existing items, and newly adopted lexis for terms previously referred to by other terms:

Phoneme/Allophone	Example	Standard form (Mihalic)	Gloss
f	fish, fis	pis	fish
	aftanun	apinun	afternoon
	faia	paia	fire
	fren	pren	friend
sh (ʃ)	pish	pis	fish
	shut	sut	shoot
	steshin	stesin	station
	shap	sap	sharp
	shuga	suka	sugar
th (θ)	thing	samting	thing
	noth	not	north
j (ʒ)	enjin	ensin	engine
	pasenjas	pasendia	passengers
	cheinj	senis	change
dj (dʒ)	vilidj	ples, viles	village
ch (tʃ)	kechim	kisim	get, catch
	ticha	tisa	teacher
	bich	nambis	beach
	chekim	sekim	check

To give some idea of the amount of variability occurring in the corpus, a list of variants is given below. Since there is an enormous number of variants, only a small sample is provided. This variability needs to be taken into consideration in any discussion of proposals for language planning, such as the revision of standardized items, if such items were to have a chance of meeting with widespread acceptability.

Standard form	Phonological variants	Gloss
abris	abiris, avris, habiris	go past
abrisim	habrisim, havrisim,	go past
abus	awus, habus	animal food
abusim	awusim	add meat
ailan	ailen	island
ais	hais	ice
amamas	hamamas, mamas	happy
animal	animol, enimol	animal
aninit	ananit, andanit, andnit, anit, nit	underneath
antap	anap, anda, andap, anta, antaf, dap	on top, above
apim	abim, api	raise
apinun	abinun, afinun, aftanun, habinun, havinun	afternoon
arasait	aratsait, arsait	other side
arere	alele, are, arele, harere	beside
as	has	cause
asde	aste, haste	yesterday
askim	aski, haski, haskim	ask
ating	ati, atin	probably
ausait	audzait, ausaid, autsai, autsaid, autsait, autseid, autseit, autshaid, autshait, autshed, autsheid, asait, atsait	outside
aut	haut	out

It can be deduced that these phonetic variants occur for a number of reasons. The first is reduction of syllables or segments due to speed of delivery, as discussed in more detail below in §3.4. Although this seems apparent from listening to rapid speech, it should be noted that the speed of extracts in this corpus has not actually been measured and correlated with the amount of reduction occurring. Note the elision of the parts in brackets in the following extract, which shows reduction apparently due to speed of delivery:

> *na ol polis ol lukim ol peles ia pinis o(l)se(m) na ol lusim gen na ol tok "maski mipla no ken fait nogut mipla - ol - <u>ba(i)</u> mipla bagarapim ol sidaun <u>b(i)lo(ng)</u> ol meri pikinini <u>b(i)lo(ng)</u> <u>m(i)pla</u>." Ol <u>to(k)</u> <u>(ol)se(m)</u> na ol no <u>tintin lo(ng)</u> fait.*

> And the police looked at the villages and <u>so</u> they left and they said "forget it, let's not fight or <u>we'll</u> spoil the lives <u>of our</u> wives and children." They <u>said this</u> and they didn't <u>think about</u> fighting. [Simbu, F, 12]

The second cause of variation is the lack of consistent discrimination between various voiced and unvoiced consonants, which is particularly common in the Highlands samples, but also occurs elsewhere:

Labial stops:

> *mipla stap lo avim niu ye, niu ye mipa - <u>mibla</u> no wok, <u>sambla</u> ol tok giaman ol sik nabaut na sampla mipla - mipla les lo wok tu*

> we stayed and celebrated New Year, <u>we</u> didn't work, <u>some</u> pretended they were sick, and the others didn't want to work either. [Enga, M, 18]

> <u>*Mibla*</u> *bin sta(p) long Rabaul na <u>mibla</u> kam tasol, na <u>mibla</u> go lo Baluan na <u>mibla</u> la go lo - wanpla taim <u>mibla</u> la go long gaden…*

> <u>We</u> were living in Rabaul and <u>we</u> came back, and <u>we</u> went to Baluan and <u>we</u> went, one time <u>we</u> were going to the garden… [Manus, F, 14]

> *Em i stap nau na em lak go <u>apim</u> disla sospen graun. Em lak go <u>abim</u> nau em lukim traipla braitpla lait i kam autsait long em. Na mama bilong em sta lo <u>kaden</u> (gaden).*

> Then he wanted to <u>lift</u> up the clay pot. He was about to <u>lift</u> it when he saw a very bright light coming from it. And his mother was away in the <u>garden</u>. [West Sepik, F, 14]

Alveolar stops:

> *"… Yu mas kam <u>andap</u> lo - yu mas flai osem pisin na kam <u>andap</u> na painim mi lo si," em tok osem.*

> "… you must come <u>up</u> to - you must fly like a bird and come <u>up</u> and look for me in the sea," he said. [Enga, F, 12]

> *Bihain lo displa em i kam bek long ples blongen na ol lain blongen i hamamas tru <u>bigos</u> em no dai na ol i <u>paidim</u> karamut na ol i danis. Em <u>dasol</u>.*

> After this he came back to his village and his family were very happy because he was alive and they <u>beat</u> the garamut (slit drum) and danced. That's <u>all</u>. [Manus, M, 14]

> *na taim ol bildim <u>rod</u> i go nau, ol ami putim dainamait n' ol blowim <u>rod</u> i go nau, ol painim disla man silip insait lo ston i stap na ol ol cheisim em.*

> And when they were building the road, the soldiers placed the dynamite and blew up the road, they found this man lying inside the stones and they chased him. [Western Highlands, M, 17]

Velar stops:

> *So mipla stap i go <u>liglig</u>, nogat graun bruk na em pudaun kam daun.*

> So we stayed <u>for a while</u> when the ground gave way and he fell down [Eastern Highlands, M, 14]

> *ol man i dai nambaut osem <u>pig</u> na <u>dog</u>, yu lukim em i dai na stap.*

> People were dying like <u>pigs</u> and <u>dogs</u>, you saw him lying dead. [Eastern Highlands, M, 18]

> *Simbu Evieishen i go daun na em i <u>gam</u> andap. <u>Kam</u> antap lo ples, mipla kisim kam lo ples, mipla krai krai i stap go go nau*
>
> Simbu Aviation went down and he <u>came</u> back up. <u>Came</u> up to the village, we took him to the village, we cried and cried [Simbu, M, 17]

Some Highlands speakers routinely voice all or most stops in medial position:

> *Long Mendi <u>mibla</u> - <u>mibla</u> sa stap <u>wandem</u> ol fren blo <u>mibla</u>. <u>Mibla</u> no sawe <u>wogim</u> <u>wanbla</u> samding <u>mibla</u> sa raun raun tasol na <u>wogim</u> ol kain <u>samding</u> olsem.*
>
> In Mendi <u>we</u> stay with <u>our</u> friends. <u>We</u> don't <u>do</u> anything, <u>we</u> just drift around and <u>do</u> various things. [Southern Highlands, M, 14]

There is occasionally the tendency to prenasalize medial voiced stops:

> *Em nau, trausel ia katim rop lo lek blo manggi ia n' em kisim em <u>gondaun</u> lo wara nau, kisim em go nau. Em kisim em go bieinim wara <u>gondaun</u> go, bringim em lo ples em ksim laulau trip <u>gondaun</u> nau, manggi ia wok ka(m) l' aus.*
>
> Then the turtle cut the rope from the boy's leg and took him <u>down</u> to the river, took him away. He took him and followed the river <u>down</u>, brought him to the village, brought the laulau (tree) drifting <u>down</u>, the boy came back home. [West Sepik, M, 13]
>
> *Mipla ple ple go, mi lusim wanpla <u>mambol</u> blo mi. Mi to(k) "mi gat planti <u>mambol</u> mi go kisi(m) kam." Mi meki(m) ose(m) go kisi(m) wanpla kam nau mi ple.*
>
> We played and played, I lost one <u>marble</u>. I said "I've got lots of <u>marbles</u>, I'll go and get them." I did go and get one and I played. [Morobe, F, 10]

Other variations involving voicing affect the sibilants 'z' and 's':

> *bas ia kilim em na ol polis putim em long <u>zel</u>. Na <u>dizla</u> man ia, <u>dizla</u> liklik manggi ia bin dai binis, na <u>dizla</u> liklik ma… - a <u>dizla</u> man ia, em ol putim lo <u>sel</u>.*
>
> The bus killed him and the police put him (the driver) in the <u>cell</u>. And this man, <u>this</u> small boy had died, and <u>this</u> man, they put him in the cell. [Enga, M, 12]
>
> *Na <u>zla</u> stori em lo wanpla wara, nem bl' em Wara Kua. Na stori i go olsem. Bipo tru, bipo tru, taim ol tumbuna stap, <u>dizla</u> wa… - ol tumbuna i save biliv osem <u>dizla</u> wara em pulap lo masalai.*
>
> And <u>this</u> story is about a river called Kua River. And the story goes like this. Long ago in the time of our ancestors, this <u>river</u> - our ancestors believed that <u>this</u> river was full of spirits. [Simbu, M, 17]

Thirdly, the presence or absence of some other phonemic contrasts related to place and manner of articulation appears to be very variable. Note the variation between 't' and 'th' (θ) by the same speaker in the following extract:

> *em repotim mipla nau ol tok osem ba mipla lukim Mista Brava lo - Mista Brava lo <u>Tesdei</u> - mipla stap i go wet i go <u>Thesdei</u> nait stadi Mista Brava singautim mipla kam lo hap*
>
> he reported us and they said we would see Mr. Brava on <u>Thursday</u> - we stayed and waited, on <u>Thursday</u> night Mr. Brava called us to go there. [East Sepik, M, 16]

A similar variability between 'd' and 'dh' (ð) by single speakers is seen in the following:

> *em i givim tupla <u>fedas</u> i go lo mama blongen lo putim lo gras, wanbla blek na wanbla red. Em tok "sapos disla blek i palai - i palai lo gras blo yu ko pundaun em yu save mi dai pinis. Sos disla redpla <u>fedha</u> i palai lo het blo yu em yu mas save osem mi stap laif."*
>
> He gave two <u>feathers</u> to his mother to put in her hair, one black one and one red one. He said "if this black one flies and lands on your hair you will know that I have died. If this red <u>feather</u> flies to your hair, you will know that I am still alive." [Manus, M, 14]
>
> *ted <u>bradha</u> bl' em kirap nau painim wanpla meri sangguma. … wanpla <u>brada</u> bl' em tu em i dai*
>
> the third <u>brother</u> started looking for a witch … one of his <u>brothers</u> had also died. [Simbu, M, 17]

The alternation between **r** and **l** is well known in second language varieties, and there is variability too among some first language speakers (Romaine 1995a). In some cases this variability was found to be quite marked. In the following extract, for example, the expected forms *lized* 'lizard', *long* 'to', *stilim* 'steal' and *lapun* 'old woman' all appear with r substituted for l, while l replaces r in *rere* 'ready':

> *em i kam araun ro disa, a kam araun ro disa haus na stirim disa kiau blo rized na ranawe pinis. Em kukim i stap na leli logen. Em stirim na go pinis na disa rapun meri i kam bek.*

> he came around to this house and stole the lizard's eggs and ran away. He cooked them and got them ready. He had stolen them and taken them away when this old woman came back. [Eastern Highlands, M, 17]

A distinction between p and f is often inconsistently applied, especially in Highlands speech samples, but also in other areas:

> *Tupla wogobaut go, tupla no, wonem ia, askim femishen lo mama papa blo tupla, tupla yet go.*

> The two went, they didn't ask permission from their parents, they just went. [Enga, F, 13]

> *Planti taim em save kisim ol bel blo fik na wasim olgeta taim, na wanpela taim em i kisim ol bel blo fik na go wasim lo wara.*

> He often got the pig's entrails and washed them, and once he got the pig's entrails and washed them in the river. [West Sepik, F, 15]

As well as general trends, there are some idiosyncratic variants in certain individuals, such as the substitution of /b/ for /r/ (*mebi* for *meri*) or the switching of the position of /r/ and /l/ (*ralim* for *larim*). These were considered to be individual peculiarities or developmental stages on the way to acquiring target phonology.

New phonological distinctions may serve a useful role in distinguishing what were homophones according to a more standard phonology. Examples from the corpus include:

Former homophones	Meaning	New distinction	Meaning
gol	gold, goal	*gold* vs *gol*	gold vs goal
hat(pela)	hard, hot	*hat(pela)* vs *hot(pela)*	hard vs hot
let	(leather) belt, late	*let* vs *leit*	(leather) belt vs late
pait(im)	hit, fight	*paitim* vs *fait*	hit vs fight
plen	plan, plane	*plen* vs *plein*	plan vs plane
sain	sign, shine	*sain* vs *shain*	sign vs shine, shiny
sak(im)	send back, shark	*sak(im)* vs *shak*	send back vs shark
sekim	shake, check	*sekim* vs *chekim*	shake vs check
sel	sail, shell	*sel* vs *shel*	sail vs shell
sol	only (*tasol*), salt	*sol* vs *solt*	only vs salt
stap	be situated, stop	*stap* vs *stop(im)*	be situated vs stop
we	where?, way	*we* vs *wei*	where vs way
wel	wild, slippery	*wail(d)* vs *wel*	wild vs slippery

However, it also appears that an equal or greater number of new homophones are appearing, especially through phonological reduction and restructuring of borrowed lexis. Although these could potentially lead to ambiguity, the context is likely to provide disambiguation in the majority of cases. Examples from the corpus are listed in the following table:

Emerging homophones

Word	Former unequivocal meaning	New alternate meaning
bai	future (etc.) marker	by (in calqued expressions such as *wan bai wan* 'one by one')
bendaun	bend down	burn down
hat	hard	heart
Holi (*Triniti*, etc.)	Holy (Trinity, etc.)	reduction of *holim*
holim	hold	haul
ista	Easter	reduction of *i stap*
ken	can	(sugar) cane
kok	penis	coca cola
kol	cold	1. reduction of *kolim*
		2. (telephone) call
mas	must	(church) mass
mi ('*m i*)	I, me	reduction of *em i*
miksim (*mi ksim*)	to mix	I get
ol	they/plural	hole
ol i (*oli*)	they + predicate marker	reduction of *holim*
pasim	to close, shut	pass (an exam or vehicle)
pres	-	1. press; 2. praise
pul	paddle	full
pusi	cat	Reduction of *pusim*
raf	rough	raft
redi	ready	reduction of *redim*
sa	reduction of *save*	reduction of *dispela*
se	say	reduction of *olsem*
sem	ashamed	reduction of *olsem*
set	-	1. shirt; 2. reduction of *husat*
sit	ashes, residue	1. seat; 2. seed
stil	steal	still, yet
sua	sore, ulcer	shore
ta	-	1. reduction of *olgeta*
		2. reduction of *taim*
tri	three	tree
wasim	wash	watch
wik	week	weak

3.3 Prosodic and suprasegmental features

Very little work on supra-segmental phonological features in Tok Pisin has been carried out. Wurm (1985) is the most detailed account of intonation patterns, mainly of Tok Pisin speakers in the Eastern Highlands. He shows that stress and intonation patterns from substrate languages have a significant effect on the patterns appearing in Tok Pisin. Faraclas (1989) investigates stress patterns among Tok Pisin speakers in East Sepik, taking account of variables such as sex, first language, and degree of education in English. He demonstrated that females show consistently less stress reduction than males, and that the amount of English schooling has a significant influence. He supports Wurm's observations about the importance of substrate languages, and shows, surprisingly, that substrate interference does not appear to be significantly less among first language speakers than second language speakers.

A detailed analysis of stress, rhythm and intonation patterns is beyond the scope of the present study, and discussion is confined to its relevance to morphophonemic and discourse features. There will also be a brief discussion of those intonation patterns which appear to have a role in the structuring of discourse in Chapter 7.

3.4 Phonological reduction

One of the most obvious features of the speech of fluent first language speakers is the speed of delivery. This 'allegro' character of speech has been commented on by Lynch (1979a) and Romaine & Wright (1987:62) in their accounts of phonological reduction among young Tok Pisin speakers. As Sankoff & Laberge (1973) noted, rapid speech is characteristically accompanied by a reduction in the number of syllables receiving primary stress, and may be difficult to understand for less fluent second language speakers.

As seen in some of the previous examples, reduction in rapid speech may give rise to clusters of consonants not normally attested in Tok Pisin. This may be taken to extremes:

mi ba kam na was <u>ken l' sla</u> (= ken long dispela) diwai

I will come and watch <u>this tree again</u> [Eastern Highlands, F, 12]

Note the cluster of four consonants from the end of the word *ken*. The extreme rapidity of the speech of some of the informants made transcription very difficult, and points to an area where there could be significant problems for inter-generational communication.

Common reductions, as noted above, include an almost universal loss of one syllable of the suffix *-pela* to *-pla*. Since the latter form is now virtually standard in spoken Tok Pisin, an alternative interpretation might be that the standard *-pla* is occasionally subject to the insertion of an epenthetic vowel. However, the full form is occasionally used in stressed or deliberately enunciated words, indicating that this might be better considered the canonical form:

Tu<u>pla</u> wet stap ia wan<u>pla</u> trai<u>pela</u> sinek go - wogobaut em krol i kam.

The two waited and a huge snake came crawling towards them. [Western Highlands, M, 16]

Other common words which frequently lose syllables appear in the table opposite. They include *mama* 'mother' to *ma* and *papa* 'father' to *pa*. *Pikinini* 'child' is often reduced to *pikini*. *Mipela* 'we exclusive' is typically reduced to *mipla*, *mpla* or *pla*. *Tasol* 'but, only' loses a syllable to become *tsol*, *chol* or *sol*. *Tok* 'speak, say' frequently loses the final consonant and becomes *to*. *Olsem* is often heard as *osem*, *ose*, *sem*, or *se*. Thus the three-syllable *tok olsem* is typically reduced to the two-syllable *to se(m)*.

Phonological reduction also has an affect on morphology as independent words become cliticized (see Chapter 4). *Long* 'in, on, at' is frequently reduced to *lo* or *l'*, and in the latter case often joins the following syllable, especially one starting with a vowel, such as *l' em* 'to him' *l' ol* 'to them' and *l' et* 'on the head'. *Bilong* 'of, possessive' behaves in a similar manner, and very commonly reduces to *bl'* as in *bl' ol* 'their' and *bl' em* 'his, her, its'. Similarly, *na* 'and' is often reduced to *n'* before vowels. The set expression *kirap na tok olsem* could be translated literally as 'got up and said that' or 'started to say', but the former is common in Papua New Guinea English. The phrase is often severely reduced to *kra na tok sem*, *kra n to se*, or even *kra t se*. Some examples of cliticization can be seen in the following extracts:

mi go silip na biain ol ksim mi go <u>l' ospitol n' ol</u> tok osem ...

I went to sleep and afterwards they took me <u>to hospital and they</u> said [Western Highlands, F, 14]

disa meri ia <u>kira n' t'</u> (=kirap na tok) "e mi sutim wanpla samting pinis."

This woman <u>got up and said</u> "hey, I've shot something" [Manus, F, 13]

> *ol meikim kastam <u>bl' ol</u> (bilong ol) na ol paiti(m) karamut na em kam*
>
> they did their traditional thing and they beat the drum and he came   [Manus, F, 13]
>
> *em go ksi' ol lain <u>bl' em</u> kam, ol ksim dsla man, ol karim go, lokim em lo aus <u>bl' ol</u> stap*
>
> he went and got <u>his</u> relatives, they got this man, they took him away and locked him in <u>their</u> house [West Sepik, M, 14]

The number of occurrences of these common reductions in the full corpus are given in brackets in the following table:

Common reduced forms

Standard form	Reduced form	Meaning
pikinini (808)	*pikini* (194)	child
mama (1113)	*ma* (88)	mother
papa (1085)	*pa* (58)	father
kirap (1237)	*kira* (469), *kra* (7)	get up
olsem (1104)	*osem* (2859), *ose* (478)	thus
save (414)	*sa* (2775)	know
laik (759)	*la* (527)	like
tok (4008)	*to* (782), *t'* (85)	say
bilong (206)	*blong* (1587), *bilo* (4), *blo* (6862), *bl'* (2673)	of (possessive)
long (4061)	*lo* (14828), *l'* (963)	in, at
mipela (208)	*mipla* (5784)	we (exclusive)
yutupela (9)	*yutupla* (110), *yutla/yutra* (161)	you two
dispela (100)	*displa* (478), *disla* (3222), *dsla* (139), *sla* (624)	this
kisi(m) (2694)	*ksi(m)* (561)	get

Syllable and stress reduction can best be seen in actual examples of discourse. The following was from a young woman at Kundiawa:

> *em katim em stret long namel blong an blongen. <u>Tso l' sla taim</u> yu save, kain taim, taim blong trabel osem bai, yu no inap tingim pen o blut nabaut*
>
> he cut him right in the middle of the arm. <u>But at this time</u>, you know, times like this, in times of trouble you won't think about pain or blood or that sort of thing

Here the standard *tasol long dispela taim* 'but at this time' with seven syllables is reduced to the three-syllable *tso l' sla taim*. A similar pattern is seen in the following extracts from an 11-year old girl at Sinasina, Simbu Province:

> *<u>l' ap</u> ol <u>mek' ose n'</u> ol tok*
>
> <u>there</u> they were <u>doing this, and they</u> said

The two-syllable *long hap* 'there' is reduced to a single syllable *l' ap*, while the 6-syllable *mekim olsem na ol* becomes the 4-syllable *mek ose n' ol*.

> *mipla kam <u>na mpl' arim</u> osem ol tok ol kisi(m) Reks i go*
>
> we came <u>and we heard</u> that they said they had taken Rex away

The six syllables of *na mipela harim* 'and we heard' become three: *na mpl arim*, with the consonants of *mpl* attaching to the preceding and following vowels. Similarly:

> *ol tok "em raskol na em gat gan, <u>n' em gim l' ol</u> na ol go fait," ol tok ose*
>
> they said "he's a criminal and he has guns, and <u>he gave them to them</u> and they went to fight" they said this

N' em gim l' ol 'and he gave them to them' is heard as three syllables, while the full standard form would be *na em givim long ol*, with six syllables.

Also very widespread is the loss of final consonants, a common feature especially in rapid speech, as shown in the following extracts:

> *wanpla dokta blong Amanab em <u>wantai</u>(m) ol femili blong em i bin go long wa... - go waswas lo bikpla wara*
>
> a doctor from Amanab <u>with</u> his family went to swim in a big river [West Sepik, F, 15]
>
> *Em go <u>anta</u>(p) lo disla buai go go stret <u>anta</u>(p) lo haus*
>
> he went <u>up</u> this betel nut palm, went straight <u>up</u> to the house [Manus, M, 14]
>
> *Nau papa blo mi <u>kira</u>(p) na tok "em mas ol tewel o <u>wane</u>(m) santing ol mas wokim ..."*
>
> Now my father <u>got up</u> and said "it must be spirits or <u>whatever</u> who did it..." [Western Highlands, F, 15]

The final *-m* of *-im* verbs and even of the pronoun *em* is occasionally lost:

> *ol <u>suti</u>(m) (di)sla boi ia l(ong) leg - boi ia lo leg na okei, ol <u>puti</u>(m) <u>e</u>(m) lo kar*
>
> they <u>shot</u> this boy in the leg, then they <u>put him</u> in the car [Simbu, F, 11]

Such reduction can have morphological implications, for example, if the final phoneme of the root is *-i* in verbs ending in *-im*, this effectively removes the distinction between transitive and intransitive, for example the use of *redi(m)* 'to prepare' discussed below.

3.5 Regional variation

The above dropping of final consonants shows conspicuous regional differences, with the feature much more common in the Momase region than elsewhere, and substrate phonology may be involved as well as reduction in rapid speech. The number of tokens of the reduced form *toki'*, for example, can be seen in the following table:

tokim **vs** *toki'* **in regional samples**

	tokim	*toki'*	ratio of *tokim* to *toki'*
Momase	548	118	4.6
Highlands	254	16	15.9
Islands	309	14	22.1

More details of this and other examples of phonological reduction which have an affect on morphology are given in chapter four.

Many Tok Pisin speakers claim to be able to recognize regional varieties, mainly on phonological grounds. Perceived deviant pronunciation is often the source of humour (Wurm, Laycock & Mühlhäusler 1984), but such stereotypes do not necessarily conform to the reality of regional variation, and informal tests by Mühlhäusler (1985n:256) show that claims to recognize regional variants may be quite unreliable. Moreover, first language speakers are less likely to exhibit some of the more marked substrate features. The following section gives a brief comparison of the more obvious phonological features of the language of the three regional samples in this corpus.

In all three regions, the phoneme inventory is basically similar, with the introduction of new phonemes from English common in loan words, but with little evidence that they are used contrastively with established phonemes. Prenasalization of stops was often depicted as a Highlands characteristic in speech mimicry by informants, and while there are some extreme cases of this in the Highlands, prenasalization of stops is also found to be quite common in the Momase and Islands samples.

The following do appear to be regional characteristics. The alternation of /t/ and /s/ in *sapos/tapos* is almost exclusively found in the Islands Region (24 tokens).

> *Na <u>tapos</u> ol man i sanap antap na ol lukluk go daun, bai ol lukim ol kaikai i stap*
>
> And <u>if</u> the men stand on top and look down they will see the food there. [East New Britain, M, 12]

There is a single attestation in each of the other two regional samples, but they are in no way typical. However, it could be argued that ***tapos*** merely represents an alternative form of this particular word, rather than a general phonological feature, as alternation of s/t in other words is not found in this corpus.

Alternation of /l/ and /r/ is found in all regions, but is most noticeable in the Highlands sample, especially in texts from the Eastern Highlands. The alternate form ***kirim*** for ***kilim*** 'kill', for example, occurred eight times in the Eastern Highlands sample, and not at all elsewhere:

> *Wanpla meri kam na - a wanpla kam na <u>kirim</u> disla pikinini. <u>Kirim</u> disla pikinini nau na em trome lo wara*
>
> A woman came and <u>killed</u> this child. <u>Killed</u> the child and threw it away in the river. [Eastern Highlands, M, 17]

Also found almost exclusively in the Highlands sample (mainly from Eastern Highlands) is a characteristic pronunciation of velar nasals as stops:

> *Nau, papa <u>blogen</u> go autsaid na tupla wet stap*
>
> Now his father went outside and the two waited. [Simbu, M, 19]

Occurrences of *b(i)logen* and *logen/log em*

	bilog en/m	*logen/m*
Eastern Highlands	73	12
Simbu	4	0
Southern Highlands	0	1
Enga	2	3
All other provinces	0	0

The lack of a voiced/unvoiced distinction is also common in the Highlands sample, but found in the other samples also:

> *<u>Wanbla</u> taim tupla <u>ririg</u> (= liklik) brata sa stap na, mama blo tupla indai pinis nau tupla <u>wogoba(ut)</u> lo bus*
>
> <u>One</u> time there were two <u>little</u> brothers and their mother had died and they <u>walked</u> into the forest. [Eastern Highlands, M, 11]

While words such as ***wanbla*** may be used to characterise lay impressions of Highlands Tok Pisin, it in fact occurred somewhat more frequently in Manus, as the following provincial breakdown illustrates:

wanbla in provincial samples

Momase: West Sepik 11, East Sepik 21, Madang 0, Morobe 0.

Highlands: Eastern Highlands 25; Simbu 3; Western Highlands 25; Southern Highlands 20; Enga 2.

Islands: Manus 107; New Ireland 0; West New Britain 0; East New Britain 1; North Solomons 0.

Alternation of /f/ and /p/ is also found mainly in the Highlands sample but also occasionally in the other samples, notably from West Sepik or North Solomons:

> *mipla putim wanpla <u>flang</u> antap nau, mipla mekim sment.*
>
> We put a <u>plank</u> on top of and made cement. [Simbu, M, 17]

> *tupla lukim wanpla wonem ia, wanpla rat i wok lo <u>plei</u> antap. Wok lo <u>flei</u> antap na tupla i lukim tasol na, torosel i go.*
>
> The two saw a rat <u>playing</u> on top. <u>Playing</u> on top, the two saw it and the turtle went. [North Solomons, M, 10]

There are some other words pronounced in a distinctive way by some of the North Solomons informants, such as *pichin* (*pisin*) 'bird' and *divai* (*diwai*) 'tree'. Finally, in all three regions, there are examples of extreme morpho-phonological reduction in rapid speech. It is to be hoped that a more comprehensive study of the phonology of first language Tok Pisin and its regional varieties will be carried out by other researchers before significant standardization measures are attempted.

4
Morphology

Morphology, the study of the internal structure of words, has traditionally been divided into inflectional morphology, where parts of words indicate grammatical relations, and derivational morphology, which deals with the processes whereby new words are formed. The distinction, however, is not absolute, for example the *-im* suffix could be considered derivational, as it affects word class membership, although it is treated under inflectional morphology by Mühlhäusler (1985d). Morphology overlaps with phonology to a considerable degree, as indicated in the previous section This chapter deals mainly with inflectional morphology, while the question of productive processes leading to the derivation of new words is dealt with in a fuller treatment of the lexicon in Chapter 5,. Morphophonemic reduction has an effect particularly on the transitive marker *-im* (§ 4.1 below) and on the trend towards cliticization of reduced forms (§ 4.5).

Pidgins have been characterized as possessing little in the way of inflectional morphology (Mühlhäusler 1985d:335), although it should be remembered that many non-Pidgin languages, notably Chinese languages such as Cantonese, are generally lacking in this feature (Matthews & Yip 1994). A number of studies of the morphology of Tok Pisin have appeared. Lynch (1979a) described some morphological changes taking place in the speech of children whose first language was Tok Pisin. Although the paper remained unpublished for many years, it was frequently quoted and was the most definitive account of Tok Pisin morphology during this time. A number of interesting observations appear in this paper, in particular the trend towards cliticization or even 'prefixization' of the future marker *bai*, preverbal aspect markers *save* and *laik*, and the prepositions *long* and *bilong*, as in the examples given in the previous chapter. Somewhat more tentative is the analysis of the reduced dual and plural forms *mitla* and *mipla*, which a synchronic description would most logically analyze as number suffixes *-t* and *-p* in combination with a non-singular suffix *-la*. Other areas discussed are the *-s* plural suffix on nouns, and the omission of the predicate marker *i* "very frequently indeed", particularly among speakers from the Highlands (Lynch 1979a:6).

Mühlhäusler (1985d) reviews inflectional morphology in Tok Pisin, noting that the only affixes normally encountered are the *-im* transitivizer and two *-pela* suffixes attached to monosyllabic adjectives and plural pronouns. However, in addition to summarizing the insights of Lynch (1979a), he points to a number of interesting trends from his own data on spoken Tok Pisin. The most notable of these are the descriptions of a present continuous *-ing* verb form among some urban speakers and a reduplicated verb form agreeing with plural subjects in a creolized variety on Manus. In addition, he considers that the *-s* plural suffix borrowed from English has now become an integral part of the grammar, disagreeing with Lynch's characterization of -s pluralization as an interference phenomenon. The most recent and most comprehensive account of current morphological changes is Romaine (1992a), where an in-depth analysis concentrates mainly on the *-s* plural form and inclusive and exclusive pronouns.

In the following discussion of morphology in the current corpus, the two well-known suffixes *-im*, indicating transitivity, and *-pela* attached to adjectives are first dealt with. Plural marking, where it occurs, is normally described as involving the pluralizing particle *ol*, but in this corpus, the use of the pluralizing suffix *-s* is frequently encountered. These alternative patterns of plural formation are described. Following this, the use of various forms of pronouns is compared to the established paradigm, and other morphological phenomena such as the cliticization of reduced forms are discussed. Finally, the use of some other borrowed affixes is described.

4.1 The transitive marker *-im*

The transitivizing marker *-im* is one of the most characteristic features of Melanesian Pidgin English, and its use has been recorded from the earliest Pidgins of the Pacific. Its etymology is no doubt from the English object pronoun 'him'. This is sometimes said to be reanalyzed according to Melanesian substrate patterns (e.g. Keesing 1988), although the suffix was present in NSWPE considerably earlier (Baker 1993) so the role of Melanesian languages was more likely to be one of reinforcement.

A number of verbs in Tok Pisin show distinct transitive and intransitive meanings depending on the presence or absence of *-im*, for example *sanapim* 'to stand something up' and *sanap* 'to be standing up'. Mihalic (1971) lists some 90 examples of this type. A few verbs, however, can clearly be used transitively, at least in some contexts, without taking the *-im* suffix, for example *gat* 'have', or, to cite further examples from Dutton (1973), *kaikai* 'eat', *pispis* 'urinate', *pekpek*, 'defecate' (as in *pispis blut* 'urinate blood' = blackwater fever, and *pekpek wara* 'diarrhoea') and from Mühlhäusler (1985h:360) *pilai* 'play' and *kuap* 'climb'. The forms *pispisim* and *pekpekim* were not thought to be permissible (Dutton 1973), but both do occur in the present corpus, and their derivation is discussed in § 5.6. In the case of *kaikai*, there is said to be a semantic distinction between *kaikai* 'eat' and *kaikaim* 'bite' (Mihalic 1971:102). However, this appears to be changing, as discussed in § 5.5.

While several writers observe that the verb *gat* 'to have' does not occur with *-im* (e.g. Mihalic 1971:26), there are a few tokens of *gatim* in the corpus, for example:

wanpela taim i gatim papa, mama na pikinini boi na gel

once there was a father mother and their son and daughter [Eastern Highlands, F, 15]

Taim fest mi kam long skul mi no gatim ol planti frens ol kam toktok long mi na mi yet mi stap.

When I first came to school I didn't have many friends coming to talk to me and I stayed by myself. [Eastern Highlands, F, 15]

Of the 10 occurrences in this corpus, seven were from the Henganofi area of Eastern Highlands. There was one each from Simbu, Enga and Western Highlands provinces:

I bin gatim tupela barata na susa. Tupela save stap ...

There was a brother and sister. The two lived .... [Western Highlands, M, 17]

Informants indicated that the form, although not standard, is not uncommon in the Highlands. This appears to be a case of over-generalization of a rule during the process of acquisition, and whether this will survive competition from the standard alternative remains to be seen.

As noted in § 3.4, the most notable change affecting the *-im* suffix in this corpus is the frequency with which the final consonant, or occasionally the whole syllable is elided. This occurs in samples from all regions, as the following further examples show. Loss is particularly noticeable before other consonants:

... osem pasin blo ol lo kili' pik nambaut em lo hia em difrent liklik ia.

like their way of killing pigs is a bit different here [Western Highlands, F, 14]

nau wanpla taim em toki' tupla n' em tok ...

once he said to the two and he said ... [Eastern Highlands, F, 12]

mi raun go daun lo aus na mi toki' dedi long onim tivi

I went back to the house and told Dad to turn the TV on [Manus, F, 16]

liklik brada bl' em askim em lo wonem hap em k(i)si' disla liklik yangpla meri

His younger brother asked him where he got this young girl [East Sepik, M, 15]

However, the final consonant of *-im* is also lost before glides:

laki na em kari' wanpla lilik naif

it was lucky that he was carrying a small knife [Eastern Highlands, F, 12]

em luki' wanpla traipla mama reinbo sneik em slip stap nau

he saw a huge rainbow serpent lying there [Eastern Highlands, F, 12]

Mi toki' yu lo go planim tsol yu les ia

I told you to go and plant it but you didn't want to [Eastern Highlands, F, 11]

It also occurs in all regions when the following word begins with a vowel, but by far the greatest number of occurrences of this are in the Momase region:

... bai yu mas <u>lukauti'</u> em gut tru ose wankain osem pikinini blo yu yet

you must <u>look after</u> him well, just like he was your own child [West Sepik, M, 16]

em sa <u>toki'</u> em na save olsem, ol man ia kam.

He <u>told</u> him and knew that the men had come [Eastern Highlands, M, 14]

Nau, man ia kam nau, em <u>aski'</u> em lo buai na em no givim.

Now the man came and <u>asked</u> him for betel nut, and he didn't give him any [West Sepik, M, 16]

em go em painim kapul em kilim em kam nau em <u>kuki'</u> em lai kaikai nau

he went and found a cuscus, killed it and came and <u>cooked it</u> and was about to eat it [Manus, F, 15]

Em no <u>luki'</u> em na em pul lo kanu kam anta(p) lo wara

He didn't <u>see</u> him and paddled the canoe up the river [Madang, M, 11]

It was seen in the preceding chapter that reduction to *-i* is generally more common in the Momase region. A further breakdown given here in the following table shows the figures for loss of *-m* before vowels in the commonest verbs *kisim* 'to get', *lukim* 'to look, see', *tokim* 'to say', *painim* 'to find, look for' and *kilim* 'to kill' in the provincial subcorpora:

Loss of final -m before vowels by province

		kisim	lukim	tokim	painim	kilim
Momase	West Sepik	4	10	10	3	-
	East Sepik	4	17	11	5	1
	Madang	2	4	6	-	-
	Morobe	6	29	3	1	1
Highlands	Eastern Highlands	-	1	4	1	-
	Simbu	-	-	-	-	-
	Western Highlands	-	-	-	-	-
	Southern Highlands	-	-	1	-	-
	Enga	-	-	1	-	-
Islands	Manus	-	-	-	-	-
	New Ireland	-	-	1	-	-
	West New Britain	-	-	-	-	-
	East New Britain	-	4	5	-	-
	North Solomons	-	2	-	-	-

It is clearly seen that the samples from the Momase area contain a far greater number of occurrences, and closer inspection of the tokens shows that this is particularly so with the verb *lukim* in the collocations *luki' em* 'see him/her' and *luki' ol* 'see them' in the Morobe samples. As noted above, in cases where a verb stem ends in *-i*, this loss of the final *-m* can eliminate the marking of the transitive/intransitive distinction:

em kirap, mama bl' em <u>redi(m)</u> kaikai bl' em pinis

he got up, his mother had <u>prepared</u> his food [West Sepik, F, 13]

Since the transitive verb *redim* 'to prepare, get something ready' is derived from *redi* 'ready' which ends in *-i*, the residual *-i* when *-m* is lost cannot be distinguished from the normal ending of the stative verb. Of 10 occurrences of *redi* used in this way, 8 were from the Momase region.

In other cases, not only the final consonant but the whole syllable is elided:

nau ol <u>kis(im)</u> em go haus nau

now they <u>took</u> him home [Eastern Highlands, M, 15]

Three occurrences of *kis* used as a reduction of *kisim* were recorded, two from Momase and one from the Highlands sub-corpora. In the above example, the meaning is not greatly affected, as there is no related intransitive form of the verb *kisim*. In other cases, loss of the final syllable results in a reduced transitive form identical with the intransitive verb. For example, in the following extract, the whole suffix *-im* is lost on one occasion in *yupla go pait(im) saksak*:

Nau em toki(m) ol meri - em toki(m) ol meri "yupla go <u>pait(im)</u> saksak, mi bai mi stap." Em nau, ol go <u>paiti(m)</u> saksak. Olgeta mer(i) yet ol kisi' bu... - e ol kisi(m) naip blong ol, k(i)si(m) tamiok ogeta go <u>paiti(m)</u> saksak ol go - ol go kati(m) saksak...

Now she told the women "you go and <u>make</u> sago, I'll stay". So they went to <u>make</u> sago. All the women took their knives, their axes, they all went to <u>make</u> sago, to cut sago... [West Sepik, F, 12.]

This could also be the interpretation in some of the cases of transitive verbs apparently used without the *-im* suffix, as in the following example, where *klaimim* 'to climb' would be expected:

papa tokim mi lo <u>klaim</u> [= klaim(im)?] diwai

father told me to climb the tree [West Sepik, M, 17]

Thus the reduction of *-im* to *-i* is a regular feature of the corpus. The relative influence of reduction through speed of delivery and substrate phonology is not clear; it is likely that normal processes of reduction are reinforced by substrate phonology. For some speakers, *-i* is the predominant variant of the transitive suffix, and it appears that loss of *-m* is particularly common in the Sepik area. It remains to be seen whether *-im* will gradually be replaced by *-i* as the standard transitive marker, or whether the normative influence of adult speakers will resist what appears to be a major change in progress. In addition, the whole suffix is sometimes lost in rapid speech. Although it would be a gross overstatement to say that the transitive suffix is being abandoned, it should be noted that occasional instances of loss do occur.

4.2 The adjectival *-pela* suffix

As noted above, the *-pela* suffix appears in two distinct morphological roles, the marking of adjectives and plural pronouns. This section is concerned with the suffix used with adjectives. It should be noted that there is considerable overlap between the category of 'adjective' applied to some of these nominal modifiers used in predicative position, and the category of 'stative verb'. The position of adjectives in Tok Pisin is quite complex, with many adjectives placed before the noun, usually with the *-pela* suffix, and a number used as post-nominal modifiers, such as *mau* 'ripe', *tambu* 'forbidden' and *nogut* 'bad'. As Mühlhäusler has pointed out (1986a:49), this appears to violate Greenberg's 19th universal, which says that if there is a general rule that descriptive adjectives precede the noun, there will be no exceptions to the rule (Greenberg 1963).

Mihalic (1971) notes that the use of *-pela* is restricted to monosyllabic adjectives, and that these forms always appear before the noun they qualify. In certain cases, forms take *-pela* when used attributively in front of nouns, but lack the suffix in predicate position. Mühlhäusler (1985d:351) lists further examples of pre- and post-nominal modifiers. The use of the *-pela* suffix with pre-nominal adjectives has obvious parallels with the 'classifiers' or 'measure words' in Chinese languages, for example as used in the following Cantonese phrase:

yat^1 go^3 yan^4

one classifier person

In this and other Chinese languages, one of a range of classifiers such as *go^3* is obligatory between numerals or adjectives and nouns (superscript numbers in the Cantonese example indicate tones). This pattern was followed in Chinese Pidgin English, with the generalized classifier *piece* or *piecee* placed before nouns. This gives a possibility of the origin of the use of *-pela* in this way, as has been suggested, for example, by Keesing (1988:113). However, Crowley (1990a:285), is sceptical of this claim and Baker (1987:180) specifically rules out this source as *-pela*'s origin. A more likely origin appears to be from 'fella' in New South Wales Pidgin being reinterpreted in its current role (Baker 1993:44).

There may also be parallels in substrate Melanesian languages such as Tolai (Mosel 1980). Mühlhäusler (1986a) has discussed at some length the question of this possible substrate influence for adjective placement before and after nouns. He demonstrates that no simple relationship exists, and although some patterns suggest substrate modelling in a synchronic analysis, they prove to be unrelated when the history of the relevant structures is traced. He concludes that neither substrate nor universalist explanations by themselves are adequate, and that grammatical reanalysis in conjunction with both processes accounts for the present situation.

In the present corpus, *-pela* is typically reduced to a single syllable *-pla*. Occasionally there is further reduction to *-la*, especially following a consonant in high frequency items such as *disla* 'this' and *gutla* 'good'. (It should be noted that *pla* on its own occurred regularly in the corpus as a reduction of *mipela* 'we exclusive'; there were altogether 91 occurrences in the corpus). The variant *-tla* also occurred quite frequently, especially in the word *wantla* (*wanpela* 'one'), with 43 occurrences in the major corpus. This was a feature more common in the Highlands, as a regional breakdown shows:

Use of *wantla* as a variant of *wanpela* by region

Momase	Highlands	Islands
1	40	0

The distribution within the region was also uneven, as a breakdown of the total attestations in the more selected provincial sub-corpora shows:

Use of *wantla* as a variant of *wanpela* in four provinces

Madang	1
Simbu	5
Western Highlands	10
Enga	16

The use of *-pla* is widespread and shows no sign of diminishing, in spite of its apparent redundancy. It should be noted that in some cases the status of *-pela* as a suffix is not unproblematic. In cases such as *dispela* or *sampela*, for example, where there is no independently occurring **dis* or **sam*, the words might better be considered as unanalysable roots.

Monosyllabic adjectives using *-pla* in attributive position constituted by far the greatest use in the corpus. These included:

Numerals	Colours	Other physical attributes
wa(n)pla 'one'	wait(p)la 'white'	bikpla 'big'
tupla 'two'	grinpla 'green'	fletpla 'flat'
tripla 'three'	blekpla 'black'	gu(t)pla 'good'
fopla 'four'	braunpla 'brown'	hotpla 'hot'
faifpla 'five'	redpla 'red'	longpla 'long'
sikspla 'six'		n(i)upla 'new'
tenpla 'ten'		naispla 'nice'
twelfpla 'twelve'		(h)olpla 'old'
festpla 'first'		smatpla 'smart'
		sotpla 'short'
		stailpla 'stylish'
		strongpla 'strong'
	Determiners	switpla 'sweet'
Quantifiers		traipla 'huge'
	na(ra)pla 'other' 'another'	trupla 'real', 'true'
sampla 'some'	dis(p)la 'this'	yangpla 'young'

The list of numerals includes the ordinal *festpla* 'first'. This is an occasional variant of *fest*, which is now preferred to the alternative standard form *nambawan*, being over four times as frequent as *nambawan* in the major corpus:

Fest, festpla and nambawan

fest	138
festpla	4
nambawan	30

In addition, a number of forms with disyllabic or multisyllabic stems occurred:

sevenpla 'seven' *levenpla* 'eleven' *tetinpla* 'thirteen' *fotinpla* 'fourteen'
fiftipla 'fifty' *fitifaifpla* 'fifty five' *yelopla* 'yellow' *narapla* 'another', 'other'
isipla 'easy' *hamaspla* 'how many?'

Yelopla, sevenpla, levenpla and *tetinpla* appear to follow the pattern of other numerals and colour terms in the use of the *-pla* suffix. The use of *fiftipla* and even *fitifaifpla* in the Enga sample is highly unusual, and is not typical of first language speakers in general, who would more typically use the English numeral unmodified. This leaves *narapla* as the only other common disyllabic form with *-pela*.

A single occurrence of *isipela* was found:

Ol sa yusim <u>isipla</u> wok - a <u>isipla</u> meted tasol lo, go na k(i)sim ol saksak.

They use an <u>easy</u> work - um an <u>easy</u> method to go and get the sago [West Sepik, M, 17]

This looks like a case of reanalysis, as *isi* 'easy, slowly' normally appears post-nominally as an adverb:

mipla stap sidaun na sinek ia i kam <u>isi tasol</u>, mi no meki(m) wanpla samting na sinek ia i kam holim mi.

we were sitting down and the snake came <u>slowly</u>, I didn't do anything and the snake came and held me. [Manus, F, 15]

However, the semantics of the first extract look decidedly English.

The form *hamaspla* is attested 11 times in the corpus, compared with 22 of *(h)amas*. Mühlhäusler lists this as a typical 'bush' form, using *-pela* indiscriminately (1985 n:247), but in the corpus there appears to be a distinction in meaning from *hamas*, the interrogative or relative pronoun. As far as can be seen from the occurrences here, *hamaspla* is used as an idiomatic or rhetorical expression indicating 'so many' or 'goodness knows how many', and is definitely not associated with incomplete acquisition:

tupla go yet, ol i no kaikai, ol i go ran <u>hamaspla</u> de, wik, ol go ran yet, na dok ia kam biein long tupla yet.

The two kept on going, they didn't eat, they ran <u>who knows how many</u> days, weeks, they still kept running, and the dog still followed them [Morobe, F, 11]

ol i bin kam na distroyim haus blo ol, kukim - kukim ol kar blong ol. <u>Hamaspla</u> kar olgeta ol bin kukim?

they came and destroyed their houses, burned their cars. <u>Goodness knows how many</u> cars they burned. [Manus, M, 18]

anti blo mipla ronim ol t(ok) "yupla go bek lo aus. <u>Hamaspla</u> taim (mi)pla toki(m) yupla?"

Our auntie chased them and said "Go home! <u>How many</u> times do we have to tell you?" [Morobe, F, 11]

The number of monosyllabic adjectives with *-p(e)la* used in predicate position was much more restricted. A total of only four were found in the corpus, although they occurred fairly frequently:

bikpla 'big' (158)   *gutpla* 'good' (81)   *traipla* 'huge' (32)   *yangpla* 'young' (7)

One feature of the present corpus is that there are a number of cases where adjectives without the *-pela* suffix are appearing before nouns instead of in the standard predicate position:

> *sampla narapla mangki ol go k(i)sim sampla <u>drai bembu</u>*
>
> some other boys went to get some <u>dry bamboo</u> [Simbu, M, 16]
>
> *Nogat do lo (di)sla haus, ol sa putim <u>drai banana lif</u> lo do ia*
>
> There was no door in this house, they put <u>dry banana leaves</u> as a door [Simbu, F, 16]

24 cases of *drai* in such a position were recorded. Others include:

> *ol mad nabaut ia em karapim lo skin bl' em na, ol <u>deti bilum</u>, ol bl' ol bifo nabaut, ol <u>deti bilum</u> nabaut ia, em anggamapim lo said said blong em ...*
>
> he covered his skin with mud and stuff, <u>dirty string bags</u>, ones from before, <u>dirty string bags</u>, he hung on his sides ... [Simbu, F, 16]
>
> *Na <u>antap ples</u> ol i kolim Pamheu lo bikpla brata ..*
>
> And the <u>upper village</u> they call Pamheu after the big brother ... [West Sepik, M, 16]

In some cases, adjectives normally appearing post-nominally were found in pre-nominal position:

> *disla man tru tru sta(p) anta(p) k(i)sim wanpla <u>mau kapiak</u>*
>
> the real man above got a <u>ripe breadfruit</u> [West Sepik, M, 14]

There were even instances where such pre-nominal adjectives were found to form opposites by prefixing *i no*. This was only attested in the Enga sample and appears to be highly unusual:

> "... *Mi ba (k)a(i)kai ol <u>mau frut</u> stap anda(p)" em tok osem nau. ... na honbil wok lo go antap na em trome ol <u>i no mau frut</u> longen ia*
>
> "... I will eat <u>the ripe fruit</u> at the top" he said now. ... and the hornbill went to the top and he threw down <u>the unripe fruit</u> [Enga, F, 12]

In other cases, the use of pre-nominal adjectives without *-pela* appears to be influenced by common English expressions, and some could arguably be analyzed as compounds rather than adjective-noun combinations. For example, Mühlhäusler (1979) lists various productive processes of (adj. + noun) to produce compounds such as *waitman* 'white man', *bikman* 'leader', *raunwara* 'lake', etc. The borderline between such compounds and less fixed expressions where adjectives appear pre-nominally appears to be fuzzy, as discussed further in § 5.5.

4.3 Plural marking on nouns

Although plural marking in Tok Pisin is mainly analytic, by the use of a pluralizing particle, affixation is increasingly used as well, so plural marking is dealt with here under the heading of morphology. The marking of plurality on nouns may be optional in Tok Pisin (Crowley et al 1995:194), but when it is important to make the distinction between singular and plural, the normal way is by the use of the particle *ol* in front of the noun or the use of other quantifiers such as *sampla* 'some' or numerals. The fact that the particle *ol* has the same form as the third person plural pronoun has received some comment in discussions of the origins of Tok Pisin, e.g. Keesing (1988), as this is the typical pattern in some of the presumed substrate languages of the Central Pacific, although the plural marker may be post-nominal rather than pre-nominal. Recently the *-s* suffix has become increasingly used to signal plurality as Tok Pisin and English come into increasingly frequent contact.

The main theoretical interest in plural marking in Pidgins and Creoles has been in connection with implicational universals. It has been suggested that marking depends not only on the syntactic position within a sentence, but also by semantic considerations, such as a hierarchy of animacy (Mühlhäusler 1981). In this section, some of these questions will be investigated. In addition, the degree to which obligatory redundant plural marking is becoming established is considered and the status of the borrowed *-s* affix is discussed.

4.3.1 The pluralizing particle *ol*

In the early stages of Pidgin formation, morphological features in the superstrate are typically ignored or at least not used productively. Early texts show that the *-s* plural morpheme was present though variable as used by English speakers in contact situations in the Pacific, but plurality was signalled in the emerging Pidgin analytically by using whatever words associated with a semantic plural were available. The most comprehensive account of number marking in Tok Pisin is Mühlhäusler (1981). He shows that in the early days of Tok Pisin, a variety of forms such as *ol* 'all', *pela* **(fela)** 'fellow', *olgeta* 'all together', *plenti* 'plenty' together with strategies such as reduplication all co-existed. As stabilization progressed, the *-pela* form became fixed for plural pronouns, while the particle *ol* came to be used before nouns. It appears that in early periods, *ol* was used sparingly, with very low redundancy (Mühlhäusler 1981:43). As Tok Pisin expanded, plural marking became more firmly established in certain syntactic environments and differentially according to an animacy scale, and moves towards greater redundancy occurred with creolization.

The order of plural marking as Tok Pisin stabilized is described by Mühlhäusler in terms of salience or prominence, i.e. the more prominent a feature in a sentence, the more likely it is to attract grammatical categories such as number marking. This prominence is in turn related to grammatical case and animacy (1981:38). The syntactic environments most favouring plural marking were in the following order: subject position, direct object, after *long* and after *bilong*. The animacy hierarchy favoured firstly humans, followed by animates, count nouns and mass nouns (1981:44).

Of particular interest to the present study are the observations made about creolized varieties. Mühlhäusler made a number of predictions about the direction of change in creolized varieties, namely that plural marking would become categorical and in a fixed position in the noun phrase, with differences in form corresponding to differences in meaning, and plural marking also appearing in other parts of the sentence (1981:55). Redundancy in plural marking was seen to increase from the time of stabilization onwards, first at sentence level then at phrase level (1981:52). It also appears that one consequence of creolization is a further increase in redundancy in this and other features (Mühlhäusler 1985d:348).

Mühlhäusler noted that while number marking had increased over the life of Tok Pisin, it was still not categorical, and a great deal of variation was still found (1981:55). The only case of apparently categorical marking he found was for animates in subject position among speakers in the sample from Malabang on Manus Island. A possible obstacle to categorical marking was identified in the phonological properties of the marker *ol*, which, in prominent pre-nominal position, does not become a clitic as easily as, for example, the English post-nominal -s.

These observations appear to be supported by data in the present corpus. Because of the size of the corpus, a full analysis of all potential occurrences was not possible without more sophisticated software and extensive tagging. However, it is seen that *ol* is generally present to mark semantic plurals, but there is a great deal of variability, and the presence or absence of *ol* is still somewhat unpredictable. For example, in the following extract, plural marking is present on *ol bet* 'beds' but absent on *spia* 'arrows' in what are apparently identical grammatical contexts and states of animacy. (It is clear from the context that *spia* is plural).

> *em i stap nau ma(ma) bl' em wokim spia nau em i kam nau ma bl' em wokim ol bet.*
>
> He stayed, his mother made arrows, he came and his mother made beds [East New Britain, M, 12]

Many other similar examples can be found where presence or absence of *ol* to mark plural is unpredictable:

> *ol step perents blo mi woki(m) liklik konfliks wantem perents blo mi tru lo - perents blo mi tru tru lo taun. Liklik konfliks bitwin tupla wantem. Em nau step perents blo mi ol tok "o nogut yu stap na ba yu bighet i go bikpla. Yu mas go bek l' ol perents blo yu".*
>
> My step-parents were in conflict with my real parents in town. A little conflict between the two. Now my step-parents said "it wouldn't be good if you stay here and get disobedient. You must go back to your parents." [Manus, M, 14]
>
> *Biain nau stap ating tu wiks bihain gen na ol gels wok lo kapsaitim ol rais lo rabis bin na ol manggi komplein. Ol tok ol i no laikim gels weistim rais nau skul kepten kirap na em tok okei nau em ol gels bai kaikai liglig.*
>
> After about two weeks again the girls tipped rice into the rubbish bin and the boys complained. They said they didn't like the girls wasting rice, then the school captain said all right, the girls will get only a little to eat. [Madang, M, 17]

nau ol i <u>kukim pis</u> ol ukim, o(l)geta ol fis bl' em na, ol - ol kukim na ol kaikai

now they <u>cooked the fish</u> they caught, <u>all their fish</u> and they - they cooked them and ate them. [West Sepik, F, 13]

na tupla i tok olsem "mitla mas painimaut wanem samting tupla sa mekim na, tupla no sa bringim <u>ol sampla abus</u> i kam." Wanpla taim, tupla lapun man meri go lo bus long <u>painim abus</u> blo tupla

and the two said "we must find out what they do when they don't bring <u>any meat</u> home." One time, an old couple went to the forest to <u>hunt animals</u> [Simbu, M, 19]

The possibility that some other distinctions, such as specific versus non-specific, may be operating cannot be ruled out.

Regarding the syntactic position of the plural marker *ol*, Mühlhäusler (1981:56) notes that it is not fixed, and subject to variation in different communities and even in the same speaker. For example, three placements of *ol* with pre-nominal adjectives co-occur: *ol*-adj-noun, adj-*ol*-noun, and *ol*-adj-*ol*-noun. Although no figures are given, he considers the form with *ol* at the beginning of the noun phrase more common (1981:56). All the above variants are found in the corpus, as seen in the following extracts.

em wanpla rul we sa(po)s yu lukim <u>ol niupla samting</u> bai yu mas no ken wokim koments o lap o kain osem.

It's a rule that if you see <u>new things</u> you mustn't make comments or laugh or that sort of thing. [East New Britain, M, 16]

tupla sa gat <u>klinpla ol kolos</u>, kloudhz na tupla sa stap lo narapla ailan.

The two had <u>clean clothes</u> and they lived on another island. [Morobe, F, 11]

Neks moning wonem <u>ol bikpla ol man,</u> ol plen pinis kisi(m) spia bl' ol, ol kam.

The next morning, what's that, <u>the big men</u>, they planned to get their spears, they came [East Sepik, M, 12]

Sometimes, each element in a sequence of determiner, adjective and noun is preceded by *ol*:

Kam daun stret lo mak blo Maprik na Yanggoru na <u>ol sampla ol yangpla ol manggi</u> ol olim ol gan, ol naip, fopla gan samting

came right to the border between Maprik and Yangoru and <u>some young boys</u> were holding guns, knives, about four guns. [West Sepik, M, 16]

Overall, it is seen that, as in Mühlhäusler's data, the pattern *ol*-adj-noun is the most common. The figures for the occurrence of adjectives with *ol* and plural nouns is seen in the following table. The case of determiners such as *dispela, narapela* and *sampela* and quantifiers such as *planti* is somewhat special, and these are dealt with separately, and so not included in the figures below.

The position of *ol* and pre-nominal adjectives

Order	Number	Proportion
ol-adj-noun	164	82%
adj-*ol*-noun	9	5%
ol-adj-*ol*-noun	26	13%
Total	199	100%

It can be seen that the great majority of occurrences follow the pattern *ol*-adjective-noun, suggesting that obligatory plural marking with *ol* immediately preceding the noun is far from well-established. The comparable figures for the determiners *sampela, narapela* and *dispela* (including contractions) are as follows:

The position of *ol* and pre-nominal determiners

Order	Number	Proportion
ol-sampela-noun	135	67.5%
sampela-ol-noun	40	20%
ol-sampela-ol-noun	25	12.5%
Total	200	100%
ol-dispela-noun	121	63%
dispela-ol-noun	50	26%
ol-dispela-ol-noun	22	11%
Total	193	100%
ol-narapela-noun	88	79%
narapela-ol-noun	10	9%
ol-narapela-ol-noun	13	12%
Total	111	100%

Again *ol*-x-noun is the predominant pattern, but here the number of occurrences of pre-nominal *ol* is considerably higher, especially in the case of ***dispela*** and ***sampela***, suggesting that the use of determiners may be associated with a greater tendency to mark pre-nominal plural. However, determiners and quantifiers preceding nouns without any involvement of *ol* were more common, for example 408 occurrences of *sampla* + noun.

Mühlhäusler's prediction that one form would become associated with one meaning (1981), was not confirmed by his data. An example is given of *sampela ol* and *ol sampela* 'some', which did not appear to have any difference in meaning (1981:57). As seen above, there were over twice as many occurrences of *ol sampela* (160) than *sampela ol* (65), (these numbers both include 25 occurrences of the double marked phrase *ol sampela ol*). While agreeing with Mühlhäusler that no categorical difference in meaning has become accepted, it did appear that there was a tendency for ***sampela ol*** to be used to indicate 'some but not all, some of them', while ***ol sampela*** more often referred to an indefinite small number 'some, a few':

Osem sampla osem ol wan tokples blo mipla, na <u>sampla ol</u> blo hia yet.

Like some of them are like speakers of our own language and <u>some of them</u> are from here. [New Ireland, M, 12]

sapos ol i lukim man em i no bilas gut em bai ol i ting olsem em i wanpla trabel man na bai ol i paitim tasol. <u>Sampla ol</u> i yusim gan barel o gan bat long paitim ol man na blut i sawe kamap.

If they saw a man who wasn't well-dressed, they would think he was a trouble-maker and hit him. <u>Some of them</u> used their gun barrel or gun butt to hit the men and make them bleed. [East New Britain, M, 18]

nau em pul i kam bek ken long aus bl' em wantem <u>ol sampla frens</u> blo em.

Now he paddled back to his house with <u>some friends</u>. [West Sepik, F, 13]

i bin sidaun nau <u>ol sampla hantas</u> ia ol i bin kam, ol man ol i kam lo sutim pisin.

He was sitting down and <u>some hunters</u> came, men who came to shoot birds. [New Ireland, F, 13]

There are, however, exceptions, and it remains to be seen whether this distinction in meaning will become established.

Mühlhäusler' prediction that plural marking would appear in other parts of the sentence was partially confirmed by the observations of reduplicated verb forms in apparent agreement with plural subjects in Malabang (1981:57). However, no instances of this kind of agreement were seen in the present corpus, and it is not clear if some instances of what appears to be partial reduplication of verbal and nominal forms were in fact no more than repetitions due to false starts. Other cases of reduplication were more associated with aspectual distinctions such as repeated or distributive action than plurality. The following two samples appear to be the most likely cases where reduplicated forms could be associated with plurality. It should be borne in mind, however, that alternative interpretations are possible, such as diminutive or distributive, following the pattern of reduplication in some Papua New Guinean languages:

Ol lukim diwai ia i gat ol lip na <u>ol nil nil</u>.

They saw the tree which has leaves and <u>spines</u>. [East New Britain, M, 17]

Na ol sampla ol sangguma meri na ol wich meri ol bin taitim ol <u>rorop</u> nabaut ia …

And some sorceresses and witches tied the <u>ropes</u> … [Simbu, F, 16]

No examples of number marking on verbs could be found. The nominal forms above too are very uncommon, so it does not appear that reduplicated forms marking number are becoming established. Increase in redundancy, however, is certainly confirmed, and a great deal of redundancy is seen in the corpus, for example, when plurality has already been indicated by other quantifiers such as *sampela* 'some' or numerals:

ol bin putim <u>ol sampla ol stiks</u> na livs nambaut osem raunim lo ol lak kukim em

they put <u>some sticks</u> and leaves around him as if to burn him [Madang, M, 17]

Tupla kirap k(i)si(m) <u>sampla ol talis</u> g(iv)im ol na ol kaikai pinis

The two got up and got <u>some talis nuts</u> to give them and they ate [East Sepik, M, 14]

Biain anti blo mi bin go kisim <u>ol sampla ol diwai</u> lo bus na kam gim em na em orait gen

Later my aunt brought <u>some wood</u> (medicines) from the bush and came and gave her them to her and she got better. [East New Britain, F, 16]

Ol sut nau ol dedi blo mi wantaim <u>ol sampla ol wok man</u> ol i wok long hevim pati i stap ia ol i harim nau

When they fired, my father and <u>some workers</u> were having a party and they heard it [Eastern Highlands, M, 16]

em bin lukim <u>sampla ol liklik manggi</u> lo wanpla ples arere lo nambis

he saw <u>some children</u> at a village by the beach [East Sepik, M 15]

Although not a feature of the corpus as a whole, it does appear that the use of *ol* immediately preceding a plural noun is approaching obligatory status for some speakers, as seen in the following examples, where *ol* has already appeared before an adjective or determiner in the noun phrase:

Na taim <u>ol yangpela ol meri</u> kam dens yu no ken lukim

And when <u>the young girls</u> come to dance, you mustn't look [West Sepik, M, 16]

<u>ol sampla ol man</u> ol fait wantem ol ami

<u>some men</u> fought with the soldiers [West Sepik, M, 14]

tupla kisi(m) <u>ol liklik ol samting</u> nambaut lo nambis ia tupla pilai pilai

the two took their <u>small things</u> to the beach and played [East Sepik, M, 13]

em rausim ol samting osem <u>ol liklik ol spia</u>

he took out the things like <u>small spears</u> [West Sepik, F, 17]

mi bin lukim <u>ol disla ol samting</u>

I saw <u>these things</u> [West Sepik, F, 17]

Em i gat <u>ol naispla ol bichis</u>

It has <u>nice beaches</u> [New Ireland, F, 15]

> *ol sampla ol yangpla ol manggi ol olim ol gan, ol naip, fopla gan...*
>
> some young men were carrying guns and knives, four guns... [West Sepik, M, 16]

In some instances, the pronoun *tupela* was also preceded by the pluralizing *ol*, although the more typical pattern is for *tupela* to be used alone. 41 occurrences of *ol tupla* were recorded, as well as nine of *tupla ol*.

> *tupla ronowe i go - kam bek long vil... - peles blong ol tupla na masalai ia ron bihain long tupla*
>
> The two ran away - came back to the village - their village and the devil ran behind them [Manus, F, 13]

> *wantla taim ol tupela mumuim pik na laikim ankol na ol lain blo tupela kam keikei ia*
>
> once the two cooked a pig and wanted their uncle and family to come and eat [Western Highlands, M, 17]

> *Na taim ol tupla susa i lukim, ol bin kirap nogut tsol ol no toktok*
>
> And when the two sisters saw it, they were surprised, but didn't say anything [West Sepik, F, 17]

> *i kam bek na ol tupla tewel ia askim em, "yu, yu wokim osem wonem na yu kechim ol fish ia?"*
>
> they came back and the two spirits asked them, "what did you do to catch the fish?" [New Ireland, M, 12]

Thus it is clear that many cases of redundant plural marking with *ol* occur. An increasing use of obligatory pre-nominal marking of plurality appears to be being made by some speakers. However, this trend has not yet reached the stage of an obligatory rule for all speakers.

Mühlhäusler's (1981) discussion of the use of *ol* concludes with a brief discussion of two observations about the particle in use. Firstly, his comments about the co-occurrence of *olgeta* and *ol* indicate some confusion. It is stated that because of their competing role as plural markers in the development of Tok Pisin, they are never found together in present-day Tok Pisin and the form **olgeta ol* is not possible (1981:43). However, later accounts of creolized Tok Pisin in the same article indicate that *olgeta ol* is obligatory in some contexts (1981:57).

Romaine (1992a:223) sheds more light on this, noting that the combination *olgeta ol* is 'not by any means rare' in her samples. In the present corpus, there are 31 occurrences of *olgeta ol*. These, however, include some cases where the *ol* following *olgeta* is a third person plural pronoun, but in most cases *olgeta* is followed by the plural marker *ol*, as in the examples below (18 occurrences in total):

> *Satadei nait ol bin tokim olgeta ol relativs blo mitupla kam bung wantaim lo antap lo ples blo mipla*
>
> On Saturday night they told all my relatives to gather outside our village [Eastern Highlands, F, 15]

> *em i go na tokim olgeta ol narapla meri, orait ol meri ia harim osem nau, ol sa kam na lukim man ia*
>
> She went and told all the other women, then the women heard about it and they came to see the man [East Sepik, M, 15]

> *wanpla kar ia fulap l(ong) olgeta ol gout na pig na ol k(i)sim na go ia*
>
> one car was full up with all the goats and pigs and they took them away [Simbu, F, 11]

> *Na ol ami yet ol kam, na olgeta ol ami, eitpla kar olgeta ol kam.*
>
> And the soldiers came, and all the soldiers, eight cars all together, came [Simbu, F, 11]

Secondly, another use of *ol* noted by Mühlhäusler (1981:43) is the indicator of 'groupiness' as in *pater ol* 'the priest and his flock', which he notes is similar to Tolai patterns (Mosel 1980), but could perhaps better be attributed to universal tendencies. This pattern is attested in the corpus a number of times, and could be alternatively considered an ellipsis of *x na ol* 'x and them'. In certain cases, there is some ambiguity, and it is not clear whether the use of *ol* indicates this kind of 'groupiness' or is merely a resumptive use of the third person plural pronoun, or simply plural marking. For example, in the following extract, it is not clear whether *meri ol* refers to a group of women and others, or is just a plural:

> *wanpla taim <u>meri ol</u> go lo sensi(m) kaikai wantem ol man lo meinlen*
>
> one time <u>the women (and the others?)</u> went to exchange food with the mainland people [Madang, F, 16]

Similarly, in the following story about a bomb explosion, *polisman ol*, could possibly refer to the 'police and other people' who attended to the girl's injuries, but is more likely to be merely a resumptive plural pronoun:

> *Na mi kam n' ol - <u>ol polisman ol</u> bin kam (ki)si(m) sampla fotos blo mipla, na biain mi go stap lo aus sik.*
>
> Now I came and <u>policemen (and other people?)</u> came and took some photos of us and later I went to stay in hospital [West Sepik, F, 17]

However, when the head noun is singular, or a proper name, then the *ol* following it is unambiguously 'groupy' (23 occurrences):

> *Lo nau moning ia mipla - <u>Z. ol</u> silip na mipla kirap nau mipla meki(m) fani na lap i sta(p).*
>
> In the morning we - <u>Z. and the others</u> were sleeping and we got up and we were joking around and laughing [Morobe, F, 11]

> *nau mi tok, "yumi nau bai yumi go we nau?" em tok, "yumi go l' aus blo <u>D. ol</u>."*
>
> Then I said, "where will we go now?", she said "let's go to <u>D. and them's</u> house." [Morobe, F, 10]

> *wanpla meri ka(m) na to(k) osem, "<u>S. ol</u> lai(k) go lo fil na plei volibol," na mi tok, "mi les ..."*
>
> a girl came and said "<u>S. and the others</u> are about to go to the field to play volleyball", and I said "I don't want to..." [Morobe, F, 12]

4.3.2 The pluralizing suffix -s

The sporadic presence of pluralizing affixes in Tok Pisin has been noted for many years. A few lexical items include the unanalyzed plural suffix from either English (*anis* 'ant' from English *ants*) or German (*binen* 'bee' from German *binen* 'bees') (Mühlhäusler 1981:39). However, neither of these suffixes became involved in widely-used productive rules during stabilization. Some use of the *-s* suffix with a pluralizing function is noted by Hall (1966), who records that it occurs with only a small number of nouns. One interesting observation arising from Hall's list is that of his 12 examples, only one is human (*bebis* 'babies') and one other animate (*kreps* 'crabs'), which suggests that an animacy hierarchy was not operating in the case of *-s* pluralization at that time. Mühlhäusler (1985b:276) notes that in urban Tok Pisin the use of the *-s* suffix is very variable, even in the speech of a single individual, and it is often difficult to say why it is used in some cases and not others. Mühlhäusler sees this as a reduction of the systematic adequacy of the language as it decreolizes, and considers that in such a case of interference between two systems in contact, animacy hierarchies would not be expected to apply. This conforms to Lynch's characterization of the use of *-s* as an interference phenomenon (1979a:6). Elsewhere, however, Mühlhäusler (1985d:339) describes the *-s* suffix as an integral part of the grammar.

Romaine devotes considerable attention to the use of the *-s* pluralizing suffix in her study of young people in Morobe and Madang Provinces (1992a:219ff). Like Mühlhäusler's account of *ol* pluralization, she, too, relates the pattern of use to an animacy hierarchy. Her study gives details of 195 lexical items to which *-s* is attached and tabulates occurrences in each of the locations investigated. She concludes that animacy does have some influence, with a larger proportion of human than animates using the suffix, and that count nouns take *-s* considerably more often than mass nouns. Phonological constraints are described as fairly unimportant (p 236). However, as the author herself acknowledges, there is something of a problem interpreting these data for phonological features, as some tokens appear to have been written phonemically (e.g. *mabos* 'marbles', *pekfeks* 'excrement'), and others in standard Tok Pisin (*pikinini* 'child') or English (*bicycles*) orthography or idiosyncratically (*blakbokkis* 'flying fox'). Romaine's figures are also interpreted in terms of urban-rural differences, although problems of definition make this a problematic area.

In the present corpus, many instances of -*s* pluralization were recorded. However, use was not always consistent, and there were cases where the same informant varied considerably in the use of -*s*:

ol i brekenenta lo <u>ol stoas</u>

they broke into <u>the stores</u>,

but:

ol i putim em klostu lo <u>ol stua</u>

They put him near <u>the stores</u> [Manus, F, 16]

This could be explained as nonce borrowings such as the English form *stoa* 'store' being more likely to take the plural -s than items with established Tok Pisin pronunciation such as *stua* 'store'. It might be expected that words newly borrowed from English which are frequently heard in the plural are more likely to retain the -*s* plural form, and even be used in this form in the singular like the earlier examples *binen* 'bee' and *anis* 'ant'. It is true that many of the words which commonly use an -*s* plural such as ***stiudents, tichas***, and ***kloudhz*** are heard in English often or mainly in the plural form. It may also be thought that -*s* marking is restricted to recent borrowings from English. However, there are now many cases where well-established Tok Pisin words are used with the -*s* affix, as also found by Romaine (1992a:238). The following are some examples:

ol alpim ol Baluan osem ol <u>piks</u> no sa go insait lo gaden na distroyim ol gaden blong ol

they helped the Baluan people to stop <u>pigs</u> from going into their gardens and destroying them [Manus, F, 14]

ol <u>kagos</u> bl' ol ia ol i pasim l' wanpla kenves

their <u>cargo</u> they wrapped in a canvas [Manus, F, 15]

ol weivs bl' ol em osem mi, mi nap lo tok em osem ol <u>mauntens</u>

the waves were like, I can say like <u>mountains</u> [Manus, F, 16]

Disla gaden em i planim ol <u>kukambas</u>, kukambas blongen

This garden he planted with <u>cucumbers</u> [New Ireland, F, 14]

na gat sem ol planti kokonat tris na ol <u>ailans</u>

and it has lots of cocoanut trees and <u>islands</u> [New Ireland, F, 15]

All the above examples are from Manus and New Ireland, where -*s* pluralization is particularly common. There were 1040 occurrences of -*s* pluralization in the corpus. Inspecting the list of the more common words occurring with -*s* plurals in the table set out on the page opposite confirms Romaine's observations about the importance of animacy in that six of the most frequent seven items are human. However, only a relatively small number of words have been adopted with -*s* pluralization, and these may have been frequently heard in the plural, or commonly used alongside an English equivalent with a similar phonological shape. It is therefore suspected that the individual circumstances surrounding the use and adoption of these words are also important.

Some of the items in the list have clearly been heard mainly or exclusively as a plural, such as ***klodhz*** 'clothes', ***luvas*** 'louvre windows', ***Hailans*** 'Highlands' and ***twins***, and it is not certain that the endings represent a plural morpheme at all rather than an unanalyzed component of the lexeme. Other words may occur in the singular, but in context, are no doubt heard mostly in the plural, such as ***perents*** 'parents', ***ruts*** 'roots', ***fedhes*** 'feathers' and ***slipas*** 'slippers'. The use of ***bois*** 'boys' and ***gels*** 'girls' is considerably more common in the Highlands and Momase samples, as the figures set out on page 74 show.

Commoner nouns with -s plurals

Plural noun	Gloss	Occurrences
bois	boys	53
frens	friends	53
perents	parents	46
wiks	weeks	44
gels	girls	41
stiudents	students	40
tichas	teachers	40
(H)ailans	Highlands	38
deis	days	31
kloudhz	clothes	31
yias	years	26
bradhas	brothers	25
fedhes	feathers	20
fruts	fruits	19
Solomons	(N) Solomons	18
sistas	sisters	15
enimols	animals	14
minits	minutes	13
soljes	soldiers	10
Geims	(SP) Games	9
manths	months	9
eshis	ashes	8
piks	pigs	8
prifeks	prefects	8
(gred) tens	grade 10's	8
twins	twins	8
reletifs	relatives	7
hausis	houses	6
kasins	cousins	6
pisis	pieces	6
Bareks	Barracks	5
ekonomiks	economics	5
klasis	classes	5
ruts	roots	5
slipas	slippers	5
weivs	waves	5
domitris	dormitories	4
flauas	flowers	4
lendounas	landowners	4
luvas	louvers	4
taims	times	4

Tokens of *boi(s)* and *gel(s)*

	boi	*bois*	*gel*	*gels*
Momase	193	24	152	25
Highlands	223	11	212	5
Islands	12	3	3	3

These rather striking figures show some clear differences among the regional samples. Both *boi* and *gel* are widely used in Momase and the Highlands, although they are marked for plural considerably more frequently in the Momase sample. In the Islands, *boi* and *gel* are rarely used, *mangki* (< *monkey*) and *meri* (< *Mary*) being the preferred terms there for 'boy' and 'girl'. Neither *mangki* nor *meri* was found to occur with an *-s* plural. Use of the *-s* suffix with *boi* and *gel* is definitely productive, as shown by the fact that semantic plurals are generally marked both with *-s* and *ol*. Only 4 occurrences of *ol boi* are found, compared with 25 of *ol bois*. The case of *gel* is even more striking; out of some 500 occurrences of *gel*, none is preceded by *ol*. Of the 41 occurrences of *gels*, all are preceded by *ol*.

With the introduction of a novel plural-forming mechanism, the possibility arises that the affix *-s* might be added to elements other than nouns. Romaine notes that *-s* is occasionally added to the plural particle *ol*, giving the following example (1992a:220):

> *ol wokim lo wonem plang, ols timbas*
>
> they made it from planks, timbers

However, it is most likely that *ols* in this case is a contraction of *olsem* 'like'. The few occurrences of *ols* in the present corpus are all explained this way. Romaine also cites the case of *-s* added to the verb (1992a:220) in the example:

> *"kisim banana hariap na kamdaun," em toks:*
>
> "get the banana quickly and come down," he said

This is almost certainly a contraction of *tok olsem* 'said thus', and many examples of such extreme reductions of *tok olsem* associated with quotations can be found in the present corpus.

One observation that has been made about *-s* pluralization is that it never occurs with words of non-English origin (Lynch 1979a:6). The common nouns taking *-s* plurals listed above are all very similar to their English equivalents. Romaine, however, found several examples, such as *kiaus* 'eggs', *pikininis* 'children' and *meris* 'women' in her data, accounting for 2% of plurals (1992:238). Since this study involved a number of young children, it is possible that developmental features of the children's acquisition of the language may have been operating. In the present corpus, where there are no very young children, only one example of a pluralizing *-s* suffix on a word of non-English origin was found, in a transcript from Manus, where the word *mapo* was used both with and without *-s*. The word *mapo* appears to have been borrowed from a Manus language. It refers to one of a group of mythical 'little people', similar to elves or leprechauns, as explained in the following extract:

> *Wanpla taim long Baluan Ailan i bin gat ol <u>mapo</u>, ol liklik man we ol - ol no sa sta(p) long osem peles, ol sa sta(p) - ol sa liv long bus tasol.*
>
> Once upon a time on Baluan Island there were <u>mapos</u>, small people who - they didn't live in villages, they just lived in the forest. [Manus F, 14]

Although initially used without the *-s* suffix, in later references there was plural agreement using *-s*:

> *ol go ronim ol <u>mapos</u> ia na ol <u>mapos</u> ia i bin ronawe nau ol disapia nating*
>
> they chased the <u>mapos</u> and the <u>mapos</u> ran away and disappeared.

Generally, then, with this one exception, *-s* plurals are avoided on words of non-English origin. It should be remembered that the plural suffix in English is realized as three allomorphs: -s, -z and -ɪz according to phonological environment, i.e. following unvoiced non-sibilant, voiced non-sibilant and sibilant phonemes respectively. Where the suffix is adopted in Tok Pisin, the *-s* form is normally used. Romaine records some examples of other allomorphs (1992a:230). In the present corpus, when a word ends in a sibilant consonant, a plural affix is not normally added:

em tokim ol go sindaun lo desk, desk blo ol, okei taim ol sindaun em gim ol <u>ol eksasais</u>, ol wokim

he told them to and sit down at their desks, then when they sat down he gave them <u>exercises</u>, they did them [East Sepik, M, 15]

Nau tupla i stap, tupla sta(p) nau tupla go ant, kolektim <u>ol fis</u>, na tupla go gi(vim) lo ankol blo tupla na anti blo tupla.

Then the two stayed then they went hunting, collecting <u>fish</u>, and the two went and gave them to their uncle and aunt. [West Sepik, F, 15]

However, there are a number of cases (38) where *-is* or *-iz* is added, not always in accordance with English morphophonemic rules:

fes dei blong skul mi bin poret liklik taim ol i wok lo kolim ol neim blo go lo <u>ol klasis</u>, tasol laki na ol i kolim neim blo mi.

on the first day of school I was worried while they were announcing the names to go to <u>classes</u>, but luckily they called my name. [New Ireland, M, 13]

tupla k(i)si(m) tamiok ia na tupla katim em ia. Katim em go <u>pisis</u> olgeta.

The two got an axe and cut him. Chopped him into <u>pieces</u>. [Simbu, F, 16]

Further instances of other allomorphs include the following:

(Mi sa) pilai tu. Pilai lo namel lo ol <u>ausis</u>, painim <u>shelz</u>.

I play too. Play among the <u>houses</u>, look for <u>shells</u>. [East New Britain, F, 12]

Em rausim ol <u>kloudhz</u> blo em, em neked, em kisim naif em katim katim lo skin blo em, blad ia i no isi.

She tore off her <u>clothes</u> and left her naked, she took a knife and repeatedly cut her body, blood was everywhere. [Morobe, F, 10]

Okei ol wok lo chekim ol <u>pasinjez</u> lo k(i)sim ol sampla mani yet

They were still checking the <u>passengers</u> to get some money [West Sepik, M, 16]

tetinpela <u>provinshes</u> long dispela kantri ol bin tek pat long kalshoral sho, ol <u>dresingz</u> bl' ol na kain kain samting i kamap na mipela bin hamamas tru long lukim displa

thirteen <u>provinces</u> of this country took part in the cultural show, their <u>dress</u> and all sorts of things were there and we were very happy to see it [Western Highlands, F, 16]

This analysis is somewhat tentative, considering that it is not always easy to distinguish between -*s* and -*z* when these are not used contrastively as separate phonemes by most speakers. It remains to be seen whether allomorphs according to the English pattern will become established in Tok Pisin.

Problems with the interpretation of -*s* pluralization can mostly be related to Mühlhäusler's observation (1981:58) that there are two developmental processes involved in pluralization; the internal development of the language along its own course, and interference phenomena as Tok Pisin and English come into renewed and intensive contact. A certain tension between competing systems was occasionally evident as informants switched between alternatives:

sapos osem <u>ol pigz</u> la go bai i no inap - <u>ol pik</u> no inap go insait long gaden

if the <u>pigs</u> want to go, they cant - the <u>pigs</u> can't go into the garden. [Manus, F, 14]

narapla tevel ia, a... - <u>wanpla ais - ai</u> blong em em bagarap, n' em wanpla ai bl' em tsol gutpla.

The other spirit, one <u>eyes - eye</u> was spoiled and one was good. [West Sepik, M, 14]

Morphological features are unlikely to be borrowed in the early stages of pidginization, and the present stage of development allowing such adoptions corresponds to Thomason & Kaufman's 'slight to moderate structural borrowing' category, which typically only occurs where there is a good deal of bilingualism (1988:78). Now that this stage has been reached, it would appear that the two processes are destined to coexist for some time, and the nature of plural marking is likely to be variable in the foreseeable future. However, the use of the -*s* plural suffix is by now common in the speech of first language speakers, even if not consistently used, and the emergence of a greater role for the suffix in other varieties would appear to be very likely. The trend towards more redundancy and obligatory marking would also seem likely to spread from first language varieties to mainstream Tok Pisin.

4.4 The pronoun system

4.4.1 The standard pronoun paradigm

Tok Pisin pronouns differ from the pronouns of the main lexifier language (English) in a number of respects, as seen in a typical paradigm shown in the following table.

The standard Tok Pisin pronoun paradigm

Person / Number	Singular	Dual		Trial	Plural
First	mi	(excl.)	mitupela	mitripela	mipela
		(incl.)	yumitupela	yumitripela	yumi
Second	yu		yutupela	yutripela	yupela
Third	em		(em)tupela	emtripela	ol

The paradigm is simpler than English in some respects, for example in that case distinctions between subject and object or gender distinctions between masculine, feminine and neuter are not normally made (the variable use of *en* in place of *em* after *long* and *bilong* is discussed below). Thus three singular forms *mi, yu* and *em* are equivalent to the English forms I, me, you (singular), he, she, it, her and him. However, the system is more complex in other respects. There is a separate plural form of the second person pronoun, and dual and often trial numbers are distinguished in addition to plural. Moreover, first person plural (and sometimes dual and trial) pronouns have distinct inclusive and exclusive forms.

As noted previously, the form of the pronoun set has received considerable attention in assessing the various contributions to the development of Melanesian Pidgin. In particular, Keesing (1988) devoted a good deal of effort to tracing the development of characteristic pronoun forms such as the inclusive and exclusive, and relating them to those of substrate languages of the Central Pacific. The presence of such marked forms in Pacific Pidgins is a major argument in favour of substrate influence in Pidgin genesis. It appears that competing superstrate forms co-existed for some time before some pronominals such as derivatives of the English 'he' and 'him' became grammaticalized as the predicate marker and transitive suffix respectively, and there was considerable variation before the present system crystallized.

4.4.2 Number distinctions: dual, trial, paucal and plural

Dual pronouns

Dual forms are commonly found in first, second and third persons in Tok Pisin to specify two referents. The first person dual exclusive form *mitupela*, normally occurring as *mitupla* or further reduced to *mitla*, is common, and the possibility of reanalysis of *-t-* as a dual marker in *mitla* in opposition to *-p-* as a plural marker (in *mipla*) has already been suggested as a new morphological rule (Lynch 1979a). However, if this tendency is operating here, it does not appear to have progressed any further than in Lynch's data. This is shown by the fact that both *mitupla* and *mitla* are often used in close proximity by the same speaker:

> tupla brata i tokim tupla sista osem "yutupla bai sta lo aus, kukim kaikai na i stap. <u>Mitupla</u> brata ba <u>mitla</u> go ant lo bus."

> The two brothers told their two sisters "you two will stay in the house and cook the food. <u>We two</u> brothers will go and hunt in the forest." [West Sepik, F, 15]

Mitupla lap nau ol raunim mitupla tasol - ol raunim mitupla nau mitla trome ogeta - mitla trome o(lge)ta plestik buai na daka na kambang mitla trome na mitla ronowe

We two laughed and they chased us - they chased us and we threw away all the plastic containers of betel nut and pepper and lime, we threw them away and we ran away. [Manus, F, 15]

Na taim mitupla kam, ankol blo mitupla em putim tupla chea blo mitupla, mitla kam sindaun.

When we two came, our uncle put two chairs for us and we sat down [Eastern Highlands, F, 17]

Furthermore, there is occasional reduction in rapid speech to *mila*, which eliminates the consonant which would be essential to distinguish between dual and plural in the proposed analysis:

lo nait, poro blo mi kam kisim mi - mipla go lo dens. Dens - dens pinis, lo moning mila kam lo haus. Mila kam, mipla i slip, go inap lo avinun, mila kirap go raun long bus.

In the night, my friend came and took me - us to the dance. When the dance finished, in the morning we came home. We came home and we slept until the afternoon, then we got up and went around in the bush. [West Sepik, M, 16]

Thus *mitla* generally appears to be a reduced alternative form of *mitupela* rather than a re-analyzed form, although the elegant re-analysis suggested by Lynch is certainly a possibility for the future.

The form *mitra* also occurs. Some Papuan languages have a "paucal" category, indicating an indefinite small number (Foley 1986:72), which is also found in Oceanic languages, and the possibility that the form *mitra* may be used contrastively as a paucal pronoun in some varieties has been suggested (S. Holzknecht, pers. comm.). This explanation, although not ruled out elsewhere, was not supported in the present corpus. The word *mitra* was attested 14 times, mainly from the Eastern Highlands sample, but in most cases it is clear from the context that it is a phonological variant of the dual form *mitla*, probably arising due to lack of consistent discrimination between [r] and [l], as in the following examples:

Oke tupla tok "moning bai mitra go sekim trep blo mitra" nau tupla (k)am sekim nau kisim ol pisin go pinis nau, tupla go ipim aninit lo as blo diwai nau, tupla painim paia.

Then they said "in the morning we will go and check our traps" then they checked them, got all the birds and the two piled them at the base of a tree and the two looked for fire. [Eastern Highlands, M, 11]

wanpela taim bikpla brata blo ol, nem blo em Jon, em kirap na tok long liklik brata blo em Pita. Em tok "Pita mitra askim ol man na ol i no givim kaikai so nau mitra yet mas painim kaikai blo mitra." So tupla lusim haus, tupla pekim olgeta kago blo tupla, tupla kisim spia, bunara, naif na ol i go.

One time their big brother who was called John said to his little brother Peter, "Peter, we two asked the men but they did not give us food, so now we two must find our own food." So the two left the house, the two packed all their things, the two got their arrows, bows and knives and left. [Eastern Highlands, M, 17]

The number of occurrences of the different forms is seen in the following table.

First person dual pronouns

Form	Number	Proportion
mitra	14	2.1%
mitla	413	61.3%
mitup(e)la	247	36.6%
Total	674	100.0%

It can be seen that in this corpus, *mitla* is now by far the commonest form in normal spoken usage. In addition to 'we two', *mitla* can also mean 'me and…' as discussed below in the section on *tupela*. A breakdown from the regional subcorpora is presented below:

Variants of *mitupela* by region

	Momase	Highlands	Islands
mitup(e)la	81	34	60
mitla	94	202	50
mitra	1	9	4
mila	5	0	0

This indicates an especially marked preference for the reduced form *mitla* in the Highlands region.

The first person dual inclusive form *yumitupela* appears in Foley's paradigm (1986:67) as well as that of Mühlhäusler (1985h:343), but it was not attested at all in the corpus. This could be partly due to the nature of the discourse, as more first person singular narratives were included in the corpus than other types. However, many of the stories and legends contained extended quotations which could have used this form, but, *mitupela, mipela* or *yumi* were used instead. It may be worth further investigation to see if *yumitupela* is becoming obsolete, as is suggested by the lack of attestations in this corpus.

The second person dual form *yutupela* was less common than the first person form in the corpus, again perhaps due to the nature of the discourse, which contained a good deal of first person narrative. Alternative forms *yutla* and *yutra* also occurred. As with the case of *mitra*, occurrences of *yutra* were almost exclusively from Eastern Highlands, and appeared to be phonological variants rather than an indication of a new semantic distinction. The numbers of the different forms of second person dual pronouns in the corpus are indicated in the table below:

Second person dual pronouns

Form	Number	Proportion
yutra	14	4.9%
yutla	147	51.6%
yutup(e)la	124	43.5%
Total	285	100.0%

A regional breakdown again shows a more marked preference for the reduced forms in the Highlands region:

Variants of *yutup(e)la* by region

	Momase	Highlands	Islands
yutup(e)la	39	26	23
yutla/yutra	45	96	13
yuta	1	5	0

Although the third person dual form *emtupela* appears as the standard form in some pronoun paradigms (e.g. Foley 1986:67), the form *tupela* is cited in other descriptions, and appears to be much more common. This is certainly the case with the present corpus, and the form *emtupela* was found comparatively rarely. Care needs to be taken in analyzing tokens of *emtupela* on computer-generated concordances, as in some cases, the combination *em tupela* does not represent a single pronoun, but other meanings. The most common is a resumptive use of *tupela* after *bilong em*:

> Go nau wanpla taim, wanpla lapun man wantem liklik <u>yangpla pikinini bl' em tupla</u> go lo disla ailen ...
>
> Some time later, an old man and <u>his young son, (the two)</u> went to this island [East Sepik, M, 17]

In other cases, the meaning is not so obvious, but involves a combination of *tupela* with *em* used as a clefting device or emphatic or focus marker as discussed in Chapter 7. In these cases, it is written in the transcripts as two words *em tupela* rather than one:

na nau sapos yumi lukim bai i gat, disla kenggaru, <u>em tupla frant lek</u> blong em i sot na dok, em lek blong em stil longpla.

And if we look, there will be, this kangaroo, <u>its two front legs</u> are short and the dog's legs are still long. [East New Britain, M, 12]

Tupla go nau ol go t(a)sol ol go, lo papa na mama blo ol, na papa na mama bl' ol no sa(ve) (ol)sem em tupla t(a)sol.

The two went to their father and mother, and their father and mother did not know that it was <u>(the two of) them</u> [West Sepik, F, 15]

The remaining tokens of *emtupela* as a third person dual pronoun amounted to only 5 occurrences compared with several thousand of *tupela*, a dramatic difference:

Nau go damblo, <u>emtupla</u> go lo (di)sla bas we tupla man bin kilim disla meri ia.

Now went down, <u>the two of them</u> went to this bus where the two men had killed this woman. [Enga, F, 12]

The word *tupela*, of course, has other functions apart from that of pronoun. Its most obvious use is as a numeral ('two') but less well known is its use as a conjunction, meaning 'together with the other of a pair' as described in § 7.1 on cohesion. The dual pronoun *tupela* and its phonologically reduced variants, then, are very common, and occur with a good deal of redundancy. Variants in connected speech included the normal form *tupla* as well as further reductions *tupl, tla* or *tul*. Once dual person has been established by the use of *tupela*, further use is strictly speaking redundant. However, one feature of many of the traditional stories in the present corpus was the high degree of redundancy involving obligatory use of this pronoun (rather than *ol*), as the following extracts indicate:

<u>tupla</u> go huk lo nambis. <u>Tupla</u> go lo nambis nau <u>tupla</u> kisim kanu blo <u>tupla</u> okei <u>tupla</u> puli(m) kanu blo <u>tupla</u> go daun lo nambis na <u>tupla</u> sidaun na <u>tupla</u> wok lo huk.

<u>the two</u> went fishing to the shore. <u>The two</u> went to the beach and <u>they (two)</u> got their canoe, then <u>they (two)</u> pulled their canoe down to the shore and <u>they (two)</u> sat down and <u>they (two)</u> were busy fishing. [East New Britain, M, 12]

Nau <u>tupla</u> ronowe go lo bus nau, dak lo <u>tupla</u> nau, <u>tupla</u> i kisim liklik naip blo <u>tupla</u>, katim ol liklik stik, wokim giaman aus, <u>tupla</u> katim kanda nau sigirapim nau paia i lait nau <u>tupla</u> silip, <u>tupla</u> kirap wokobaut.

<u>The two</u> ran away into the bush, it got dark, <u>they (two)</u> got their small knife, cut little sticks, made a pretend house. <u>The two</u> cut some cane and rubbed it and made fire and <u>the two</u> slept, <u>the two</u> got up and set off. [East New Britain, M, 12]

However, as noted in § 4.3.1, *ol* occasionally appears as an additional redundant feature preceding *tupela*:

Em singaut singaut go tsol nogat ol pulim <u>ol tupla</u> go namel go antap nau.

He shouted and shouted but it was no good, they pulled <u>the two</u> into the middle and pulled them up. [Madang, M, 16]

ol to(k) (ol)se(m) na ol polis olim gan na pointi(m) lo ol sta, <u>ol tupla</u> ol boksing go na, angkol blo mipla em vin ia.

They said this and the police pointed their guns at them, <u>the two</u> were boxing and my uncle won. [Simbu, F, 12]

Na tupla kisim disla man ia, <u>ol tupla</u> mumuim em i kam lo - lo disla bikbos blo peles ia nau

Now the two got this man, <u>they (two)</u> roasted him and brought him to the chief of the village. [New Ireland, M, 12]

A summary of the occurrence of dual pronouns in the corpus is given in the following table. The forms in the first column include phonological variants. The figures for *tupela* are approximate, as a full analysis was not made of every token of *tupela* as a pronoun and as a numeral.

Dual pronouns

Form	Number of occurrences
emtupela	3
tupela	3000
yutupela	285
mitupela	674
yumitupela	0

Trial pronouns

Trial forms were extremely uncommon in the corpus. The number of tokens recorded and their frequency can be seen below:

Trial pronouns

Form	Number of Tokens
emtripela	0
tripela (pronoun)	9
yutripela	0
mitripela	1
yumitripela	1

From these figures, it appears that the trial distinction is not regularly marked in the pronoun morphology. Instead, *tripela* is used occasionally as a modifier of a pronoun already in plural form, or in conjunction with *ol*:

So mi tokim em osem mipla - <u>mipla tripla</u> i orait wantaim mami, mipla stap gut tasol, tsol mipla misim em stret

So I told him that <u>the three of us</u> were all right with mother, we were fine, but we really miss him [Manus, F, 15]

narapla meri ia em tambu bl' em na <u>ol tripla</u> kam nau ol askim mipla na mipla tok - mipla no toktok.

Another woman was her in-law, and <u>the three</u> came and asked us and we said - we didn't say anything. [Morobe, F, 11]

m(a)ma bl' em karim tripla muli na, ... tupla bans, em karim kam na sinautim <u>ol tripla</u> kam kaikai.

His mother brought three oranges and ... three bunches, she brought them and called <u>the three</u> to come and eat [West Sepik, F, 13]

The bare forms *tupela* and *tripela* are both more common than morphologically complex forms, suggesting that numerals might also be used with pronominal reference for numbers greater than three. However, this is most uncommon with only seven occurrences in the corpus, four of which were preceded by *ol*:

tupla brada ia tok ose ba tupla kisi(m) tupla susa ia ose(m) meri blo tupla nau <u>ol fopla</u> marit na ol kamapim oun ples blo ol

the two brothers said they would get two sisters and marry them and <u>the four</u> got married and founded their own village. [East Sepik, F, 16]

Mühlhäusler notes that the dual pronoun *tupela* cannot be used for inanimates (1985h:344), and this is supported by data from the present corpus. This also seems to apply generally to trial pronouns, although there are single occurrences of *tripela* and *fopela* to refer to plant material and plastic containers respectively:

meri i tokim em, "sapos yu go bek lo ailan blo yu, yu mas putim displa kokonas baksait lo kanu na yu no ken lukluk baksait inap yu harim <u>tripla</u> pairap okei bai yu tanim na bai yu lukluk."

The woman told him, "if you go back to your island, you must put these coconuts in the back of the canoe, and you mustn't look back until you hear <u>the three</u> explode, then you can turn round and look." [East New Britain, F, 14]

tupla plestik ia pulap pinis lo daka nau, em kirap nau, em holim <u>fopla</u> lo han bl' em nau...

the two plastic containers were filled with betel peppers then he got up and held <u>four</u> of them in his hand... [Morobe, F, 14]

Plural pronouns

Mühlhäusler notes that the singular/plural pronoun distinction is somewhat variable, and that *em* may occasionally denote a plural referent among some speakers, giving the example *ol wasman em i stap* 'the watchmen were there' (1985h:344). This was described as particularly common when the plural noun was an inanimate. In the present corpus, this appears to be uncommon; plural referents are generally indicated by overtly plural pronouns. On the occasions where a plural referent is followed by *em*, an interpretation in terms of topicalization or switch reference is often more appropriate (see Chapter 7 below):

Na (di)sla tupla yangpla meri, ol - i no ol tru tru meri, <u>em ol masalai</u> blong Wagi.

And these two young women, they were not real people, <u>they were spirits</u> of the Waghi River. [Simbu, M, 15]

If extreme pressure from English were to influence Tok Pisin morphology, it might be expected that the distinction between singular and plural second person pronouns could become eroded in favour of a generic *yu*, following the English pattern. However, no examples of loss of plural marking on second person plural pronouns were found, and *yupela* was always used with plural referents.

4.4.3 The inclusive/exclusive distinction

As we have seen, the standard pronoun paradigm maintains a distinction between inclusive and exclusive uses of the first person plural pronouns - *yumi* and *mipela* respectively. In the majority of cases, this distinction is also maintained in the corpus. However, there are instances where this is not the case. In the following extract, for example, the informant is explaining the 'pay-back system' in pre-contact Western Highlands, and the listener, an expatriate, is obviously not included:

Lo taim bilong tumbuna, loenoda i no bin kam, n' ol tumbuna blo <u>yumi</u> go wail tru long said blo peibek sistem. Sapos lain blo traib blo naratla lain i kam kam paitim <u>yumi</u> - wanpela man blo <u>yumi</u> o samting olsem ...

In the time of our grandparents there was no law and order, and <u>our</u> grandparents were really wild because of the pay-back system. If a group from another tribe came and attacked <u>us</u>, one of <u>our</u> men, or something like that ... [Western Highlands, M, 16]

In this example, the informant is using what is normally described as the inclusive form when relating a narrative to a listener who clearly was nowhere near the action in time or place. An alternative interpretation is thus called for. Romaine (1992a) discusses this problem in some detail in her analysis of children's speech from Morobe and Madang provinces. In her data she noted several occurrences of this anomalous use of *yumi* and termed it 'communal', as it appeared to refer to cultural items or property held in common by the speaker's community. This explanation is a useful insight, and a non-inclusive use of *yumi* can sometimes be interpreted in this way in the corpus. However, it does not account for all the anomalous uses of *yumi* in the present corpus. For example, in the following extract, *ples bilong yumi* could reasonably be categorized as communal, but the other occurrences appear to refer simply to a 'we' unmarked for the inclusive/exclusive distinction:

Wanpla taim ia, <u>yumi</u> sa stap long ples bilong <u>yumi</u> nau, <u>yumi</u> sa go - <u>yumi</u> wantaim brata blong <u>yumi</u>, <u>yumi</u> sa go hukim fis na kam kaikai na, ... na <u>yumi</u> sa go kisim banana nabaut

one time, <u>we</u> were in <u>our</u> village, <u>we</u> went, <u>we</u> and <u>our</u> brother went fishing and came to eat, and <u>we</u> went to get bananas and things [Eastern Highlands, F, 11]

With second language speakers such as those in the rural villages in Romaine's study, it may be that the inclusive/exclusive distinction of standard Tok Pisin has not been fully mastered, and interlanguage phenomena may be operating. As Mühlhäusler notes (1985h:343) confusion of these forms is common as an 'interference phenomenon' among second language Tok Pisin speakers for whom the inclusive/exclusive distinction is not made in the first language. In many parts of mainland Papua New Guinea in particular, there is no substrate motivation to preserve the inclusive/exclusive distinction as there is, for example, for speakers of Austronesian languages of the New Guinea Islands. In the following example, note the alternation of *yumi* and *mipela* without any apparent change of referent, suggesting that the forms may simply be used interchangeably:

Nau mipla karim ol dok, mipla go antap. Taim yumi go antap, mipla arim wanpla pik singaut, na taim mipla go insait, mipla lukim em i karim ol pikinini sanap i stap.

Now we carried the dogs and we went up. When we went up, we heard a pig calling, and when we went in, we saw it giving birth. [West Sepik, M, 17]

The inclusive/exclusive distinction appears to be maintained in the New Guinea Islands regions more than in either the Highlands or Momase Regions.

4.4.4 *Em* and *en*

In the basic pronoun paradigm presented in 4.4.1, no case distinctions were made. However, there are two forms of the third person singular *em* and *en* in common use. *En* cannot appear in subject position, and is only used as an enclitic after *long* or *bilong*. Because *en* cannot have an independent existence, *longen* and *bilongen* are written here as single words. However, *em* also appears after *long* and *bilong*, and the significance of the choice between *en* and *em* in this position is by no means clear. Dutton describes the difference in terms of emphasis (1973:39). He describes the normal unstressed possessive pronoun as *bilongen*, with *bilong em* putting the emphasis on the person to whom it belongs. In the corpus, *em* is considerably more common than *en*. In addition to the usual explanations of the distribution of *em* and *en* in terms of case or emphasis (Dutton 1973, Mihalic 1971), there appears to be a relationship to the degree of contraction of *long* and *bilong*, as can be seen in the following table:

Use of *en* and *em* with *long* and *bilong*

long variants

with *em*	Number	%	with *en*	Number	%
l' em	133	25%	len	15	6%
lo em	225	42%	loen	74	29%
long em	180	33%	longen	164	65%
Total	538	100%	Total	253	100%

bilong variants

with *em*	Number	%	with *en*	Number	%
bl' em	1584	54%	blen	156	16%
blo em	575	20%	bloen	272	29%
blong em	710	24%	blongen	517	54%
bilong em	44	2%	bilongen	8	1%
Total	2913	100%	Total	953	100%

The first comment to be made about these figures is that it was often very difficult to distinguish between *en* and *em* in the recordings, especially in fast or indistinct speech, or when unstressed. So, although every effort was made to identify the difference, it was not always possible to be sure that one form rather than the other was used. Keeping this caveat in mind, a number of interesting observations emerge.

The first is that there is an overall preponderance of *em* forms. Over twice as many occurred with *long*, and more than three times as many with *bilong*, even when unstressed, suggesting that this is the canonical form:

Nau em slip l' aus sik (ta)sol taim ol g(iv)im keikei l' em, em sa keikei (ta)sol em kaikai no save raun, keikei em sa traut olgeta

Now he slept at the hospital, but when they gave <u>him</u> food, he ate but the food did not go round, the food was vomited out. [Simbu, M, 17]

Mipla wari l' em mipla karai l' em long faif ouklok moning go inap tulait, ol man i kam ol karai l' em i go i go

We worried <u>about him</u>, we cried <u>for him</u> from five o'clock until dawn, people came and cried and cried <u>for him</u>. [West Sepik, M, 15]

Em tokim mama bl' em, mama bl' em gi(vi)m em naif ia na em katim katim go lilik nogut.

He told <u>his</u> mother, <u>his</u> mother gave him a knife and he cut it into small pieces. [Morobe, F, 13]

Em nau tewel ksim tamiok bl' em tsol tamiok bl' em i no sap.

So the spirit got <u>his</u> axe, but <u>his</u> axe was not sharp. [New Ireland, M, 14]

Also noteworthy is the fact that the use of *en* occurred more frequently with less contracted forms, suggesting that other functions might be replacing that of the normal unstressed pronoun. One of these appears to be in relative clause formation, as shown in the following extract, where *longen* and *long em* have quite different interpretations:

ol lain bl' ol man indai longen sa givim amaunt ol lagim ol baim long em na ol sa lainim ap ol pig.

The clan of the men <u>who have died</u> give the amount which they want them <u>to pay for him</u> and they line up the pigs. [Southern Highlands, F, 14]

The role of *longen* and *long em* and their contractions in relative clause delimitation is discussed more fully when considering relativization in § 6.6.4.

4.4.5 Other pronoun forms

A number of other pronoun forms do appear, for example, a compromise first person plural form *yumipela* occurs from time to time. Romaine (1992a:217) found this as an occasional variant in the Madang Province sample, while Mühlhäusler (1985h:343) relates the form to a lack of distinction between inclusive and exclusive in the first language. In Romaine's data, *yumipela* has inclusive reference, and this also appeared to be the case with the single occurrence in the present corpus, although a communal interpretation would also be possible:

"*... meri ia yu save olsem em ticha blong yumipla ia na, blo wanem yu mekim (di)sla kain pasin?*"

"… this woman, you know she is <u>our</u> teacher, so why are you doing this?" [Simbu, F, 19]

Romaine's speech samples contain one or two other unusual forms, such as *miplu*, which appears without comment (possibly a misprint), and *empela*, which is a possible relic of an earlier form (1992:213). The use of *mipela ol* as a pronoun also occurs in Romaine's data in the phrase *mipla ol go nau* (1992a:215). In the corpus, the collocation *mipla ol* is quite frequently attested, but not as a pronoun, as the *ol* usually acts as a plural marker to following nouns:

Wanpla meri Finshafen ia em sa - em sa raun raun nau, mipla ol meri sa, mipla ol meri sa jeles lo em.

A Finschhafen girl goes around, we girls are jealous of her. [Morobe, F, 12]

Alternatively it may be used as a resumptive third person plural pronoun:

Sutim em lo leg nau, tupla ol angkol blo mipla ol beinim em raun raun l' em ia, ol ranawe go pinis ia.

They shot him in the leg, then two of our uncles who had chased him, they ran away. [Simbu, F, 12]

4.5 Cliticization

One of the striking findings of Lynch's (1979a) review of morphological change was the reduction of some particles to clitics or prefixes. For example, the future or irrealis marker *bai*, already a reduction of the sentence-level adverbial *baimbai*, was typically further reduced to *ba* or *b'* as in *em ba kam* or *b' ol i kam*, while *long* and *bilong* were typically reduced to *(b)lo* or *(b)l'* as in *(b)lo em* or *(b)l' em*. These reductions, as some of the examples above have already shown, were very typically found in the present corpus:

> *wanpla taim nau ol man tok osem b' ol aid na olim em*
>
> one time the men said <u>they would</u> hide and catch him [West Sepik, F, 13]

> *disla susa bl' em sori nogut tru l' em*
>
> this sister <u>of his</u> was very sorry <u>for him</u> [Western Highlands, M, 17]

> *em ronowe go stret lo, wonem, ples blo papa bl' em, kisim binatang l' em nau, em no go tokim papa bl' em ...*
>
> he ran straight to <u>his</u> father's village, got the grubs <u>from him</u>, he didn't tell <u>his</u> father [West Sepik. M, 16]

The above examples show reduction to a single consonant before vowels, but the same reduction can also be found before glides:

> *Em digi(m) ol lo disla ples ia, i go kamap l' wanpla nupla ples*
>
> He dug a hole in this village which went <u>to a</u> new village [West Sepik, M, 15]

> *tupla to(k)(ol)sem, "yutupla kam na bai mi painim l' aus bl' yutupla."*
>
> The two said "you two come and I will look for it in <u>your</u> house." [Manus, F, 11]

> *Maunt Hagen em osem, bikpla strit, mipla bin stap l' wanpla liklik ples we ol sa kolim Keltika*
>
> Mount Hagen is like, big streets, we stayed <u>in a</u> little village which they called Keltika. [Manus, F, 12]

> *ol sampla mipla go daun lo tamblo ia l' Wara Wagi ia*
>
> some of us went down <u>to the River</u> Waghi [Simbu, F, 12]

Reduction can also occur before other consonants, especially when articulation of adjacent consonants occurs in a similar position. The first of a pair of consonants may also attach itself to a preceding vowel:

> *ol ksim ogeta ol spia n' ol displa samting na ol kilim em, na i rausim em l' sla (= long dispela) ples.*
>
> They got their spears and these things and they killed him, and threw him <u>out of this</u> village. [West Sepik, M, 17]

> *em tokim em "orait yu go anta(p) l' sla kokonas long hap i go ia go antap, taim anis kaikai yu, yu pilim wanem samting, no ken singaut."*
>
> she told him "all right, you climb <u>that</u> coconut tree over there, climb up, when the ants bite you, whatever you feel, do not cry out." [Manus, M, 12]

> *em kirap na em tok olsem "em fest taim blo yupla na sapos seken taim ken mi lukim nem bl' yupla ken, em nau b' mi puti(m) yupla lo panishment."*
>
> He got up and said "it's your first time, and if there's a second time, I will see your names, then <u>I'll</u> put you on punishment." [Manus, F, 16]

> *Tupla pikinini stap go, papa na mama bl' tupla indai, na papa i wokim wanpla sel kanu blo tupla*
>
> The two children stayed there, <u>their</u> mother and father died, and their father made them a sailing canoe [West Sepik, M, 17]

Lynch also comments on the cliticization of the habitual and inceptive aspect markers *save* and *laik*, normally reduced to *sa* and *la* respectively. Again, many instances of this reduction are attested in the corpus, and these in fact appear to be the standard spoken forms of these aspect particles:

na tupla sa go painim abus lo bus, kilim na kam ba kukim ba kaikai

and the two <u>would go</u> hunting, kill it and bring it back to cook and eat [West Sepik, F, 13]

nau ol sa yusim lo taim ol la go anting lo bus ol sa yusim go na kilim ol planti abus nambaut

now they <u>(habitually) use</u> them when they are <u>about to/want to go</u> hunting, they <u>use</u> them and kill lots of animals [Western Highlands, F, 14]

em sidaun stap nau em la apim hed bl' em, nogat em lukim wanpla sta(p) ia man shain nogut tru.

He was sitting down and <u>about to raise</u> his head when he saw one, a man really shining bright. [Morobe, F, 14]

Em gat tupla pikini meri na ol sa stap lo wanpla aus lo bus na wanpla taim mama blo ol em la dai, em - em wok gaden...

She had two daughters and they <u>stayed</u> in a house in the bush and one time, their mother was <u>about to die</u>, she was working in the garden... [Madang, F, 12]

The reduction of *save* to *sa* as a habitual aspect marker could effectively differentiate it from the *save* meaning 'to know', which is generally not reduced. Lynch is more definite, and states that both *sa* and *la* are reduced only in their aspectual role, and not in their regular verbal use (1979a:8). However, there are a few instances in the corpus where *save* 'to know' is also reduced to *sa*, eliminating this semantic distinction:

Mi bin sidaun na mi poret nogut stret. Mi no sa ba mi mek(im) wonem

I sat down and I was very afraid. I didn't <u>know</u> what to do. [Manus, F, 15]

man em no - em no sa haus blo usat tru

the man didn't <u>know</u> whose house it really was [Western Highlands, M, 16]

The numbers were as follows:

Sa and *save* as 'to know' and aspect marker	
save 'to know'	255
save (aspectual)	159
sa 'to know'	19
sa (aspectual)	2756

Thus, the reduced form *sa* does appear to be the aspectual particle in the great majority of cases, with both functions widely used for *save*. The dual role of the full form *save* appears to show little differentiation in different regions:

Save as aspectual particle and 'to know' by region			
	Momase	Highlands	Islands
save (know)	68	42	90
save (aspectual)	48	27	67
Ratio	1.4	1.6	1.3

Thus the potential ambiguity between *sa*/*save* as a verb and an aspect particle still remains. This is complicated further by the fact that *dispela* may also be reduced to *sa* in rapid speech:

em go mekim nupla haus bl' em nau, em sa - em sa stap na taim em luki(m) ol sa (= disla) muruk na em la toktok l' ol, ol muruk ia tup... - ol tupla sa ranawe.

He went and made a new house for himself, he (habitually) stayed there and when he saw these cassowaries and he wanted to talk to them, the two cassowaries would run away. [Eastern Highlands, F, 12]

Na moning em slip, kirap nau em to(k), "yu klaim sa ko(ko)nas. Anis kaikai yu, yu no ken kilim, yu klaim tasol."

In the morning he got up from sleep and said "you climb this coconut tree. If ants bite you, you mustn't kill them, just climb." [Morobe, F, 12]

mi no inap lo bilivim tasol em bin tru, em bin rausim ol sa samting lo dsa (=dispela) bodi blo (di)sla liklik sik manggi ia.

I couldn't believe it but it was true, he took these things from the body of the sick little boy. [West Sepik, F, 17]

tupla sa slip lo has blo wanpla traipla diwai. Lo sa diwai ia wanpla traipla sneik sa stap antap lo wonem, het blen nau ...

the two slept at the foot of a huge tree. In this tree a huge snake lived up at the top... [Eastern Highlands, F, 12]

The status of the reduced form **la** is less certain due to the closer relationship between the two meanings. As with the distinction between *save* and *sa*, *la* appears to be normally used as an aspect particle indicating 'about to do something' and the full form **laik** as a verb 'like, want to'. However, especially with the reduced form **la**, the distinction between the possible meanings is not always clear-cut, and there are some cases where both interpretations would be possible:

Disla, wanem ia sangguma man ia em la dring wara, na em giaman go putim et blong em ia, man ia pushim disla sangguma man go long wara.

This sorcerer, he was about to/wanted to drink water, and he pretended to put his head down, the man pushed the sorcerer into the river. [Enga, M, 18]

Em ronim ol nau, em rausim belt ia na wipim ol nau, em la beltim ol nau, ol ronowe.

He chased them and took off his belt and whipped them, he was about to/wanted to belt them and they ran away. [Morobe, F, 12]

lo moning nau taim tupla la go long, am wara tupla lukim mama blo tupla i dai na stap lo said blo wara.

In the morning when the two wanted to/were about to go to the river, they saw their mother who had died standing beside the river. [Manus, F, 14]

The reduction and cliticization of some other aspect markers was found, including **wok long**, and what could turn out to be a newly emerging aspect particle **kirap** as discussed in Chapter 7. **Wok long** is used to indicate that an action is in progress, and can be best translated as 'engaged in' or 'busy' doing something, although this may sound unnatural in normal English, and the present continuous would often be used for a more natural-sounding translation:

Mipla kam lo rot na mitla (w)ok lo kaikai - mitla ok lo kaikai buai kam lo rot na mitla o lo (= wok long) spak na mitla o lo laf na singsing na kam lo rot.

We came along the road and we were busy chewing - we were (busy) chewing betel nut as we went along the road and we were intoxicated and we were laughing and singing and came along the road. [Manus, F, 15]

Wok long is often reduced to *wo lo, ok lo, o lo* or *wo*, especially in the Manus and Sepik samples. A regional breakdown shows the following:

	Variants of *wok long* by region		
	Islands	Momase	Highlands
wok lo(ng)	284	190	124
wo lo(ng)	32	8	5
ok lo(ng)	12	9	4
wo + verb	5	9	2

The syntactic functions of **laik, save, wok long** and **kirap** are further discussed in § 6.6. on aspect markers.

4.6 Other suffixes

A number of other occurrences of what are suffixes in English can be found in the corpus, although the extent to which they are analyzed as suffixes in Tok Pisin is open to question. In most cases they appear to be adopted unanalyzed in borrowed lexical items, although there is evidence that some morphological analysis is being made by bilingual speakers.

4.6.1 The *-ing* suffix

Mühlhäusler (1985d:339) observes that the English *-ing* suffix was used in some creolized varieties he investigated and he suggests that the suffix entered first as an unanalyzed attachment to borrowed verbal forms and then came to acquire a continuous aspect function in distinction to other verbal forms among some speakers.

In standard Tok Pisin, words ending in -ing are very common, mainly those derived from the English 'thing' or 'think', for example, *samting, nating, ting, tingting, ating*. Other common words ending in -ing include *ring, king, wing, sting, moning*, etc. There is thus no phonological impediment to the adoption of -ing forms. In the corpus, a number of more recent verbal derivatives ending in *-ing* are also found, based on present participial forms in English. These are almost exclusively used in an unanalyzed way, usually adjectivally or as noun (gerundial) forms. Adjectival *-ing* forms appearing in the corpus are seen in the table below. The choice of following noun may be severely constrained by a unique or limited collocation, and some of these are indicated in the table. The number of tokens is given in brackets:

Adjectival *-ing* forms

boding (2)	boarding (school)
boring (8)	boring
ekting (4)	acting (prefects)
flaing (10)	flying (fox)
folowing (1)	following
fraitning (2)	frightening
haiding (1)	hiding (place)
intresting (4)	interesting
isigouing (1)	easy going
komending (1)	commanding (officer)
mising (1)	missing
pleying (1)	playing (mate)
saraunding (1)	surrounding
seving (7)	surfing (board)
shoking (1)	shocking
swiming (8)	swimming (pool)

Meanings appear to be generally equivalent to the English forms, except for *boring*, which has shifted the meaning to the personal state 'bored' and could also be considered as a stative verb 'to be bored'. The other forms, which are more clearly adjectival in nature, appear before the noun they qualify. Some are not structurally identical to the English forms from which they were derived, for example *seving bod* 'surf board' and *pleing meit* 'play mate' have adopted an *-ing* ending on what are in English nominal compounds.

Nominal forms were suprisingly numerous, with 27 different types, although the number of token is most cases is small.

Nominal *-ing* forms

bigining (4)	beginning
bilding(s) (3)	building
blesing (2)	blessing
dresing (2)	dress(ing)
droing (1)	drawing
faiting (1)	fighting
faking (1)	fucking
fandreizing (1)	fundraising
filing(s) (4)	feeling
kiling (1)	killing
laitning (7)	lightening
maining (1)	mining
mining (3)	meaning
miting (11)	meeting
nesing (2)	nursing
ofring (1)	offering
raiting (2)	writing
riding (2)	reading
rikoding (1)	recording
seving (7)	surfing
shiping (1)	shipping
s(h)oping (4)	shopping
swiming (8)	swimming
tiching (1)	teaching
treining (4)	training
woning (1)	warning

Although the lexemes in the table above are primarily used as nouns, in one or two instances, a supplementary verbal use may also appear, but usually the *-ing* ending is unanalyzed, and the form is used as a single morpheme:

Na em go em <u>treining</u> lo karim ston

And he went and <u>trained</u> to carry the stone [Manus, M, 14]

The most common verbal use of *-ing* forms involves borrowing from two English lexical phrases 'to go fishing' and 'to go hunting', which appear as *go fishing* and *go (h)anting*:

Go na wanpla taim moning, pikinini bl' em i <u>go fishing</u>

then one morning his son <u>went fishing</u> [Manus, M, 11]

ol tripela brada ol sa go anting nabaut

the three brothers would go hunting [Western Highlands, M, 16]

Okei wanpla taim wanpla man i go - i go hanting

OK once a man went hunting [New Ireland, M, 12]

The phrasal verb may even incorporate a prepositional element:

wanpla taim tupla bin go haut fishing na tupla bin kisim sampla fis

once the two went out fishing and caught some fish [Manus, M, 14]

These examples are interesting, as they suggest that an early stage of the differentiation of morphological function could be emerging in the context of language mixing. However, it appears that, like the earlier examples, the *-ing* continues to remain unanalyzed in most cases:

taim yangbla brada i go fishing, na em i fishing stap...

when the younger brother went fishing, and he was fishing [Manus, M, 14]

Another verbal use of an *-ing* form was:

ol relativ blong em i sawe kam na mipla sawe singing lo nait i go inap moning

his relatives come and we sing in the night until morning [East New Britain, M, 17]

Only in a single case is there the suggestion of continuous aspect associated with the *-ing* ending:

Em i stap osem tenpla krismas tiching, nau em lusim na kam.

He stayed teaching for ten years then left and came (home). [Eastern Highlands, M, 18]

4.6.2 The *-ed* suffix

As with English *-ing* forms, past participial forms usually appear to be borrowed unanalyzed, like the established examples of ***tan*** 'cooked' (from English 'done') and ***maret*** or ***marit*** 'married'. A number of unanalyzed *-ed* past participle forms appeared in the corpus, for example:

planti man meri nau ol i intrested yet lo kalcha blo yumi

a lot of people are still interested in our culture [New Ireland, F, 15]

Mipla priperim ol speshel mil blong ol speshel gest, ol invaited gest na mipla bin mekim bikpla kaikai tru

we prepared a special meal for the special guests, the invited guests, and we really made a feast [Manus F, 16]

In the following extract, the past participial form is used as a base to which a transitive marker is added:

rein i kam na bagarapim, na hedmasta tok nogat, em kenselim disla. Em pospondim na em tok Fraide neks wik bai ol gi(vi)m olgeta praisis

rain came and spoiled it and the headmaster said no, he cancelled this (graduation). He postponed it and said Friday next week they would give out the prizes. [Southern Highlands, F, 16]

Other similar examples included the use of ***disaided*** 'decided' (1), ***krauded*** 'crowded (1), ***taied*** 'tired' (6), ***adopted*** 'adopted' (1), ***disapiad*** 'disappeared' (2), ***shotsaited*** 'shortsighted' (1) and ***injed*** 'injured' (1). Also similar to the case of continuous *-ing* forms, occurrences of the use of *-ed* endings to indicate aspect, tense or participial functions were rare. In the few instances that they occurred, they may better be considered nonce borrowing or code-switching. The following were found:

Biain lo moning lo narapla dei nau, brata blen disaided olsem bai em bai stilim et blong em.

After another morning, his brother decided he would steal his head [East New Britain, F, 14]

Em tok osem nau em bin go lo namel stret na em bin, wonem disapiad na man ia bin belhat

He said this then he went right into the middle and disappeared, and the man was angry. [Enga, F, 12]

> *Fes taim stret taim mi bin go visitim Buka mi bin saprais bikos mi bin go na i bin <u>weldivelopt</u>*
>
> The very first time I went to visit Buka I was surprised because I went and it was <u>well-developed</u>. [East New Britain, F, 16]

The tension between the Tok Pisin and English systems can be seen in the following attempted repair of a form with a borrowed ending to a more standard form:

> *ol wanwan tasol ol no bin ronowe bikos ol bin <u>diskavad</u> - diskava - diskava, osem na ol bin stap na ol cheinj i go lo plents*
>
> only a few didn't run away because they <u>were discovered</u>, so they stayed and changed into plants [East New Britain, M, 16]

To what extent examples such as those detailed above represent a precursor of morphological change remains to be seen as Tok Pisin develops. The above example suggests that the speaker is resisting morphological change, and is preserving the distinction between the English and Tok Pisin systems.

4.6.3 Phrasal elements in verbs

Many established Tok Pisin words incorporate an element derived from an English adverb, most notably 'up' 'down' and 'out', such as **karamap** 'to cover (up)', **litimap** 'to lift (up)' **painaut** 'to find out', **singaut** 'shout', **kamdaun** 'come down' etc. The extent to which these elements can be regarded as distinct morphemes is debatable, and in most cases it seems that, whatever the ultimate derivation, the item is used as a single unanalyzed lexeme.

> *em la kam bek lo aus ia nogat em arim wanpla dok <u>singaut</u>.*
>
> He was about to come home when he heard a dog <u>barking</u>. [Eastern Highlands, F, 16]

> *mipla wokobaut i go go <u>kamap</u> lo haus sik, ples blo kisim marasin na mipla bin go insait.*
>
> We went on walking and <u>arrived</u> at the hospital, the place to get medicine, and we went inside. [Madang, F, 17]

> *Nau katim wanpla brensh blo galip na i <u>pundaun</u> antap lo pikinini blong em.*
>
> Now he cut a branch of the tree and it <u>fell down</u> on top of his son. [New Ireland, M, 15]

In the last example, there is no separate word **pun*, showing that *pundaun* is clearly a single morpheme. However, *aut* 'out', *daun* 'down' and *ap* 'up' do exist as independent items, and a good case can be made for a morphemic analysis of words such as *kamaut* 'to come out' into component morphemes *kam* 'come' and *aut* 'out'. Indeed, it is not clear whether forms such as this and *godaun* 'go down' should be written as one word or two.

> *em nau manggi ia i kirap <u>kam daun</u> (kamdaun?). <u>Kam daun</u> long kokonas nau na <u>kam daun</u> lo tupla lek nau. Em nau wok lo <u>kam daun</u> na i <u>pundaun</u> i <u>kam daun</u>. <u>Pundaun</u> i <u>kam daun</u> na i pas lo diwai na hed blongen i buruk olgeta.*
>
> So the boy started to <u>come down</u>. <u>Come down</u> the coconut tree on two legs. He was <u>coming down</u> and he <u>fell down</u>. <u>Fell down</u> and caught on the tree and his head was really broken. [North Solomons, M, 14]

> *em lukim olsem disla balus pas nau em <u>kamaut</u> (kam aut?) na tokim ol manmeri insait lo disla balus lo <u>kamaut</u> na pusim disla balus*
>
> he saw that the plane was stuck and he <u>came out</u> and told the people inside the plane to <u>come out</u> and push the plane. [Eastern Highlands, F, 14]

> *Wanpla taim tupla brada blo mi bin <u>go aut</u> (goaut?) na <u>go aut</u> lo si, na tupla ksim wanpla bikpla trausel tru.*
>
> Once two of my brothers <u>went out</u> and <u>went out</u> to sea, and they caught a really big turtle. [West Sepik, F, 13]

Even the adverb *in* can be found in the corpus (four times), although these occurrences could also be interpreted part of a single borrowed verbal expression:

> *em sa stap em yet olsem na taim manggi ia kam <u>pip in</u> ia em i no fil gud.*
>
> He liked to stay by himself and when this boy came and <u>peeped in</u>, he didn't feel good. [East New Britain, M, 19]

In English, many phrasal verbs incorporate an adverbial or prepositional element, but act as single lexical items, shown by the fact that they can often be replaced by single words. For example, the phrasal verb 'to look after' is synonymous with 'to nurture'. The literal meaning of the word 'after' is irrelevant to the meaning of the phrasal verb, as with many other examples, where the apparently arbitrary nature of the prepositional element makes learning English phrasal verbs so difficult for speakers of other languages. In the corpus, a variety of new lexical items derived from English phrasal verbs can be found. In most cases, the item is borrowed as an unanalyzed chunk and becomes part of the idiomatic competence of the speaker (cf Pawley 1993). In some cases the prepositional or adverbial element is semantically transparent, while in others, it has no semantic relevance. For example, there appears to be no semantic significance in the phrasal element in the following:

> *Ol i bin flai lo balus nau ol i bin laik <u>traimaut</u> ol parashuts.*
>
> They flew in the plane and they wanted to <u>try out</u> the parachutes. [New Ireland, M, 12]

> *Na ol man tok osem mi mas <u>watsaut</u> long pukpuk ia, sapos yupla lukim nau bai yu mas ripot o kain osem.*
>
> And people said I should <u>watch out</u> for the crocodile, if you see one now, you are supposed to report it or something [Manus, M, 15]

> *Nau man em ksim wanpla osem faia lait stap, em ksim tasol na em go paitim meri ia ... Nau tupla kisim pikinini nau tupla <u>kuldaun</u> na tupla yet stap.*
>
> Now the man got a burning stick, he got it and went to hit the woman ... Now the two got their child back and the two <u>cooled down</u> and they still live there. [Enga, F, 13]

> *Na i stap go nau, moning ol Lombrum kam n' ol stopim paia ia na, i bin <u>sloudaun</u>. Nau i bin pinis.*
>
> And it stayed like that and in the morning the Lombrum people came and fought the fire and it <u>slowed down</u>. It was put out. [Manus, F, 15]

> *Ol sanap na ol <u>holdap</u> l' wanpla piemvi blo Drekikir, wanpla ples anta(p) lo Maprik. Ol <u>holdap</u> n' ol kisi(m) ol mani.*
>
> They stood (on the road) and <u>held up</u> a PMV (public motor vehicle) from Dreikikir, a village past Maprik. They <u>held it up</u> and got the money. [West Sepik, M, 16]

> *Biain mipla piknik pinis, lo leit lo aftanun dedi bl' em tokim mipla lo <u>pekap</u> na biain mipla kam bek gen lo haus lo taun.*
>
> After we had had our picnic, in the late afternoon his father told us to <u>pack up</u> and afterwards we came back to the house in town. [Manus, F, 14]

However, in other cases, although a phrasal verb appears to be unanalyzed, there is nevertheless some semantic information to be gleaned from the individual parts. For example, in the following extract, *bendaun* 'burn down' implies that a building has been burned right down to the ground. Although there is no word **ben* 'burn', and the term looks like an unanalyzed borrowing, there is nevertheless the possibility that the *daun* component is not altogether without meaning:

> *ol bin kisim mipla - sampla - wanwan manggi lo go intaviu lo fainaut lo usait i bin kukim disla tasol nau ol no fainaut yet nau ol polis i investiget yet lo fainaut lo disla bilding i bin <u>bendaun</u>.*
>
> They took a few of us boys to interview to find out who set fire to it, but they haven't found out yet, and the police are still investigating to find out about the building which was <u>burned down</u>. [East Sepik, M, 17]

Similarly, although there is no word **spred* 'spread', information could be obtained from the *aut* part of the word *spredaut* 'spread out':

> *Ol go wantem nau liglig brada kirap na tok "mipela bung wantem i no gutla, mipela <u>spredaut</u> na bai mipela painim keikei blo mipela yet." Okei ol <u>spredaut</u>.*
>
> They went together and the younger brother said "staying together is not good, we should <u>spread out</u> and find our own food." So they <u>spread out</u>. [Western Highlands, M, 16]

Likewise, the term *hensapim* 'to hold up, rob' is derived from the English imperative expression 'hands up!', which may be semantically transparent:

> *Ol i go na ol i <u>hensapim</u> em lo masket na ol i askim em lo brata blo Pita.*
>
> They went and <u>held him up</u> with a shotgun and they asked him about Peter's brother. [Manus, M, 15]

Occasionally a phrasal verb is calqued to give a parallel expression using Tok Pisin words, for example in the following extract, the English expression 'deal with' is translated as ***dil wantaim***:

> *ol difens no hamamas lo, am, hau ol polis ol i <u>dil wante</u>* (= *dil wantaim*) *disla sityuesen so ol yet ol i kisim i go lo han blong ol.*
>
> The soldiers were not happy about, um, how the police <u>dealt with</u> this situation so they took it into their own hands [Manus, F, 15]

In cases where the verb is immediately followed by an adverbial element, it may not be clear if morphological analysis is appropriate or not. Use of ***daun*** and ***aut***, for example, is almost always immediately following a verb, especially the verbs ***go*** and ***kam***. Only in a very small percentage of occurrences is it separated from the verb. For example, out of 1091 tokens of ***daun*** 'down', in only 3 cases was the object separated from the verb. However, such occurrences where the phrasal element is separated from a verbal stem could indicate that an incipient change towards constructions analogous to English expressions is taking place or has the potential to occur:

> *Ol bringim go <u>putim em daun</u> lo graun nau em tok "putim mi isi go daun lo graun," nau ol putim em.*
>
> They brought him and <u>put him down</u> on the ground and he said "put me down gently on the ground," and they put him down. [West Sepik, F, 13]

> *Mipla singsing pinis nau, mipla statof stret ia ren bin kam ia. Mipla laik <u>givim setifiket aut</u> l' ol skul pikinini taim, so ol kensolim*
>
> We had finished dancing and started off when the rain came. Just when we were about to <u>give the certificates out</u> to the school children, so they cancelled it. [Southern Highlands, F, 14]

> *papa blo mi i ring i kam long Hengganofi Hai nau o(l) tok sem "bai mipla <u>skwizim yu tasol in</u>," so mi tok okei tasol na ol salim mi kam tu lo peles.*
>
> My father rang up Henganofi High School and they said "we can just <u>squeeze you in</u>," so I agreed and they sent me to the village. [Eastern Highlands (ex-North Solomons), M, 16]

Other phrase-level lexical items are discussed in the following chapter dealing with the lexicon.

5

Lexicon

Chapter 5 looks at the composition of the lexicon - the words used by first language Tok Pisin speakers. As noted in Chapter 1, the Tok Pisin lexicon is derived mainly from English but contains items from a number of other languages. The words in current use as exemplified by the corpus appear to include an increased number of English-derived items, whereas, for example, most items of German origin have dropped out of use. Even familiar names of flora and fauna from Melanesian languages now co-exist with English-derived alternatives. In the following sections the newly appearing words are examined to determine their source, i.e. either as borrowing or a product of internal developmental processes. The frequency of the most common items in the three regional sub-corpora is indicated.

5.1 Identifying new lexis

A significant number of lexical items outside the standard dictionary entries appear in the corpus. As noted previously, Mihalic's (1971) dictionary was used as the standard for the purpose of identifying 'new' words, as this continues to be the standard dictionary of Tok Pisin. It must be remembered, however, that Mihalic's dictionary was last revised in 1971 and, as Mihalic himself has observed (1990), many of the entries now appear to be obsolete. Words such as ***dadap*** (a kind of tree), surely unknown to the majority of Tok Pisin speakers today, are included, while items which are shown in this corpus to be common and widespread, such as ***dedi*** 'daddy, father', ***siksti*** 'very fast' (see below) and ***okei*** 'all right', are missing. The choice of some of the entries also appears a little inconsistent, for example ***daiva*** 'diver' is present but not ***daiv*** 'to dive', while ***draiv*** 'to drive' is present but not ***draiva*** 'driver'. The present corpus, however, is too small to give an accurate guide to all the words in current use.

Some of the entries and omissions in Mihalic appear to be worthy of mention. As Laycock has shown, there are often inconsistencies in the written standard, and substratum elements can give clues as to the basic identity of certain forms (1985:305), for example regional variations in pronunciation suggest that ***tispela*** would be a better standard than ***dispela*** for 'this' (< *this fellow*). Similarly, the word ***draipela*** 'very large' almost always appears to be rendered as ***traipela*** in the corpus, and this is probably a better version of the standard form.[20] Mihalic lists ***daunbilo*** for 'below', but this form is not found here, and a closer approximation would be ***tambolo*** or variants such as ***tamblo***. In some cases it is not clear whether a word in the corpus is a variant of an established Tok Pisin item or a separate borrowing, for example the word ***kechim*** often appears in place of ***kisim*** 'catch', and is nearer to the presumed superstrate source, but is more likely to be a case of renewed borrowing than developmental change. Words not present in Mihalic but very commonly occurring in the corpus are discussed in more detail in § 5.2 below.

To examine the inventory of words occurring in the corpus but not included in Mihalic's dictionary, a preliminary analysis using simple word-processing macros was used.[21] First, phonological variants were restored to their standard spellings, e.g. ***mipla*** was restored to ***mipela*** (< *me fellow*), by global search and replace operations. 'Words' consisting of fragments from false starts were also eliminated. Then each item occurring in Mihalic's inventory of head words was systematically deleted and replaced with a single space. This had the same net effect that a Tok Pisin spell checker would have had, i.e. to display those words which do not appear in the dictionary, but since no such spell checker appears to be available, these macros were used instead.

The result of the elimination of dictionary-based words by the operation of these macros was a 'residue' consisting of all the words in the corpus not present on Mihalic's basic list. This residue, minus proper nouns, constituted the raw material on which this analysis of lexical innovation is

---

[20] Mihalic assumes it to derive from English 'dry' but Ross (1992:371) suggests a conflation of English 'dry' and Ramoaaina *tarai* 'big'. (Ramoaaina is spoken on the Duke of York islands, East New Britain.)

[21] A macro is a series of instructions suitable for use with a standard personal computer word-processing programme, in this case Word for Windows used in conjunction with the Windows 95 operating system. Macros were devised to eliminate all words appearing in Mihalic's (1971) dictionary from a text file of the whole corpus so that the remainder could be more easily seen.

based. In addition, new combinations of existing words with new idiomatic meanings were investigated by inspection of the transcripts of the corpus.

An examination of the residue of words left by eliminating the dictionary's head words did reveal some interesting points. Firstly, the sheer number of the several hundred new lexical items was noteworthy, indicating that considerable change in the lexicon is in progress. Secondly, the overwhelming majority of new items appear to originate from English. This is in spite of the many internal productive processes available for producing new words, as described in § 5.6.

Thirdly, the status of some of these words as Tok Pisin items rather than *ad hoc* or nonce borrowings is open to question. The distinction between code-mixing and borrowing is not always easy to make, and even if a word is established as a borrowed item by certain speakers, the degree to which it is integrated into the language of the speech community needs to be examined. The area of borrowing, code-mixing and code-switching is a controversial one, and no general agreement has yet been established. Pioneering work by Myers-Scotton in East Africa has generated considerable interest in recent years, and has given legitimacy to an area of study once regarded as marginal. Her notable contributions to the field include a description of social (1993a) and linguistic (1993b) constraints on code-switching in multilingual communities. Other work on code-switching appears in Poplack (1980 1988), Poplack & Meechan (1995) and Milroy & Muysken (1995).

Romaine (1992a) discusses nonce borrowing in some detail, and words appearing only once in the transcripts are not considered further in her analysis. However, this practice is problematic in a number of ways. In a small corpus, items may not appear with great frequency, and many unequivocally Tok Pisin items may be unrepresented or severely under-represented in a small sample. Secondly, the circumstances determining whether an item is once-only or occurs more than once may be somewhat arbitrary. To take a practical example, if an informant repeated an item because it was not clearly heard the first time, this would appear twice in the corpus and therefore not be classified as a nonce borrowing. Thus a more satisfactory means of deciding whether an item should be regarded as Tok Pisin or not is needed. The problem of deciding what should be included and what excluded as ad hoc borrowing is not easily resolved. Healey (1975) discusses the question of when a word should be considered part of Tok Pisin, expressing unease at the number of English words being used in the language, and drawing the rather unsatisfactory conclusion that a word is a pidgin word:

> when it is included in a Pidgin dictionary, kept modern and up-to-date by a specific group whose task it is to constantly rewrite the official dictionary, to provide the appropriate people and organisations with words to use, and to force the pace of Pidgin development so that it will keep pace with the nation's total development (Healey 1975:42)

In the absence of such an administrative resource in the foreseeable future, a lexical item is included as a Tok Pisin word in the present corpus if it appears with reasonable certainty to be phonologically, morphologically and syntactically integrated into the text. Such a criterion is not without difficulties, as there is a considerable degree of variation in phonological features, and some morphological and syntactic restructuring also appears to be taking place. Nevertheless, the criterion is retained as more satisfactory than an arbitrary counting of tokens or reliance on external standards.

The problem can be illustrated by looking at a number of examples in the corpus. In the following, the use of the *-im* transitive marker shows that the words ***saspektim*** *'suspect'* and ***distroyim*** *'destroy'*, although clearly recent English borrowings, are integrated morphologically:

> *Ol bin kisim em go bek long Lombrum na narapla ol man nambaut ol <u>saspektim</u> ol ia ol i bin kam na <u>distroyim</u> haus blo ol*

> They took him back to Lombrum, and the other men that they <u>suspected</u>, they came and <u>destroyed</u> their houses [Manus, M, 18]

In other cases, the border-line between borrowing and code-switching is more fuzzy. In the following extract, the informant started to use the English expression 'out of control', but then corrected himself, finding, however, that the available alternatives did not quite encapsulate the meaning he required.

> *Ol kar sa osem go <u>out of c...</u>- go - ron go nogut na pundaun go insait lo maunten na go daun lo Wara Simbu*

> The cars go <u>out of c...</u> - go, run badly and run off the road in the mountains and down into the Chimbu River [Western Highlands, M, 17]

Another informant uses a whole phrase which is phonologically, morphologically and syntactically English and this can thus be considered a switch:

Okei lo Mande moning <u>the following day</u> *mipela i go lo gaden*

Then on Monday morning, <u>the following day</u> we went to the garden [Western Highlands, M, 15]

However, if such a phrase were to become commonly established, perhaps with the substitution of *long* for 'the', it might reasonably be considered a Tok Pisin item. Many established Tok Pisin words have the same phonological shape as the corresponding English item, and similarly for recent borrowings, where a single word, or short expression is used, it is sometimes difficult to determine whether it should be written as Tok Pisin or English:

tupela tanim kamap ston nau tupela stap lo (di)sla hap[22] *na stap* <u>for good</u> / *fogud*.

the two turned into stone and they stayed in this place for ever [Western Highlands, F, 14]

Once again, the tension between the two phonological systems is sometimes revealed as a switch between two forms:

Mipla wetim bas go go go, nogat <u>afta... - abinun</u> nau, mi belat nogut tru.

We waited and waited for the bus until <u>afternoon</u>, I was very angry [Simbu, F, 18]

Similarly, a more recently borrowed lexical item may be used initially, but abandoned in favour of more standard items:

So ol i bin <u>disaid - ol i bin pasim tok</u>, ba ol kam daun long nambis, na kisim solwara na karim go

So they <u>decided, they decided</u> they would come down to the coast and get salt water and bring it back [East Sepik, M, 17]

A closer look at the role of the linguistic and social factors influencing code-mixing and code-switching will be found in the discussion of the relationship between Tok Pisin and English in Chapter 8.

The 'new' words identified here have been classified into a number of categories. Phonological variants of words already present in Tok Pisin were discussed in Chapter 3. Then there are those relatively recent innovations which have become so common and widespread that they must surely now be regarded as standard vocabulary items in Tok Pisin. Merging into this category are words which are not so common, and attested by a smaller number of tokens in the corpus. They are nevertheless considered to be Tok Pisin words in that they appear to be fully integrated morphologically and syntactically into the language without any overt indication of a switch. These are grouped into those words which are introduced from English, those which come from other languages, and those which appear to have been formed by the internal productive processes of the language, including idiomatic expressions.

5.2 Established new words

Some words which do not appear in Mihalic are now so common and well-established that they deserve special mention if only for the rapidity with which they have taken their place as high frequency items in the lexicon. These include kin relations, connectors, time measurement and terms specifically connected with school and other contemporary institutions.

The first group comprises kinship terms. In Mihalic's (1971) dictionary, the number of such terms is rather limited. *Mama* and *papa* are used for the parents, with *brata* and *susa* used for siblings, but he mentions some apparently declining use of *brata* for siblings of the same sex and *susa* for siblings of the opposite sex. In-laws are referred to as *tambu*,[23] while the reciprocal term *tumbuna* (a Tolai[24] word) is used for both grandparents and grandchildren, although the alternatives *lapun mama* (grandmother) and *lapun papa* (grandfather) are given.[25] Religious fathers, brothers and sisters are distinguished as *pater, bruder* and *sista* respectively. Cousins are

---

[22] *Hap* is generally assumed to derive ulitmately from English *half* via e.g. *hap graun* 'piece of ground'.
[23] *Tambu* also means 'taboo', a word of ultimate Polynesian origin.
[24] Here and below, note that many of the words attributed to Tolai by Mihalic also occur in other, neighbouring languages - see Ross 1992.
[25] *Lapun* 'old (person)' comes from a language of New Hanover.

grouped with siblings as ***brata*** and ***susa*** apart from maternal cousins, who are included in the general term for maternal relatives, ***kandere***.[26]

A number of departures from this system appear in the corpus. The word ***sista*** is frequently used to refer to siblings without any religious connotations, and ***kasen*** (31 occurrences) is commonly used to refer to cousins of various types. ***Brata*** and ***susa***, sometimes shortened to ***bro*** and ***sis***, now refer only to male and female individuals, respectively, and no longer to same sex and opposite sex. The use has also been extended to non-related close friends. Reference to maternal or paternal cousins may be ignored in favour of the sex of the cousin, as ***kasen sista*** or ***kasen brata***, although ***kandere*** (48) is still in common use, especially to refer to the parents' generation. However, 24 (50%) of these were recorded in the West Sepik Province, suggesting that it is much more frequently used there. The words ***angkol*** (138) and ***anti*** (99) are often used loosely to refer to siblings of either parents, and the words ***papa*** and ***mama*** for parents themselves are often replaced by ***dedi*** (138) or ***mami*** (70), the latter sometimes shortened to the familiar ***mams***. ***Bubu*** or ***pupu*** is the commonest term for grandparents (88), although there are other alternatives, such as ***grendedi***, ***bubu mami*** and ***bubu dedi***. The use of the generic term ***meri***[27] 'woman' is frequently replaced by the word ***gel***, often in the plural form ***gels***, to refer to unmarried females. Mihalic's definition of ***boi*** is mainly related to labouring, regardless of age, but this colonial usage seems to have been largely abandoned, and ***boi*** is widely used as an alternative to ***mangki*** (< *monkey*), meaning a young male person, and in compounds such as ***haus boi*** 'house for unmarried men'. The terms ***boi*** and ***gel*** are more common in the Highlands and Momase samples, as discussed previously.

Another area where a number of new words have become well established is in the use of connectors. The use of ***bat*** 'but' in place of ***tasol*** (< *that's all*) is widespread in the data. In cause and effect relationships, the use of ***so*** is frequently encountered, where the use of ***olsem na*** would previously have been more likely.[28] The phonetic similarity of reduced forms of ***olsem na*** or ***tasol*** to ***so*** may well have hastened this change. As Romaine has noted (1992a:146), the use of ***orait*** as a connector appears to be losing ground in favour of ***okei***. In the present data, ***okei*** is certainly very commonly used in this way, approximately six times more frequently than ***orait***. There appears to be a differentiation of meaning, with ***orait*** virtually reserved for the use meaning 'all right, satisfactory', with 87 occurrences against only seven of ***okei*** used in this way. ***Bikos***, too, is frequently used instead of ***long wanem***,[29] and ***wai*** for ***bilong wanem***, often in the form of ***wai na***, an example of the "serial" use of ***na*** as described by Verhaar (1991b). Some of the figures for connectors in the corpus appear in the following table, showing the marked extent to which new connectors are becoming established:

Traditional and borrowed connectors

oke/okei	940	*orait*	149
bat	59	*tasol*	211
so	366	*olsem na*	408
bikos	157	*long wanem*	28
wai (na)	28	*bilong wanem*	17

The use of ***yes*** and ***nogat***[30] as connectors is also worthy of note, as are a variety of other connectors borrowed from or calqued on English expressions. These are discussed in § 7.1.4.

The third area where a number of new words have become common is the domain of animals, and it is likely that school lessons have been largely responsible for this. A similar phenomenon was noted by Romaine (1992a:157). Thus, for example, ***igel*** is used in the present corpus almost as much as ***taranggau***, the Tolai word for 'eagle' (32 vs 35 occurrences), while ***frog*** (70) is much more common than ***rokrok*** (another Tolai word; 39). The form ***blakbokis*** (< *black* + *box* and/or *fox*) seems to have been totally abandoned in favour of ***flaingfoks***. With domesticated animals, ***ship***

---

[26] The origin of this word remains to be established. Mihalic (1971) derives this from English *kindred* but it seems unlikely that this word would have occurred frequently in contact situations.
[27] This word is first recorded in Queensland in the 1840s (Baker 1993) and is generally assumed to derive from *Mary*.
[28] *Olsem* derives from 'all the same as', forms of which are found in many English-lexicon Pidgins and Creoles.
[29] *Wanem* comes from 'what name' which has a number of different grammatical functions in varieties of Australian and Melanesian PE.
[30] The immediate source of *nogat* is the negator *no* and the verb *gat* 'have' (which sequence also translated English 'there isn't/aren't'. As a single word (with final stress) *nogat* may normally be glossed 'no' or 'nothing' and occurs mainly in answer to questions. As discussed in § 7.1.4, it has acquired an additional role as a connector.

'sheep' is appearing for *sipsip*, and *kau* 'cattle' for *bulmakau* (< *bull and cow*). The Tolai words *muruk* (32), *palai* (14) and *kalangar* (7) are still commonly used, but tokens of the English-derived alternatives *kasowari* (17), *lized* (6) and *perot* (2), respectively, are also appearing. *Lized* also has the advantage over *palai* of not being homophonous with *palai* 'to fly'.

Since many of the recordings were made in schools, often the topics are to do with school life, and it should remembered that the present corpus has this bias. As the language of instruction is (in theory) English, many terms relating to school life are commonly used and have considerable importance for the students, and have been adopted wholesale. Not surprisingly, terms such as *gredueishen* 'graduation', *prifeks* 'prefects', *tem brek* 'term break', *holidei* 'holiday', *rises* 'recess', and *hedmasta* 'headmaster' appear to have become firmly established items in Tok Pisin discourse among schoolchildren.

Perhaps also related to the school routine, the terms used for days, calendar time and clock time were largely English-based, for example *T(h)esdei* had completely replaced *Fonde*,[31] with 15 attestations against zero, and phrases such as *tu manths* and *tu wiks* now appear in place of the expected *tupela mun* or *tupela wik*. Clock time is often expressed as a rather awkwardly integrated expression based on English. Time is usually approximated to *tu ouklok*, *siks ouklok* etc. or *hapas siks*, *hapas nain*, etc., and finer distinctions were less common. Common institutionalized aspects of PNG life have also left a mark on the lexicon, reflected in such common items as *difens* 'defence force, soldier', *patrol* 'patrol' and *polis stesin* 'police station'.

Finally, some words have moved rapidly into the language more unpredictably. The prime example is *siksti* meaning 'very fast' (i.e. 60 mph), which is now almost universal, having apparently entered the language as a catch phrase based on a popular song (see § 5.6 below). It is attested in the corpus from almost all provinces in a wide variety of contexts (136 occurrences), in spite of the existence of adequate alternatives for 'fast, quickly', such as *spit* and *hariap*:

mi laf nogut tru na wanpla liklik meri siksti *kam na ma(ma) bl' em to(k) "yu go pumapim wara." Nau em* siksti *kam ia noga(t) em go pundaun. Em pundaun na mi kira tok "sori", mi tok osem. Mi no woki(m) tasol mi tok sori nating.*

I really laughed and a small girl came quickly and her mother said "you go and fill the water container." Now she came quickly but she fell down. She fell down and I said "sorry", I said. It wasn't my fault, but I said sorry anyway. [Morobe, F, 12]

em lugim kaswari ia wok lo pinisim pinisim olgeta mau frut. Nau em siksti *go tasol nau lo eli moning em* siksti *go nau pinisim olgeta.*

He saw the cassowary finishing all the ripe fruit. Now he went fast but now in the early morning he went fast and finished them all [Enga F, 12]

Taim sista bilong ol i lukim ol, ol siksti *- em* siksti *go long ol na em holimpasim ol na karai.*

When their sister saw them they - she quickly went to them and hugged them and cried. [East New Britain, M, 12]

It is also occasionally used alone as a verb meaning 'to go very fast':

tiages go lo nus blo mipla na mipla pilim osem pein lo nus blo mipla, lai fait na yumi siksti, *em ia mipla olgeta go lo wara*

tear gas went into our noses and our noses really hurt, (they were) about to fight so we ran fast, we all went to the river. [Morobe, F, 12]

na tupla tok "wantla man karim ol bedshit na sanap namel stap na mitla lugim na mitla siksti *ia."*

And the two said "a man was carrying bed sheets and standing in the middle, and we saw him and we ran fast." [Simbu, F, 14]

Nau, ol no gi(vi)m mipla rop blo hos nau mi tok "okei" nau mi, mi no sa(v)e mi kikim hos na hos stat lo siksti *nau. Em* siksti *nau mi wel antap lo hos...*

Now they didn't give us the horse's reins and I said "OK" and I didn't know, I kicked the horse and the horse ran fast. It went fast and I was sliding around on top of the horse... [Eastern Highlands, F, 16]

Other common words appear to fill a need for greater referential adequacy, for example the words *werim* 'to wear' (49) and *chekim* 'to check' (55) are needed in commonly encountered situations:

---

[31] From *four day* (with a prenasalized *d*); cf *tunde* 'Tuesday' (< *two day*) and *trinde* 'Wednesday' (< *three day*).

Em wasim olgeta (y)et em puti(m) lo san na em nogat samting lo <u>werim</u>. Em as nating na em go lo dog lo askim em lo ol sampla klouths bl' em bai em <u>werim</u>.

He washed them all and put them in the sun and he had nothing to <u>wear</u>. He was naked and he went to the dog and asked him for some of his clothes for him to <u>wear</u>. [West Sepik, F, 16]

Nau tupla tok osem nau tupla burukim dua kam <u>chekim</u> disla aus ia.

The two said this and broke down the door and <u>checked</u> this house. [Enga, F, 12]

These common additions to the Tok Pisin lexical inventory are significantly all derived from English, with the single exception of *bubu* 'grandparent', presumably originating as a diminutive of *tumbuna* (see above). As will be seen in the following section, this is also the case for the great majority of less common borrowed items.

5.3 Borrowed items of lower frequency

A very large number of less frequently occurring borrowed items appeared in the corpus. Firstly, the following tables show samples of words borrowed from English. As noted above, a word was accepted as Tok Pisin if it appeared to be fully integrated into the utterance. The items are divided for convenience into verbs/adjectives, nouns and other parts of speech, but it should be borne in mind that this is a rough distinction, and it is often not possible to assign such labels at anything more than a superficial level of confidence, and many items can operate in different part-of-speech categories. A full list of the novel items would be very long, and so a selection only is presented in the tables below. Proper nouns such as names of people and places have been excluded. A full list of the verbal forms introduced from English in the Manus sample appeared in Smith (1998b).

Sample lexical items borrowed from English - verbs/adjectives

Tok Pisin lexeme	English gloss	Tok Pisin lexeme	English gloss
alauim	allow	*intaviuwim*	interview
anserim	answer	*kanselim*	cancel
aptudeit	be up-to-date	*kolektim*	collect
atekim	attack	*komperim*	compare
bildim	build	*othoraizim*	authorize
blid	bleed	*ovatenim*	overturn
dekoreitim	decorate	*panisim*	punish
enjoyim	enjoy	*prodyusim*	produce
fosim	force	*stebim*	stab

Sample lexical items borrowed from English - nouns

Tok Pisin lexeme	English gloss	Tok Pisin lexeme	English gloss
agrikalcha	agriculture	*medjik*	magic, sorcery
bilding	building	*meinlend*	mainland
domitri	dormitory	*pemishen*	permission
douza	bulldozer	*perents*	parents
fiunrel	funeral	*poket*	pocket
hanta	hunter	*problem*	problem
keten	curtain	*saprais*	surprise
komplent	complaint	*sisho*	sea shore, beach
likwid	liquid	*waif*	wife

Most borrowed items adopt the morphology of Tok Pisin where appropriate, such as the transitive marker *-im*, and there is little evidence of analysis of English morphological structure. For example, a term such as *othoraizim* is found with the *-im* marker in spite of its English-like phonology, while the term *brekanenta* is used as single lexical item, with no attempt to break up the phrase into component parts. The main question is how far these borrowings can be considered to be standard Tok Pisin items, which is discussed further in Chapter 8.

Sample lexical items borrowed from English - other categories

Tok Pisin lexeme	English gloss	Tok Pisin lexeme	English gloss
abaut	approximately	insted	alternatively
afpas	half past the hour	oklok	o'clock
agou	ago, before	oldhou	although
antil	until	onli	only
au	how	oun	own
bat	but	ov	of, belonging to
da	the, definite article	samhau	somehow
det	that (complementizer)	wai (na)	why
eli	early (adverb)	yes	well, then

The ease with which English words are borrowed and incorporated into Tok Pisin speech is quite striking. The phenomenon is not by any means confined to high school students, and primary school students also exhibited the tendency to some degree. This wholesale borrowing of words from English demands some explanation, and it appears that borrowed items are adopted for a number of reasons.

Firstly, borrowed words may encapsulate finer distinctions of meaning not currently made by more generic existing items. Although other means are available for making finer distinctions, the availability of ready-made terms encourages the use of borrowing by those with a reasonable command of English. Examples of such items are given in the following table:

Borrowed items with greater semantic specificity

Adopted item	English gloss	More generic Tok Pisin term
bildim	build (a house)	wokim (< work)
disapia	disappear	go pinis (< finish)
djeles	jealous	kirap nogut (< get up no good)
fraim	fry	kukim
gel	unmarried female	meri (see note on p 96)
intaviuwim	interview	askim, tokim
kolektim	collect	kisim (< catch)
lekshara	lecturer	tisa (< teacher)
ovatenim	overturn	kapsaitim (< capsize)
rimaindim	remind	tokim gen (< talk + again)

However, there are many other cases where borrowed items co-exist with referentially adequate alternatives, so borrowing must be taking place other than for purely referential reasons, presumably for greater stylistic flexibility:

Borrowed items with referentially adequate alternatives

Adopted item	English gloss	Referentially adequate Tok Pisin term
araiv	arrive	kamap (< come up)
bihevia	behaviour	pasin (< fashion)
frog	frog	rokrok (see p 97)
kenggaru	kangaroo	sikau (origin not established)
ripitim	repeat	wokim gen (< work + again)
toch	torch	sutlam (< shoot + lamp)
treinim	train	lainim, skulim
wachim	watch	lukim
weding	get married	marit

In other cases, borrowing may disambiguate existing homophones. Some examples of these were tabulated in § 3.2. (p 52). Lastly, the effect of English-medium education is likely to be the major force dictating the nature of the lexicon for a newly emerging generation who are effectively bilingual in Tok Pisin and English. Many new concepts are introduced first through the education system in English and ready-made terms for these concepts provide an easy means of expanding the Tok Pisin lexicon.

Although the overwhelming majority of borrowed items were adopted from English, there were a few cases of borrowing from other languages. Some are fairly well-known, such as *moka* (a traditional exchange ceremony) and *puripuri* 'sorcery', but in most other cases, exotic items from local languages are used with an explanation of the meaning for the purposes of the narrative of traditional stories. The following is a list of borrowings of non-English origin occurring in the samples:

Borrowed lexical items of non-English origin

Lexical item	Possible source language/area	English gloss
aidik	Tolai	kind of fish
aif	Enga	salt
ainga	?	magic power
ate	West Sepik	ancestor?
karakap	Tolai	green vegetable
kau	Manus	aromatic substance used in magic
korkor	Tolai	black mourning clothes
kyo	Enga	sorcerer
mapo	Manus	leprechaun, fairy
moka	Melpa	traditional payment ceremony
nafau	Simbu/WH	father
palai	Manus?	bush rope, vine
pikus	?	type of tree
puripuri	Hiri Motu?	magic, sorcery
simar	West Sepik	stump of breadfruit tree?

The word *pikus*, apparently meaning a type of tree, is found in the Manus and West Sepik samples. This could be a variant of the word *fikus* recorded in Mihalic (1971:85) meaning 'banyan tree' from the Latin generic name *Ficus*.

5.4 Regional variation in word frequency

The first stage in the lexical analysis of the three regional corpora was the compilation of word frequency lists.[32] Word frequency is somewhat unreliable for lower frequency words unless an enormous corpus is available. However, for high frequency items, which tend to include many grammatical words, the exercise can be very revealing.[33]

Before analyzing the sub-corpora, each word was first restored to standard spelling. This made it easier to see the results, and variants such as *bilong, blong, blo* and *bl'* are treated as a single item. For the purposes of this analysis, the clitic *en* was also separated from words such as *longen* and *bilongen* and treated as a separate word. The table below shows the 30 most frequent items in the three regional sub-corpora. In the 'frequency' column headed 1/n, a word with, for example, 100 in this column occurs with a frequency of one out of every hundred words in the sample. Thus the lower the number, the higher the frequency, or the commoner the word.

---

[32] This was done using the Longman Miniconcordancer (Chandler 1989) and Oxford Microconcord (Scott & Johns 1993) programs. Unfortunately the more powerful *Wordsmith* programme was not available at the time of analysis.

[33] In an earlier paper (Smith 1995b), some practical details of the use of concordance programmes were presented, and a preliminary analysis of samples collected in Western Highlands and New Ireland was carried out. It should be noted, however, that strict criteria for residence for inclusion in the samples were not applied to this earlier study, which was essentially exploratory.

The 30 most frequently occurring words in three regional samples

	Momase (94,000 words)			Highlands (66,000 words)			Islands (66,000 words)		
Rank	Word	No.	Freq. (1/n)	Word	No.	Freq. (1/n)	Word	No.	Freq. (1/n)
1	em	7302	13	em	4791	14	i	5121	13
2	na	5123	18	na	3959	17	em	3989	16
3	nau	5029	19	long	3049	22	long	3546	18
4	go	4889	19	ol	2772	24	na	3450	19
5	long	4170	22	go	2540	26	ol	3137	21
6	ol	3957	24	nau	2430	27	go	2712	24
7	ia	3160	30	ia	2349	28	nau	2274	29
8	bilong	2826	33	bilong	2070	32	bilong	2138	31
9	mipela	2496	38	mi	1365	48	mi	1448	45
10	kam	2428	39	kam	1286	51	ia	1367	48
11	mi	2322	40	i	1273	52	bin	1133	58
12	i	1896	49	tupela	1257	52	kam	1123	58
13	stap	1751	53	stap	1191	55	tupela	1097	60
14	tok	1463	64	dispela	1077	61	dispela	903	73
15	tupela	1295	72	olsem	1048	63	wanpela	900	73
16	wanpela	1022	92	tok	1007	65	stap	819	80
17	kisim	906	103	wanpela	800	82	mipela	759	86
18	olsem	902	104	man	765	86	taim	713	92
19	man	898	104	save	756	87	man	674	97
20	yu	884	106	mipela	681	96	save	635	103
21	meri	837	112	yu	597	110	tok	573	114
22	dispela	828	113	meri	571	115	olsem	571	115
23	haus	663	141	kisim	551	119	kisim	530	124
24	bai	655	143	bai	517	128	en	497	132
25	save	638	147	taim	499	131	bai	490	152
26	taim	628	149	bin	467	140	meri	486	135
27	kirap	605	155	en	446	147	tasol	485	135
28	lukim	604	155	tasol	408	161	no	457	143
29	pinis	557	168	haus	401	164	yu	452	145
30	tasol	553	169	no	388	169	kirap	417	139

The figures in the table show striking uniformity for the majority of items, with some notable differences in one or two specific instances. In the three regional samples, no fewer than 26 out of the commonest 30 words are the same. In the Highlands and Islands samples – the most widely separated geographically – no fewer than 28 out of the 30 are the same, with very similar frequencies for most items. Of the items present in the most frequent 30 on one list but missing from others, most are just outside. For example, in the Islands sample, *haus* is ranked 36, *lukim* 33 and *pinis* 39. In the Highlands sample *pinis* is ranked 37 and in the Morobe sample, *no* is ranked 32 and *bin* 33. As a general observation, the figures indicate a remarkable uniformity of lexical frequency in speech samples from widely separated parts of the country.

Other statistics also demonstrate this uniformity, for example, in the following table, broad similarities can be seen in the number of different words in the samples, the type/token ratio and average word length:

Lexical statistics - three sub-corpora

	Momase	Highlands	Islands
Words	93675	65498	65543
Different words	1858	2022	1803
Type/token ratio	22.79	23.21	22.77
Average length (letters)	3.72	3.79	3.65

There are nevertheless one or two conspicuous exceptions which demand some comment. The grammatical particle *i* is by far the most common word in the Islands sample with a frequency of one in every 13 words, but it is well down the list in the Highlands and Momase samples with frequencies of only one in 52 and 49 respectively. The enclitic *en*, which is ranked 24th in the Islands sample and 26th in the Highlands sample is not even ranked in the top hundred in the Momase sample, and has a frequency of only 1/867. Similarly, **kirap** is a common item in Islands and Momase samples, but is only ranked 70 in the Highlands sample.

Much has already been written about the predicate marker, but the statistics presented here add an important piece of evidence to the debate. It can be seen very clearly that regional variation is an important factor in the absence or presence of *i*, with about four times the number of occurrences in the Islands sample than in other regions. No future discussion of constraints on the use of *i* can afford to ignore this fact. The finding that *en* is so uncommon in the Momase sample, only about one sixth as frequent as in the other two samples, was something of a surprise, and no really convincing explanation is offered. The only possibility that comes to mind concerns the relative youth of the subjects from Morobe, whose speech makes up a considerable portion of the Momase sample. The major contributors were aged 10 to 13, younger than the mid-teen adolescents typical of the corpus as a whole. As will be seen in Chapter 6, *en* has come to have an increasingly important role in relative clause marking. It is known that younger children generally use fewer relative clauses (Romaine 1985), and this may account for the smaller number of tokens of *en*.

The difference in the occurrence of **kirap** is also quite striking. The frequency of 1/516 in the Highlands sample is much less than either the Islands (1/139) or Momase (1/155) samples. This difference appears to be accounted for by the much greater use in the latter two samples of **kirap** as an introduction to quoted speech, as described in detail in Chapter 7. It remains to be seen whether this feature of speech will spread into the Highlands in future.

Although not so marked, some other frequency differences are also apparent - in particular, the use of **bin** as a past marker is considerably more frequent in the Islands sample, with a frequency there of 1/58, compared with 1/140 in the Highlands sample and 1/194 in the Momase sample. The use of *ia, stap* and *tok*, on the other hand, are all considerably more frequent in the Highlands and Momase samples than the Islands sample.

Greater variability in the next thirty words is to be expected, and the figures for the three samples in the table (opposite) show that this is indeed the case. Nevertheless, there is still considerable uniformity, with 19 of the words common to all three lists.

Again a number of specific examples stand out as indicating regional differences. The word **nabaut** is ranked 32 in the Highlands sample, but is very infrequent in the other two samples. The distinctive Highlands use of **nabaut**, especially after nouns, to mean 'and that sort of thing' can account for this. Among some speakers, the item is very frequently used and in some cases appears to carry very little meaning, acting as little more than a conversational filler while searching for words:

> *Em wokobaut go, <u>haus nabaut</u> ia em <u>sain nabaut</u> osem daimon ia.*
>
> He walked on, the <u>house or what's it</u> was <u>shining or whatever</u>, like diamonds. [Western Highlands, M, 16]

The frequency of the words **gel** and **boi** for 'girl' and 'boy' also stands out in the Highlands sample, as discussed in the previous chapter. The word **nogat** is considerably less frequent in the Islands sample than the other two, while **manki** is used more often in the Islands sample. The most frequent word outside the standard dictionary was **okei** 'all right, connector', with a frequency of 1/356, the 50th ranked word in the Momase sample. Some words have variant regional forms, such as **arasait**, which is commonly substituted for **autsait** 'outside' in the Islands sample. The over-representation of the word **kilim** 'kill' in the Highlands sample no doubt reflects the choice of the topic of many of the stories.

Second 30 most frequently occurring words in three regional samples

	Momase (94,000 words)			Highlands (66,000 words)			Islands (66,000 words)		
Rank	Word	No.	Freq. (1/n)	Word	No.	Freq. (1/n)	Word	No.	Freq. (1/n)
31	nogat	551	170	lukim	370	177	laik	350	197
32	no	509	184	nabaut	364	180	wok	333	197
33	bin	483	194	kaikai	337	194	lukim	330	199
34	kaikai	458	205	liklik	332	197	kaikai	314	209
35	wanem	439	213	nogat	325	202	manki	297	221
36	liklik	399	235	wanem	312	210	haus	294	223
37	antap	380	247	pinis	286	229	bek	282	232
38	tokim	380	247	laik	272	243	wanem	274	239
39	daun	358	262	ples	252	260	pinis	272	241
40	ples	355	264	insait	245	267	ples	269	244
41	wantaim	348	269	antap	238	275	liklik	262	250
42	brata	337	278	wara	237	276	tokim	246	266
43	insait	330	284	kilim	229	286	bihain	238	275
44	yumi	316	296	lapun	229	286	antap	237	277
45	mama	295	318	manki	224	292	wantaim	220	298
46	laik	293	320	boi	223	294	gat	218	301
47	wara	285	329	brata	222	295	a	212	309
48	olgeta	266	352	tokim	219	299	brata	212	309
49	tru	266	352	painim	214	306	ken	212	309
50	okei	263	356	gel	212	309	papa	209	314
51	putim	261	358	papa	209	313	mama	199	329
52	bek	256	367	a	196	334	olgeta	198	331
53	wok	246	381	tru	196	334	pikinini	185	354
54	yupela	236	397	bek	195	336	insait	170	386
55	ken	234	400	wok	194	338	lapun	164	400
56	slip	234	400	karim	192	341	yet	164	400
57	was	233	402	yet	191	343	mekim	161	407
58	narapela	232	404	olgeta	190	345	okei	158	415
59	karim	228	411	pikinini	186	352	samting	158	415
60	papa	227	413	wantaim	182	182	daun	157	417

5.5 Semantic changes

As pointed out by Mühlhäusler (1985a:187), the same word may mean very different things to different people, and it is often impossible in a brief investigation to know the semantic range of an item. That Tok Pisin words derived from English may have a very different semantic range from the English source word is well-known. Thus the English word 'die' does not have the same range of meanings as the Tok Pisin *dai* 'to die, cease, be unconscious', and the latter is semantically closer to many languages of Papua New Guinea. Words which are phonologically similar to English words with extra or unexpected meanings are a hazard that English-speaking learners of Tok Pisin continually face (Smith 1988). For example, the word ***resis*** has a meaning 'race' or 'races' which can be easily understood without realizing that there is an extra meaning 'to compete'. The underlying semantics in different areas are likely to be influenced by substrate patterns, but as Mühlhäusler notes (1985a:187), this area has been neglected, and a word's meaning to dictionary makers may not be the same as the meaning to speakers of the language in various localities.

It would thus be expected that recently borrowed items may also differ in their semantic properties once they are adopted into Tok Pisin. The full range of meanings of all the words used cannot be known from an investigation such as this. However, it is evident that some of the adopted words are being used with meanings different from that in the source language. The adoptions listed in the table below seem to have changed from or added to the English meaning, although they may be fairly closely related. Without a detailed knowledge of the languages of the different areas, it is not known whether or not these changes are influenced by substrate semantics.

Adopted English words with changed or additional meanings

Lexical item	English meaning	Changed/additional meaning in sample
ami	army	soldier
boring	boring	bored
deti	dirty	personal residue collected for sorcery
difens	defence (force)	soldier
eimim	aim (intrans.)	take aim at
gaidim	to guide	to guard
patrolim	to patrol	to give a lift to
shedo	shadow	reflection
tumoro	tomorrow	the next day

In other cases, semantic distinctions already in place in the standard lexicon appear to have changed. For example the inclusive/exclusive distinction commonly made between the pronouns *yumi* and *mipela* is not always maintained, as noted in § 4.4.3. Similarly, the distinction between *kaikaim* 'bite' and *kaikai* 'eat' (Mihalic 1971:102; a word of Polynesian origin) appears to have been replaced by a semantic distinction between the agents or objects involved. In many cases it appears that *kaikaim* is used to mean 'to eat' when a non-human agent such as a *masalai* 'spirit'[34] or wild beast is doing the eating, or the object of the eating, by beasts or other humans, is a human. The following examples illustrate this usage, where the translation 'bite' would be inappropriate:

disla tewel em i stap na em kaikaim olgeta ol pisin blong em

this spirit stayed and ate all his birds [West Sepik, M, 14]

tupla karim em i go lo haus blo tupla na kilim boi ia na tupla kaikaim boi ia

the two carried him back to their house, killed the boy and ate him [Eastern Highlands, M, 17]

Taim em i go em i harim masalai tok "klostu bai san i go daun nau bai yumi kilim disla liklik pikinini na yumi kaikaim."

When he went he heard the spirit say "the sun will soon set, then we'll kill this child and eat him." [Manus, M, 14]

Na long nait wanpela bikpela sneik i stap insait long wara i smelim ol smel bilong abus na i kam antap. N' em i kaikaim olgeta abus bilong man na i daunim man tu na, go daun gen long wara.

And in the night a big snake living in the river smelled the game and came up. And it ate all the man's game and swallowed the man too and went back to the river. [West Sepik, F, 17]

In the corpus, out of 117 occurrences of *kaikaim*, 103 or 88% were used with a human object. There were almost two thousand occurrences of *kaikai* and its variants, but this was only rarely used with a human object.

The overlap of the semantic range of polysemous items appears to be an important factor in grammaticalization. A notable example is the word *yet*, whose various semantic and grammatical functions have been described by Sankoff (1993). It appears from her analysis that the adoption of the English word 'yet' as the Tok Pisin *yet* 'still', and its resemblance to the Tolai *iat*, led to Tok Pisin *yet* acquiring some of the other functions of *iat*, such as reflexivity and focus marking. The range of functions of *yet* is discussed more fully in § 6.8 on focus marking.

---

[34] Mihalic (1971) attributes this word to a New Hanover source.

5.6 New words formed by internal productive processes

Although the English lexicon is providing a source for wholesale borrowing into Tok Pisin, internal development is proceeding in parallel. Mühlhäusler (1979, 1985j) has shown that Tok Pisin has an extensive and sophisticated facility for producing new words through internal productive processes. These processes consist of compounding to produce new series of lexemes, multifunctionality, where a new item is derived from a different part of speech, and reduplication. It is well known that modern Tok Pisin has a lively repertoire of idiomatic expressions, and these will be looked at here also.

5.6.1 Compounding, multifunctionality and reduplication

In an exhaustive analysis, Mühlhäusler (1979) describes 21 'programmes' for compounding, 21 for multifunctionality, and 12 for reduplication. In the corpus, these productive processes continued to operate in parallel with the borrowing of items from English. One or two examples from each category are cited for illustration. For example, the productive program producing such compound words as *wantok* 'person who speaks the same language' and *wanwok* 'workmate', described as (*wan* + N) N → *mitupela i gat wanpela* N (Mühlhäusler 1985j:432) is continuing to produce novel items:

> *lo aste moning ia mi go lo skul nau ol wanklas blo mi ol kam nau ol wokim fani lo mi nau mi laf.*
>
> Yesterday morning I went to school and my classmates came and joked around and I laughed. [Morobe, F, 12]
>
> *Na naratla samting em osem ol ba intamaret o, ba mi to wone(m), ol ba maret klostu klostu osem ol maret - maretim ol lain lo osem wanlain bl' ol yet.*
>
> And another thing is that they inter-marry, or what shall I say, they marry close together, that is they marry people who are their own (clan) relatives. [Western Highlands, F, 14]
>
> *So ol kilim ol nau, man, mi bin sore tru lo lukim wanskul blo mi plas ol man i dai nambaut osem pig na dog.*
>
> So they killed them, man, I was really sad to see my school mate plus (other) men dying like pigs and dogs. [Eastern Highlands, M, 18]

As noted in § 4.2, the program (adj. + N. to compound noun) raises the problem of how far such constructions can be considered compounds, and whether an alternative interpretation is possible whereby adjectives are being used pre-verbally without the use of *-pela*. Multifunctionality programmes producing derived items of different parts of speech are still productive. For example Mühlhäusler described the following programme producing transitive verbs from nouns (1985j:434):

> (N + *im*) Vtr → *jusim* (sic) N *long mekim wanpela samting*   'to use N to do something'

New examples from the corpus include the verb *pedelim* 'to paddle' from the noun *pedel* 'canoe paddle' and *trepim* 'to trap' from *trep* 'a trap':

> *ol i wok lo kaikai manggo na lukluk go daun lo solwara na ol i lukim wanpla lapun meri pedelim kanu blongen i kam nau*
>
> they were eating mangoes and looked down to the sea and they saw an old woman paddling her canoe towards them [East New Britain, M, 14]
>
> *tupla laik go painim kaikai nau, taim tupla go stret nau disla - wanpla diwai trepim disla narapla meri, wanpla liklik meri.*
>
> The two were about to go and look for food, and as they were going a tree trapped this other girl, a small girl [East New Britain, M, 12]

However, the possibility that such verbs have been borrowed directly from English rather than derived from existing Tok Pisin nouns cannot be ruled out. In the following cases, a derived item with no English parallel follows the programme 'derivation of transitive verbs from intransitive verbs' (Mühlhäusler 1985j:437):

> *Ol i pul i go long solwara i go i go i go i go i go i go arasait stret nau, kapul i kirap tasol nau i kapupuim[35] kanu nau i buruk.*
>
> They paddled on the sea, paddled and paddled right to the other side, the cuscus got up and 'farted' the canoe to pieces. [East New Britain, M, 12]

> *Mama blo disla mauspas manggi sidaunim mauspas manggi sta na em ... lukim wanpla frog na frog ia em kirap nau em pokim tang blo em kam autsait lo disla mauspas manggi ia na mauspas manggi ia karai nogut tru*
>
> The mute boy's mother made him sit down and he ... saw a frog, and the frog poked its tongue out at the mute boy and the mute boy really cried. [East Sepik, F, 15]

> *Anta lo diwai i bin gat wanpla sneik we wok lo taim rokrok bin slip, em wok lo pudaunim ol nats antap lo baksait blong em*
>
> Up the tree was a snake who was working while the frog slept, and he was throwing down the nuts on to his back [East New Britain, F, 15]

An example from a younger informant excluded from the corpus is also interesting in this respect. The word **pekpek** 'defecate' (< Tolai *pekapeke*, Label *pekpeke*) is normally unmarked by *-im*, but in the following, the added *-im* suffix changes the meaning:

> *Em i wok lo wonem pekpekim kiau lo sait ia. Tupla lukim em nau na tupla laik kilim. ... Em wok lo pekpekim kiau blong em nau, tupla ia ol laik kisim rop na pasim em tasol nogat.*
>
> It (turtle) was laying eggs on the side. The two saw it and wanted to kill it. ... It was busy laying its eggs, the two wanted to get a rope and tie it up, but they couldn't. [North Solomons, M, 9]

In the following two examples, the word **pispisim** derived from the verb **pispis** 'urinate' (intransitive or transitive unmarked by *-im*), appears to have developed independently into two different meanings:

> *Frog singaut nau binen flai go nau pispisim ai blo pig nau, pig dai.*
>
> The frog called out and the bee flew and stung the eye of the pig and the pig died. [Madang, F, 11]

> *Tupla wantem bin ksi(m) (di)sla faia go, na liklik brada bin go na pispisim (di)sla faia, na faia i bin dai.*
>
> The two took this fire away, and the younger brother went and extinguished/pissed on the fire and the fire went out. [East Sepik, F, 16]

Some other productive 'programmes' not included in Mühlhäusler's exhaustive account were also found, such as the following nominal compound:

> *Papa i wokim wanpla selkanu blo tupla*
>
> (Their) father made them a sailing canoe [West Sepik, M, 17]

Following Mühlhäusler's conventions, this could be analyzed as:

> *selkanu = kanu i gat sel*   (N1 + N2) N → N2 *i gat* N1

More problematic are those derived phrase-level collocations which act as single lexical items, as noted in the case of items derived from English phrasal verbs in § 4.6.3. Similarly, the distinction is often fuzzy between what is a derived fixed expression and what is normal syntactic structure. However, certain collocations appear to represent conventionally understood concepts. For example, in the following extract, the expression *daiman pati* has a specific meaning in West Sepik as a celebration to honour ancestors, and acts as a single lexical item:

> *Tupla wokim pati pinis singautim olgeta man kam nau, ol selebreitim olsem blo tenkim tumbuna bl' ol olsem mipla sa tok daiman pati.*
>
> The two made a feast and called all the men to come, they were celebrating to thank their ancestors, or as we say 'dead man party'. [West Sepik, M, 16]

Similarly, other two-word items such as **sutim tok(tok)** 'to blame' (< *shoot* + *talk*) or **karim lek** 'courting ceremony' (< *carry* + *leg*; see Mihalic 1971 for details) refer to specific concepts which are conventionally understood, and are equivalent to single lexemes:

---

[35] The origin of this word has not been established. It could well be onomatopoetic.

> *Ol <u>sutim to(k)tok</u> kam lo em na ol tok "em raskol na em gat gan, n' em gi(vi)m l' ol na ol go fait," ol tok ose(m) na, em na ol polis kam na painim disla manggi ia.*
>
> They <u>blamed</u> him and said "he's a criminal and he has a gun and he gave it to them and they went to fight." They said this and the police came looking for this boy. [Simbu, F, 12]
>
> *Lo pasin blo ol Simbu ol sa go <u>karim lek</u> ia na ol tok "bai mipla go <u>karim lek</u>" na ol tok lo mi go wantem ol.*
>
> The Chimbus' way is to go <u>courting</u> and they said "we are going <u>courting</u>" and they asked me to go with them. [Eastern Highlands, M, 18]

Other idiomatic expressions also fall into this category. For example, the meaning of the phrase *tu kina meri* 'prostitute' (lit. 'two **kina** woman' - **kina** is the PNG unit of currency) cannot be extracted from the sum of its parts, but this conventional meaning is now well established:

> *Na meri ia em em dring bia n' em <u>tu kina meri</u> ia, em spak nau (w)ogobaut lo rot i go ia, noga(t), ol man ia ol paitim em nogut tru nau ol polis kam na sutim - sutim wanpla bl' ol, man Sipik ating.*
>
> And the woman was drinking beer, she was a <u>prostitute</u>, and she was drunk and walking around on the road and these men beat her up, then the police came and shot one of them, a Sepik man, I think. [Morobe, F, 12]

A fuller discussion of idiomatic language can be found in § 5.6.2.

Mühlhäusler also discusses lexical redundancy rules (1985j:427), and notes various phonological, morphological and semantic constraints on word formation processes. Many of the phonological rules such as restriction of lexical items to three syllables and insertion of epenthetic vowels seem now to be routinely contravened as borrowing from English becomes more widespread. Some examples of consonant clusters were given in § 3.1, and they are commonly found. The speakers of the following complexes of consonant clusters, for example, exhibited no tendency to insert epenthetic vowels:

> *Mipela spendim wanpela nait lo Lae, mipela stap, <u>nekst</u> moning lo Sandei mipela <u>flai</u> i go lo <u>Finsh</u>.*
>
> We spent one night in Lae, we stayed and <u>next</u> morning on Sunday we <u>flew</u> to <u>Finsch(hafen)</u> [Western Highlands, M, 15]
>
> *Neim blo mi yet em <u>Kristopa</u> na <u>krismas</u> blo mi em <u>fiftin</u>.*
>
> My name is <u>Christopher</u> and I am <u>fifteen years old</u>. [West Sepik, M, 15]

Many of the semantic redundancy conventions described by Mühlhäusler (1985j:427) appear to be retained. Examples include conventions such as that the name of a place can also refer to the people from that place; the name of an animal also refers to the meat of that animal; and the name of a material can also refer to an object made from that material:

> *Em tok olsem, "yupla baim mi siks kina," na <u>ol Makam</u> ia, ol tok olsem, "disla hap ia ol no sa baim siksti, a siks kina lo go antap lo Watarais na kam, ol sa baim - ol sa baim fo kina tasol ia."*
>
> He said "you must pay six kina," and <u>the Markham people</u> said "from here people don't pay sixty - er six kina to go to Waterais, they pay only four kina." [Morobe, F, 11]
>
> *Em i go stap aninit long haus ... na taim ol i <u>kaikai kapul</u> na tromoi bun i kam aninit long haus long ol dok em i kisim na kaikai.*
>
> He stayed underneath the house ... and when they <u>ate cuscus</u> and threw the bones under the house for the dogs he got them and ate them. [Manus, M, 13]
>
> *lo moning taim win sa blowim duwai em ol manggo ol sa pudaun kam daun na mipela sa kisim ol <u>plestik</u> na go kolektim na putim insaid lo fridj.*
>
> In the morning the wind blows the tree and the mangoes fall down to the ground and we get <u>plastic containers</u> and go and collect them and put them in the fridge. [Western Highlands, M, 15]

Of particular interest are the morphological redundancy rules described by Mühlhäusler (1985j:428). The rule that words cannot have more than two morphemes was illustrated by the unacceptability of forms such as **grasnaipim* derived from bimorphemic compounds. While this tendency is no doubt in operation, examples were found in the corpus of words with more than two morphemes. For example, the word *toknogutim* could be analyzed into four distinct morphemes: *tok-no-gut-im* (say-negative-good-transitive), and this form was attested eight times:

Okei ol stop nau ol ting osem ankol blo mi <u>toknogutim</u> ol

Then they stopped, they thought my uncle was <u>insulting</u> them. [New Ireland, M, 12]

Nau wantok bloen trikim em na tok "em sa <u>toknogutim</u> yu na em tok 'ba mi bekim..."

Now his friend tricked him and said "he is <u>saying bad things</u> about you and says 'I will get revenge...'" [Madang, M, 13]

Em bin kam sanap na tokim ol olgeta olsem "usait <u>toknogutim</u> mi?"

He came and said to them all "who is <u>saying bad things</u> about me?" [East New Britain, M, 12]

The rule that transitive verbs should not be derived from items containing three or more syllables (Mühlhäusler 1985j:428) is routinely broken, (although Mühlhäusler indicates that the rule does not apply to all speakers):

Na l' aus sik ol laik <u>opereitim</u> em lo wednisde wan oklok ...

And in the hospital they wanted to <u>operate on</u> him on Wednesday at one o'clock [Simbu, M, 17]

mipla bin mekim bikpla kaikai tru lo ol speshel gest na mipla <u>dekoreitim</u> araund lo skul insait lo mes lo redim lo disla grediueishen bl' ol greid ten.

We made a very big feast for the special guests and we <u>decorated</u> around the school inside the mess to get it ready for this grade 10 graduation. [Manus, F, 16]

Tupla wokim pati pinis, singautim olgeta man kam nau, ol <u>selebreitim</u> olsem blo tenkim tumbuna bl' ol ...

The two had a party, called all the men to come and <u>celebrate</u> to thank their ancestors... [West Sepik, M, 16]

(Di)sla wara em <u>sepereitim</u> (di)sla tupla klen na, olsem, ol sa brukim maret na maret i go kam na em, ol stat lo fomim ol narapla djenereishen

This river <u>separated</u> these two clans and they divorced and married in various places and they started to form a new generation [Simbu, F, 16]

It should also be remembered that many well-established verbs such as *hamamasim, karamapim* and *bagarapim* have more than three syllables.

As noted in Chapter 1, some Tok Pisin lexical items have been formed by conflation of two or more different words, sometimes from different languages. A number of instances were found of new items in the corpus which appeared to result from conflation, as shown in the following table:

Words arising from possible conflation of two items

Word	Meaning	Possible dual origin
chus	choice	Eng. 'choice' and 'choose'
dranggim	drown	Eng. 'drown' and TP 'dring'
flet	number plate	Eng. 'plate' and 'flat'
pispom	fish farm/pond	Eng. 'fish farm/pond'
solapim	beat	Eng. 'slap' and 'swell up'
stes	steps outside house	Eng. 'steps' and 'stairs'
wevim (tel)	wag (tail)	Eng. 'wave' and 'wag'
zel	jail	Eng. 'jail' and 'cell'

Borrowed items may also be re-interpreted to suggest a derivational morphology which is not present in the original, e.g. *windua* 'window', which appears to be a combination of *win* 'wind, air' and *dua* 'door', and *merigoraun* 'merry-go-round' which has the apparent components *meri go raun* 'girl goes round'.

5.6.2 Idiomatic language

Idiomatic language usually refers to fixed expressions whose meanings are conventionally understood, and not retrievable from the individual words. The internal structure of such idioms may bypass normal grammatical rules, for example, the English expression "by and large".

Closely related are metaphorical expressions, which may lose some of their expressive force and become clichés after regular use. Both of these are the subject of this section, as well as two further categories; the distinctly Papua New Guinean use of catch phrases in jocular banter and borrowed expressions which appear to be calqued on other expressions which are already idiomatic. A fuller account of idiomatic Tok Pisin, especially in relation to referential and stylistic needs, appears in Smith (1990b). A similar account of idiomatic language in Bislama appears in Crowley (1988).

It is likely that the chosen genre for these recordings did not favour the maximal production of idioms. Idiomatic phrases tend to be used in more naturalistic and informal exchanges rather than the slightly formal setting of producing unscripted monologues for a researcher. The following tables record some idiomatic expressions used in the corpus, especially those which appear to be relatively new, and compare them with some of the expressions catalogued in Smith (1990b). Some were quite frequent, such as *siksti* 'go fast' (< 60 [miles per hour]) with over 130 tokens, while most were attested only a single time or very infrequently. For convenience, these are classified into the headings outlined above, although it should be borne in mind that there may be some overlap between categories. Numbers of occurrences are given in brackets.

Idioms of the first type, regular fixed expressions with conventional meanings greater than the sum of the parts, occur regularly in Tok Pisin. Some examples from Smith (1990b) include the following:

Common Tok Pisin idioms

Expression	Literal meaning	Idiomatic meaning
kisim taim	get time	suffer a misfortune
masta mak	European who makes marks	surveyor
mekim save	make know	punish
sutim tok	shoot talk	blame
taitim bun	tighten bones	try hard, stretch
tok hait	talk hide	secret

Masta mak at work at Unitech (Lae)

In the present corpus, many more expressions of this kind were found of which some such as *dis nating* 'disappear' have not previously been recorded. These are set out in the following table.

Idioms in the corpus

Expression	Literal meaning	Idiomatic meaning
(h)apim bia (1)	to lift up beer	drink (beer)
as nating (5)	arse nothing	naked
daiman pati (1)	dead man party	mortuary feast
dis nating (2)	disappear nothing	disappear
fes bon (64)	first born	eldest sibling
givim wanpela (1)	give one	hit with fist
go pas (3)	go first	be a leader
hatim slip (1)	heat sleep	to be fast asleep
i no isi (13)	not easy, gentle	(to eat, hit) with enthusiasm
i no pilai (1)	not playing	extreme
kalap nogut (3)	jump badly	get a fright or shock
kalapim kokonas (17)	jump coconut	climb coconut tree
kirap bek (4)	get up back	recover, revive
kirap nogut (44)	get up badly	get a shock, be disturbed
kisim taim (2)	get time	suffer
kisim tingting (1)	get thought	realize
lek mak (18)	leg mark	footprint
lus tingting (3)	lose thought	forget
mekim save lo toilet (1)	punish toilet	be busy defecating
Not Solo (1)	(abbreviation)	North Solomons
paia lait (1)	fire light	burning brand
painim indai (2)	find death	kill oneself
pasim tok (12)	close talk	agree, decide
paul lus (1)	mix up lose	get lost
putim was (4)	put watch	pay attention, guard
putim yau (1)	put ear	listen

Metaphorical expressions are also commonly found in Tok Pisin. Some of the examples given in Smith (1990b) are:

Metaphorical expressions in Tok Pisin

Expression	Literal meaning	Idiomatic meaning
daunim spet	swallow saliva	be afraid
givim beksait	give one's back	leave, ignore
kapsaitim wara	pour water	urinate
karim kaikai	bring food	give the desired effect
tanim plet	turn the plate	commit incest

Some of the derivations are quite obvious, while in other cases more subtle imagery is employed. For example in the case of *tanim plet* 'incest', a member of the family such as a sister or daughter is associated with providing food. A man guilty of ***tanim plet*** turns the plate upside down, making a mockery of its purpose (Smith 1990b:280).

In the corpus, a number of such expressions were found:

Metaphorical expressions in the corpus

Expression	Literal meaning	Idiomatic meaning
ai gris (7)	eye flirt, eye flatter	covet, desire
bagarap lo anggre (10)	spoiled with hunger	very hungry
bekim an (10)	give back hand	retaliate
bel sut (1)	belly shoot	be afraid, aroused
Bikpela (1)	big one	God
brukim binggo (2)	break bingo	win at bingo (gambling game)
das kirap (2)	dust get up	they went fast
dring wara (2)	drink water	drown
hatim bel (4)	heat belly	to anger
hatim (1)	to heat	the be angry with
hensapim (16)	to 'hands up'	hold up, mug, rob
kaikai wara (1)	eat water	drown
kisim balus (1)	get aeroplane	die
maus bilong rot (1)	mouth of road	junction
mumuim (1)	cook on hot stones	beat (tribal fight)
nus (bilong kanu) (1)	nose (of canoe)	prow
painim ples (1)	look for place	run for cover, be ashamed
sem krangki (2)	shame badly	very ashamed
skin tait (1)	skin tight	?active, motivated
tamiok bai wokobaut long yu (1)	axe will walk about on you	You will be chopped with an axe

Some of these may be influenced by similar expressions in PNG languages.

The third group consists of idioms which appear to have been borrowed from English and calqued on terms which are themselves idiomatic, as the examples from Smith (1990b) illustrate:

Borrowed or calqued idioms in Tok Pisin

Expression	Literal meaning	Idiomatic meaning
givim han	give hand	help
katim kona	cut corner	no do properly
kisim tamiok	get axe	be eliminated
soim pes	show face	put in an appearance
tanim tebol	turn table	get revenge
bulsit	bullshit	attempt to deceive

Occasionally, idioms are borrowed but the meaning is changed, for example in current urban Tok Pisin, ***ful swing*** 'full swing' is sometimes used to indicate a hard connecting punch in a brawl, or ***wan drop*** 'one drop' to drink a whole bottle of beer without pausing for breath. Such borrowed idioms were also well represented in the corpus. A selection of them is set out in the table overleaf.

Borrowed or calqued idioms in the corpus

Expression	Literal meaning	Idiomatic meaning
dil(im) wantaim (2)	deal with	administer etc.
filim omsik (2)	feel homesick	miss home
fogud (1)	for good	permanently
fulim raun (1)	fool round	to fool around
fultaim (2)	full time	continuously
get yus(t) (long) (6)	get used to	to become familiar (with)
givap (2)	give up	abandon
katim long bus (2)	cut in the bush	take a short cut
mekim frens wantaim (2)	make friends with	to befriend
painim hat (10)	find (it) hard	to have difficulty
plei tach (6)	play touch	to play touch rugby
ronim bisnis (1)	run business	operate a business
ranim skul (2)	run the school	administer the school
souof (6)	show off	show off
spendim nait (2)	spend the night	stay overnight
tekim wan mun (etc.) (5)	take one month	require one month to complete
tekof (9)	take off	depart
tekpat (8)	take part	participate
wok pered (2)	work parade	working bee in schools

A final group consists of exclamations and catch phrases which become fashionable fads. This is a well-known social phenomenon in Papua New Guinea, where certain expressions unpredictably become popular and are used repeatedly to elicit laughter. Some of those recorded in Smith (1990b) were popular over the last couple of decades:

Catch phrases in Tok Pisin

Expression	Literal meaning	Idiomatic meaning
givim siksti	give it 60 [mph]	go fast
laik gutwan	like good one	you are putting on airs as if you are somebody important or attractive
sais o?	Right size?	Surely we are sexually compatible?
stail manggi	style boy	stylish young person
strong tru	very strong	you are very cheeky
yu okei o waia lus?	are you all right or have you a wire loose?	are you crazy?

The fate of these catch-phrases is variable. Some stay around for a period of intense use and then drop rapidly out of fashion, while others become established items. For example, the expressions *sais o?* 'are you my size?', was heard constantly in the late 1980s as a vulgar but jocular verbal play between the sexes, but has since dropped almost completely out of use. *Givim siksti* 'go fast', on the other hand, has shifted from being a catch phrase and has taken its place in modern Tok Pisin as a standard expression for speed, among younger speakers at least, as the examples given in § 5.2 attest. Indeed, no fewer than 136 occurrences of this were found in the corpus. The number of other catch phrases in the corpus was small, because they tend to be used in more informal exchanges between groups.

Catch phrases

Expression	Literal meaning	Idiomatic meaning
em bai hat (1)	it will be hard	rejection of a sexual proposition
man! (33)	man	goodness!, wow!
wari bilong yu! (5)	your problem	that's just tough!

It is noteworthy that many idiomatic expressions do not function primarily to overcome referential inadequacy, but to increase the stylistic or expressive capability of the language. Euphemisms also fall into the category of idioms, and terms such as ***bagarapim*** 'spoil' meaning 'rape' and ***tromoi pipia*** 'throw away rubbish' for 'defecate' are regularly used. Occasionally there can be potential confusion about whether a literal or metaphorical interpretation is intended. A case in point is the song ***Kela*** recorded by Willie Sebas of the Sagothorns, a Lae-based Sepik band, on the cassette *Sagothorns: i gat kik* (Pacific Gold Studios, 1993). Complaints about the use of *kela* (literally 'bald head'[36] but widely used idiomatically to refer to the penis) were eventually referred to the censorship board. However, the board (in public at least) recognized only the literal interpretation, and ruled that the song was innocuous (*National* 17/8/94).

The following brief collection records those onomatopoeic inventions which describe noises heard around, and various other exclamations used in the corpus:

Onomatopoeic words, etc.

Word	Meaning
chts!	sound made by marbles bumping together
ss!	shoo! Go away!
u!	ooo! (wailing noise)
uish!	ouch!
us!	shoo! go away!

Man! Samting tru, ia! Yumi lukim fri tasol!
Watching the Mendi show for free (I), Southern Highlands

---

[36] Apparently from German *kahl* 'bald' (Mühlhäusler, p c).

Another category which is included here for convenience is that of acronyms. A number of institutions and organizations are commonly referred to by acronyms, the meaning of which may or may not be transparent to the speakers.

Acronyms

Sound	Acronym	Full expression
dipiai	DPI	Department of Primary Industry
eiarsi	ARC	ARC Titan Company
emtivi	Em TV	EM TV (television station)
espi	SP	South Pacific (Games, Brewery etc.)
nip	NIP	New Ireland Province
oueleseich	OLSH	Our Lady of the Sacred Heart
piemvi	PMV	public motor vehicle
piendji	PNG	Papua New Guinea
piendjibisi	PNGBC	PNG Banking Corporation
pipisi	PPC	Provincial Police Commander
siaibi	CIB	Corrective Institutions Bureau
siembi	CMB	Copra Marketing Board
sisiarai	CCRI	Cocoa and Coconut Research Institute
viesou	VSO	Voluntary Service Overseas
yupiendji	UPNG	University of Papua New Guinea

Somewhat similiar to the above, but not strictly an acronym, is the abbreviation **Balopa**, taken from initial syllables of Baluan, Lou and Pak, which is commonly used in Manus Province to refer to the inhabitants of these three islands.

Finally, included here for interest, is the single recorded case of a children's rhyming song or jingle used in play, not recorded from the transcripts, but heard in schoolyard activities:

as i hanggere! kaikai andewe!

(your) arse [US: ass] is hungry, (it's) eating your underwear!

This is a vulgar but good-natured taunt when other children's underwear is seen 'riding up' or twisted out of place between the buttocks. An intensive study of children's playground language and games would make a most useful and interesting study, and no doubt reveal some fascinating insights into linguistic innovations taking place.

6

Syntax

In this chapter, word order is discussed first (§ 6.1), followed by a consideration of the 'predicate marker' *i* (§ 6.2), and aspects of the verb phrase, in particular the use and ordering of tense, mood and aspect particles (§ 6.3). Verb serialization is then reviewed (§ 6.4). This is followed by the noun phrase but, since certain aspects of this, such as adjective-noun placement, were dealt with in § 4.2, the focus here is on the use of determiners (§ 6.5). Then there is an account of some of the innovations taking place in relative clause formation (§ 6.6). Finally, the somewhat neglected areas of complementation (§ 6.7) and focus (§ 6.8) are discussed.

6.1 Word order

One of the most basic features of syntax is word order. The usual arrangement of constituents, or canonical word order, provides a convenient criterion for typological classifications of the world's languages (Greenberg 1963). Tok Pisin is clearly an SVO language; the subject is typically first, followed by the verb and then the object. In this, it follows the pattern not only of its principal lexifier language (English), but also a number of putative substrate languages. Austronesian languages are typically SVO compared with the more common SOV pattern among Papuan languages (although it should be noted that many Austronesian languages in the New Guinea region are in fact SOV). However, it has also been suggested that SVO word order may be a 'natural' pattern which is typical of Creole languages because of universal tendencies or ease of processing rather than the characteristics of substrates or superstrates (Romaine 1988a:30). There is still considerable debate on this issue, but all the likely sources of origin of Tok Pisin syntax would indicate the development of an SVO order.

Whatever its origin, SVO has been the canonical word order since Tok Pisin stabilized. Typical sentences, then, proceed in the following manner:

Nau lapun man ia kirap tsol ksim ol pik ia go nau em kaikai

Now the old man got up and took the pigs away and he ate [Eastern Highlands M, 14]

However, there are occasional variations, as shown by the following extracts taken from the same speaker quoted immediately above:

ol go tokim mama bl' ol tok "<u>man ia yumi kilim em pinis</u>, n' ogeta samting em pinis nau."

they went and told their mother and said "<u>this man we have killed</u>, and everything is finished now."

Taim em kilim na <u>ol bel blen nambaut</u> em sa rausim

when he killed (the pigs) <u>the entrails and things</u> he took out

This appears to be more a question of focus than basic word order, as the SVO pattern is maintained in the great majority of cases. Front focus or other types of dislocation of elements can offer a stylistic variation where the most significant element in the clause is moved for emphasis. A more detailed treatment of focus and topicalization appears in § 6.8.

6.2 The particle *i*

The particle *i* has been a prominent feature of Melanesian Pidgin in one form or another since early in its history (Keesing 1988). The form *i* and its precursors have variously been described as the 'predicate marker', 'resumptive pronoun' and 'subject-referencing pronoun' and it is rather hard to pin down its exact function. According to Keesing (1988:133), it appears that what was originally a pronoun ('he') in the lexifier language came to be reanalyzed in a role analogous to substrate syntactic patterns as a subject-referencing pronoun and thence as a marker indicating the onset of the predicate. Mühlhäusler (1990a:247), considers that there is little evidence for the grammaticalization of *i* in Tok Pisin before 1885, and suggests a development independent of that of Solomon Islands Pijin and Bislama.

Although of considerable theoretical interest, the origin of *i* will not be further considered here, and the emphasis will be on how *i* is used today in syntactic constructions. A great deal has been written about the role and function of this particle, but as Smeall (1975:1, quoted in Mühlhäusler 1985h:373) observes:

> *i* stands out, in the sea of polysemy which is Tok Pisin, as an element to which no functional status has been assigned with any success.

The traditional interpretation of *i* as a "predicate marker" is exemplified by Mihalic (1971:23), who gives a detailed list of rules for its use between subjects and predicates of sentences. He notes that the particle is "always" used when the subject is a noun or the third person singular pronoun, and "never" used with second and third person singular pronouns. Other rules for use are qualified with "sometimes" or "usually", indicating even in this prescriptive account the variable nature of its use. Such categorical rules have been institutionalized to some extent in written standards such as *Nupela Testamen* (Bible Society 1966). Mundhenk (1990) gives some details of the regularization of these rules, while admitting that *i* remains "one of the most troublesome items in the language" (1990:348). The effect of the written standard, however, may well come to be a significant factor in the perception of speakers concerning the use of *i* in formal registers.

Dutton (1973) is similarly prescriptive about the use of *i*, although his purpose is primarily pedagogical, pointing out a difficult concept for English-speaking learners and appealing for attention to its presence. He also notes that the presence of *i* may fundamentally affect the meaning of the modals *laik* and *ken*, (see § 6.3) and while this is frequently referred to, it has not been generally confirmed elsewhere. With reference to Highlands varieties, Wurm (1971) and Franklin (1980) have proposed some rules for use, although as Mühlhäusler points out (1985h:373) some of the patterns are restricted to certain speakers and it seems clear that substrate patterns influence these second language varieties.

Attempts to specify more precisely the exact constraints governing the presence or absence of *i* were carried out by Smeall (1975) and Woolford (1979b). Smeall suggests that the phonological environment is a significant factor determining the presence or absence of the particle. Woolford, investigating the same corpus of Sankoff's speech samples, suggests that the grammatical environment is more significant. She is able to draw some fairly definite conclusions, such as the statement that:

> A grammatical analysis ... reveals that *i* is actually categorically present or absent in many environments and that its variable occurrence in other environments is implicationally patterned. (Woolford 1979b:37)

However, she also considers that there are indications that *i* may be "dropping out of Tok Pisin altogether" (Woolford 1979b:37). The problem with the above analyses, as Mühlhäusler notes (1985h:373), is that a larger and more varied data base would be needed to draw conclusions applying to more than a small number of speakers in a restricted location. Lynch's study shows that the use of *i* to introduce predicates may be greatly reduced in the speech of certain first language Tok Pisin speakers (1979a:6), and this is confirmed by Smith (1990a:204). Romaine's "The decline of predicate marking in Tok Pisin" (1993) offers further evidence that the particle is becoming less frequently used. Based on a large corpus of recorded speech from informants, mainly children, in Morobe and Madang provinces and a collection of written materials, it is suggested that developments point to a "decline and possible eventual loss" of the predicate marker (1993:259). However, this conclusion is problematic in a number of respects. Firstly, as the author acknowledges, the term "predicate marker" is unsatisfactory, and there may be considerable differences in the use of *i* where the particle's main function is more than separation of subject and predicate, e.g. before and after modals or before verbs of motion. Secondly, although a small part of the overall database, much of the written corpus, used was written by expatriates, and while their work has no doubt been influential in standardizing written Tok Pisin, it does not necessarily have much relevance to today's spoken usage. Thus comparisons of spoken data with standardized written samples may over-emphasize the rate of loss of *i*. Thirdly, while the corpus of spoken language used is impressive in size, it is from a somewhat limited geographical area, and large gaps remain in our knowledge of usage in other parts of the country. Generalizations about the whole country based on regionally situated samples may thus be misleading. This limitation has also been commented on by Nekitel (1994:196), who suggests that a more broad-based study should be undertaken before such generalizations can be made, and points out that Romaine's suggestion that *i* may be in terminal decline goes against his own intuitions as a Creole speaker.

However, in spite of clear indications that the use of *i* is declining in certain situations or among certain speakers, an analysis of the present corpus shows that rumours of its demise are certainly premature. Although observations of reduced use may be evident from certain samples, there is significant regional variation, and *i* is in fact the most frequently occurring word in the New Ireland sample (Smith 1995b) and the New Guinea Islands corpus as a whole. A comparison of the frequency of use of *i* in the different regional samples shows that the Islands provinces also use the particle a great deal more than in other regions, with a frequency about four times as great as those in the Momase and Highlands regions:

Frequency of *i* in three regional samples

	Momase	Highlands	Islands
Frequency (1/n)[37]	49	52	13

There is a strong preliminary indication, then, that *i* is still in frequent use in certain parts of the country, and that there is considerable regional variation. To examine this further, an attempt will be made to look at the different functions of the particle, both in its traditional role separating subject from predicate, and also in other uses, such as in post-verbal aspectual constructions *i stap*, *i go* and *i kam*, and in collocation with other words such as *dai, no* and *bin*. In the present corpus the particle *i* occurs 13,220 times, and a full syntactic analysis of all these occurrences plus the slots where *i* could occur but is not present was considered to be beyond the resources of the current project. Instead, some samples will be examined and a closer examination of some of the lexical collocations with *i* will be carried out to shed some further light on its use.

6.2.1 Separation of subject and predicate

By examining some samples of speech, confirmation of the reduction of predicate marking by many individuals is readily seen. In the following extract from Western Highlands, for example, *i* is not used in a single one of the 15 locations in which it might be expected to appear, showing that Woolford's generalizations cannot be applied to all speakers, and confirming Romaine's observations that there may be considerable loss of the particle among certain speakers. In the following extract and the remainder of this section, positions where *i* does not, but might be expected to occur, will be marked by [Ø].

> *wanpela Fraide mi - mi wantem bikpela brata blo mi mipela [Ø] pinisim skul na mipela [Ø] go l' aus na [Ø] stap nau mipela [Ø] ting osem [Ø] nogat wantla problem ba [Ø] kamap osem na mipela femli olgeta mipela [Ø] go [Ø] stap lo aus, t(a)sol lo nait, tu ouklok wantla man [Ø] kam na [Ø] tok osem "nogat ol [Ø] kilim Malipu Balakau," na mipela [Ø] fret nau mipela [Ø] pekim olgeta samting, mipela [Ø] go putim l' aus blo wan(pe)la masta man nau mipela [Ø] go slip lo wantla apatment.*

> One Friday my big brother and I finished school and we went home and at home we didn't think that any problem would come up, so we just stayed at home, but in the night at 2 o'clock a man came and said they had killed Malipu Balakau and we were afraid and we packed all our things and went and put them in a European's house and we went to sleep in an apartment. [Western Highlands, F, 14]

By contrast, frequent (but still not categorical) marking with *i* is seen in the following New Ireland samples:

> *Na taim <u>mipla i kam</u> long Utu mipla [Ø] bin [Ø] stap na long moning lo Sarere <u>mipla i bin go</u> bek long taun. [Ø] Go raun long taun na mi lukim olsem <u>taun blong Kevieng i no</u> bikpla tumas we long Madang, we long <u>Madang i bik</u>, <u>taun i bikpla</u> na planti olsem <u>planti man i sae</u> raun long taun na <u>i gat</u> planti ol stua na <u>ol ka i wok long</u> ron long rot.*

> And when <u>we came</u> to Utu we stayed (the night) and in the morning on Saturday <u>we went</u> back to town. Going round the town I saw that <u>Kavieng town is not</u> very big, whereas <u>Madang is big</u>, the

---

[37] The figures mean that *i* occurs once every 13 words in the Islands data, once every 49 words in the Highlands, and once every 52 words in the Highlands.

town is big and lots of people walk around town and there are lots of stores and <u>cars running</u> on the road. [New Ireland, M, 16]

Ye bikos <u>em i laikim</u> bikos <u>i gat</u> am <u>mipla i stap</u> klostu lo solwara na sem em [Ø] sa - em [Ø] sa gat lak lo [Ø] go hariap lo maket na [Ø] go kisim ol kaikai lo maket na <u>em i laikim</u> bikos <u>ol skul i stap</u> longwe so <u>em i ken</u> go lukim ol peles tu. <u>Mami blo mi tu i laikim</u> bikos <u>em i ting</u> Kavieng em [Ø] wanpla gutpla peles. Em [Ø] tasol.

Yes, <u>he likes it</u> here because <u>there are</u>, um <u>we stay</u> close to the sea and he likes to be able to go to the market easily and get food, and <u>he likes</u> (his job) because <u>the schools are</u> far away and he can go and see new places. <u>My mother like it too</u>, because <u>she thinks</u> Kavieng is a nice place. That's all. [New Ireland, F, 14]

liklik brada bilong mi <u>i bin kam</u> na, <u>em i kam</u> kros, <u>em i laikim</u>, <u>em i laikim</u> pensil.

My small brother <u>came</u> and <u>he was angry</u>, <u>he wanted, he wanted</u> a pencil. [New Ireland, F, 15]

Other New Guinea Islands extracts also frequently use *i* in this way, and short samples may give the impression that categorical marking is taking place:

<u>ol man i bin paitim</u> garamut, na <u>tupla i go</u> dens lo hap we <u>ol man i paitim</u> garamut long em. <u>Wanpla i dres</u> lo grinpla tradishnel dres na <u>wanpla i dres</u> lo braunpla.

<u>The men beat</u> the slit drum and <u>the two went</u> to dance at the place where <u>the men were beating</u> the drum. <u>One was dressed</u> in green traditional dress and <u>one was dressed</u> in brown. [Manus, M, 14]

However, there may be considerable variation, and further samples from the same speaker indicate an unpredictable variation in presence or absence of *i* in similar situations:

Na <u>ol man i haskim</u> tupla lo kaikai, tasol tupla [Ø] tok tupla [Ø] gat kaikai, tasol <u>ol man i fosim</u> tupla, na tupla [Ø] bin go kaikai. So <u>tupla i kaikai i stap</u> inap lo <u>ol man i tok</u> <u>kaikai i pinis</u>, na tupla [Ø] no save kaikai, tupla [Ø] sa giaman ksim kaikai [Ø] kam arasait na [Ø] trome go l' ol dok.

And the men asked the two to eat, but the two said they had food, but they forced them, and the two went and ate. So they ate until the men said the food was finished, and the two didn't eat, they pretended to take food and threw it to the dogs. [Manus, M, 14]

Samples from the Momase region also tend to show reduction in the occurrence of the predicate marker compared with New Guinea Islands samples. In the following sample from Madang, apart from one instance, the marker is routinely omitted:

Last wiken ol manggi ol [Ø] kros lo rais na, ol [Ø] no kaikai. Nau ol [Ø] go daun lo domitri na ol [Ø] kros. Ol [Ø] kros [Ø] stap na narapla boi, skul kep... - skul kepten [Ø] bin totok osem "maski lo osem sherim wansait rais. Rais [Ø] mas fea. Bois [Ø] mas <u>eat equal</u>, osem kaikai ikwal na gels." Na biain ken em [Ø] sensim toktok blongen ken na <u>em i tok</u> "bois [Ø] mas kaikai mo na gels [Ø] mas kaikai liglig" nau ol manggi [Ø] kros.

Last weekend the boys were angry about rice, and they didn't eat. They went to the dormitory and they were angry. They were sulking and another boy, the school captain said "don't share rice unequally. It must be fair. The boys must <u>eat the same amount</u> as the girls." And afterwards he changed his mind and <u>said</u> "boys must eat more and girls must get less," and the kids were angry. [Madang, M, 16]

It is most likely that there is substrate motivation for the retention of *i*, as many Austronesian languages spoken in the Islands region mark predicates in a way that is similar to the standard Tok Pisin pattern, while in many other areas, there is no analogous pattern in substrate languages, and *i* is more likely to be a source of interference or ambiguity for second language acquirers. The informants in this study are, of course, first language speakers, so the influence of substrate languages would necessarily be indirect, via the norms of the second-language-speaking community.

To get an idea of geographical variation in the occurrence of *i* in its predicate marking role, a sample of the first hundred possible slots were examined from each of the provincial sub-corpora. Only the separation of third person subject and predicate was counted, ignoring, for example, post-verbal aspect such as *i go* and *i stap* and first and second person subjects. It should be remembered that this sub-corpus includes only those informants who had lived for all or nearly all their lives within the province in question. Furthermore, those with parents from other provinces were excluded from this particular analysis:

Percentage of predicates marked by province (sample)

Momase	West Sepik	14
	East Sepik	38
	Madang	1
	Morobe	16
Highlands	Eastern Highlands	12
	Simbu	5
	Western Highlands	6
	Southern Highlands	29
	Enga	3
Islands	Manus	73
	New Ireland	61
	West New Britain	73
	East New Britain	69
	North Solomons	55

Since these are only samples, conclusions should be drawn with caution; individual speakers may differ within the same provincial sample. However, a pattern is clearly seen where marking of predicates is much more frequent in all the five provinces in New Guinea Islands region, and the particle is omitted very frequently indeed in some of the other provinces.

Having established a broad pattern, it is interesting to observe when the particle is omitted in the New Guinea Islands samples, and when it is present in the other regions. It appeared that in some cases, the presence of another particle influenced the omission of *i*. For example, in the East New Britain sample, in 16 of the 39 cases where *i* was omitted, the habitual marker *sa* was present in the slot it would normally occupy. Where *i* was atypically present, for example, in the Highlands samples, its occurrence appeared to be limited to collocations with a very limited number of words such as *dai, stap* and *no*. The co-occurrence of *i* and other markers is discussed further in the next section.

A final observation about subject-predicate marking involves the question of whether a plural form of the predicate marker exists. A case could be made for a plural form when examining some of the New Guinea Islands transcripts. In Bislama, Crowley (1990a:231) gives an account of a plural form of the predicate marker *oli* following plural subjects. This pattern does occur quite frequently in the New Guinea Islands samples:

wanpla taim nau ol narapla neiba lo narapla ailan <u>ol i laik kam</u> na <u>ol i wo(k)</u> wantem ol na <u>ol i kam</u> nau na <u>ol i wok (l)o kilim</u> olgeta

once the other neighbours from another island <u>were about to come</u> and <u>they worked</u> together and came and <u>they killed</u> them all [East New Britain, M, 13]

Yes, ol man blong Kevieng <u>ol i</u> gutpla man, <u>ol i</u> frendli na isigouing.

Yes, the Kavieng people are good people, <u>they</u> are friendly and easy-going [New Ireland, F, 15]

Out of 47 occurrences of *ol N ol i* only one was recorded in the Highlands and three in the Momase regions. It is difficult to say whether *ol i* is best considered as a plural predicate marker or merely a repetition or recapitulation of the subject pronoun.

6.2.2 Collocations of *i* with other words

In areas where the predicate is seldom marked, when *i* is used, it is usually in collocations where *i* is placed before *no, gat, dai* or *bin*:

Na disla taim laki na wanpla kar <u>i no bin kam</u> bigos sapos wanpla kar <u>i bin kam</u> em [Ø] ken [Ø] krukutim mi tsol [Ø] nogat kar [Ø] bin kam.

And at this time it was lucky that a car <u>did not come</u> because if a car <u>had come</u> it could have run over me, but one didn't come. [Western Highlands, F, 16]

Ol [Ø] wok lo tingting [Ø] go [Ø] go ol [Ø] tok "bifo bifo tru samting i no sa kamap. Na nau olsem wanem?" Ol toktok i go [Ø] go, ol [Ø] go nabaut, [Ø] painim dsla samting [Ø] go [Ø] go nait ol [Ø] go aut nabaut, ol samting ia ol i no sa lukim, ol [Ø] sa lug(i)m wanpla pisin tsol [Ø] sa plai.

They thought hard about it and said "in the old days this <u>didn't happen</u>? But how about now?" They <u>talked and talked</u> and they went looking for this thing looking until night they <u>didn't find</u> these things, they just saw a bird flying. [Simbu, F, 14]

Ol [Ø] wok lo sut [Ø] kam ausait na disa meri <u>i gat bel</u> ia em [Ø] kam daun, em [Ø] kam, bel bl' em [Ø] buruk na blad bl' em ...

They were shooting outside and this <u>pregnant</u> woman came down, she came and her waters broke and she was bleeding [Eastern Highlands, M, 17]

The use of *i* before *dai* is common in all regions, and often the form *indai* is used as the standard:

wanpla taim displa meri ia [Ø] sa go lo bus, na dsla man <u>i dai</u> ia, em sa - em sa [Ø] ka... - [Ø] tanim kamap dog nau, em sa [Ø] kaikai disla nambatu waif.

Once this woman went to the forest and this man <u>who had died</u>, he turned into a dog and ate this second wife. [Enga, F, 12]

mipla kukim ol tasol ol i no <u>indai</u> yet.

We burned them (sorcerers) but they haven't <u>died</u> yet [Simbu, M, 17]

Indeed a case could be made for writing the word *i(n)dai* as a single unanalyzed root in the same way that *inap* is usually written as a single word.

Another factor which may affect the presence or absence of *i* is the presence of other preverbal particles and *ia*, which may or may not occupy a pre-verbal slot. The influence of other particles on the presence or absence of *i* has been discussed in some detail by Woolford (1979b) and Romaine (1992a:275ff). The latter describes a general reduction of occurrences before and after tense, mood and aspect particles. She observes that:

> Predicate marking is now virtually non-existent in urban children of Morobe Province for [i.e. before] *mas, bai* and *ken*, and nearly so for *save*. It is sporadically present in small numbers before *laik* and *bin*. Likewise, the appearance of the predicate marker after tense, mood and aspect markers is very marginal now in urban areas. It is non-existent for *bai* and *bin*, nearly so for *mas* and *ken*, and very weak before the others. (Romaine 1992a:282)

This is borne out to some extent by data in the present corpus, although there is again considerable regional variation. One feature of the urban Lae population, including the suburb of Taraka from which many of Romaine's Lae informants were drawn, is that there is now a large proportion of people from the Highlands provinces. Thus comparisons with Sankoff's earlier Morobe data may not be valid. Investigation of the corpus shows that *i* occurs both before and after all the above-mentioned particles, although much more commonly with some than others. A full breakdown of the occurrence of *i* before and after preverbal particles can be seen in the following table:

Use of tense, mood and aspect and negative markers with *i*

TMA marker	Total occurrences	before *i*		after *i*	
		No.	%	No.	%
mas	596	15	2.5	19	3.1
ken	983	17	1.7	24	2.4
sa(ve)	3370	10	0.3	246	7.3
la(ik)	1639	3	0.2	179	10.9
stap	5477	155	2.8	1239	22.6
bai	2927	46	1.8	2	0.1
bin	3969	55	1.6	918	23.1
no	2704	6	0.2	756	28.0

It appears that the word following *i* is more closely correlated with the presence of the particle than the word preceding it. When analysing tokens of *ken* preceding *i*, for example, it was noticed that the word following *ken i* is restricted to only three choices, *stap*, *go* or *kam* in the majority of cases (76%). The corresponding percentages for these three items following *mas*, *save* and *bin* preceding *i* are 64%, 50%, 58%. In fact figures show that the occurrence of *i* is severely constrained by collocation with a small number of following words, and it is possible that the force of these collocations may be at least as significant as syntactic considerations in those areas where predicate marking is not common. More than half of all the 13,220 occurrences of *i*, for example, are followed by only four words, *go*, *kam*, *stap* or *bin*, and the most common 14 words following *i* account for over three quarters (76%) of all occurrences:

Words following *i*

Word following *i*	number	%
go	3 354	25.4
kam	1 280	9.7
stap	1 145	8.7
bin	918	6.9
no	756	5.7
gat	596	4.5
dai (incl. *indai*)	362	2.7
tok(im)	316	2.4
kirap	300	2.3
sa(ve)	246	1.9
lukim	236	1.8
kisim	229	1.7
la(ik)	179	1.4
wok	147	1.1
Total	10 064	76.2

There is thus the possibility that *i* may be losing its grammatical function to some extent, and being re-analyzed as an integral part of a collocation which is approaching the status of a lexeme, such as *igo, ibin, ino, ikam, idai, istap* or *igat*.

The term *inap* meaning 'until' 'capable' 'can' is usually written as one word, reflecting its derivation from the English 'enough', but Mühlhäusler has noted that it could also be analysed as *i* + the root *nap*. If this analysis is made by speakers, it would be expected that the form *nap* would become common in areas where *i* is routinely omitted. There is support for this in the present corpus. There are approximately equal numbers of the two forms, 236 tokens of *nap* compared with 255 of *inap*, suggesting that *nap* may be on the way to becoming the standard form. It might be expected that *nap* would occur more frequently in the Highlands samples, where *i* is more frequently omitted, and this does appear to be the case:

inap and *nap* by region

	Momase	Highlands	Islands
inap	92	38	96
nap	73	54	66
ratio	1.3	0.7	1.5

6.2.3 Use of *i* with post-verbal aspect markers

As noted above, even in areas where there is considerable loss of *i* between subject and predicate, the particle may still be used post-verbally with **stap**, **go** and **kam** to encode aspectual distinctions. In the following extracts, *i go* and *i stap* indicate continuing action:

> Em [Ø] wokim li(k)lik bilum <u>i stap</u>, string bek. Wokim [Ø] stap na lapun ia em [Ø] pasim suga <u>i go go</u> na biain nau em [Ø] anggre
>
> She <u>was making</u> a bilum, a string bag. Making it, the old man <u>was tying up</u> the sugar cane and afterwards he was hungry. [Eastern Highlands, M, 17]

> Neks moning em [Ø] wokobaut i go bek. <u>i go i go i go</u>, em [Ø] go lukim, tupla [Ø] maret ia, wokim - kukim ston na tupla [Ø] mumu <u>i stap</u>.
>
> Next morning he walked back. Walked and walked, he went and saw that the two were married, heating stones and making an earth oven. [Eastern Highlands, M, 17]

> mipla [Ø] lukim osem ol lain ia [Ø] laik lukim mipla na [Ø] laik autim mipla ia mipla [Ø] ron [Ø] go lo lain kokonas na mipla [Ø] <u>ait i stap</u>. Taim mipla [Ø] <u>ait i stap</u> nau mipla [Ø] lukim tupla tewel.
>
> We saw that they wanted to find us and throw us out, we ran to a row of coconut trees and hid. While we were hiding we saw two spirits. [New Ireland, M, 12]

In addition, *i go* can be used in serial verb constructions such as **klaim i go antap** 'climb up' in the following extract (*i stap* here again indicates continuing action):

> Em [Ø] go antap, <u>klaim i go</u> antap, <u>i go antap</u>, em [Ø] go antap lo diwai na em [Ø] pikim ol diwai nambaut <u>i stap</u> - frut nambaut na em [Ø] kaikai <u>i stap</u>.
>
> He went up, climbed up and up, he climbed up the tree and he was picking the trees - the fruit and he was eating it. [Eastern Highlands, M, 17]

However, *i* is also frequently omitted before **stap** and **go** in such constructions:

> mipla [Ø] kam lo dens na, mipla [Ø] dens lo Kundiawa Hotel [Ø] <u>stap [Ø] go [Ø] go</u>, dens [Ø] finis nau mipla [Ø] la go lo fles na mipla [Ø] go ia, wanpla man [Ø] ronim mipla.
>
> We came to the dance and were dancing and dancing at the Kundiawa Hotel, the dance finished and we were about to go to the village but as we were on our way a man chased us. [Simbu, F, 15]

> ankol [Ø] bin poisinim em ia [Ø] kam na em [Ø] <u>tanim [Ø] go</u> long masalai na em [Ø] tromei han bl' em
>
> the uncle who poisoned him came and he turned to the devil and aimed a punch. [Western Highlands, M, 17]

> Em [Ø] <u>wok [Ø] go [Ø] go</u> nau, disla meri ia [Ø] wok lo stretim haus [Ø] stap nau, no(g)at em [Ø] swipim haus nau,
>
> She worked and worked, this woman was busy cleaning the house, she was sweeping the house. [Eastern Highlands, F, 11]

> tupla [Ø] go stilim paia blo wanpla tewel meri - tupla [Ø] stilim [Ø] go tupla [Ø] <u>katim [Ø] stap</u> tupla [Ø] katim [Ø] stap tewel meri [Ø] kam - tewel [Ø] ronim ol <u>bi i karim</u> ol hap kaikai blo em
>
> the two went and stole some firewood from a witch, they stole it and were cutting it, the witch came and chased the bees which were carrying her food. [East Sepik, M, 17]

It is interesting to note that the only occurrence of *i* in the last extract is not in any of the traditional roles, but to introduce a relative clause.

As with **go**, the use of *i* before **kam** indicates directionality or serial verb use:

> tupla [Ø] lukim wanpla liklik <u>i bin</u> kalap <u>i kam</u> antap long sho na disla taim <u>tupla i bin</u> ran <u>i go</u>, <u>tupla i bin</u> kisim pinis, tupla [Ø] bin go bek lo aus blo tupla
>
> the two saw a little one (kangaroo) jumping towards them on the shore and at then they ran and got it and went back to the house. [East New Britain, M, 14]

em [Ø] to(k) (ol)sem "usat [Ø] k(i)sim tauel blo mi, uset man [Ø] kisim ... em [Ø] mas <u>karim i kam</u> bek na [Ø] givim mi."

he said "whoever took my towel, whoever took it must <u>bring it</u> back and give it to me." [Simbu, F, 14]

The particle *i* is again more frequently omitted in the Highlands region in this collocation:

Post-verbal *i kam* by region

Momase	Highlands	Islands
74	36	73

The use of *stap (i) go* to indicate staying for a length of time is found in all areas, and the use of *stap go* vs. *stap i go* can also show the regional variation inherent in the use of *i* as well as the much greater use of *stap go* in the Momase and Highlands provinces:

Stap go and *stap i go* by province

		stap i go	stap go	ratio
Momase	West Sepik	16	58	0.3
	East Sepik	21	19	1.1
	Madang	5	11	0.5
	Morobe	17	94	0.2
Highlands	Eastern Highlands	24	12	2.0
	Simbu	9	43	0.2
	Western Highlands	10	13	0.8
	Southern Highlands	2	1	2.0
	Enga	1	4	0.3
Islands	Manus	12	16	0.8
	New Ireland	2	2	1.0
	West New Britain	1	1	1.0
	East New Britain	27	8	3.4
	North Solomons	0	0	0

6.2.4 The role of *i* in discourse

The role of *i* in discourse patterning is seen when looking at collocations of *i* with the preceding words *na* and *nau*. The use of *na i* and *nau i* to introduce clauses in sequence is common in New Guinea Islands region samples, but rarely found in other regions:

em <u>i go</u> kalapim kapiak okei <u>i salim</u> em [Ø] go kalapim buai <u>na i tokim</u> em, "no ken [Ø] go kisim displa <u>i tamblo</u> ia i - <u>i mau</u> pinis ia, go kisim displa i - <u>i yangpla</u> yet." Okei <u>em i go</u> kisim <u>nau i kam</u> daun [Ø] go putim lo kanu blong em.

he climbed the breadfruit tree then he sent him to climb the betel nut tree and said to him "don't get the ones below that are ripe, go and get the unripe ones." So he went and got them and came down and put them in his canoe. [New Ireland, M, 12]

em i pudaun i go nau i silip [Ø] go [Ø] go [Ø] go nau [Ø] go <u>i trip</u> <u>i go</u> lo disla hap liklik wara <u>i go</u> nau [Ø] go lo edj blo wara stret nau

He fell down unconscious and drifted to this small creek now right to the edge of the water. [New Ireland, F, 13]

liklik manggi [Ø] kirap nau <u>na i tok</u>, "usat ia?". <u>I lukluk</u> nambaut <u>na i nogat</u> man <u>na i lukim</u> tasol disla rokrok ia <u>i sidaun</u> anta lo ston <u>na i kira(p)</u> [Ø] tok, "ating ston ia <u>i toktok</u>."

The small boy got up and said "who's that?" He looked around and there was no-one and he just saw this frog sitting on the stone and he said "it must be the stone talking." [New Ireland, F, 13]

Statistics for the occurrence of these constructions in the different regions are found in the table in § 7.2.2 on temporal sequencing in discourse.

The use of *i*, then continues to be highly variable, and categorical rules for its use are still very difficult to formulate. However, an analysis of this corpus has shown clearly that *i* is still used very frequently in some parts of the country while little used in others, and future discussion of the decline of predicate marking must take this regional variation into account. In addition, it is suggested that the collocational force of a small number of words following *i* may be highly significant in determining the presence or absence of the particle.

One factor relevant to the loss of *i* after the third person singular pronoun which does not appear to have been considered previously is related to possible ambiguity at a high speed of delivery. At the extremely rapid rate of speech normal to many first language speakers, it is often difficult to distinguish *mi* from *em + i*, (e.g. *mi kam/em i kam*), but less so when the *em* is not followed by *i* (*mi kam/em kam*). Thus the need to eliminate this potential source of ambiguity could be one contributing factor in the loss of the particle *i* after third person singular pronouns in allegro speech.

6.3 The verb phrase: marking tense, mood and aspect

6.3.1 The scope of tense, mood and aspect (TMA)

The terms 'tense', 'mood' and 'aspect' refer to theoretical constructs which are still being refined, and the borderline between them is sometimes fuzzy. This is compounded by the fact that some of the categories that have traditionally been referred to as 'tenses' in English grammar, such as the present continuous, are really aspectual categories. In simple terms, tense, mood and aspect (hereafter TMA) markers grammaticalize various phenomena related to verb phrases, such as time, type of action and possibility of outcome. Tense relates events to a certain time, usually to the present as defined by the moment of speaking. This is absolute tense, whereas relative tense relates events to some other specified reference point (Comrie 1985:16). Aspect is somewhat more difficult to define, but Comrie's definition of aspect as "different ways of viewing the internal temporal constituency" of a situation (Comrie 1976:3) is one of the most satisfactory. Fundamental distinctions include the concept of 'perfective', where a situation is viewed in its entirety, in contrast with that of 'imperfective', which refers to progressive or continuous aspects (Comrie 1976:12). Situations are divided into 'states', which are static, and 'events' and 'processes', which are dynamic, and respectively viewed from a 'perfective' and 'imperfective' perspective (Comrie 1976:13). The term 'perfect' is reserved for a past situation which has present relevance.

Mood is even more problematic, and the grammatical mood and modal categories exist in relationship to the semantic domain of modality, specifying various attitudes towards possibility, obligation and existence. Epistemic modality, referring to various aspects of knowledge, is sometimes distinguished from deontic modality, which generally concerns individual obligations and capabilities, and a variety of other metalinguistic labels have been used to refer to other categories, as discussed below. The 'mood' of English grammar (indicative, subjunctive, etc.) is of little relevance to the modal categories of Tok Pisin.

The question of TMA marking in Pidgin and Creole languages has received a great deal of attention in recent years, and this topic has been the focus of much of the discussion of the origin and essential nature of Creole languages. It had long been observed that there are certain uniformities in the structure of TMA markers in diverse Creole languages (Singler 1990a:vii), but it was Bickerton who triggered a more vigorous debate.

Bickerton (1974, 1980) observed that various Creoles tend to mark only one tense, one mood and one aspect, and that markers occur in that order in syntax. Where his views became more controversial was the attribution of these features to an innate cognitive faculty or 'natural semantax' common to all human beings, a concept later refined as the 'bioprogram' (Bickerton 1981). This has spawned a lively debate involving widely differing opinions, and no consensus has yet resulted. However, the somewhat less controversial aspect of Bickerton's TMA analysis has provided a theoretical framework which has been extremely useful to Pidgin and Creole linguistics in general. Typical Creoles are described as having markers for anterior tense, irrealis mood and non-punctual aspect (Bickerton 1981), i.e. a more generic system than that possessed by most natural languages. Zero marking indicates present tense for stative verbs, but past for non-statives. This classification has continued to form the basis of much of the subsequent discussion of TMA in Creole languages, and has been a useful point of departure for discussing categories which can too easily be seen in terms of inappropriate comparisons with English or other languages.

However, as Winford has pointed out (1996), there is a good deal of terminological confusion, and a serious deficiency in many of the cross-linguistic comparisons of TMA systems is the fact that different descriptions use different terminology and frameworks of analysis. In particular, Winford points to the lack of awareness of what is being done in other branches of linguistics, where theoretical refinement of such categories as perfect, relative past and imperfective has made considerable progress in recent years. He attacks the use of broad categories such as 'irrealis', 'non-punctual' and 'anterior' rather than a more thorough analysis of the syntax, semantics and pragmatics of particular linguistic features.

This confusion is in evidence when considering Tok Pisin TMA markers. For example, Tok Pisin *bai* has been variously described as an adverbial, modal, tense marker and aspect marker, with functions such as irrealis, iterative and punctual. Indeed, diachronic studies have shown that all these descriptions may have been accurate for some speakers at some time in Tok Pisin's development (Sankoff 1991:69). Thus instead of dealing with tense, mood and aspect as separate and distinct phenomena, in the following account, the various particles involved in TMA marking will be dealt with in turn, and their overlapping functions described as appropriate.

In the following sections, there is a brief review of the common TMA particles, especially as exhibited in the present corpus, in relation to descriptions in standard accounts. Comparisons of figures with the various statistics available are made to highlight similarities and differences. A final section deals with a question which has not received much attention previously, the co-occurrence of particles in combination and constraints on their use.

6.3.2 The particle *bai*

The problem of classification referred to above is highlighted in the case of the Tok Pisin TMA marker which has perhaps received the most attention, the so-called 'future marker' *bai*. 'Future' refers unequivocally to tense, and this is the meaning which has been prominent in early descriptions such as Mihalic (1971) and Dutton (1973). The origin of the particle is the adverbial expression *baimbai*, derived ultimately from the English 'by and by', which was shown in Sankoff & Laberge's well-known study (1973) to have become reduced to a single syllable, lost stress and become positioned closer to the verb.

Sankoff also followed up her earlier work on *bai* in a 1991 article which pointed out a confusing array of functions which can be assigned to the particle. She identified the association of the use of *bai* with present and past as well as future time, irrealis and hypothetical mood and iterative-habitual and punctual aspect, indicating the complexity of the semantic interpretation of TMA markers and their shifting nature.

Romaine (1992a) followed up and refined Sankoff's work, and looked at the distribution of *bai* in various contexts in samples from several different areas of Morobe and Madang provinces. A number of interesting observations emerge from her detailed study. The sequence of grammaticalization described by Sankoff & Laberge (1973) is questioned, as a number of instances of preverbal *baimbai* are cited from early Pacific Pidgin materials and other varieties of Melanesian Pidgin (confirmed by Baker 1993) as well as samples from contemporary speakers. Thus, the phonological reduction of *baimbai* and the move to preverbal position may be separate processes, although the analogic remodelling of pre-verbal *baimbai* from pre-verbal *bai* is not ruled out. It is interesting to compare the situation in Solomons Pijin, where the reduced form *bai* is commonly used, but the move to pre-verbal position does not appear to be taking place at the same rate as in Tok Pisin (Jourdan 1985a:81). Another possible explanation of the reduction of *baimbai* is also presented by Romaine (1992a:258): re-analysis of *baimbai* as *bai em bai*, a sequence which is occasionally attested in her data.

Since so much attention has been given to this marker, it is worth seeing how the use of *bai* in the present corpus compares with that described in the above accounts. A number of observations are relevant. The first concerns the status of *baimbai*. Sankoff (1991:62) noted that the use of the form *baimbai* appeared to be decreasing in the late 1960s, although still a feature of the speech of some of the older conservative speakers. Romaine (1992a:256) found that the form was still in sporadic use by both children and adults in some locations. However, not a single token of *baimbai* appears in the present corpus. The same situation obtains for *baibai*. The few occurrences of repeated *bai* located by a concordancer turn out not to be the reduplicated form *baibai* attested in earlier times, but a repetition of *bai* while hesitating and searching for words. A single token of *babai* was recorded. Thus it can be said with a fair degree of certainty that *bai*, (including its reduced forms *ba* and *b'*) is now the only one of these forms in regular use by first language speakers.

Next the syntactic position of *bai* will be examined. Sankoff (1991:65) maintains that one crucial indication that *bai* has not become fully integrated into the verb phrase is that is always occurs to the left of the predicate marker *i*. This does generally seem to be true, with just one exception from the corpus:

em i togim mama blongen lo <u>em i ba i stap</u> lo disla hol na pekpek go daun.

He told his mother that <u>he would stay</u> on this hole and defecate into it. [Manus, M, 14]

Even in the extract above, *i* is repeated after *ba*, although this may be conditioned by the presence of the following *stap*. Similarly, *bai* is reported invariably to occur before the left-most particle in the verb phrase, the negative *no* (Sankoff 1991:65). Again this normally appears to be the case, but a few counter-examples can be found:

"... yupla kisi(m) displa boi R kam gi(vi)m mipla okei <u>ba mipla no ba kam</u>, paini(m) yupla o bagarapim peles blo yupla."

"... if you get this boy R and give him to us, then <u>we won't come</u> and look for you or destroy your village." [Simbu, F, 14]

As in the case above, *ba* is repeated after the negative particle.

Sankoff (1991) also made some interesting observations concerning the positioning of *bai* in various grammatical environments. The particle tended to occur to the left of first and second person, and third person plural pronouns, but to the right of the third person singular (Sankoff 1991:63). The 'heaviness' of the noun phrase was also seen to influence placement; longer more complex noun phrases tended to be associated with pre-verbal *bai*. Romaine's more detailed analysis (1992a) generally confirmed these results. She examined various variables such as age, sex, urban or rural residence and locality, and the grammatical environment, such as differences in use with the different pronouns and full noun phrases. The figures provide evidence of a spread or progression of a move towards the preverbal use of *bai* from clause-initial placement. A discussion of the 'irrealis' function of *bai* in relation to Bybee's paradigm is also presented (Romaine 1992a, 1995b).

The finding that different pronouns differ with respect to their placement before or after *bai* is borne out by an analysis of the present corpus. Even a rough indication as shown by a concordance confirms this. Here, the number of occurrences of the sequence pronoun-*bai* is compared with that of *bai*-pronoun, for example *em bai kam* versus *bai em kam*, as seen in the following table.

Occurrences of *bai* before or after different pronouns

Tokens	Pronoun before *bai*		Pronoun after *bai*		Total %
	No.	%	No.	%	
mi	216	31	478	69	100
yu	56	22	194	78	100
em	381	81	91	19	100
mipela	73	36	132	64	100
yumi	14	18	66	83	101
yupela	11	21	42	79	100
ol	178	42	246	58	100

These figures are rough, as concordance results merely show the occurrence of certain sequences, ignoring significant syntactic and semantic distinctions. For example, they do not distinguish between the use of the pronoun as subject, such as in *em bai kam*, from a noun phrase ending in *em*, such as *mama bilong em bai kam*. A more systematic tagging of grammatical morphemes would be needed to show this distinction clearly. Similarly, the use of *bai* as a future is not distinguished from other modal uses. However, even in a rough analysis, some differences are immediately apparent. The most striking is the position of the third person singular pronoun *em*, which is much more commonly placed before *bai*, in contrast to all the rest, which are more often place after *bai* to varying degrees. A look at regional sub-corpora shows that there are differential patterns here:

Bai (and variants) before and after *mi*, *yu* and *em* by region

	Momase	Highlands	Islands
bai mi	163	106	146
mi bai	89	81	23
ratio	1.8	1.3	6.3
bai yu	84	33	58
yu bai	18	24	8
ratio	4.7	1.4	7.3
bai em	40	8	23
em bai	134	121	62
ratio	0.3	0.07	0.37

In the case of the first person singular pronoun *mi*, the Islands sample shows a much greater tendency for *bai* to appear first, some six times more freqeuntly than *mi* appearing before *bai*. In the other two regional samples, *bai* still appears first in the majority of cases, but the distinction is much less pronounced. A similar situation obtains for *yu* with the Islands and Highlands samples, with Momase in intermediate position. The most marked differentiation is seem with the placement of *bai* after *em* in the Highlands sample, which has reached an almost categoriacal status. The other two regional samples show *bai* after *em* about three times more often, but there is much greater variability.

The reduction of *bai* leading to cliticization was noted by Lynch (1979a) and Sankoff (1986). As observed in § 4.5, *bai* is frequently reduced in the present corpus to *ba* or *b'* and often attached to following pronouns as a proclitic. Reduction to *b'* occurs especially where it precedes the pronoun *ol* (30 occurences):

> *Sapos ol i gutpla, em b' ol i stap na ol - ol i bagarap olgeta b' ol i dai.*
>
> If they are in good condition <u>they will stay</u> (in hospital) and (if) they are really badly wounded <u>they will die</u>. [Manus, F, 15]

It is also occasionally attested before *yupela*:

> *sapos yupla les lo mi suwim lo yupla, ba mi kamautim na putim lo floa, na b' yupla ple ple longen.*
>
> If you don't want me to push it to you, I will take it out and put it on the floor and <u>you can</u> play with it. [East Sepik, M, 15]

Reduction of *bai* to *b'* before consonants was less frequent, with only a single occurrence of *b' mi* meaning 'I will':

> *em kirap na em tok olsem "em fest taim blo yupla na sapos seken taim ken mi lukim nem bl' yupla ken, em nau b' mi puti' yupla lo panishment."*
>
> he said "this is the first time for you, but if I see your name a second time, I will give you punishment" [Manus, F 16]

However, reduction of *bilong* to the identical form before *mi* or *mipela* did occur 11 times, indicating the potential for ambiguity with such extreme reduction:

> *Na lo naintin eiti siks, papa b' mi bin, koros wantem mama blo mi na em bin k(i)s(im) nupla meri.*
>
> And in 1986 <u>my father</u> was angry with my mother and he got a new wife. [West Sepik, F, 13]

The reduced *b' (bai)* is less often cliticized on following verbs, but this did occur once, where the following verb began with a vowel:

> *mi lugim tupla stap nau, meri ia ting mi b' ait lo gras na wokim pret ia...*
>
> I saw the two of them, the girl thought I <u>would hide</u> in the grass and scare them... [Simbu, F, 14]

6.3.3 The particle *laik*

This particle, often appearing in the reduced forms *lai* and *la*, has a dual role to indicate 'wanting to do something' or 'being about to do something'. In many cases it is difficult to distinguish between the two meanings, and both could equally apply, and for this reason, a complete statistical account of the different functions of *laik* has not been attempted:

> *wanpla taim em <u>laik go</u> lo bus na painim ol bus rop.*
>
> Once he <u>was about/wanted to</u> go to the bush and find some bush rope. [Simbu, F, 16]

Certain uses, however, such as with the verb *dai*, can usually be assumed to indicate the 'about to' meaning:

> *man ia <u>laik dai</u> taim, em bin tokim brata bloen na tok "mi dai, yupla mas go troim mi blo wara."*
>
> When the man was about to die, he told his brother "when I die you must go and throw me in the water." [Enga, F, 12]

The meaning of *laik* as 'about to do something' can be made unequivocal by the use of the adverbial *klostu* 'nearly, soon to happen':

> *so biknait nau, <u>klostu laik tulait</u> nau, ol meri blo em go daun nau ...*
>
> so in the middle of the night, <u>almost about to become dawn</u>, his wives went down ... [West Sepik, F, 15]

This can apply not only to time but to events which almost happen:

> *em <u>laik tromoi</u> ston go lo brukim stua bl' em ia nogat ston ia bauns bek na <u>laik klostu paitim</u> het bl' em.*
>
> he wanted to throw the stone to smash his store but the stone bounced back and <u>was almost about to (= nearly)</u> hit his head [Morobe, F, 12]

The use of *klostu* meaning 'about to' followed or preceded by *laik*, however only occurred in the Morobe sample. Only two occurrence of *klostu* + verb without *laik* were found:

> *i go nau, masalai ia <u>klostu kilim</u>, wonem ia, liklik brata blo fesbon.*
>
> Then the spirit was about to kill the what, the little brother of the first born. [Madang, M, 12]

The alternative *klosap* is described in some accounts (Dutton 1973:101), but this form does not occur in the present corpus.

Dutton (1973:23) draws a distinction between *laik i* meaning 'want to' and *laik* indicating imminent action. However, this distinction is not supported by the data in the present corpus. Out of some 1500 tokens of *laik*, only three are followed by *i*, showing that the form *laik i* is not in common use. In one of these three, *laik i* clearly refers to incipient action rather than volition:

> *Na mama i bin sik na em i klostu i <u>laik i dai</u>*
>
> And his mother was ill and shortly <u>about to die</u>. [West Sepik, F, 17]

It seems that the presence of *i* in this case is determined more by the following *dai* than the preceding *laik*. Similarly, *laik* without *i* can be used to indicate desire rather than incipient action, even when the reduced form *la* is used, as the following extract clearly shows:

> *"... ol tumbuna meri, yupla opi(m) do. Mi kol ia, mi la ka(m) sta(p) wante(m) yupla."*
>
> "... old women, open the door! I'm cold and I <u>want to come in</u> and be with you!" [West Sepik, F, 12]

Thus if the distinction described by Dutton still exists, it would appear to be confined to second language varieties or restricted in distribution.

As with *bai*, and *save*, Lynch (1979a) reports that *laik* is often reduced and cliticized to a following verb. In the corpus, reduction as *la* frequently occurs, but there is only a single instance of further reduction to *l'*:

Na meri ia kira(p) na em <u>la ka(m)</u> paitim mipla, noga(t) sista blo mipla bung na ol <u>la paitim</u> em nau

And the girl came and <u>was about to/wanted to</u> hit us, but our sisters got together and <u>were about to/wanted to</u> hit her now. [Morobe, F, 12]

Em i go i go na i kisim, wanem ia, kokonas na i <u>l' go</u> kam daun nau, na anis sa kaikai em tu

He went and got a, what's it, a coconut and <u>was about to come</u> down when the ants bit him [Manus, M, 13]

Mundhenk (1990:369) notes yet another meaning for *laik*, and gives the example of the phrase *mi no laik* meaning 'I ought to have'. This appears to be unusual, but one or two instances in the corpus could possibly support this interpretation, especially when rising intonation is used:

Tupla laik bekim na man ia i ronowe pinis. Nau tupla ia tok, "man, yu <u>no laik paitim em gut</u>."

The two wanted to reply and the man ran away. Now they said "gee, you <u>ought to have hit him</u> (?) properly." [North Solomons, M, 12]

Boi ia tok, "mi no toki(m) yu kilim ol pig, usat toki(m) yu lo kilim tupla pig, <u>yu no la larim ol</u> i stap na mi yet ba kam kilim na kaikai."

The boy said "I didn't tell you to kill the pigs, who told you to kill two pigs, <u>you should have left them</u> and I would come and kill them myself." [Eastern Highlands, M, 15]

6.3.4 *Bin* - past time reference

The particle *bin*, derived from the English 'been', is well known as a marker of past tense in a variety of Creoles. The use of *bin* is recorded in descriptions of Tok Pisin such as Mihalic 1971, Dutton 1973, and Mühlhäusler 1985h. However, it should be noted that past tense is unmarked in many cases, which tends to confirm Bickerton's assertion (1981) that the normal past tense form in Creoles is the unmarked form, for non-stative verbs at least.

If the standard form of past for non-statives is unmarked, there would appear to be no compelling reason for retaining the marker *bin* apart from designating past in past. Indeed, Sankoff, states that *bin* is now 'extremely rare, particularly in the speech of native speakers' (1991:73). This observation, however, is puzzling, as other indications show otherwise. It could be due to regional differences, with *bin* under-represented in Sankoff's Morobe sample, but Mihalic (1971:72) notes that *bin* is found "especially in the Rabaul and Morobe areas. It is gradually becoming more common." Mühlhäusler (1985h:378) makes the somewhat controversial claim that *bin* "was virtually unknown in most areas 20 years ago" but notes that it "is vigorously present in the speech of most younger speakers and is found with many second-language speakers of the language today". Current information concerning the use of *bin*, then, is conflicting and incomplete.

The present investigation does not support the suggestion that loss of *bin* is related to first language use. Almost 4,000 tokens of *bin* were recorded, making it one of the most frequently occurring words in the corpus. Thus it appears that Sankoff's result is something of an anomaly. It is not reserved for past before past, and is frequently used to indicate simple past with non-stative verbs:

mi <u>bin witnesim</u> stret lo ai blo mi na mi <u>bin harim</u> pairap blo gan

I <u>witnessed it</u> with my own eyes and I <u>heard</u> the guns fire [Eastern Highlands, M, 18]

The particle *bin* can occur very frequently and is almost categorically followed directly by a verb or adjective (in some cases the distinction between adjectives and stative verbs is somewhat fuzzy).

mitupla go daun na mi <u>bin niupla</u> tu na ol, ol lain lo peles i <u>bin kam</u> tok ples lo mi na mi no save. Mi <u>bin go</u> tasol na mi <u>bin stap</u>.

We went down and I was new to the place and they, my family in the village came and spoke to me in the local language and I didn't understand. I just went and stayed there. [East New Britain, F, 15]

The few exceptions are where *i* ('predicate marker') or *no* 'not' intervene between **bin** and the verb. The use of *i* in such instances is restricted to co-occurrence with **stap, go, kam** or **dai**:

> *Ol enemi stap klostu klostu long ap na ol i no <u>bin i go</u> lo narapla hap.*
>
> The enemies stayed very close by, and they didn't go to another place. [Madang, M, 17]

> *ol <u>bin nogat</u> aus na ol i <u>bin nogat</u> awus (abus) na tupla sista i plen lo go long bus long kisim, painim awus*
>
> they had no house and no meat so the two sisters planned to go to the bush to find meat. [East Sepik, M, 12]

The use of **bin** is frequently redundant, for example, in the following extract, past time reference has clearly been established by the use of *apaste (hapasde)* 'the day before yesterday':

> *apaste lo nait <u>em bin go</u> lo wanpela pati na <u>em bin spak</u> liglig na em kam slip.*
>
> The day before yesterday he went to a party and he got a bit drunk and he came to sleep. [Western Highlands, F, 16]

Many other examples of the redundant use of **bin** can be found:

> *lo aste lo nait mipla <u>bin stap</u> lo dometris na wanpla manggi, wanpla manggi Sentrol na wanpla manggi Tolai <u>ol bin fait</u>*
>
> last night <u>we were</u> in the dormitories and a boy from Central and a Tolai boy <u>had a fight</u> [East New Britain, M, 18]

> *Aste <u>mipla bin</u> go lo fil na mipla lukim ol sista blo mi plei soka*
>
> Yesterday <u>we went</u> to the field and we watched my sisters playing soccer. [North Solomons, F, 12]

> *aste taim ol la wokim lo ia, wedha i no <u>bin gutla</u> tumas bat ol greid ten <u>bin</u> - ol laik kisim setifiket bl' ol*
>
> yesterday, when they wanted to do it here, the weather <u>wasn't very good</u>, but the grade 10 students <u>were</u> - wanted to get their certificates. [Southern Highlands, F, 16]

Thus it appears that **bin** has an important role in past tense marking which is showing no sign of disappearing. Since some unmarked forms may indicate present as well as past, the use of **bin** is an extra resource for disambiguating time reference. There is definite regional variation here, with the use of **bin** considerably more common in the New Guinea Islands sample:

Occurrences of bin

Momase	Highlands	Islands
849	626	1722

6.3.5 *Pinis* - completed action

It appears that in earlier forms of Melanesian Pidgin English, various forms such as **bin** and **pinis** competed for past time reference before the stabilization of **bin** as a past tense marker and **pinis** as a completive aspect marker. Mühlhäusler notes that **bin** may still imply some idea of completion (1985h:388). The word **pinis** occurs as a lexical verb as well as an aspect marker. The intransitive form **pinis** and transitive **pinisim** both refer to finishing or terminating something.

> *olidei bin <u>pinis</u> nau, mipla ba go lo Sande lo epot.*
>
> The holiday had <u>finished</u> and we were to go on Sunday to the airport. [East Sepik, M, 15]

> *em <u>pinisim</u> wanpla kaikai. Em tok "mi <u>pinisim</u> disla." Em <u>pinisim</u> kaukau, em tok "mi <u>pinisim</u> kaukau," na em tok "yu kaikai ogeta."*
>
> She <u>finished</u> one lot of food. She said "I <u>have finished</u> this one." She <u>finished</u> the sweet potato and said "I have <u>finished</u> the sweet potato," and he said "you eat it all." [Eastern Highlands, F, 15]

> *nau disla manggi ia tokim mi olsem "bai mipla go daun lo Kimbe na stap lo Kimbe inap sik blo em bai <u>pinis</u>." Taim sik blo em <u>pinis</u> - taim mipla go daun lo Kimbe em bin - sik blo em <u>pinis</u> nau na sip i bin tekof go lo Lei*
>
> now this boy said to me "we'll go down to Kimbe and stay in Kimbe until his illness <u>is over</u>." When his illness <u>had finished</u> - when we went down to Kimbe he was - his illness <u>was finished</u> now and the ship took off for Lae. [East New Britain, N, 15]

The difference between transitive use with *-im* and intransitive without *-im*, however, is not always clear-cut. In the following, for example, the use of *pinis* without the *-im* suffix is clearly transitive, and there is the possibility of a calque from a similar phrase borrowed from English:

> *Taim mi <u>pinis</u> skul mi laik go stap lo ples na helpim ol perents blo mi.*
>
> When I <u>finish school</u> I want to go back to the village and help my parents. [Southern Highlands, F, 14]

In addition, *pinis* is sometimes used on its own to indicate 'that's all' or 'it's finished'. This is presumably derived by ellipsis from an expression such as *em i pinis* 'it is finished'.

> *i stap na i go, ol no stretim na nau i stap yet - disla koros stap yet. <u>Pinis</u>.*
>
> It kept on like this, they didn't sort it out, and it's still there, this dispute is still continuing. <u>That's all</u>. [Manus, M, 15]

As a completive marker, *pinis* is a common item, with some 1200 tokens in the corpus. The use in the corpus is generally similar to published descriptions. It is more frequent in the Momase sample than those of the other two regions:

Pinis in three regional sub-corpora

Momase	Highlands	Islands
772	342	379

Sometimes the translation of the completive into English suggests the perfect 'has done', but in other cases a past tense is a more appropriate rendering:

> *Nau mipla <u>go lo aus pinis</u> na mama blo mipla kam na askim mipla lo, em askim mipla, "yupla stap we na kam?"*
>
> When <u>we had gone home</u>, our mother came and asked us, she asked us "where have you come from?" [Morobe, F, 12]

> *antap ia i gat ol diwai nambaut stap na em <u>lukim pinis</u>, smuk i kam antap lo haus ia em <u>lukim pinis</u>.*
>
> Above there were trees and things and he <u>saw them</u>, smoke came from the fire and he <u>saw it</u>. [Eastern Highlands, M, 17]

The fact that *pinis* indicates completion has led to a role for *pinis* in sequencing discourse. Mihalic (1971:48) notes that:

> Sentences are often connected in narration by repeating the main verb of the preceding sentence in the perfective e.g. *Yu mas mekim gutpela wok. Mekim pinis, orait, nau yu ken go limlimbur.*

This kind of pattern occurs regularly in the corpus:

> *ol woki(m) seim - seim ose(m) ol woki(m) lo brada blong em. <u>Wokim pinis</u> nau n' ol k(i)si(m) tupla nau na kari(m) tupla go*
>
> they did the same as they had done to her brother. <u>After doing it</u>, they got the two and took them away. [West Sepik, F, 17]

However, there are a number of variants on this basic theme. Further discussion of this feature appears in §7.2.2 on temporal sequencing in discourse.

6.3.6 More aspect distinctions: *save, wok long, (i) stap, (i) go and (i) kam*

Habitual aspect is marked in Tok Pisin by the pre-verbal particle *save*, while continuous aspect is marked by pre-verbal *wok long* or post-verbal *(i) stap*. Other indicators of continuing action are *(i) go* and *(i) kam* following verbs, which can also indicate direction.

Save

The particle *save* is used to indicate regularly recurring or habitual action, and also appears as the variants *sawe, sae*, and the most common of all, *sa*. The unreduced *save* has the same form as the lexical word meaning 'to know'. As noted in §4.5, the reduced form *sa* is often used as the aspect particle with the unreduced form reserved for the lexical use, as suggested by Lynch (1979a:8), but this distinction is by no means absolute, and the lexical verb is also seen in reduced form.

An example of the typical use of the habitual aspect marker is seen in the following extract, where the verbs indicating the habitual actions associated with attempts to cut a hard sago stump are marked with *save*:

> *Dispela drai saksak, olgeta yangpela man long ples i <u>save traim</u> long katim, tasol em i strong mo. Ston tamiok blong ol i <u>save buruk</u> nating.*

> This dry sago, all the young men in the village <u>tried (habitually)</u> to cut it, but it was very hard. Their stone axes <u>would just break</u>. [West Sepik, M, 18]

In the following description of militant action in Bougainville, the recurring events described are marked with *sa*, while the single past actions of the final sentence are unmarked.

> *Mipla stap lo skul, ol ami ol <u>sa pait</u> wantem ol man ia. Mipla olgeta taim mipla <u>sa harim</u> ol gan i pairap. Nau ol militants <u>sa kam</u> ol <u>sa brukim</u> ol sto nambaut taim ol ami ol i kam. Em nau mipla kirap nau mipla ronowe kam lo ia.*

> (when) we were in school, the army <u>would fight</u> with the men. All the time we <u>would hear</u> guns firing. Now the militants <u>(habitually) come</u> and <u>break</u> into the stores when the army come. So we got up and ran away to here. [East New Britain, M, 16]

The marker is often used repeatedly and redundantly. In the following, for example, the habitual nature of the action has been established by the adverbial phrase *olgeta taim* 'every time, always', and further use of *sa* is therefore redundant:

> *... sampla man i stap na <u>olgeta taim ol sa go</u> lo bus na painim kapul lo wanpla hul blo ston.*

> ... some men lived there and they <u>would always go</u> to the bush to look for cuscus (possum) in a cave. [Simbu, M, 18]

This interpretation of *save* as a habitual, however, is not universal in the corpus, and there were some puzzling instances where *save* is used in situations which are clearly punctual in nature:

> *Wanpla taim displa meri ia <u>sa go</u> lo bus, na dsla man i dai ia, em <u>sa tanim</u> kamap dog nau, em <u>sa kaikai</u> disla nambatu waif.*

> One time the woman went to the bush, and this man who had died turned into a dog and ate the second wife. [Enga, F, 12]

Similarly, in the following extract, single punctual events in a narrative are marked by *sa*. A habitual interpretation would not be possible:

> *Nau, ol polis damblo ol <u>sa kam</u> antap osem na ol polis lo ia ol <u>sa go daun</u>. Nau ol <u>sa blogim</u> disla Daina ia damblo na ol <u>sa olim</u> ol (di)sla man. Nau ol <u>sa ensapim</u> ol nau, ol <u>sa tog</u> osem "yupla lukim wanpla samting kamap?"*

> Now the police below <u>came up</u> and the police here <u>went down</u>. Now they <u>blocked</u> the (Toyota) Dyna below and they <u>arrested</u> these men. Now they <u>held them up</u> and <u>said</u> "did you see something happen?" [Enga, F, 12]

This use mostly occurs in samples from the Highlands, and especially Enga Province, and it appears that *sa* has been re-interpreted as a past tense marker by a number of speakers in this area. This would appear to have the potential for considerable confusion, and it is likely that a more standard interpretation will follow increased contact between speakers in this area and the rest of the country.

Wok long

The phrase ***wok long*** has a lexical meaning, 'work in/at', unrelated to aspect, when preceding a noun phrase, for example:

Okei, meri ia <u>wok lo</u> gaden yet ...

So the woman was still <u>working in</u> the garden ... [Simbu, F, 13]

As a preverbal marker, ***wok long*** implies that the agent is busy doing something, or actively engaged in an action. It would often be rendered in an English translation as the continuous aspect:

Em i kam sanap lo rot na i <u>wok lo singaut</u>. I <u>wok lo singaut</u> lo man i prich. Em <u>wok lo tok</u> se ol man i prich ol <u>wok lo giaman</u>.

He came and stood on the road and <u>was shouting</u>. He <u>was shouting</u> at the preacher. He <u>was saying</u> that people who preach <u>are telling lies</u>. [New Ireland, F, 16]

The use of ***wok long*** as continuous aspect marker is frequent with some 750 tokens in the corpus. It is attested regularly in all regions, but somewhat less in the Highlands:

Wok long **(and variants) by region**

Momase	Highlands	Islands
201	130	299

As discussed in section 3.5, there is a noticeable tendency in the corpus for *wok long* to be greatly reduced in rapid speech. It is frequently reduced to *wo lo* or even *o lo* or *wo l'*:

Em nau tupla <u>wo lo sidaun</u> wari nau, na tupla i laik lukluk go arasait lo rip na tupla i lukim disla man tupla i mumuim ia <u>wo lo sanap</u> lo rip, painim pis i stap.

So the two <u>were sitting</u> and worrying and they wanted to look to the other side of the reef and they saw this man that they had cooked <u>standing</u> on the reef, looking for fish. [New Ireland, M, 12]

Mipla <u>wok lo wokim</u> go na peles ia i go nogut olgeta. Ol man <u>o' lo kilim</u> ol yet.

We <u>are doing this</u> and the place is really deteriorating. People <u>are killing</u> each other. [Manus, F, 15]

na taim shak <u>wo lo</u> kaikai, tupla hariap pul i go lo nambis

and while the shark <u>was busy eating</u>, the two quickly paddled to shore [West Sepik, M, 14]

em kirap tasol giaman apim bonet blo kar i go antap na em <u>wo lo giaman fiksim</u> nabaut

he just lifted the bonnet of the car (as if he knew what he was doing) and <u>he was pretending</u> to fix it. [Manus, M, 18]

em i kam olgeta stap insait lo bus ia ol <u>wo l'</u> wokobaut i kam

he came and stayed in the forest, they <u>were coming</u> (on foot) [Manus, M, 14]

The possibility that the marker will become further reduced and cliticized is also suggested by the further reduction by some young speakers to *wo*:

tupla <u>wo mekim fani</u> na mipla <u>wo laf</u> lo frant stap ia

the two <u>were making fun</u> and we <u>were laughing</u> at the front. [Morobe, F, 12]

Tupla <u>wo sutim</u> go go na ol i gat pisin pinis nau

The two <u>were shooting</u> and they got a bird [Simbu M, 15]

lek blo meri ia go sting nau na sinek i <u>wo kamap</u> longen.

The girl's leg went rotten and worms <u>were growing</u> in it [East New Britain, M, 12]

Stap

The word ***stap*** is an existential verb meaning 'stay' or 'be situated' or simply 'be'. When placed after other verbs it indicates continuing action i.e. durative aspect. If the main verb has an object, *stap* usually appears after the object:

> Ol <u>slip lo (di)sla aus stap</u> na, wanpla taim ia traipla ren stret.
>
> They <u>stayed in this house</u>, and once there was very heavy rain [Simbu, F, 16]

A similar function of durative aspect marking is attached to ***wok long***, and the distinction between the two, if any, is not clear. Indeed, verbs are frequently marked by both the pre-verbal ***wok long*** and the post-verbal ***stap***. It is particularly difficult to determine the difference between them when they are applied to stative verbs:

> ol klaim i go antap lo tri nau, ol <u>wok lo sidaun i stap</u>.
>
> They climbed up the tree and they <u>were sitting there</u>. [North Solomons, F, 12]

As far as can be determined from the present corpus, ***wok long*** tends to be used with more active non-stative verbs, while ***i stap*** is commoner with statives, but there are instances where the two constructions appear to have identical meanings.

One notable syntactic difference between Bislama and Tok Pisin is that *stap* can appear before the verb in Bislama as follows (Crowley 1990:10):

> hem i stap dring
>
> he drinks/he is drinking

In Bislama, ***stap*** can be a continuous as well as a habitual aspect marker, while in Tok Pisin, ***stap*** is restricted to continuous aspect and is almost always following the verb. There are one or two instances of ***stap*** preceding the verb in the present corpus, but whether these are best considered cases of aspect marking or serialization is not clear.

One interesting feature is the widespread use of ***stap*** and ***go*** together after verbs, particularly in the Highlands and Momase samples

Use of the collocation *stap go*/*stap i go* by region

	Momase	Highlands	Islands
stap go	182	53	21
stap i go	58	43	32

> tupla <u>stori stap go go</u>, nau klostu ndelait nau em togim sla meri na tok ...
>
> the two <u>talked and talked</u> until nearly daybreak, then she told the woman ... [Simbu, F, 16]

In the following, repetition of the verb, use of post-verbal *stap* and repeated *go* leave no doubt about the continuing nature of the activity:

> mipla dring, mipla <u>stori stori stap go go</u> nau noga(t) yu kam.
>
> We drank, we <u>talked and talked</u>, then you came. [Morobe, F, 12]

The particles (i) go and (i) kam

The verbs ***go*** 'go' and ***kam*** 'come' are frequently used as lexical words, but can also indicate directional movement and continuing aspect. There appears to be a gradation between the full lexical role and that of aspect marking, as shown in the following sequence of extracts. The first shows the full lexical use of ***go***. The second contains ***go*** as the second part of a serial construction while the third is somewhat similar, indicating movement away from something. The fourth represents the aspectual use indicating continuing action:

i. *full lexical use of go*

> Ai blongen i pas nau em <u>go daun</u> tasol nau em i <u>go daun</u> lo ples blo ol daiman.
>
> His eyes were closed and he <u>went down</u>, and he <u>went right down</u> to the dead people's place. [East New Britain, M, 12]

ii. *go* in serial constructions

Nau angkol blo tupla la <u>putim balus i go andap</u> tasol nogat.

Now their uncle wanted to <u>take the plane up</u>, but he couldn't. [East Sepik, M, 12]

iii. directional use of *go*

taim em pinisim wok ol <u>salim i go bek</u> lo peles.

When he had finished work, they <u>sent him back</u> to the village. [East New Britain, M, 16]

iv. aspectual use of *go*

ol bin sutim em nau em pudaun nau barta bl' em bin <u>weit weit i go</u> nau em no kam nau ol karai karai i go.

They shot him and he fell down and his brother was <u>waiting and waiting</u>, he didn't come and they <u>cried and cried</u>. [East New Britain, M, 12]

Whether this gradation reflects a diachronic pattern of development would need confirmation from historical sources. However, it seems likely that the extension by analogy from verbs of motion to other verbs may have been involved, as suggested by the sequence of the following examples:

Na tupela mangki ia tupela i no trastim lapun meri ia, tupela poret nau tupela <u>wokabaut i go</u> yet.

The two boys did not trust the old woman, they were afraid and they <u>kept on walking</u>. [Morobe, F, 14]

Em <u>bieinim i go i go</u> n' em paini(m) laulau i sanap i sta(p).

He <u>kept on following</u> (the river) and he found the laulau tree standing there [West Sepik, M, 13]

em <u>krai krai i go i go i go</u> nau, em sidaun antap - andanit lo wanpla kokonas diwai nau, em <u>krai krai i go</u> ia

he <u>cried and cried</u>, he sat on - under a coconut tree and <u>kept on crying</u>. [Eastern Highlands, F, 11]

All the above examples show the use of ***go*** with *i*, but the *i* is frequently omitted:

<u>Dring go go</u> em pilim osem, em i no nap pinis wara, bel blo em go pen nating.

He <u>drank and drank</u> and felt that he could not finish the water, his stomach was hurting. [East Sepik, M, 16]

The use of *kam* is more limited, and apart from its normal lexical role, it is usually restricted to indicating motion towards the speaker, or similar meanings:

"Yu aitim abus blo mi sta(p), oke <u>k(i)sim kam</u>."

"You are hiding my meat, just <u>bring it here</u>." [Eastern Highlands, M, 11]

However, it can also indicate continuing action, especially when repeated:

Mipla go na mi to(k) "mi nog(at) ofring" na ol gi(vi)m mi ten toea nau. Nau ol <u>puti(m) kam kam</u> ia noga(t) mi no putim.

We went (to church) and I said "I have no offering" and they gave me 10 toea. Now they <u>kept on putting</u> the offerings in, but I didn't put mine in. [Morobe, F, 12]

6.3.7 Modal particles

Mood and modality are separate concepts: mood is a formal grammatical verbal category, whereas modality expresses a number of semantic categories dealing with the way the world is viewed by individuals. Modality is subdivided into a confusing array of types. As Bybee & Fleischmann (1995:2) note:

> It covers a broad range of semantic nuances - jussive, desiderative, intentive, hypothetical, potential, obligative, dubitative, hortatory, exclamative, etc. - whose common denominator is the addition of a supplement or overlay of meaning to the most neutral semantic value of the proposition of an utterance, namely factual and declarative.

Indeed, there seems to be little constraint on further metalinguistic elaboration as new distinctions such as "apprehensional epistemics" in To'aba'ita (Lichtenberk 1995: 294) or the "delayed imperative" in Buriat (Bybee & Fleischmann 1995:2) are found in other languages. One difficulty which has complicated discussion of modality is that there may be an uncomfortable fit between the formal and semantic categories both within languages and especially cross-linguistically. This has been true of Creoles as much as other languages, and the over-general use of such concepts as 'irrealis' has come in for some criticism recently (Winford 1996:73; Bybee & Fleischmann, 1995:3). In Tok Pisin, the commonest modals are *mas, ken* and *inap,* associated with obligation, permission and possibility.

Mas

The particle *mas,* from English 'must', can imply not only personal obligation to do something, but also an assumption that something must be true, corresponding to a distinction which is sometimes made between deontic and epistemic modality. More recently, the category of deontic modality has been further refined as "agent-oriented" modality, which includes such categories as obligation, desire, ability, permission and root possibility (Bybee 1985). The use of such "agent-oriented" and "epistemic" uses of *mas* can be seen respectively in the following extracts:

> *N(a) em tok osem mi mas pasim egdjem blo mi na mi mas go l(ong) aiskul na mi mas bekim bek ol mani blong em em bin baim*
>
> And he said I must pass my exams and I must go to high school and I must repay all the money he had paid. [West Sepik, F, 15]

> *Bas kam nau mi tok, "em mas Djef mas kam" nau mipla kam sidaun sta(p)*
>
> The bus came and I said "it must be Geoff coming", so we came and sat down. [Morobe, F, 12]

Occasionally both are used in close proximity:

> *tupla sista ia tok "o mitla mas go na lukim, ol mas mekim sampla samting lo papa ia."*
>
> The two sisters said "we must (agent-oriented) go and look, they must (epistemic) have done something to father." [East Sepik, F, 16]

Almost 600 tokens were recorded in the corpus. The agent-oriented use was considerably more common than epistemic use, as the following table indicates:

Agent-oriented and epistemic uses of *mas*

Agent-oriented		Epistemic		Indeterminate		Total	
No.	%	No.	%	No.	%	No.	%
436	76	129	22	11	2	576	100

Indeterminate cases were generally false starts or otherwise difficult to interpret. There was rarely any ambiguity between the two meanings. In the following, however, it is not entirely clear whether the predictions for the future entail a determination that something must come to pass, or whether it is just a supposition of what is likely to occur:

> *Mi ting osem lo hia tu tausend mi mas gat wanpla haus blo mi yet na mi mas stap longwe lo ol perents blo mi. Na mi mas - mi mas gat - mi mas gat wanpla kar na mi mas gat - mi mas gat wokboi we bai em i sa klinim insait lo haus blo mi.*
>
> I think in the year 2000 I must/should/will have my own house and I must/should/will stay far from my parents. And I must/should/will have a car and I must/should/will have a servant to clean my house. [East New Britain, F, 16]

In a single case, the more English-sounding variant *mast* was used:

> *Tupla bamp na mast fopla man bin dai lo disla taim*
>
> The two crashed and there must have been four people killed at this time. [West Sepik, M, 16]

Normally *mas* appears alone preceding a single verb, but an interesting serial construction following *wokim* 'to make' is found in the following:

Ol papa i sa go antap lo suga na ol sa rausim skin bl' em, pasim lo rop lo <u>wokim suga mas gro</u> go longpla.

The old men go to the top of the sugar cane and the take off its skin, tie it with rope to <u>make it grow</u> long. [Eastern Highlands, M, 17]

Other serial constructions found with *mas* following another verb were the following:

mama ia tok ose em la <u>kisi(m) olge(ta) tripla pikini bl' em mas go</u> bek lo ples bl' em.

mother said that she <u>would like to take all three children</u> back to her village. [West Sepik, F, 16]

Ol tok "wanpla meri ia em laik, em laik lo karim lek osem na ol man <u>laikim yupla mas kam</u>"

They said "a girl wants to have courting ceremony, so the men <u>want you to come</u>," [Morobe, F, 13]

Ken and inap

The word *ken* for many speakers is homophonous with the word *ken (gen)* meaning 'again'. A role in marking future has been described, but it is better known as a modal indicating permission. The role in marking definite future events has been reported by Dutton (1973:166). As with the reported case of *laik* and *laik i*, the predicate marker *i* is said to distinguish the meanings. In this case, *ken* is said to relate to permission and *ken i* to definite future. However, again this corpus can not provide examples to support this distinction. The combination of the modal *ken* with *i* is not common, only two examples being found out of some 1,000 tokens of *ken* in the corpus. In each case, the meaning is clearly *not* definite future.

Na meri ia i singaut na em tok "yu no <u>ken i go,</u> yu kam bek."

And the woman shouted "you <u>can't go</u>, come back." [Southern Highlands, M, 17]

In its modal use, *ken* normally indicates permission:

em i tok "Yu no <u>ken go</u> skul, stap tasol lo aus, na kisim pei blo yu na stap nating."

He said "you <u>shouldn't go</u> to school, just stay at home and collect your pay and do nothing." [Simbu, F, 19]

It is sometimes also used to denote physical capability, which is usually expressed by *inap*. In fact, the distinction between *ken* and *inap* appears to be becoming blurred, as shown by the following, where the normal roles are reversed:

Sapos ol i lainim ol dok nau ol i <u>ken arim</u> toktok tasol ol no sa(v)e lo toktok.

If they teach dogs nowadays they <u>can understand</u> (capability) the words, but they don't know how to speak. [East New Britain, F, 15]

em tokim disla ol liklik manggi "<u>inap mi baim</u> disla trausel l' yupla?" na ol tok "okei."

He said to these boys "can I (permission) buy this turtle from you?" and they said "OK." [East Sepik, M, 15]

6.3.8 Other TMA markers

Borrowing of English TMA particles such as 'might', 'will', 'should', 'could' and so on might be expected, considering the close relationship between Tok Pisin and English and the massive change in the lexicon which has taken place due to borrowing from English. However, it was somewhat surprising to find that borrowing of English TMA markers does not seem to have occurred to any significant extent in the corpus. The only example found was *shud* 'should' with a similar meaning to English, attested in three instances:

osem <u>mipla shud stap</u> yet tasol mipla gat liklik femili problem

so we <u>should still be there</u> but we had a bit of a family problem [Manus, F, 16]

Dedi blo mi <u>em shud letim</u> mi lo go na lukim solwara blo ples blo mami blo mi.

my father <u>should have let</u> me go and see the sea at my mother's village. [East New Britain, F, 15]

> em kar eksident, angkol blo mi yet bampim em na na *em shud dai*
>
> it was a car accident, my uncle bumped him and he should have died [Eastern Highlands, F, 16]

Although the number of tokens is small, they occur from widely separated areas, and it is conjectured that having gained a foothold, structures such as this are likely to increase in use as more bilingual individuals emerge.

Kirap

This is not a TMA marker, but there is a possibility that it could be in the process of developing into an incipient aspect particle (Smith 1996). Many quotations or indirect reports of speech begin with the phrase *kirap na tok (olsem)* 'got up and said (that)'. Although the literal meaning of *kirap* is 'to get up' (and also 'to begin'), it is often used where there is no physical action or intention to 'get up' and the actual function is usually to indicate the initiation of an utterance or conversation exchange. Because *kirap* can also mean 'to initiate' or 'to begin' it would appear at first sight that the best translation would be 'started to say'. However, a similar construction is common in Papua New Guinea English expressed as 'got up and said'. A typical use is illustrated below:

> Go na, man tru tru i *kirap na tok* "em orait, maski, kros maski yu kam na mitla wok wantem na katim kapiak, ksim ol binatang."
>
> Then the real man said "it's all right, never mind, let's not argue, let's work together and cut the breadfruit tree and get the grubs." [West Sepik, M, 16]

However, the use of *kirap* does not always indicate the first move in a conversation, as is clearly shown by the following exchange:

> Na ol *kira tok*, "yu tasol disla man mipla mumuim yu?" N' em *kira tok*, "ye mi tasol", na tupla *kira tok*, "yu onem kain man ia..."
>
> Now they said "are you the man we cooked?" And he said "Yes, it's me." And the two said "what kind of man are you?" [New Ireland, M, 12]

It does, however, appear to represent the first time of speaking in a given turn. *Kirap na tok* is frequently reduced to *kira na tok, kira tok, kra tok, kra to* or even *kra t*. It is usually followed by *olsem* or one of its reduced variants, although this too may be omitted. In the longer versions, *nau* may be used instead of *na*. These changes, phonological reduction and pre-verbal placement, suggest that at some time in the future *kirap* could possibly undergo grammaticalization to an aspect marker. The following examples show progressively reduced forms:

> nau mi *kira na tok osem* "a mi go tokim mama blo mi..".
>
> Now I said "I'm going to tell my mother..." [Western Highlands, F, 15]

> meri ia *kira nau tokim* ol "oke yupla no (k)en slip, yupla mas stap was..."
>
> the woman told them "you mustn't sleep, you must keep watch..." [West Sepik, F, 12]

> em kam nau lukim em nau em *kira nau tok* "yu la mekim wonem lo d(isp)la meri nau?"
>
> he came and saw him and said "what are you going to do to this woman?" [West Sepik, M, 13]

> Olgeta skin blogen em ol kati(m) kati(m) pinis wantem naif na het tsol stap na em *kra n' t' s'*, "o man blo mi em sawe osem mi wokim rong na lo fogivim mi em - em yet i dai."
>
> All his body was cut away with a knife and only the head remained and she said "oh my husband knew I had done wrong and to forgive me he himself died." [Eastern Highlands, F, 16]

> Nau mi *kira t' se*, "plis mi laikim wanpla raid lo hos bl' yutla."
>
> Now I said "please, I would like a ride on your horse." [Eastern Highlands, F, 16]

> disa meri ia *kira n' t'* "e mi sutim wanpla samting pinis."
>
> This woman said "I've speared something." [Manus, F, 13]

> *em go sanap antap nau wanpla man <u>kira tok</u>, "yu kam daun."*
>
> He stood on top and a man <u>said</u> "you come down." [Morobe, F, 11]

> *Em go nau olsem ol polis kot ol narapela ol lain ia i stap nogat, em <u>kra sem</u> wanem ia, "putim mi long sel nau."*
>
> he went and the police charged the others who were there and he <u>said</u>, what was it "put me in the cell now." [Morobe, F, 12]

> *N' em <u>kira tok</u>, "mi - mi no inap dai."*
>
> And he <u>said</u> "I can't die." [New Ireland, M, 12]

Sometimes the *tok* is left out altogether, leaving *kirap* to signify the whole phrase:

> *Na papa blo em <u>kra</u> "sh pikinini yu stap tasol ia..".*
>
> And his father <u>said</u> "sh, son, just stay there..". [Manus, M, 16]

Thus while *kirap* at the moment cannot be considered an aspect marker, it is a possible contender for such a status, considering the grammaticalization of other such lexical items from constant use in discourse. It is noteworthy that significant changes to *kirap* in rapid speech are taking place in all regions.

Bek

The status of *bek* as an aspect marker is not certain, and it is usually used as an adverb. However, it appears to have expanded its semantic range from its basic meaning 'to return (something) to its original place' and is another possible contender for the development of a new 'resumptive' aspect distinction. The great majority of occurrences of *bek* are adverbial uses with the verbs of motion such as *go* and *kam*, often in conjunction with the adverb *ken* 'again':

> *Orait tupla i <u>kam bek</u> tamblo na lo havinun displa man i <u>kam bek ken</u>.*
>
> So the two <u>went back</u> down and in the afternoon this man <u>came back</u> again. [Manus, M, 13]

> *Na nau narapla man ia kirap nau tokim em "orait nau ba yu <u>go bek</u>, ba yu kari(m) disla kundu, na ba yu <u>go bek</u>."*
>
> Now another man said to him "so now you should <u>go back</u>, take your drum and <u>go back</u>." [East Sepik, M, 16]

In one or two instances, however, analogic remodelling is suspected where *bek* is found with non-motion verbs which nevertheless involve an element of location, indicating that something is being returned to its original position:

> *em tok "ei usat tru sa kam kamautim kaikai blo mi lo gaden ia?" Em - em mekim osem go nau em <u>planim bek</u>.*
>
> He said "Hey, who comes and uproots the food in my garden?" He did this and later he planted them <u>back again</u>. [West New Britain, M, 12]

> *man bl' em raun raun na em kam na em laik <u>putim bun bl' em go bek</u> ia i no nap em ad tumas.*
>
> Her husband walked around and he came and wanted to <u>put her bones back</u>, but he couldn't, it was too hard. [Simbu, F, 16]

This appears to have been extended even further in meaning, to include any resumption of activity, more or less equivalent to the 're-' prefix in English:

> *Orait mipla bin kam bek gen lo Rabaul na <u>spendim bek</u> laif lo hia.*
>
> So we came back again to Rabaul and <u>resumed our life</u> here [East New Britain, F, 16]

> *Taim mi bin go - go antap lo peles mi bin endjoyim laif blo mi stret lo wonem mi <u>go mitim bek</u> ken ol kasins blo mi na ol bin welkamim mipla gut tru.*
>
> When I went back up to the village I really enjoyed life because I <u>renewed acquaintance with</u> my cousins and they really welcomed us. [East New Britain, F, 16]

Na em nau i kirap i tokim tupla pikinini blongen blo <u>mumuim papa blo tupla bek</u>.

So he got up and told the two children to <u>roast their father again</u>. [New Ireland, M, 12]

em i tok "yu wokobaut traim." Em nau manggi ia wokobaut. Em nau manggi kirap nau na i <u>hamamas bek</u> lo brata blong em i mekim gut

he said "try to walk." Then the boy walked. The boy <u>cheered up again</u> that his brother was doing well [North Solomons, M, 14]

em go lo wanpla glasman lo ples na, em givim wara, kol wara nau na, em <u>kirap bek</u> na nau em stap.

He went to a healer in the village and he gave him cold water, <u>he was revived</u> and he's still alive. [West Sepik, F, 16]

Expressions such as *marit bek* 'remarry' are now in widespread use, suggesting that this new role for the particle is becoming established.

6.3.9 TMA particles in combination

According to Sankoff's schema (1991:64), the ordering of the various particles in the verb phrase is as follows:

```
              bin                              igo
    no              save    laik    aux    V   istap   pinis
              ken                              ikam
```

The particle *bai* is considered outside the verb phrase, and *wok long* and *mas* are ignored. It is interesting to consider what happens when particles are used in combination, as this does not appear to have received much attention in previous accounts.

In the following table, the number of occurrences of different combinations of TMA markers is shown. For example, the entry '18' in the *bin* row, *save* column indicate that the combination *bin save* in immediate proximity, in that order is found 18 times in the corpus. Use of words such as *save*, *laik* and *pinis* with their full lexical meaning is excluded, as is fortuitous juxtaposition of particles affecting verbs in different clauses.

TMA markers in combination

	bai	bin	sa(ve)	mas	la(ik)	wok long	pinis	ken	(i) stap
bai		0	10	4	1	1	0	1	0
bin	0		18	0	30	23	0	0	0
sa(ve)	0	1		0	18	0	0	0	1
mas	0	0	1		0	0	0	0	1
la(ik)	7	0	0	0		0	0	0	1
wok long	0	0	0	0	0		0	0	0
pinis	0	0	0	0	0	0		0	4
ken	0	0	1	0	0	0	0		0
(i) stap	0	0	0	0	0	0	6	0	

The combination *laik bai* would contradict Sankoff's characterisation of *bai* outside the verb phrase, but its use here requires further scrutiny. As noted, there is often difficulty in distinguishing the meanings 'like to' from 'about to', but in the examples in the corpus, it appears that the combination *laik bai* is usually interpreted as 'desire that something happen':

taim mi maret, mi <u>laik bai</u> mi - bai mi mas - bai mi wantem man blo mi mas gat fopla pikinini ... mipla <u>laik bai</u> mipla gat wanpla kar blo mipla yet.

When I am married I <u>would like to</u> - my husband and I should have four children ... we <u>would like to</u> have our own car. [East New Britain, F, 17]

Thus combinations like this containing a clause boundary do not appear strictly to be combinations of TMA particles and are excluded from further consideration. The only regularly occurring combinations remaining are *bai save, bai mas, bin save, bin laik, bin wok long, save laik*, and *i stap pinis*. The ordering of these combinations all conform to Sankoff's schema above.

Some of these combinations do appear to have a productive role; in particular, there is a case for describing a 'past habitual' marked with **bin sa**, or a 'past continuous' marked with **bin wok long**. These do not occur uniformly throughout the sample, however. All the tokens of *bin wok long*, and all but one of *bin sa* were recorded in the New Guinea Islands region:

Wanpla taim lo peles ol man <u>bin wok lo koros</u> koros nambaut long ol gaden blong ol

Once upon a time, in the village the men <u>were arguing</u> about their gardens [New Ireland, M, 12]

Ol bin no laikim bai disla fait ia bai kam daun olgeta lo ples blo mami blo mi na <u>ol bin wok lo lukluk</u> lukluk tasol tok osem sapos ol biarei bai kam bai ol i ronim ol tasol ol no bin kam klostu lo ailan ia disla taim

They didn't want this conflict to spread to my mother's place, and they <u>were keeping watch</u> and said that if the BRA came, they would chase them out, but they didn't come near the island at that time. [East New Britain, F, 16]

Displa pik <u>em i bin sae kaikaim</u> ol man na, i bin traipla tru ia, traipla pik osem na i sa kaikaim ol man. Na <u>i bin sa ronim</u> ol man nambaut, na ol man i bin kirap lusim displa ples.

This pig <u>used to eat</u> people and it was huge, huge and ate people. And it <u>used to chase</u> people, and the people abandoned the village. [East New Britain, M, 18]

lo displa taim ol klen <u>i bin sa fait</u> na wokim nambaut, am disla ol - i bin gat wanpla traipla moran tu we <u>i bin sa kam</u> na kilim ol disla ol man na meri

At this time the clans <u>would fight</u> and things like that, um these - there was a huge python which <u>used to come</u> and kill these men and women [New Ireland, F, 15]

The speaker in the latter example, however, did show a certain amount of uncertainty when this combination was used in the negative:

Am bifo bifo tru tru lo taim blo tumbuna <u>ol man i no bin sa</u>, <u>ol man i bin no sa stap</u> gut.

Long ago in the olden days, the people <u>didn't live</u> well. [New Ireland, F, 15]

Only in a single counter-example in the corpus does the order *sa bin* occur:

ol lain lo ples ol bin osem kam gritim mipla osem, hamamas lo lukim mipla na <u>ol i sa bin tok ples</u> long mipla.

My relatives in the village came to greet us, they were happy to see us and they <u>talked to us</u> in the local language. [West Sepik, M, 16]

There are some other combinations which occur, albeit with single or very few tokens, namely *bai laik, bai wok long, bai ken, mas save, laik bin*, and *ken save*. Since these could possibly be variants which might develop a productive role in the future, they are recorded here as they occurred in the speech extracts.

Na em stap lo aus na em sa, olgeta taim bai em stap go bai em korosim mipla, <u>em bai laik kilim</u> mipla wantem naif.

And he stayed at home and he, all the time he stayed there he would get angry with us, he <u>?could have been about to</u> kill us with a knife. [Morobe, F, 14]

Ol i stap gut o ol i stap nogut, mi no sawe na ol tu i no sawe hau mi stap long hia. Na bikos long displa ating ol femili blong mi long ples tu <u>bai wok long wari</u> liklik long mi.

Whether they are all right or not, I don't know, and they too don't know how I am here. And because of this I think that my family at home <u>must be a bit worried</u> about me. [East New Britain, M, 20]

"... ba mi go lo narapla ples ia, na ba mi painim narapla meri we kam <u>bai ken sta(p)</u> (w)antem yu na elpim yu lo wok gaden."

" ... I will go to another village and find another wife who will come and <u>can stay</u> with you and help you with garden work." [East Sepik, M, 15]

em i go hait long has blo wanpla diwai i stap nau, em i go - em i holpasim man ia i tokim em <u>ol i mas save stap kaikai gut</u>.

He went and hid behind a tree stump, he went and caught the man and told him they <u>must live and eat well</u>. [West New Britain, F, 12]

mipla sa laik go putim lansh blo mipla insait lo klasrum na ol sa koros se bai mipla <u>i no ken sa go insait</u>

we like to put our lunch in the classroom and they are angry because we <u>are not allowed to go inside</u>. [East New Britain, F, 12]

Since some of these may be novel combinations, the translations are somewhat tentative. However, it does appear that retention of multiple particles could indicate an increase in redundancy and obligatory use of TMA marking in the speech of first language speakers, with unpredictable consequences for future semantic distinctions.

6.4 Verb serialization

Serial verbs constitute another aspect of the syntax of Pidgin and Creole languages which has received considerable attention in recent years. Unfortunately the area has been bedeviled by vagueness of definition, but a clearer picture is gradually emerging both of serial verbs in natural languages, and their occurrence and significance in Pidgins and Creoles.

The field of verb serialization is relatively new, indeed, as Seuren pointed out (1993:193), the term was only coined some 30 years ago with reference to West African languages (Stewart 1963). Escure (1991) defines the requirements of true serial verb constructions as (i) a surface string of verbs or verb-like structures and (ii) a semantic relationship between them. However, other definitions are used by other writers, making cross-comparison of data more difficult. A discussion of definitions can be found in Seuren (1991).

Much of the debate on serial verbs has concerned Atlantic Creoles, e.g. Byrne (1991) on argument structure, and Lefebvre (1991), Sebba (1987) and Winford (1993) on directional serial verbs. A major motivating factor has been the question of origins. Bickerton's proposal (1981) that universals account for such structures has been contested by those seeking to demonstrate a plausible West African substrate, where serializing constructions are widely found (Schiller 1993).

Crowley (1990b) notes that, although attention to serial verbs in Pidgin and Creole studies had concentrated almost exclusively on Atlantic Creoles, serial verbs are found in languages of New Guinea (Bradshaw 1982, Siegel 1984), and Vanuatu (Crowley 1987a). His account of serial verbs in Bislama (1990b) provides some much-needed data for Pacific contact languages. He reports the widespread use of serialized verbs of motion and posture and their use in marking verbal aspect, noting that their serial nature is demonstrated by the obligatory insertion of the predicate markers *i* or *oli*. Another set of serial constructions is shown to have developed into prepositions.

Crowley's work is highly relevant to the present study, and a comparison of his findings with data from the corpus is in order. In the following discussion, a comprehensive evaluation of the problems of definition will not be attempted, but an account of serial-like constructions as they occur in the corpus will be given to provide some up-to-date data from first language Tok Pisin speakers. Thus, not all the constructions described below as "serial" are analogous, and different structures or origins may be involved.

As seen in the previous section, the use of serial constructions with *go, kam* and *stap* is extremely common. Givón (1990:27) describes these as verbs of motion, but in many cases not only directionality but also continuous aspect is expressed. One difference from Bislama is that the predicate marker *i* is not obligatory in such constructions, and it is frequently omitted, especially in some regions (see §6.2). In some cases, repetition of the verb of motion is used as a further device to indicate the intensity of the aspect:

Na mipela <u>stap go go go go</u> nau, mi skul lo Hagen na ol naratla bradhas blo mi tu ol skul lo Hagen na mipela sta(p) lo Hagen.

And we <u>stayed for a long time</u>, I went to school in Mt. Hagen and my other brothers also went to school in Hagen and we live in Hagen. [Western Highlands, F, 14]

> *Tupla <u>wokobaut kam kam kam</u> olgeda lo aus nau, tupla lugim, tupla lugim aus blo tupla em, nogat man stap.*
>
> The two <u>came all the way back</u> home, they saw their house had nobody in it. [Simbu, M, 18]

The verb *kirap* 'get up, start', as noted in § 6.3, is often involved in serial constructions with aspectual characteristics, but the degree to which they encode single propositions is open to question. Although *kirap* is most frequently used with the verb *tok*, the following examples show combinations with other verbs:

> *dewel ia <u>kirap holim</u> em na em karim go lo aus blo em.*
>
> the devil <u>got up and held him/started to hold</u> him and carried him to his house [East Sepik, M, 17]

> *Nau, ol lain blo mipla belat nau, ol go andap nau, ol <u>kirap pait</u> na ol pait.*
>
> Now my clan members were angry, they went up and <u>started to fight</u> and they fought. [Simbu, M, 15]

The verb *stat* too is often used with what approaches an aspectual role for actions which are just beginning:

> *ol sa kukim kaikai lo paia ia, ol lusi(m) nau ol <u>stat kuk</u> lo kleipot.*
>
> They would cook food on the fire, then they stopped and <u>started to cook</u> in clay pots. [Madang, M, 17]

Other examples from the corpus could fall into the category of serial verb constructions depending on the definition employed. The verb *traim* 'try' is often followed by other verbs as 'to try to do something'. This type of construction could be considered rather as a verbal complement, although in English, for example, single verbs such as 'emulate' (= 'try to equal') encode what would be serial constructions with 'try':

> *Olsem nau em i tingim wanpla aidia we bai em i pasim yau blong em, bai em i <u>traim chenshim</u> pes blong em liklik.*
>
> So he had an idea that he would bind his ears so that he would <u>try to change</u> his face a little. [East Sepik, M, 15]

> *Em nau bikpla brata kirap tokim liklik brata, "mitupla <u>traim digim</u> displa diwai ia."*
>
> So the big brother said to his little brother "let's <u>try to dig</u> this tree up." [East New Britain, M, 17]

Another verb frequently involved in what appear to be serial constructions is *kamap*. The extent to which it encodes meaning or aspect when it follows another verb is not clear. It usually follows the verbs *go* 'go' and *kam* 'come', but sometimes other verbs as well, as in the following examples:

> *em i wokobaut i go lo narapla ples lo fainim ol meri. Taim em <u>go kamap</u> lo rot em i bungim wanpla lapun meri.*
>
> He walked to another village to look for the women. When he <u>arrived</u> at the road he met an old woman. [East Sepik, M, 15]

> *Na taim ol i kirap nogut em i <u>kam kamap</u> na em i askim ol "yupela wokim dispela pati lo wonem?"*
>
> And while they were surprised (at what they heard), he <u>appeared</u> and asked them "why are you having this party?" [Manus, M, 13]

> *Peibek sistem ... em wantla kastom blo yumi ol lapun i bin <u>bringim kamap</u>*
>
> The 'payback system' ... is one of our customs which our ancestors <u>introduced</u> [Western Highlands, M, 16]

> *Ol pul kam kam kam, kamap lo seim ap nau, o(l) lukim wara <u>boil kamap</u>*
>
> they paddled and paddled back to the same place and they saw the water <u>boiling up</u>. [West Sepik, F, 15]

> *Nau Pek i kirap kamap loen lo driman na i tok, tok, "lapun meri yu go yu go kisim stem blo mi stret, stem blo mi em i swit."*
>
> Now Pek <u>appeared</u> to her in a dream and said "old woman, go and get my stem, my stem is sweet." [New Ireland, F, 13]

> *tupela stap lo (di)sla hap go nau, tupela tanim kamap ston nau tupela stap lo sla hap*
>
> they stayed in this place and <u>turned into</u> stone and stayed there. [Western Highlands, F, 14]

In languages such as Kalam (Madang Province), serial verb constructions are commonly used to increase the referential power of a limited verbal lexicon (Givón 1990). The number of serial constructions used for this purpose in Tok Pisin appears to be severely limited, and the option of borrowing English verbs is generally exercised where greater referential power is required (Smith 1994a). However, there are a number of examples where serial constructions appear to be used to encapsulate more specific meaning. Combinations with *save*, for example, such as *luk save* 'recognize' and *tok save* 'inform', have been known for some time, (Mihalic 1971) and are well represented in the present corpus (8 and 26 tokens respectively):

> *I go nau em i stap antap lo maunten i lukluk go lo nabis na lukim kadere blongen i kam na em i luk sawe pinis longen.*
>
> Later he was on the mountain looking to the coast and saw his uncle coming, and he <u>recognized</u> him [West New Britain, F, 15]

> *Nau man bl' em ia lukim nau em go tok save l' ol man nabaut, na ol kam painim em ia*
>
> And his wife saw it and she went and <u>informed</u> everyone, and they came to look for him [Simbu, F, 13]

The verb *tanim* 'turn' may be followed by other verbs, but whether the meaning encoded is a single action or consecutive actions may not be clear:

> *em man bl' em, luki(m) osem man bl' em tanim wokobaut go bek ken l' narapla said.*
>
> It was her husband, looked like her husband <u>turning back</u> again to the other side [West Sepik, F, 13]

> *na meri ia i tanim lukluk na em lukim man Buka i sindaun smail long em.*
>
> and the girl <u>looked round</u> and saw the Buka man <u>sitting smiling</u> at her. [East Sepik, M, 17]

In the use of *sindaun smail* 'sit smiling' in the last example, it is similarly difficult to tell whether one or two actions are involved. This is also the case with the following:

> *ol i sindaun raunim sekel, na ol i sindaun, wanpla boi lo namel, narapla ken osem, ol i sindaun miks miks i go*
>
> they <u>sat round</u> in a circle, and they sat, one boy in the middle, another one like this, they <u>sat down all mixed up</u>. [Eastern Highlands, M, 18]

> *Wanpla blo narapla ples, sampla blo narapla ples ol ka(m) na, ol miks wandem na ka(m) sindaun was lo em i stap.*
>
> One (sorcerer) from one village, some from another came and they mixed with one another and <u>lay in wait</u> for him [East Sepik, M, 12]

Some other examples of serial constructions apparently encoding specific meanings greater than the sum of the individual parts are as follows:

> *ol go kari(m) fes ston raunim as lo kalip go, raunim ol ples kam bek, puti(m) lo namel lo ples na (di)s(pel)a ston i stap nau, blupla ston. Narapla ken ol kisi(m) raunim na sa ston i sta lo ples blo mi*
>
> they <u>took</u> the first stone <u>around</u> the base of the nut tree, round all the villages and back, put it in the middle of the village and this stone is still there, the blue stone. The other one they took and <u>put round</u> and this stone is in my village. [East Sepik, M, 16]

Ogeta taim em ba kisim rop, em wokim bilum, ba ol rop i pudaun go anda l' aus, na ol sa <u>brumim rausim</u>

He always got string and made string bags and the string would fall underneath the house and they would <u>sweep it away</u>. [East Sepik, M, 18]

Nau mama papa bl' ol bin <u>dai lusim</u> ol taim ol liklik yet, na tupla stap i go

They had been <u>orphaned</u> by their parents when they were still small, and the two lived there. [West Sepik, F, 13]

tupla puti(m) anta(p) lo liklik kanu nau, na kanu <u>sel kari(m) go</u> go ogeta lo narapla ailan

they put it on a small canoe and the canoe <u>bore</u> them to another island [West Sepik, F, 13]

Ol i bin stap, na ol i wonem - sampla lain bin <u>kros pait</u>, na ol i rausim em, wande pikini blong em.

They stayed there and some people <u>quarrelled</u> and they threw him and his children out. [West Sepik, M, 19]

narapla poro bl' em wonem, <u>putim ipim</u> bl' em, ipim blo tupla wante(m) go go, pinis nau, tupla kisim ogeta wonem, mumut kam putim nau tupla tilim.

His other friend <u>piled up</u> his (bandicoots), heaped both of theirs, then the two got all the bandicoots and put them down and divided them up. [East Sepik, M, 12]

em presim go daun tasol, em <u>putim pasim</u> em, em stap sting na nau binatang blo saksak i kam em sa keikei.

He pressed him down, he <u>trapped</u> him, he went rotten there and now sago grubs came and he ate them. [East Sepik, M, 16]

mipla kisim ol ap limbum blo Mista B., mipla <u>k(i)sim putim</u> andap lo trakta, mipla kam wantem.

We got Mr. B's bits of palm stem, we <u>loaded</u> them on to the tractor and we came with them. [East Sepik, M, 17]

Worth mentioning here is Verhaar's (1991b) description of what he terms the "serial" use of *na*. In this article he notes uses of *na* which have more than a coordinating role, and produce structures similar to serial constructions which he calls "co-lexical serialization". He notes that various critics of a first draft of the paper suggested that this may be better described as a subordinating function of *na* (1991b:138), and this criticism does seem to be valid. As Siegel notes (1998:5) two of the principal criteria for categorization as serial verbs, the absence of coordinating or subordinating structures, and being part of the same action or event, are not met, especially if alternative translations are given to some of the examples.

In Bislama, a number of serial verb constructions involving the verbs *agensem, kasem, bitim, raonem* and *folem* have developed into prepositions (Crowley 1990b). This does not appear to have occurred to any significant extent in Tok Pisin, although occasional uses in the corpus do have parallels with the Bislama examples. The verb *agens(t)im* occurs only rarely in the corpus, and the equivalent *sakim* is not observed in serial constructions. However, two examples of the use of *agens(t)im* are open to re-interpretation in a prepositional role as well as a verbal one:

Tupla bin laik kamap frens na maret tasol ol no bin laik. Ol lain blo meri <u>bin agenstim disla pasin</u>.

The two wanted to be friends and get married, but they did not like this. The girl's family <u>opposed/were against</u> this behaviour. [East New Britain, F, 16]

Ol biarei ol i bin kilim sampla man husat ol i bin ting olsem ol i wok lo <u>go agensim ol</u>.

The BRA (Bougainville Revolutionary Army) killed some men who they thought were <u>working against them/opposing them</u>. [East New Britain, M, 20]

The verb **bitim* is not found, but the equivalent *winim* occasionally suggests the meaning 'more than'. The closest examples from the present corpus are the rather ambiguous uses shown in the following, where *winim* has the meaning 'be bigger than':

Taim tupla stap go winim krismas, ol - boi winim krismas olsem ten, em i bikpla pinis.

When the two stayed there <u>over the age</u> - the <u>boy was over ten years old</u>, he was already big. [Simbu, M, 18]

bifo em olsem draipela dok winim haus, na nau em, yumi gat ol liklik liklik dok

before it was a huge dog, <u>bigger than a house</u>, and now it's, we have small dogs. [Morobe, F, 15]

The verb ***folim** is not found in the corpus, but some interesting constructions involving **bihainim** and **lusim** in serial constructions echo the Bislama prepositions, or at least allow for the possibility of an alternative interpretation as a preposition:

em kam go daun lo nambis na meri krai biainim em wantem li(k)li(k) boi ia.

He came down to the beach and his wife <u>cried behind him/followed him crying</u> with the small boy. [Madang, F, 14]

Em kirap i ronowe lusim em go insait lo bus. Meri ia kirap ron biainim em.

He got up and <u>ran away from him</u> into the forest. The woman got up and <u>ran after/chased</u> him. [New Ireland, F, 14]

Nau ol i bin kisim ol naif na ol katapel na ol spia na ol i ron biainim ol man i go antap lo bikpla ples blo mipla antap.

So they got their knives and catapults and spears and they <u>ran behind/chased</u> the men up to our big village. [West New Britain, F, 15]

However, none of the examples with **bihainim** is similar to the use reported by Crowley (1990b:80) of 'according to'. The verb **raunim** is often used as an alternative form of **ronim** in this corpus. There are one or two examples where a prepositional interpretation would be a possibility:

Okei kirap na i tok osem bai go na bai wokobaut raunim disla ailan.

So he got up and said he would go and <u>walk round</u> this island [New Ireland, F, 13]

ol sa mekim ol ston raunim ol gaden.

They <u>built stones around</u> the gardens [Manus, F, 14]

ol lain i olim paia ba ol i go na putim paia raunim disla kunai pinis nau ba ol i sanap was i stap.

The ones holding fire would go and <u>make fire around</u> this area of grassland and they would keep watch. [East Sepik, M, 15]

It should be noted that an alternative English borrowing, **araun** 'around' is also attested (14 tokens). This is most often used with time expressions to mean 'approximately', but is also occasionally used to mean 'around' in the spatial sense:

mipla wantem bikman go was go go, a samting araun tu ouklok o tri ouklok lo moning nau mipla go bek lo ples.

We stayed and watched with the leader, something <u>around two o'clock</u> or 3 o'clock in the morning we went home. [West Sepik, M, 14]

olgeta man meri kam bum araun l' ofis na ol bin ksim setifiket bl' ol

all the people <u>gathered around the office</u> and they got their certificates [Southern Highlands, F, 14]

The alternative form **araund** is also used with the same range of meanings:

(di)sla boi mas araund sikstin yias ould na ol i kisim em.

this boy must have been <u>around sixteen years old</u> and they caught him. [Manus, M, 18]

mipla dekoreitim araund lo skul insait lo mes lo redim lo disla grediueishen bl' ol greid ten.

We decorated <u>around the school</u>, in the mess to get it ready for this grade 10 graduation. [Manus, F, 16]

The verb **kasem** is used in Bislama to mean 'up to' or 'until' (Crowley 1990b:79), but the equivalent **kisim** in Tok Pisin does not seem to be used at all in this way, **inap (long)** being used instead in such situations. The only other example where re-interpretation as a preposition would be possible appears to be the example involving *kamap* mentioned earlier:

> *na dsla man i dai ia, em sa - em sa ka... - tanim kamap dog nau, em sa kaikai disla nambatu waif.*
>
> and this man who had died, he <u>turned into a dog</u> and ate this second wife. [Enga, F, 12]

Thus it can be stated that the use of these serial constructions as prepositions is not a productive pattern in Tok Pisin, but a number of examples illustrate potential ambiguity where re-interpretation presumably did occur in Bislama, and could occur in Tok Pisin, especially with the prospect of "koineization" if Tok Pisin and Bislama come into increased contact.

6.5 The noun phrase

The noun phrase in Tok Pisin can consist of a pronoun or a noun, either bare or accompanied by pre- or post-modifiers. Sankoff & Mazzie have classified these into quantifiers, other pre-nominal modifiers and post-nominal modifiers (1991:4). In a more detailed breakdown (1991:18) they list quantifiers as numerals and the terms *ologeta, planti* and *sampela*; other pre-nominal modifiers as *wanpela, dispela, narapela* and *ol*; and post-nominal modifiers as the demonstrative *ia*, possessive constructions with *bilong*, and restrictive relative clauses or adjectives. Mühlhäusler (1985h:352) adds *liklik* to the list of quantifiers.

The main focus of Sankoff & Mazzie (1991) is an investigation of the extent to which determiners have become grammaticalized, especially into definite and indefinite articles. They showed that the candidates for indefinite article, *wanpela* 'one', and definite article, *dispela* 'this', were used sporadically and there was by no means obligatory marking of these categories. The post-nominal *ia* was shown to occur far more frequently in subject position, indicating that its function may be more related to subject- or topic-marking. Furthermore, the high frequency of bare nouns encountered for known or specified referents contradicts Bickerton's claim (1981) that the zero determiner marks non-specifics. Sankoff & Mazzie also showed that an unusually high proportion of possessives were found in those categories which are often implicated in the marking of inalienable possession in Austronesian languages, i.e. body parts and relatives. Thus the study which set out to investigate universal processes of grammaticalization ended up providing further evidence of substrate influence.

A number of observations concerning the present corpus can be made in the light of Sankoff & Mazzie's study. Firstly, their observation that body parts and relatives (kin) tend to be followed by possessives is generally borne out by the present study. The possible status of *wanpela* and *sampla* as indefinite articles is not so clear. It should be noted that these two items do not only act as pre-nominal indefinite determiners, and other functions overlap to some extent. *Wanpela* is also used as a numeral where the quantifying meaning is primary, as in the following examples:

> *Yes, papa mama blong mi ol i gat <u>wanpla tokples tasol</u>. Em tokples Telei.*
>
> Yes, my parents have one (i.e. the same) language, Telei. [East New Britain, M, 19]

> *Tsol <u>wanpla manggi tasol</u> em bin stap lo bus, em bin kisim tulip, tulip em kumu,*
>
> But <u>only one boy</u> stayed in the bush, he collected "two-leaf" leaves, "two-leaf" is a kind of green vegetable [East Sepik, M, 17]

Sampela could be used in a similar way to specify some but not all, but no tokens of pre-nominal use occur in the corpus apart from use as a pronoun:

> *olgeta dog indai. Na <u>sampla</u> i go blek nogut tru na <u>sampla</u> i go osem faia kukim ol*
>
> all the dogs died. And some of them went very black and some went like fire had burned them [East Sepik, M, 15]

Wanpela is used pronominally in a similar way:

> *Djaiant i sut lo spia bl' em na sutim lek blo <u>wanpla</u>. Na <u>wanpla</u> i pundaun nau*
>
> The giant threw his spear and pierced the leg of <u>one of them</u>. And <u>(this) one</u> fell down [East New Britain, M, 12]

This is discussed further in § 7.1 on reference and cohesion.

The use of *wanpela* and *sampela* as quantifiers, however, represents only a small minority, which are usually further distinguished by the presence of *tasol*. In the majority of cases, *wanpela* and *sampela* do appear to have a role analogous to that of indefinite articles, indicating the non-specific nature of something or someone:

> *mipla kaikai buai pinis na mipla wetim man blo <u>wanpla anti blo mipla</u>.*
>
> We finished chewing betel nut and waited for the husband of <u>an aunt</u>. [Morobe, F, 12]

> *masalai tokim em "yu stap ananit na mi go anta(p) lo diwai na mi traim lukluk. Bai mi ken lukim <u>sampla abus</u> o nogat."*
>
> The devil said to him "yu stay down here and I'll go up the tree and try to look. I'll see if I can see <u>some animals</u> or not." [Manus, F, 15]

While there are many tokens of *wanpela* and *sampela* in this role, there are still instances of bare nouns indicating both definites and indefinites:

> *ol salim wanpla dog go na tok, "s(ap)os yu <u>lukim man</u> stap antap okei wevim teil blo yu na yu kam."*
>
> They sent a dog and said "if you <u>see a man</u> up there, just wag your tail and come." [Eastern Highlands, F, 16]

> *Taim em go insait n' em i lukim man ia hait i stap. Arait (=orait), <u>meri i save</u> osem sista blong em i <u>haitim man</u> i sta(p) insai(t) l' aus.*
>
> When she went in she saw a man hiding. Then <u>the woman</u> knew that her sister <u>had hidden the man</u> inside the house. [East Sepik, M, 15]

However, the occurrence of bare nouns, especially human nouns, appears to be considerably less frequent in the corpus than indicated in Sankoff & Mazzie's sample, suggesting that the process of grammaticalization may be continuing. Furthermore, the status of some of the bare nouns as specific may be open to question.

In particular, the use of postposed *ia* does appear to be approaching an obligatory use for known human referents among some speakers. Frequently such marking is highly redundant. A full analysis cannot be made without an extensively tagged corpus, but samples from some speakers show the tendency to mark known human referents very frequently. The following extended passage, for example, is typical of many speakers. Marking of the known nouns with human reference is highlighted. The unmarked *pikinini* and *boi* in the first two sentences are introduced for the first time. All the previously introduced human nouns except one are marked with *ia* or a possessive:

> *Em stap go na <u>meri ia</u> gat bel na <u>meri ia</u> karim [Ø] pikinini. <u>Meri ia</u> karim [Ø] boi, beibi boi. Go <u>beibi ia</u> go bikpla stret na ol go lo gaden, wanpla taim ol go lo gaden. Ol go lo gaden na <u>boi ia</u>, liglig <u>boi ia</u> sidaun lo seid na <u>mama blongen</u> planim taro lo gaden na <u>papa blongen</u> was lo <u>beibi ia</u> na tupla sidaun stap na [Ø] <u>beibi</u> krai na <u>papa bloen</u> singaut na <u>meri ia</u> kirap na tokim <u>man blongen</u> "yu no sa wok, yu sa slip nating lo nambis."*
>
> After a while the woman got pregnant and <u>the woman</u> had (a) <u>child</u>. <u>The woman</u> had <u>a boy</u>, a <u>baby boy</u>. <u>The baby</u> grew up and they went to the garden, once they went to the garden. They went to the garden and <u>the boy</u>, <u>the small boy</u> sat at the side and <u>his mother</u> planted taro in the garden and <u>his father</u> watched <u>the baby</u> and the two were sitting down and <u>the baby</u> cried and <u>his father</u> called out and <u>the woman</u> got up and said to <u>her husband</u> "you don't work, you just lie around at the beach." [Madang, F, 14]

It might be expected that if grammaticalization is proceeding, it would be accompanied by phonological reduction and loss of stress. Thus, if *wanpela* were to be reduced to or replaced by a grammatical marker equivalent to an indefinite article, the existing lexeme *wan* would surely be a prime candidate. However, the use of *wan* in the corpus is almost exclusively with a quantitative meaning, including numerals, dates and some other fixed expressions:

> *Na em sa kisim tupla <u>wan kina</u> ia, olsem em reprisentim disla tupla pikinini bl' em na em silipim ol, wasim ol disla tupla <u>wan kina</u>, sa givim susu lo disla tupla <u>wan kina</u>.*
>
> And she takes two <u>one kina (coins)</u> which represent her two children and she puts them to bed, washes these two <u>one kina coins</u>, breast-feeds these two <u>one kina coins</u>. [Morobe, F, 13]

> *Go na afta twelf ouklok, <u>wan ouklok</u>, <u>hafpas wan</u> mipla bin go na mipla go pilai.*
>
> Then after twelve o'clock, <u>one o'clock</u>, <u>half past one</u> we went and played. [North Solomons, F, 11]

Na mi go lo ples blo mi, mi stap lo ap, <u>wan wik</u>, nau mi kam bek lo skul.

I went to my village, I stayed there for <u>one week</u>, then I came back to school [Enga, M, 18]

Similarly, ***sampela*** does not appear to be undergoing much reduction, apart from the almost universal attenuation of ***-pela*** to ***-pla***. In the corpus, only three examples of further reduction were found:

disla narapla man lukim ia em tokim ol, <u>samla lain</u>, ol wantaim ol go.

This other man who saw it told them, <u>some people</u>, they went with them. [Simbu, F, 16]

mi save helpim ol papa mama blo mi, lo wokim ol wok, <u>sama taim</u> mi sa go raun wantem ol frens go pilai nambaut

I help my parents to do things, <u>sometimes</u> I go round with my friends, go and play around. [East Sepik, M, 15]

Na tupla lukim nau tupla sa sem, <u>sama samting</u> mas rong lo ples

And the two saw it now and they knew that <u>something</u> must be wrong in the village. [West Sepik, M, 16]

The demonstrative ***dispela***, on the other hand, as seen in Chapter 3, does seem to be undergoing considerable reduction and loss of stressed syllables, indicating possible future grammaticalization as a definite marker. It is often used in conjunction with *ol* for plural referents:

Kati(m) leg an bl' em na ed bl' em na o(l)g(et)a samting na ol larim em <u>l' sla ap</u> (long dispela hap) ia.

Cut off his arms and legs and his head and everything and they left him <u>at this place</u>. [Simbu, F, 16]

narapela ankel (b)l' mi em tok osem "Bil, yu kisim, yu kisim <u>sa buk</u> (dispela buk) mi givim yu pinis."

another of my uncles said "Bill, you get <u>this book</u> I gave you." [Morobe, F, 12]

(em) i givim ol ples long <u>ol sla ol man meri</u> long i stap long em.

(he) gave the villages to these people to live in. [Madang, M, 19]

Kaikai nau tupla i trautim <u>ol sla ol fish</u> ol bonim lo faia ia

After eating the two vomited <u>the fish</u> that they had heated on the fire [Manus, F, 16]

The extent of the reduction is indicated in the following table, which shows reduced forms of *dispela*:

Reduction of *dispela*

Form	Number	%
dispela	101	2.2
displa	478	10.2
disla	3101	66.1
dsla	139	3.0
disa	136	2.9
dsa	88	1.9
sla	623	13.3
sa	22	0.5
Total	4688	100.0

This clearly shows a progressive reduction to ***disla*** and ***sla***. The further reduction to ***sa***, however, creates a homophone with the normal reduced form of the habitual aspect marker ***save***, which places a considerable constraint on productive use. If this process were to proceed along these lines, one can extrapolate to the future existence of grammaticalized definite singular and plural markers *sla* and *slol*, but this is only conjecture at present.

It seems, then, that the marking of known, definite or specific nouns by pre-posed reduced forms of *dispela* or post-posed possessives or the particle *ia* is now a regular feature of first language speech.

6.6 Relativization

Mühlhäusler (1985h:415) notes a number of ways of signaling relative clauses. These include the absence of overt markers, often accompanied by distinctive intonation (Wurm 1971), pronominalization with personal pronouns or the relative pronouns *wonem, husat* and *we*, and bracketing with *ia (ya)*. In this section, such relativization strategies in the corpus will be investigated with reference to the findings of more detailed treatments by Romaine (1992a), Siegel (1985a) and Sankoff & Brown (1986).

6.6.1 Standard relativizing structures

The types of relative constructions typical of earlier periods of Tok Pisin were simple juxtaposition or pronominalization (Mihalic 1971). Unmarked relatives occasionally appear in the corpus, although it is perhaps worth noting that these very often involve the use of the word *dai*:

ol man i sa kam singsing na lo moning bai ol i lotu lo disla man i bin dai na go planim.

The people come and sing and in the morning they will have a service for this man who has died and go and bury him. [East New Britain, M, 17]

Tupla mangki na meri lukim desla (= dispela) pasin ankol blo em wokim, tupla lukim na tupla ronowe i go...

The two children saw the kind of thing their uncle was doing and ran away [Western Highlands, M, 15]

tupla brata mama i bin dai na tupla stap wantaim papa tasol.

two brothers whose mother had died were staying with their father [Western Highlands, F, 15]

Em nau ol i karim man ia nau ol i go troim em lo solwara, disla man ol i mumuim em na i dai.

Then they carried the man and threw him into the sea, this man who they had cooked and who had died [New Ireland, M, 12]

More often, relative clauses are introduced by *em* or the appropriate personal pronoun:

... i kam lo prifeks em ol i bin votim mi olsem Skul Vais Kepten...

... came to the prefects who elected me school Vice-captain [Eastern Highlands, F, 14.]

na disla ailan nogat man i sa go. I gat wanpla lapun meri em sa stap long hap.

And nobody went to this island. There was one old woman who stayed there. [East New Britain, M, 12]

"san yupla no ken go aut i gat pik osem desla (= dispela) pik em sa kaikai ol man em sa raun."

"During the day you mustn't go out, there is a pig, this pig which eats people going around." [Madang, M, 17]

i gat sampla ol militens em ol faitman blo Bogenvil i bin sta(p) lo rod

there were some militants, who are fighters from Bougainville, on the road. [East New Britain, M, 14]

6.6.2 Relative pronouns: *husat* and *we*

According to Bailey & Maroldt (1977:51), the English interrogative pronouns *who?* and *where?* acquired the function of relative pronouns during the Middle English period under the influence of French, although it may be that they had this function in Old English. It appears that a similar adoption of a relativizing function for the interrogatives *husat?* and *we?* is in progress in Tok

Pisin. As noted above, some syntactic means of relativization have been adopted which do not involve the use of relative pronouns. However, the pronouns *husat* and *we* are being increasingly used, especially in written Tok Pisin. Long complex sentences including these relative pronouns are becoming a common feature of the formal register of *Tok Pisin* now typical of *Wantok* newspaper reports, as reported in Siegel (1981). Siegel (1985a) further discusses the proliferation of the use of *we* and *husat* as relativizers in media Tok Pisin, as exemplified by the following:

Ol man husat i gat dispela sik bilong bia i ken ringim Alkoholiks Anonimas

Men who are alcoholics can ring Alcoholics Anonymous

i gat planti ples balus we Des 7 balus na ol liklik balus nabaut i save pundaun long en

there are many airstrips where Dash 7 and all sorts of small planes can land (Siegel 1985a:526)

These relative pronouns appear to be related to the English 'where' and 'who' as relativizers, and, although they have become especially popular in news items translated from English (Siegel 1983, 1985a), until recently they appeared to be much less common in spoken Tok Pisin. Mühlhäusler (1985h:416) for example, notes that *husat* as a relative pronoun is normally restricted to varieties in contact with English, and Romaine describes its use as marginal (1992a:297). Aitchison (1981) in her study of several young women in Lae remarked on the use of *we* as a relative pronoun referring to people, which was apparently a new development. However, it is seen in the present corpus that, for some speakers at least, the use of these relative pronouns has become a regular feature of speech also.

Husat

A number of variants of *husat* appear in the main corpus, as interrogative pronoun, relative pronoun, and as a filler *husat ia* while thinking of the identity of a person.

Variants of *husat* in the main corpus

husat	23
usat	90
husaet	3
usaet	4
husait	14
usait	30
huset	1
uset	40
set	4
sat	3

Husat as a relativizer is used exclusively with human referents. Although some informants intuitively rejected the relativizing use of *husat*, considering it a phenomenon of written or Anglicized Tok Pisin, it does appear occasionally in the corpus. The numbers of tokens were fairly small, and in the regional sub-corpora, the following figures were obtained:

Husat and variants as relative pronoun by region

Momase	Highlands	Islands
2	5	5

It is not clear whether the use of *husat* is modeled on English or has evolved through use in discourse. The examples below suggest that the latter is a possibility, and show a route of transition from an interrogative expression not functioning as a relative to a relative expression. The standard use as an interrogative is illustrated by the following:

> *em korosim meri ia, tokim em tok, "<u>usat</u> toki' yu na yu laitim paia na yu wokim smok go lo ap blo mi?"*
>
> It (the *masalai*) was angry with the girl and asked her, "<u>who</u> told you to light a fire and send the smoke to my place?" [East New Britain, F, 16]

In the following four examples, ***husat*** possesses elements of an interrogative meaning and all cases deal with situations in which the identity of a person is being sought:

> *Na mi ka(m) daun lo balus na mi painim <u>usat man bai kisim mi</u> stret lo eapot*
>
> And I got off the plane and looked for <u>who would pick me up</u> at the airport [Eastern Highlands, F, 18]

> *Na mi bin wanda osem usat stret raitim disa leta*
>
> And I wondered <u>who had written this letter</u> [Manus, F, 16]

> *ol i tokim wanpla meri na osem bai stap lo gaden na was inap bai painim <u>usat man bai kam</u> na kisim ol kaikai*
>
> They told a woman to stay in the garden and watch to find out <u>who would come</u> and take the food [East New Britain, M, 18]

> *lo narapla dei ol plen osem ol bai traim (l)o ketsim <u>husat tru sa kam</u> lo haus na sa klinim haus blong ol*
>
> On another day they planned to catch <u>who it was who came</u> and cleaned their house [West Sepik, F, 17]

In the following, the structure is similar, but the identity of the referent is known:

> *Taim apinun tupla brata i kam, tupla i bin hamamas nogut tru lo lukim <u>husat i bin klinim haus blong tupela.</u>*
>
> When the two brothers came in the afternoon they were very happy to see <u>who had cleaned</u> their house. [Manus, F, 15]

In the next examples, however, ***husat*** refers to an antecedent noun phrase, where the identity of the party in question is known, and there are no interrogative connotations.

> *mipla i go kisim kar blo wanpla ankol na loudim olgeta disla olgeta <u>ol man usat bin bagarap</u> lo eksident*
>
> We went and got a car from our uncle and loaded up all the people <u>who were injured</u> in the accident [Eastern Highlands, M, 18]

> *Brata blo JP <u>usat i bin stap</u> ... wantem ol manggi hia lo Papitalai vilidj*
>
> JP's brother <u>who stayed</u> with the boys here in Papitalai village [Manus, M, 15]

> *tupla manmeri <u>usat i sawe kilim man</u> na dai tupla bin kechim boi ia*
>
> a couple <u>who killed people</u> caught the boy [Eastern Highlands, M, 17]

> *edmasta kolim neim blong ol pikinini nambaut na osem ol greid seven tu nain <u>usat bai ksim prais bl' ol</u>*
>
> the headmaster called the names of the children, like the grade seven to nines <u>who would get prizes</u> [Southern Highlands, F, 14]

One or two interesting examples suggest that the form ***usat ol*** could become differentiated for plural referents:

> *ol i bin kilim sampla man <u>husat ol i ting</u> olsem ol i wok lo go agensim ol*
>
> they killed some men <u>whom they suspected</u> of going against them [East New Britain, M, 17]

> *Em i kam insait na wok long bungim gen ol man meri na ol pikinini <u>usat ol i biket</u>*
>
> He came inside and met the men women and children again <u>who had disobeyed him</u> [Madang, M, 16]

It is seen that *husat* is used in all regions as a relative pronoun, and although numbers are small, this use seems sufficiently widespread to appear likely to consolidate in the future.

We

We as a relative pronoun is present in both Bislama and Solomons Pijin (Crowley, p c), and it may be an old usage which has survived marginally as a regionalism and been subsequently taken up by younger speakers. Alternatively, just as *husat* could have developed from an interrogative pronoun, a similar route is posited for the development of *we* as a relative pronoun from *we?* 'in what place?' This transition of functions is illustrated in the following sequence. The use of *we?* in clause final position is the most common way to enquire about location:

> *wanpla rat kam na em tok "ai poroman yu go we?" em tok osem.*
>
> A rat came and said "hey friend, where are you going?" [Enga, F, 12]

As a relative pronoun, *we* is also very often associated with location, often in collocation with *ples*, *hap* or a similar locative expression:

> *Em suwim em i go insait lo mambu na haitim i stap antap long ples we ol sa putim faia lo em*
>
> he pushed it into the bamboo and hid it above the place where they put the fire [Eastern Highlands, M, 17]

> *em no bin save olsem disla hap em wanpla baret we wara sa ron*
>
> he didn't know that this place was a drain where water flowed [East Sepik, M, 16]

> *yu go lo disla ples we yu waswas*
>
> you go to this place where you wash [Eastern Highlands, F, 16]

> *Em wokbaut i go i go i go nau em abrisim ap we brata blong em i go longen ia*
>
> He walked and walked and passed the place where his brother went [Manus, F, 15]

The next set of examples shows what appears to be an extension of the function - the use of *we* in relative clauses which do not have a clearly locative function, but qualify an inanimate or non-human animate being without referring to its position:

> *em kisim narapla antil em finisim olgeta disla karuka we bikpla brata blo em bin putim*
>
> he took another until he finished off the pandanus nuts which his big brother had put (there) [Eastern Highlands, M, 19]

> *yu go kisim kokonas we i no drip, i no kulau, em mas jast - a rait -wanem sais*
>
> You go and get a coconut which is not too young, not ready for drinking, it must be just the right size [Manus, M, 13]

> *dedi blo mi bin lukim wanpla krokodail we em i traim lo atekim mipla*
>
> my father saw a crocodile which tried to attack us [Manus, F, 14]

> *... ol militan kam antap long wata saplai tenk ia we wata i save saplaim ol man long Noth Solomon...*
>
> the militants went up to the water tank which supplies water to the people of North Solomons [Western Highlands, M, 16]

Finally, human referents, too, may be relativized using *we*:

> *dens wok lo ko (=go) gutpla tasol i kat (= gat) ol sampla man we ol i spak i stap namel.*
>
> The dance was going well, but there were some men who were drunk among them [Manus, M, 13]

> *Olsem ol man we ol nogat wok ol stap nating long taun ol i wokim ol raskol pasin, ol i stil, burkim stua na raun raun nating*
>
> So men who have no work hang around in town and get involved in criminal activities, they steal, break into shops and just wander around. [East New Britain, M, 19]

Long agou i gat - i gat wanpla meri we em i liv aloun long wanpla peles.

Long ago there was a woman <u>who lived alone</u> in a village. [Manus, M, 13]

disla lapun man, em papa bl' em we elpim em

this old man, it was his father <u>who helped him</u>

bai mi go na maretim disla man we sta lo disla haus ia

I will go and marry the man <u>who lives in this house</u> [Eastern Highlands, F, 15]

Lo disla ples i ga(t) wanpla sangguma man we i sa kilim ol man nambaut na man lo ples.

In this village there was a sorcerer <u>who killed people</u> including the village men. [West Sepik, M, 17]

Aitchison (1981:205) remarked upon this as an innovation in Lae, but the above examples show occurrences throughout the country. Its use was particularly noticeable in corpus samples from the Manus Province, and a regional breakdown shows that the spread is not even. The table below shows the total number of tokens of *we* as a relative pronoun in the regional sub-corpora, and further shows use in locative constructions such as *ples we* 'the place where', with human referents and with non-human referents in non-locative contexts:

We as a relative pronoun

	Momase	Highlands	Islands
total *we* as relative pronoun	36	50	84
use in locative contexts	23	28	27
use with human referents	5	8	26
use with non-human referents	8	14	31

It can be seen that the use of relative pronouns is generally greater in the Islands region according to these figures, and particularly so for non-locative contexts, especially where the referent is human. Thus it appears that the use of relative pronouns is a significant feature of first language speech. This could be influenced by the lexifier, English, or could be due to independent development or substrate influence, as suggested by the extension of the use of *we* to human referents. It should be noted that the English relative 'who', while not dissimilar in phonological shape to the Tok Pisin *we*, is not used at all, suggesting that independent development or substrate explanations may be more convincing than straight borrowing from English.

6.6.3 The particle *ia* in relative clause delimitation

The particle *ia* (also spelled *ya* and *hia* in some references), presumably derived from 'here', has a number of functions. The only one described by Mihalic is that of adding a verbal exclamation on to a statement:

Man Goroka i ples kol ya!

Golly, Goroka is a cold place [Mihalic 1979:206]

Dutton (1973) does not separate the particle from the adverbial *hia*, but does footnote the observation that it has other functions in discourse (1973:90).

Apart from use as an exclamatory particle, *ia* is commonly used for anaphoric reference. This can be particularly useful in disambiguation, considering the problems of identifying the referent of the third person singular pronoun *em*, which is unmarked for gender or case. Thus subsequent mentions of particular persons will often appear as *man ia* or *meri ia*, rather than the pronoun *em*, as noted in § 6.5:

em i lukim wanpla lapun man em stap tasol na lo arere lo faia ... na lapun man ia kirap na tok ...

he saw an old man alone beside the fire... the old <u>man (already mentioned)</u> said ... [Eastern Highlands, F, 14]

Such anaphoric use of *ia* is now well established in written *Tok Pisin*, and also frequently heard in the written-like style of the National Broadcasting Corporation's news broadcasts in *Tok Pisin*. *Ia* also commonly adopts exophoric reference in typical replies to letters to *Wantok Niuspepa*. The following example is from Lomax's study:

> *Mi laik bekim pas bilong <u>brata ya</u> Mathew Minape*
>
> I would like to reply to <u>this man</u> Mathew Minape (Lomax 1983:24)

Other instances of the use of *ia* indicate more general deixis (Sankoff & Brown 1976) and a role in indicating focus discussed more fully below in § 6.8.

With such a multiplicity of functions, *ia* is likely to be subject to reinterpretation. Sankoff & Brown's landmark paper "Origin of syntax in discourse" (1976) first pointed out the emergence of *ia* as a bracket to mark off relative clauses, demonstrating how discourse features can come to be reanalyzed and adopt a syntactic role. They found that both the head noun and the co-referential noun phrase in such relative constructions can occupy the three basic syntactic positions: subject, complement and oblique (1980:212). A typical example is given below:

> *Dispela <u>man ia, lek bilong en idai ia</u>, em istap insait nau*
>
> This man, <u>whose leg was injured</u>, stayed inside. (Sankoff & Brown 1980:213])

This kind of clause bracketing is by no means a universal feature of Tok Pisin, and it is very unlikely to be found in written texts, for example none was found in the written corpus used in Siegel's analysis (1981). It might be expected to be common among first language speakers, and occurrences are indeed found in the present corpus. However, one could gain the impression from Sankoff & Brown's examples of *ia* bracketing, especially those quoted by other writers, that it is a conventional, neat and orderly delimitation of relativized components. In fact, the position of *ia* in relativization appears to be much more messy. Clauses bracketed in the "classic manner" such as in the following extract do occur, but they are in the minority:

> *... <u>trausis ia mi werim ia</u> i no inap long mi ...*
>
> the <u>trousers which I was wearing</u> did not fit [Morobe, F, 12]

> *Na laki tru wanpla liklik redio, <u>stereo ia mitla putim lo kout ia</u>, em no lukim na disla samding stap yet*
>
> Luckily one small stereo <u>radio which we had put in our coat</u> he did not see, and this thing is still here. [East New Britain, M, 16]

More often, one or other of the potentially bracketing occurrences of *ia* is omitted (as Sankoff & Brown acknowledge). In the following two examples, only the first and second *ia* respectively are present:

> <u>*man ia i gat et tasol*</u> *em i stap tamblo lo has blo diwai na <u>man ia i gat lek</u>, houl bodi em i klaimim diwai.*
>
> The <u>man who only had a head</u> stayed below at the bottom of the tree and the <u>man who had legs</u>, a whole body, climbed the tree [East New Britain, M, 16]

> *Disla <u>man kisim pik blo tupla ia</u>, em kam lo haus blo tupla nau, em save lo haus blo tupla na em kam.*
>
> This <u>man who took their pig</u>, he came to their house, he knew their house and he came. [East New Britain, M, 17]

In other cases, the function of *ia* itself is open to question. Often examples of *ia* which at first sight appear to be of this type turn out on closer inspection of the context to be not so clear-cut; they are ambiguous or have an anaphoric or other function. For example, consider the following:

> *ol stap nau, disla <u>pisin ia wok lo lukautim liklik pikinini ia</u> go nau em gro go bikla nau*
>
> they stayed and <u>this bird looked after the small child</u> until he grew big [Enga, F, 14]

At first sight, this might be interpreted as containing a *ia*-bracketed relative clause, meaning 'the bird which looked after the child'. However, on looking at the extract in context, it is more likely that *ia* is used anaphorically in both instances to refer to the child and the bird which have appeared earlier in the discourse. Other examples, too, are not easy to interpret unequivocally.

Often it is difficult to assign an exact function to the particle, which seems to be highly variable, and may merely mark the end of a section of discourse or stress a particular feature:

Wanpla taim ia lo Wapenamanda ia i gat tupla sista, liklik gel osem - liklik gel ia na osem mi

Once upon a time in Wapenamanda there were two sisters, little girls like - little girls just like me. [Enga, F, 12]

Em go ia em lukim ia insait ia man, osem pales ia,

He went and saw it, the interior, wow, it was like a palace [Western Highlands, M, 16]

In other cases, what is delimited may not be a clause at all, but a noun phrase in apposition which serves to define or otherwise qualify the referent:

desla bus ia, renforest ia long Inglis ia ol i save kolim olsem ia...

this forest, rain forest in English, it's called that [Western Highlands, M, 16]

Ankol blo mipla ia Rex ia em kisim mipla

My uncle Rex, took us [Simbu, F, 13]

Em blo Popondeta tsol lilik peles lo - lo disla - klostu lo maunten faia ia Maunt Lamington ia klostu lo em.

He is from Popondetta, a small village near this - near the volcano called Mt. Lamington, close to there [Simbu, F, 13]

In the present corpus, there are nearly 10,000 tokens of *ia* with emphatic, anaphoric and deictic functions as well as use in clause bracketing. This large number makes a comprehensive analysis somewhat difficult. A sample of 100 occurrences from each of the regional samples was thus analyzed to give a rough indication of how the particle is most often used. It was sometimes difficult to separate the functions, especially the anaphoric and deictic, and the category "clause bracketing" is used loosely to include noun phrases in apposition and even adverbial phrases. Thus the following breakdown of the functions of *ia* is somewhat tentative. However, it can be seen that "clause bracketing" only accounts for a small percentage of all occurrences of *ia*, and anaphoric reference is the most common function by far in all regions:

Functions of *ia*

	Momase	Islands	Highlands
	Number (%)	Number (%)	Number (%)
"Clause bracketing"	7	9	9
Anaphoric reference	79	78	63
Emphasis/focus	8	12	24
Other or ambiguous	6	1	4
Total	100	100	100

6.6.4 The use of *longen/long em* in relativization

In locative relative expressions, it can be seen that *we* is often accompanied by a clause-final **longen** or **long em**. As noted in chapter two, in transcriptions of the texts, **longen** and its variants (*logen, loen, len*) were written as a single word, as *-en* does not have an independent existence, as it is always attached as an enclitic to **long** or **bilong**. The *en/em* distinction is the only example of case-marking normally found in Tok Pisin. The usual meaning of **longen** is 'of it' or 'its' or 'to it' or 'to him', etc., as in the following:

mi kirap, mi lap longen nau...

I got up and laughed at him now...'. [New Ireland, F, 14]

This is quite similar to the meaning of **long em**, although, as noted previously, Dutton (1973:39) draws a distinction between *em* and *-en* in terms of emphasis or focus. However, among some speakers in the present corpus, ***longen*** appears to have an additional role in delimiting relative clauses in a significant number of cases. This tendency has also been noted by Mundhenk (1990:354), who states that this form is favoured in *Nupela Testamen* over the use of *we* as a relative pronoun in locative contexts. A typical example is seen in the following extracts from the corpus:

> *em karim tupla i go, putim tupla lo wanpla <u>ples we ol sa putim man lo(n)gen</u>*
>
> he took the two away to a <u>place where they put people</u> (in it) [Eastern Highlands, M, 17]

> *I gat wanpla traipla <u>klab ol sa dens longen</u>*
>
> There was a big club <u>where they danced</u> (in it) [Manus, F, 15]

> *ankol blo em sindaun ... insaid tru long <u>kona we dak longen</u>*
>
> his uncle was sitting right inside in a corner <u>which was dark</u> (at it). [Western Highlands, M, 17]

The use of ***lo(n)gen*** in the examples above clearly refers to a location, but appears to have a secondary clause delimiting role. This is more easily seen in other cases where reference to location is not so easy to demonstrate, and the clause delimiting function appears primary:

> *i man Wabag ia em poisinim em longen ia wokobaut kam i go*
>
> It was the <u>Wabag man who poisoned him</u> approaching [Western Highlands, F, 15]

In the above example, *ia* bracketing as described above also contributes to the delimitation of the relative clause, although in some other examples *ia* is not present:

> *em kam brukim paiawud long bus nau em smelim pik <u>tupla bin kilim longen</u> na em kam klostu*
>
> he came collecting firewood in the forest and he smelled the pig <u>which the two had killed</u> and he approached [East New Britain (ex-Western Highlands), M, 18]

> *Kirap nau wokobaut i go bek, bihainim dispela ol liklik ston <u>tupela bin tromei long rot longen</u>*
>
> He got up and walked back, followed these little stones <u>which they had thrown on the road</u> [Western Highlands, M, 16]

> *na disla pikinini <u>tupla karim lo(n)gen</u> em gutpla pikinini tru*
>
> and this child <u>whom the two bore</u> was a very good child [Eastern Highlands, M, 17]

> *ol lain bl' <u>ol man indai longen</u> sa givim amaunt ol lagim (=laikim) ol baim long em*
>
> the family of the <u>men who die</u> give the amount they want them to pay for him [Southern Highlands, F, 15]

The distinction between ***longen*** and ***long em*** made by some speakers can be clearly seen in the last example, where ***baim long em*** indicates 'pay for him' while ***indai longen*** means 'who die'. The clause delimiting function is rarely seen with ***long em***, although it was found to occur in the extract below, and the distinction is not absolute:

> *em bin go lo disla <u>hap em sa go kechim fish long em</u> na em bin go ait*
>
> he went to the place <u>where he went to catch fish</u> and he hid [East New Britain, F, 14]

The use of ***longen*** in relativization is much more common in certain areas, such as the Highlands in general and Western Highlands in particular. Here it appears to be undergoing semantic bleaching, i.e. losing its semantic content and being grammaticalized as a relative marker. It is difficult to quote exact figures, as frequently there is a certain amount of ambiguity about whether a construction should be construed as a relative or not. Indeed, such ambiguity could have been instrumental in the reinterpretation of the word as a relative marker. When all constructions which could be interpreted as relatives are included, the regional breakdown for ***longen*** relatives is as follows:

Relative clauses with *longen* and variants (*logen, loen*)

Momase	Highlands	Islands
5	63	34

These figures indicate that this construction is found considerably more often in the Highlands samples, and very seldom in the Momase sample.

6.7 Complementation

A number of words are used to introduce complements in Tok Pisin. Woolford (1981) lists *long*, *olsem* and *na* as the main complementizers, while Mühlhäusler (1985e:116) adds *bilong*, *baimbai* and *se* and more recent additions *sapos* and *we* in creolized varieties (1985e:153). This list represents a variety of word types: prepositions, adverbs, conjunctions and serial verb constructions, which have presumably developed during discourse to adopt the role of complementizer. Woolford (1981) has suggested a route for this development by a process of syntactic reanalysis. For example, in the following sentence (Woolford 1981:130), such reanalysis may not alter the surface appearance of the text.

ol (i no) save long ol i mekim singsing

they (neg) knew about/that they would have a dance.

She likewise suggests a similar route for the reanalysis of *olsem* from an adverb to a complementizer, which is a reasonably common process in other languages (1981:134). Similarly the conjunction *na* has been reanalyzed in this way due to its frequent placement before complements. Thus, the sentence *gutpela na yu kam* 'it is good that you have come' would no longer make sense if *na* were to be analyzed merely as a conjunction (Woolford 1981:136), similar to Verhaar's "serial" use of *na* (1991b). Woolford notes that there is no obvious similar route for the development of *we* as a complementizer.

6.7.1 Olsem

Of the above words, *olsem* (< *all the same as*) appears to be the most widely used, and this is by far the most common complementizer in the present corpus, very often following the verb *tok*. The phrase *tok olsem* can feature *olsem* as both an adverb and a complementizer as shown respectively in the following two examples:

"... *mi bai stap lo aus blo mi*" *em tok <u>olsem</u> na em go.*

"... I will be in my house" he said <u>thus</u> and he went [Simbu, M, 15]

em bin tokim boi Sipik ia <u>tok olsem</u> "yu save lo manggi biarei tu?"

he said to the Sepik boy "do you know the BRA boys?" [Manus, F, 15]

In addition to its use with *tok*, *olsem* is used in conjunction with a variety of other verbs as well:

S(ap)os disla redpla fedha i palai lo het blo yu, em yu mas <u>save osem</u> mi stap laif.

If this red feather flies on to your head, you must <u>know that</u> I am alive. [Manus, M, 14]

Em nau man ia <u>tingting bek osem</u> em bin askim em, na em les lo em.

Now the man <u>remembered that</u> he had asked him and he didn't want him. [West Sepik, M, 16]

mi <u>ting osem</u> taim mi winim skul mi laik tru long stadi long akauntants

I <u>think that</u> when I leave school I really want to study accountancy [Southern Highlands, M, 14]

Rabaul i <u>luk olsem</u> i gutpla ples stret taim mi kamap.

Rabaul <u>looked like</u> it was a good place when I arrived [East New Britain, M, 18]

The term *olsem* occurs very frequently and has a number of reduced variants. The number of occurrences in the full corpus and the regional samples are as follows:

Olsem and variants in corpus and regional sub-corpora

	Full corpus	Momase	Highlands	Islands
olsem	1104	271	371	367
osem	2859	965	958	474
ose	478	269	93	51
sem	349	143	88	75
se	123	37	17	44
s'	10	3	2	3
Total	4923	1688	1529	1014

It can be seen *osem* is the most frequently occurring form in all regions, but that the Momase sample shows a tendency towards greater reduction than the other two regions. It should be noted that reductions of *olsem* create a number of homophones with other words as mentioned in Chapter 3. The word *sem* 'ashamed, shy', for example, is similar in form to a common reduction, and cases of this were removed before the count was made. The extreme reduction *s'* occurs in the corpus for *dispela*, *save* and *stap* as well as for *olsem*, and these too were removed from the count. The above figures, however, do include what may be two forms of *se*, which may represent a convergence of two distinct items, as discussed in the next section.

6.7.2 *Se*

The term *olsem* as a complementizer in Tok Pisin corresponds to *se* in Bislama. Crowley (1989c) notes that the particle *se* in Bislama has a much wider range of functions than *olsem* in Tok Pisin. In addition to its role as a complementizer, it can also function as a copula, transitive verb of locution and interrogative as well as being used in focus constructions. He traces the origins of some of these constructions, noting that the French *c'est* ('it is') may have had an influence as well as the English verb *say*. In Tok Pisin, Crowley (1989c:204) also points to the fortuitous convergence which has led to *olsem* being reduced to *se* in rapid speech. He notes that *se* is otherwise virtually absent in most varieties of Tok Pisin except perhaps in New Ireland.

The present corpus supports Crowley's suggestion that *se* may be a regional feature, although it is not confined to New Ireland. 123 occurrences of *se* are found, some of which are clearly reductions of *olsem* in allegro speech, leaving some 50 tokens of the non-reduced *se*, mostly from the East New Britain, New Ireland or Manus samples. The lack of attestation in the North Solomons and West New Britain provinces could be due to the small size of these samples. Almost two thirds of these tokens of *se* occur immediately following the verbs *ting* 'think' and *tok* 'say', as in the following:

> *Wanpla meri Tolai nau em i bin go skul lo Ostrelia na em i kam bek na em i <u>ting se</u> em nau ia.*
>
> One Tolai girl went to school in Australia and she came back and she <u>thought that</u> she was quite something. [East New Britain, F, 18]

> *liklik brata blo tupla i <u>tok se</u> kaikai bl' ol i stap lo haus kuk*
>
> their little brother <u>said that</u> their food was in the kitchen. [New Ireland, M, 14]

> *Holim pasim em nau na meri ia i <u>ting se</u> em tewel ia na em i pret liklik*
>
> (It) grabbed her and the woman <u>thought that</u> it was a spirit and she was a bit afraid. [East New Britain, M, 18]

> *Ol go bek ken lo taun, chekim bebi blong ol nau ol <u>tok se</u>, "ye bebi blo yupla orait."*
>
> They went back to town and checked their baby and they <u>said</u> "yes, your baby is all right." [New Ireland, M, 12]

Further discussion of the reporting of speech appears in § 7.2.3. As noted by Crowley (1989c), Mihalic (1971) glosses *tingse* as 'to guess' rather than 'to think'. However, in the present corpus, all the occurrences appear to mean 'to think'. The use of *se* with other verbs of locution or intellectual activity is also attested:

brata blong em nau go <u>askim em se</u>, "yu kisim disla ... yangpla meri we?"

his brother went and <u>asked him (thus)</u> "where did you get this young woman?" [New Ireland, M, 12]

ol i <u>save se</u> papa blong ol i no blong ples blo mi olsem na ol i no laik tichim ol pikinini blo mi lo tok ples

they <u>knew that</u> their fathers were not from my place so they did not want to teach my children the local language [East New Britain, F, 19]

Most interesting is the use of *se* to introduce complements unconnected with verbs of locution or intellectual activity:

I <u>bin hepen se</u> wanpla yangpla meri em bin go daun lo wara ...

<u>It happened that</u> a young woman went down to the river ... [East New Britain, F, 15]

So ol man ol i kam bek na ol i <u>painim se</u> displa pik ia i dai na ol bin tok tenkyu tru lo disla tupla brata ia.

So the men came back and <u>found that</u> this pig was dead and they thanked the two brothers very much. [East New Britain, M, 18]

Thus it appears that the use of *se* as a complementizer is not uncommon in first language Tok Pisin. It generally has a restricted distribution in the New Guinea Islands provinces and is most often used in collocation with *ting* 'think' and *tok* 'say', but use with other verbs suggests an extension of its role.

Regional samples are as follows:

Use of *se* by region

Momase	Highlands	Islands
17	1	33

The provincial samples exclude many of the informants on residence criteria, but some figures show the tendency to the use of *se* as complementizer in certain areas. The figures here include some cases where it is difficult to be sure whether *se* is a reduced form of *olsem* or not. The large number from New Ireland Province is the most noteworthy figure.

Use of (unreduced) *se* by province

Momase	West Sepik	6
	East Sepik	1
	Madang	0
	Morobe	4
Highlands	Eastern Highlands	0
	Simbu	0
	Western Highlands	0
	Southern Highlands	0
	Enga	0
Islands	Manus	3
	New Ireland	17
	West New Britain	0
	East New Britain	3
	North Solomons	0

6.7.3 *We*

The use of *we* as a complementizer is rare in the present corpus, and only two tokens can be found:

> *Fransis Ona i tok em i les lo wok. Em i koros wantem ol bisiel (BCL) na em tok we ol no gim em planti mani.*
>
> Francis Ona said he didn't want to work any more. He was angry with BCL (Bougainville Copper Ltd.) and he said that they did not pay enough. [Manus, F, 14]

> *Olsem nau em i tingim wanpla aidia we bai em i pasim yau blong em, bai em i traim chenshim pes blong em liklik.*
>
> So he had an idea that he would tie his ears, to try and change his face a bit. [East Sepik, M, 15]

6.7.4 Other complementizers

The use of *long* and *sapos* in this role appears to be declining. No occurrences of *sapos* as a complementizer were found, and only a single token of *long* with *save* was recorded:

> *nau ol disla man ol kaikai maleo ia, ol i silip na ol i no sae lo wanpla i kamap.*
>
> Now the men who has eaten eels were asleep and they did not know that one had arrived. [East New Britain, M, 12]

The construction *save long* in the corpus is almost totally reserved for the meaning 'know of' or 'know about':

> *Ating em tasol mi save lo disla hap.*
>
> I think that's all I know about this place. [Manus, M, 18]

Where the meaning 'know that' is required, *save olsem* is used instead:

> *Taim tupla wo lo wokbaut i kam, meri ia i no save olsem em man blong em.*
>
> When the two approached, the woman did not know that it was her husband. [Manus, M, 14]

One interesting development is the occasional adoption of *dhet* 'that' from English as a complementizer, of which five tokens were found, representing all three regions:

> *Tasol mipla fainim dhet sapos i kam lo Inglis em i save, ... - em inap lo andastendim mo beta*
>
> But we found that if it switches to English, he knows, he can understand better. [East New Britain, F, 19]

Having gained a foothold, it is likely that a greater role for *dhet* will be seen in the future.

6.8 Focus and topicalization

One consequence of the traditional analysis and description of languages such as Tok Pisin in terms of mainstream grammatical categories is that areas such as focus and topicalization have been given little attention. Focus and topicalization are, however, important features of many languages, including those Austronesian languages which may reasonably be assumed to have made a contribution to Tok Pisin's early development, and those languages which continue to exert an influence on contemporary second language Tok Pisin speakers.

Focus and topicalization generally refer to means of emphasizing important information in a sentence or utterance. They include various means of highlighting the most recent subject of discussion, as opposed to comments about that subject, or new information as opposed to what is already given and understood. The functional grammar of Halliday emphasized the importance of this kind of analysis in English, as seen in his description of theme and rheme in information structure (see e.g. Halliday 1978). While languages such as English may be termed subject-prominent, many other languages such as Chinese languages could be termed topic prominent, as the topic of discussion is usually presented first in spite of basic SVO word order. In Cantonese, for example, the emphasized constituent is fronted as in the following example:

> *fo^2 gai^1 ngoh^5 mei^6 sik^6 gwoh^3 la^1*
>
> fire chicken I not yet eat ever exclamation
>
> I have never eaten turkey

Although these analyses mainly concern information content rather than grammar as traditionally conceived, there are various syntactic means by which focus or topicalization can be communicated. Formally, a distinction is sometimes made between topicalization and focus in terms of the presence or absence respectively of co-indexed pronouns. For example, in the sentence "this boy at our school, yesterday he hit the teacher", the topicalized "this boy at our school" is the referent of "he" which appears in situ. Focus involves emphasis without the presence of such co-indexed pronouns.

Typical focus mechanisms include movement, clefting and the use of specific focus markers. Movement of constituents such as fronting or left- or right-dislocation serve to emphasize the constituent moved from its normally expected position. For example, emphasis can be given to the moved constituents in such sentences as "he's a bit of devil is our Mr. Jones" (right dislocation) or "justice is all we are asking for" (left dislocation or fronting). Clefting is another focusing device well-known from English. For example, in restating the straightforward sentence 'John married Mary' as 'It was Mary that John married', emphasis is given to the importance of Mary in the information presented by splitting the sentence into two, each part with its own verb. Pseudo-clefts are sometimes distinguished from clefts, where a wh- clause is used for similar emphasis, for example, 'what we need is rain'. Recently such clefting mechanisms have received attention in Caribbean Creoles, for example, Lumsden (1990) and Lefebvre & Ritter (1993); and Indian Ocean Creoles (Seuren 1993). Focal particles are not well known in English, but may be important in other languages, including many Austronesian languages, for example a description of Sundanese focal particles (Müller-Gotama 1996), and the Manam (Lichtenberk 1980) and Kilivila (Senft 1986) data cited by Sankoff (1993:134). In the case of Tok Pisin, the most important of these focal particles is *yet*.

6.8.1 Existing studies of focus and topicalization in Tok Pisin

Until the work of Sankoff (1993), focus and topicalization were largely neglected in studies of Tok Pisin. Mihalic (1971) does give one or two examples of recapitulation of pronouns after a subject in his section on idiomatic usages. These appear to be examples of topicalization, but he merely notes that these are "primarily for clarity's sake" (1971:48). Romaine briefly discusses subject focus and object focus in her discussion of relativization (1992a:289), but does not examine focusing strategies in detail. Dutton (1973:131) deals with 'emphatic pronouns' which are followed by *yet*, *tasol* and *wanpela* and reflexives (1973:188). Anticipating Sankoff's discussion of the position of wh-questions, he notes that *watpo*, *westap* and *wasmara* are always placed at the beginning of sentences, which is no doubt related to their role in 'impatient questions' (1973:231).

Similar discussion of these topics appears in Dutton & Thomas (1985). The latter source also mentions "focus" and verb grouping (1985:304), but this is a somewhat different use of the word "focus", used in relation to whether verbs are separated by conjunctions or used in serial constructions. Ross (1985:548) notes that a number of post nominal emphasizers including *tu*, *stret* and *yet* have been adopted from Tok Pisin into a variety of Austronesian languages, describing them as 'replacive', i.e. similar in function to existing focal particles in these languages. Mühlhäusler (1985h:344) also discusses pronoun emphasis with the particles *yet*, *ia*, *tasol* o r *wanpela* and the reflexive with *yet*. Faraclas (1990:115) discusses focal and antifocal pronouns, classifying *i* as a subject referencing pronoun.

In other regional varieties, Shnukal (1988:86) discusses focussing mechanisms in Torres Strait Broken, including fronting of focused objects, subject pronoun repetition and the use of *nau* as a focal particle. Keesing's (1988) extensive discussion of the role of pronouns in Melanesian Pidgin English, especially Solomons Pijin, traces the reanalysis of the resumptive pronouns commonly used in informal English (Hall [1966:83] refers to "substandard English"). According to Keesing's analysis, resumptive pronouns were interpreted as subject referencing pronouns, hence their subsequent inclusion in the verb phrase as a predicate marker, while the English object pronoun 'him' became reanalysed as a focal pronoun. Sankoff (1977b) also reviews this process, whereby what appeared to be topicalization soon lost this function in favour of predicate marking.

Byrne & Winford's landmark volume on focus and grammatical relations in Creole languages (1993) contains references to Tok Pisin by Bickerton, and an important contribution by Sankoff. Bickerton (1993) looks at subject focus with reference to pleonastic or resumptive pronouns in a number of Creoles including Tok Pisin. Bickerton's analysis is a useful synthesis, but deals with Tok Pisin as though it were a unitary whole rather than a complex phenomenon with extreme variability in time and space (although the author does acknowledge in a footnote that there is some variation). It is not clear, for example, whether the examples given are intuitive or taken from actual attestations and thus some of the grammaticality judgments appear to be open to question. For example, the sentence *em i singautim mi i bringim i go wara longen* 'he shouted to me to bring him water' (1993:211) looks decidedly strange from the perspective of most contemporary varieties.

Sankoff (1993) deals with focus and topicalization in some detail, and because of its comprehensive treatment of the subject, this work will be used as the starting point for this discussion. She first reviews word order and fronting, noting that fronting does occur as an occasional departure from the standard SVO order. She also discusses the position of wh- forms, and Woolford's (1979a) assertion that they nearly always appear *in situ*. The use of cleft-like structures involving *em* and their role in focus are also discussed, and related to a similar pattern in Austronesian languages of the region. Her most significant finding is that the particle *yet* is a prominent focus marker, differing from many other Creole markers in that it is postposed. The probable origin is traced to the Tolai *iat*, a multi-functional particle, which appears to have given rise to a generalization of these extra functions to the Tok Pisin equivalent of the English 'yet' through fortuitous phonological resemblance, or what Sankoff (1993:136) calls "a happy surprise". Her findings will be compared with evidence from the present corpus.

6.8.2 Word order

Word order was discussed briefly in § 6.1. It was noted that the canonical word order is SVO, but there is occasional movement for emphasis. As also mentioned above, fronting of emphasized constituents can be accompanied by a replicated pronoun in situ (topicalization) or a zero element (focus) as in the following examples:

Morota mipla putim andap lo trakta, go wanpla manggi statim trakta, mipla kam.

The sago thatch we put on the tractor, then a boy started the tractor and we left. [East Sepik, M, 17]

pipia blen yu sa trome go na yumi sa k(i)sim na kaikai.

The worthless residue (of the food) you throw away and we get it and eat it. (i.e. all we ever get are your crumbs) [Eastern Highlands, M, 14]

Em sindaun i stap nau, *dsla lapun man em* kam na em sindaun i stap

He was sitting down, this old man (he) came and was sitting down [Simbu, F, 16]

Topical constructions such as the last example above appear to be more common in the corpus than focus by fronting as in the first two examples.

6.8.3 Wh- question forms

Sankoff looks at wh- question particles, agreeing with Woolford's (1979a) analysis that they appear in situ most of the time as far as wh- nominals are concerned. In other words, questioned subjects would be expected in subject position and questioned objects post-verbally. However, Sankoff's corpus has some instances of sentence initial wh- + noun phrases, where a post-verbal position would be indicated, as in the following (Sankoff 1993:122):

wonem skul yu givim em?

What schooling did you give him

She interprets this as a probable focus construction, but notes that it always occurs with double object verbs, indicating that this may be a stronger motivation. In the present corpus, there are some 1500 tokens of *wanem* (or *wonem*), but the overwhelming majority of these are used as a filler when thinking of an appropriate word:

pikinini man bl' em ia em wok lo kisim *wonem* bonara wante spia bl' em na em wok lo sutim ol liglig palai na ol grasopa nambaut

his son got his, what's it? his bow and arrow and was shooting at little lizards and grasshoppers. [Madang, M, 16]

Of the remainder, some are used as determiners:

> ... *em no lukim tupla nau, em smelim lek blo tupla, smelim <u>wonem daireksen</u> tupla wok lo go ...*
>
> ... it didn't see the two, it smelled their legs, smelled <u>what direction</u> the two were going ... [Manus, F, 11]

Of the remaining occurrences of *wanem* as a question particle, most are in situ, as in the following examples in subject and object position:

> *em lukim aus bl' em paia na em tok "ai aus blo mi paia ia, <u>wanem samting mekim</u> ia?"*
>
> he saw that his house was on fire and he said "hey, my house is on fire, <u>what caused this</u>?" [Simbu, F, 13]

> *em i go na lapun meri ia i askim em, "yes - yes yangpla, <u>yu laikim wonem</u>?"*
>
> He went on and the old woman asked him "well young man, <u>what do you want</u>?" [East New Britain, M, 12]

However, there are a few cases where movement appears to be for emphasis:

> *long avinun em bin askim em, askim mama blong em "<u>wonem em 'shit'</u>?" Na em tok, "em ia narapla wed lo ... sidaun lo sit".*
>
> In the afternoon he asked his mother "<u>what does 'shit' mean</u>?" And she said "it's just another word for 'sit on a seat'." [New Ireland, M, 12]

> *... disla ples em rits long kain kain kaikai. <u>Wonem kain kaikai yu nemim</u> em rits ...*
>
> this place was rich in all kinds of food. <u>Whatever kind of food you name</u>, it was rich [Eastern Highlands, M, 17]

In the case of wh- adverbials, Sankoff notes that the position appears to be specific to the lexical items concerned (1993:123). While *we*, *olsem wanem* and *long wanem* usually appear post-verbally, *watpo* and *bilong wanem* are normally found in sentence-initial position. In the exceptional case involving *we (stap)* in initial position, Sankoff interprets this as being due to a long following relative clause. *Watpo* is considered an archaism or possible regional variant. However, as noted above, Dutton has identified a number of what he terms 'impatient' questions, *westap*, *watpo* and *wasmara*, where there sentence-initial position is presumably for rhetorical emphasis. Unfortunately the present corpus cannot shed any light on this question, as none of these forms are attested in the speech of these informants; the only collocation of *we* and *stap* involves *we* as a relative pronoun:

> *"... bai mi go na maretim disla man <u>we sta(p)</u> lo disla haus ia."*
>
> "... I will go and marry the man <u>who lives</u> in this house." [Eastern Highlands, F, 15]

An analysis of other wh- adverbial question forms (including phonological variants) in the present corpus is summarized in the following table:

Position of wh- question adverbials

	Tokens	Initial		Postverbal	
		Number	%	Number	%
we?	133	2	1.5	131	98.5
bilong wanem?	36	36	100	0	0
long wanem?	7	0	0	7	100
olsem wanem?	16	1	6	15	94

It can be seen that these figures strongly support Sankoff's findings. The position of individual items appears to be almost categorical, and the main comment here concerns an explanation for exceptional positions.

In the case of *we*, of the 400 or so occurrences in the corpus, over two thirds were relative pronouns. *We?* as a question particle sometimes occurred in collocation with *long* as *long we?* and *nau* as *we nau?* It can be seen from the table that the overwhelming majority of occurrences were in postverbal position, as in:

> *Em nau em kirap nau em tokim em "na displa sneik sa stap lo <u>we</u>?"*
>
> So he asked her "and <u>where</u> does this snake live?" [East New Britain, M, 12]

In many cases, *we* indicates 'is/are where' without the presence of another verb, and these are included in the above figures:

> *... tupla pikinini ia tok "mama blo mitupla <u>we</u>?"*
>
> ... the two children said "<u>where</u> is our mother?" [Simbu, F, 16]

The only two exceptions were the following:

> *Lo avinun em kam nau em tokim - askim brata, liklik brata blo em, uset Airina na tok, "<u>we</u> ol karuka we aste mitupla kisim?"*
>
> In the afternoon he came and said - asked his brother, his younger brother, who's that Airina "<u>where</u> are the pandanus nuts that we collected yesterday?" [Eastern Highlands, M, 19]

> *meri bloen tsol sa stap na em sa askim "<u>we</u> liklik brada blo mi?"*
>
> only his wife was there and he asked her "<u>where</u> is my younger brother?" [Enga, F, 12]

In the first case, it is evident from the intonation that the question is asked in an impatient tone, and this is thus a possible example of focal dislocation. In the second, as with some of the other Enga samples, there are a number of departures from usual conventions, including the use of *sa* for what are clearly punctual rather than habitual events. However, this too could be fronting for emphasis of a question forcefully or impatiently asked. Notwithstanding these exceptional cases, it is clear that *we* is almost categorically post-verbal for most speakers.

Bilong wanem? as a question is placed in initial position in all samples attested in the corpus apart from two cases where *bilong wanem* was used in isolation:

> *Na disla frog kirap na tok osem "ei, yu kam, yu kam klostu pastem." Na gel ia tok "<u>blo wanem</u>?"*
>
> And this frog said "hey, you come, come close". And the girl said "<u>why</u>?" [Simbu, F, 15]

Otherwise, the categorical position was as in the following example:

> *na displa man tok osem "<u>blo wonem yu laik</u> kam hait lo haus blo mi?"*
>
> and the man said "<u>why did you want</u> to come and hide in my house?" [Manus, F, 13]

Occasionally, the word *na* follows *bilong wanem* (12 occurrences in the corpus):

> *... em singaut "yutla kam daun. Yutla meri blo mi, <u>blo wonem na</u> yutupla ranawe?"*
>
> He called out "you (two) come down. You are my wives, <u>why</u> did you run away?" [West Sepik, F, 15]

Sankoff (1993) cites ***long wanem*** as a question form, but in the present corpus *long wanem* usually indicates 'because' and *bilong wanem* 'why?', although it is not always easy in allegro speech to distinguish the two. There were six cases of the use of *bilong wanem* meaning 'because'. Out of 155 tokens of *long wanem* in the corpus, only 7 had the meaning 'why'. Of these, all occurred postverbally, as in the following:

> *em pairapim haus bl' ol nau, em tok "hei ol meri, yupla slip <u>l' wonem</u>? Bus graun bl' yupla na yupla slip ia?"*
>
> He shouted into their house "hey, you women, <u>why</u> are you sleeping? Is this your own land for you to sleep on?" [West Sepik, F, 12]

Of the 16 tokens of *olsem wanem* 'how?', all but one were clause-initial, which appears to be the definitive position. The exception, in a story from New Ireland, appeared to be a case of emphasis for rhetorical effect, as other occurrences of *olsem wanem* (*wonem*) by the same speaker were clause-initial. However, the exceptional case was also used with a clause which was long and complex, similar to Sankoff's example of a fronted *wanem*, and this may also have been a factor:

> *Em kirap i askim "yu kam <u>olsem wonem</u>?"*
>
> He asked "<u>how</u> did you get here?"

Kisim disla meri nau, tupla go lo aus nau brada blongen askim, "yu kisim disla meri <u>olsem wonem</u>?"

He got the girl and the two went to the house and his brother asked "<u>how</u> did you get this girl?"

... (em i) go bek nau lo peles nau brata blen askim "<u>olsem wonem yu gat</u> wonem ia kukamba i cheinj osem gutpla meri tu?"

(he) went back to the village and his brother asked "<u>how did you get</u> the cucumber to change into a nice girl?" [New Ireland, F, 14]

6.8.4 The role of *em*

Dutton (1973:39) draws a distinction between a stressed or emphasized *em* and an unemphasized *en* in such expressions as ***bilum bilong em*** and ***bilum bilong en***. This is a useful distinction, but does not appear to be made consistently in this corpus. Sankoff notes that, whatever their origin, the *i* predicate marker and *-im* suffix now do not have a role in marking topicalization or object case, and that it is now the pronouns *em* and *ol* which mark topic changes. She notes that *em* frequently expressed more than the third person singular pronoun (1993:129) including replies to yes-no questions, hesitations, equative sentences and use in fixed expressions such as *em nau* and *em tasol*. In addition, *em* sometimes precedes noun phrases in constructions which appear to be similar to clefts in English as in the following example:

Nogat, em wantok i putim long maunten ia

No, it was my friend who was wearing it on the mountainside [Sankoff 1993:130]

However, Sankoff's analysis of her Buang material showed that this type of focus construction was not common among adult speakers, and almost completely absent among younger speakers. A look at the present corpus supports Sankoff's suggestion that *em* as a focal construction is not particularly common, although instances can readily be found of the '*em*-cleft' type of construction.

Equative sentences appear to be the source of such focal constructions, and equatives beginning with *em* are not uncommon:

Mama blong em dai pinis, <u>em tewel blo mama</u> blong em tasol

Her mother was dead, it was only her <u>mother's spirit</u> [Madang, F, 12]

Cleft-like structures where *em* introduces a relative clause are less common, but do appear regularly throughout the samples from all regions:

tasol ol man lo ples kira(p) na ol tok "<u>em mama bl' em yet sanggumaim man ia</u> na kilim em indai."

But the village men said "<u>it is his own mother who poisoned the man </u>and killed him." [Simbu, F, 16]

Ol man ron go, o(l) la(ik) paitim masalai, <u>em masalai chenj osem pik</u> i kilim wanpla man ...

The men ran, they wanted to attack the devil, <u>it was the devil who changed into a pig</u> and killed a man ... [Manus, M, 11]

Nau em disla labun meri - <u>em disla save meri kirap nau</u>, em to(k) osem...

Now it was this old women, <u>this wise woman who got up</u> and said... [Simbu, F, 14]

<u>Em disla meri blo disla man ia</u> em i dai ia

<u>It was this man's wife</u> who died [East New Britain, M, 12]

na taim em wogobaut lo rod yet <u>em disla labun meri silip are(re) lo faia</u> em kirap ...

and while she was still walking on the road, <u>it was this old woman who was sleeping beside the fire</u> who got up ... [East Sepik, M, 11]

The following extract shows the fronting of the object *disla tupla bun* 'these two bones', and an apparent cleft with *em disla*:

> *na i tok "disla tupla bun em ba(i) yu kisim i go lo ma(ma) blo yu na ma blo yu ba planim. <u>Em disla bai tanim</u> i go olsem banana blong em."*
>
> and he said "<u>these two bones</u> you should take to your mother and she should plant them. <u>It is these that will turn</u> into a banana." [West New Britain, F, 15]

Em may also be used with plural subjects:

> *ol bin go planim em long peles blo m(i)pla long Noth Kous. <u>Em ol ami bin eskotim</u> em …*
>
> they went and buried him in our village on the North Coast. <u>It was the army who escorted</u> him … [Manus, F, 14]

Thus constructions similar to clefts do appear occasionally in the data.

6.8.5 The particle *yet*

Since *yet* is the principle focus marking mechanism cited by Sankoff, it is worth looking at this and other focal particles in some detail. As noted above, the Tok Pisin *yet* combines some of the meanings of the English 'yet' and the Tolai *iat*, presumably through generalization of the other functions of the Tolai *iat* to the Tok Pisin *yet* adopted from English. The English 'yet' can mean 'still', in the sense of 'still continuing', but is more often used negatively 'not yet' to indicate that something has not happened, or in questions to ask whether something has happened or not. Both these uses occur with Tok Pisin *yet*, and many examples could be found in the present corpus.

1. *yet* meaning 'still':

   > *lo moning tru ol painim em ka(m) na <u>mipla silip yet</u>*
   >
   > very early in the morning they came to look for him and <u>we were still asleep</u> [Simbu, F, 11]

   > *Na tudei i gat displa wara <u>i stap yet</u>…*
   >
   > And today this stream <u>is still there</u>… [Manus, M, 13]

   > *na i tokim em, "no ken go kisim displa i tamblo ia i - i mau pinis ia, go kisim displa <u>i yangpla yet</u>."*
   >
   > and told him "don't get the one underneath that is ripe, go and get this one which <u>is still young</u>" [New Ireland, M, 12]

   > *long naintin eiti nain, taim <u>mi stap manggi yet</u> ati(ng) lo greid fo, mi mi bin lukim wanbla djingka*
   >
   > In 1989, when <u>I was still a young boy</u>, I think in grade 4, I saw a jinker (large timber truck) [West Sepik, M, 16]

2. *yet* with negative, meaning 'not yet'

   > *mipla bin kam kamap long nait na mipla bin, mi <u>no bin save yet</u> long taun i luk olsem wonem na <u>mi no save yet</u> long ol ples long Kevieng*
   >
   > We arrived at night and we - I <u>didn't yet know</u> what the town looked like and I <u>wasn't yet familiar</u> with the villages around Kavieng [New Ireland, M, 16]

   > *em tok "mitla weitim man blo mi. Man blo mi <u>no kam yet</u>."*
   >
   > She said "we are waiting for my husband. My husband <u>has not come yet</u>." [Western Highlands, M, 16]

   > *Long bipo tru ailan Ali <u>i no kamap yet</u>…*
   >
   > Long ago Ali island <u>was not formed yet</u>… [West Sepik, M, 15]

   > *tapos bik moning, nambawan kakaruk <u>i no karai yet</u> yutupla kisim ol bombom…*
   >
   > when it is very early in the morning, when the first rooster <u>hasn't crowed yet</u>, get coconut fronds… [East New Britain, M, 12]

> *Nau olgeta samting redi tasol ol <u>no paini(m) abus yet</u>, so ol - ol man wok lo go*
>
> Now everything was ready but they <u>hadn't found any meat yet</u>, so they all went (hunting) [Eastern Highlands, F, 15]

3. *Yet* in questions was very uncommon. Only one example was found:

> *em tok poro bl' em "wanpla kona <u>stap yet a</u>?" Na em to "<u>i no yet</u>."*
>
> He asked his friend "is there still another corner?" And he said "not yet." [East Sepik, M, 12]

The extra function of the Tolai particle *iat* suggested by Sankoff as the source of the use of *yet* as a focal particle gives emphasis, usually to a pronoun, and can often be translated as the equivalent of 'himself', 'ourselves' or 'my own', 'our own', etc. The following are examples of this kind of emphasis involving *yet*:

> *em kisi(m) liklik brada bl' em na lukautim osem pikinini <u>blong em yet</u>*
>
> He took his little brother and looked after him like <u>his own</u> child [Southern Highlands, F, 15]

> *man blo meri ia tok "mi lusim yu nau, <u>yu yet</u> yu les lo mi."*
>
> the woman's husband said "I'm leaving you now, <u>you yourself</u> are tired of me." [Madang, F, 14]

> *lo peles ol i kolim Lengmundrau em lo hap blo <u>mipla yet</u>*
>
> at the village called Lengmundrau, that's <u>our own</u> place [Manus, M, 13]

> *papa blo mi em stap lo narapla aus blong <u>em yet</u>*
>
> My father stayed in another house, <u>his own</u> house [West Sepik, F, 13]

> *sa(po)s ol tokples blo <u>mipla yet</u> lo Rabaul em mi ken sawe*
>
> If they speak <u>our own</u> language in Rabaul then I can understand [New Ireland, M, 12]

Sankoff notes that the use of *yet* in this way is restricted to pronouns in her corpus, and does not occur as a focal particle with nouns, although she admits that "to my ear, the use of *yet* with full nouns sounds fine" (1993:131). Some examples from the present corpus suggest that Sankoff's ear may have been reliable after all, and indicate that the use of *yet* to intensify nouns is indeed possible:

> *wanpla pupu - pupu blo <u>peles yet</u> i kam nau i kam askim tupla...*
>
> an old man from <u>the village itself</u> came and asked the two... [New Ireland, M, 12]

> *em go kaikai na tupla <u>tambu yet</u> stap lo haus*
>
> he went to eat and two <u>in-laws themselves</u> were in the house [Enga, F, 14]

> *disla pilai bai sa go on olgeta taim tasol bai sa go long <u>wanwan ilektoret yet</u> o wanwan ples*
>
> these games will go on all the time, but they will go only to <u>some electorates</u> or some villages [East New Britain, M, 19]

> *Em sa trikim ol na ol sa ting ol <u>brada yet</u> na em sa stap.*
>
> He fools them and they think they are <u>really brothers</u> and he stays there [Southern Highlands, M, 18]

> *ol <u>ami yet</u> ol kam na olgeta ol ami, eitpla kar olgeta ol kam*
>
> the soldiers <u>(by) themselves</u> came and all the soldiers, eight cars all together came [Simbu, F, 15]

In the last example, *yet* 'themselves' appears to be more than mere emphasis, and seems to imply 'only themselves' or 'by themselves', as it was in direct reply to a question about whether police came with the soldiers or not.

It should also be noted that a competing emphatic form derived from the English 'own' is occasionally heard. The two tokens in the corpus are given below. Note that the word order follows that of the expression borrowed from English with the emphatic modifier before the noun:

tupla brada ia tok ose ba tupla kisi(m) tupla susa ia ose(m) meri blo tupla nau ol fopla marit na ol kamapim <u>oun ples blo ol</u>

the two brothers said they would get two sisters and marry them and the four got married and founded <u>their own village</u>. [East Sepik, F, 16]

ol bin kisim ol man lo vilidj, lo peles blo mipla na ol wok long lainim ol lo tokples blong ol na singsing na lotu long ol god giaman blong ol, long <u>oun tokples blong ol</u>.

They (the Japanese) took the men to the village, to our village and they set about teaching them their language and songs and religious rituals to their false gods in <u>their own language</u>. [East New Britain, M, 18]

The use of *yet* with pronouns includes a purely reflexive as well as focal function. Use as a reflexive differs from the emphatic or focal use in that *yet* is an essential argument to the verb, as in the English 'he looked at him<u>self</u> in the mirror'. However, Mühlhäusler points out that *yet* is often omitted in reflexives if *-im* verbs without an object are used, as in *tel bilong kapul i hukim long diwai* 'the possum's tail hooked itself on a branch' (1985h:345).

Examples of a reflexive use of *yet* from the corpus include the following:

liklik brata i wok wanda hau na brata blen i sa painim planti fish. Biain em - <u>em bin askim em yet</u> na em bin tok osem wanpla taim bai em i go na i go lukluk stil

the little brother wondered how his brother caught so many fish. Later <u>he asked himself</u> and he said one time he would go and spy [East New Britain, F, 14]

na tupla katim dilim ol mit blo pik <u>go lo tupla yet</u>...

and the two cut and gave the pieces of pork <u>to themselves</u> [Madang, F, 12]

<u>tupla kukim tupla yet</u> insait lo pot nau tupla bin dai

<u>the two cooked themselves</u> inside the pot and died [New Ireland, M, 12]

tupla kisi(m) olgeta samting, lusim ol ples ia wantem ol lain ia na tupla go stap <u>blo tupla yet</u>

the two got their things, left their villages and their families and went to live <u>by themselves</u> [East Sepik, F, 16]

em traim stret lo <u>rausi(m) em yet</u> lo rop go, <u>em rausi(m) em yet</u> lo limbum pinis

he tried hard to <u>free himself</u> from the rope, <u>he freed himself</u> from the palm sheath [West Sepik, F, 17]

Calquing of borrowed expressions may also be involved, as in the following example, where the reflexive use of *yet* appears to have been derived from the English expression 'enjoyed ourselves'

mipla waswas nais stret, mipla <u>endjoyim mipla yet</u> stret

we had a nice swim, we really <u>enjoyed ourselves</u> [East Sepik, F, 15]

The final use of the particle *yet* is as an intensifier to adverbs or adjectives. It was fairly uncommon (see table below), and used mainly in collocation with the words *bipo* and *mo*.

<u>Long taim bifo yet</u> i gat wanpla yangpla meri

<u>Long ago</u> there was a young girl [Southern Highlands, F, 15]

em testim ia, man, i swit <u>mo yet</u>

he tasted it, man, it was <u>exceptionally</u> tasty [Eastern Highlands, M, 18]

Biain em bin drink na em bin teistim wara blen i <u>swit mo mo yet</u>

Later he drank and tasted it - its liquid was <u>very sweet</u> [East New Britain, F, 14]

Although this intensifying function usually accompanies adjectives or adverbs, there are cases where this is not strictly the case, as in the following, where the nominal compound *bikmoning* refers to the early morning, although it could be argued that *yet* intensifies the whole of the adverbial phrase:

Papa blo em go lo bikmoning yet, em i go lo bus

His father went <u>very early in the morning</u>, he went to the bush [West Sepik, M, 13]

Sankoff notes (1993:132) that for four groups of speakers in her corpus the function of *yet* has changed over time, from a preponderance of uses as a 'temporal negative polarity' item (i.e. 'not yet') through 'still' to its present most common application as a focal or intensifying particle with the negative function dropping out of use. It would be illuminating to compare the various functions of *yet* in the present corpus. Out of 811 recorded instances of *yet* the breakdown of the different functions is seen in the following table.

Functions of *yet*

Function	Number	Percentage
focus	359	44.3
'still'	291	35.9
'not yet'	91	11.2
reflexive	41	5.1
adv./adj. intensifier	27	3.3
unclassified	2	0.2
Total	811	100.0

A number of observations need to be made here. Over 80% of occurrences involve the focal or continuous function, although 'not yet' is still frequently attested. As noted, the focal use is not limited to pronouns, but occurs with nouns as well. Focus on pronouns appears to have led to some specialization in meaning, implying 'by oneself' or 'alone' as well as 'one's own' or unspecified emphasis. In some cases, this 'by oneself' meaning also seems to occur with nouns followed by *yet*:

em daunim tupla - fopla olgeta, em daunim olgeta na em kaikaim ol nau noga(t) man sa sta(p) lo disla ailan. <u>Krokodail yet sta(p)</u>...

it (crocodile) swallowed all two - four, it swallowed them all and it ate them all and now there were no people left on the island. <u>The crocodile stayed by itself</u>. [Morobe, F, 12]

The most common focal use involving nouns is with places:

ol bin dens nau na <u>ol man lo Los Nigros yet</u> ol bin gat kros l' wanpla man we em sa wok long - em seila blong ol difens.

they were dancing and <u>the men from Los Negros itself</u> got cross with a man who worked with - he was a sailor with the Defence Force. [Manus, F, 15]

With a multiplicity of functions, the possibility of ambiguity arises. However, ambiguity appears to be avoided by the context in which *yet* appears. Occurrences following noun phrases are almost always focal, while those following verbs are usually continuous, especially in the common collocation *stap yet*. Use as an intensifying particle is limited to certain lexical collocations, such as *bipo yet* and *moa yet*. Occasionally further disambiguation is provided by additional signalling, such as the use of *stil* to indicate continuity, or the phrase *bilong em yet* to indicate 'by himself':

na nau yu go andap bai yu lukim disla ston i <u>stil stap yet</u> sheip blo man na dok.

And now if you go up there you will see that this stone <u>is still there</u> in the shape of a man and a dog. [East Sepik, M, 16]

ol no totok wantem disla meri ia, na meri ia belat na em go stap <u>blong em yet</u>.

They didn't talk to this woman, and she was upset and went to stay <u>by herself</u>. [Morobe, F, 13]

Out of the 800 or so occurrences, only a very few appeared to be ambiguous:

Ating mi no save lo sampla hap blo Rabaul <u>yet</u>.

I think I don't know some of the places around Rabaul <u>itself/yet</u> [East New Britain, M, 17]

Nau mama blong ol i tok "yupla no nap kilim em, em bikpla stret ia." Tasol tupla <u>strong strong yet</u> *na ol tok osem, "bai mipla traim tasol."*

And their mother said "you can't kill it, it's too big." But the two <u>insisted really strongly/still insisted</u> and said "we'll just try." [East New Britain, M, 11]

em go anta(p) lo kisim pikinini blo frut ia. Em go <u>antap yet</u> *na wanpla man blo ples em kam...*

he climbed up to get the fruit. He <u>climbed right up/was still climbing</u> and a village man came [Madang, M, 13]

Na em luki(m) tupla <u>longwe yet</u> *na em sa(v)e ose(m) em papa na mama blo em*

She saw them from <u>very far away/still a long way away</u> and she knew that it was her parents [West Sepik, F, 15]

This kind of ambiguity presumably served as the raw material on which generalization of the different functions of *yet* developed.

6.8.6 Other focussing devices

Sankoff also notes the use of other intensifiers, such as *tru*, *moa* and *stret*, with adverbials but not with nominals (1993:132). Other particles to which a focal role has been attributed include *ia* (Mühlhäusler 1985h:344), *nau* (Shnukal 1988:86) and *tasol* (**Dutton** 1973:131). These particles are all well attested in the corpus, as seen below. The numbers of tokens represent the following words only when used with an emphasizing, focal or intensifying function:

Intensifying particles

Item	Tokens
tru	1020
stret	541
tasol	80
moa	59

Although Sankoff precludes the use of *stret* and *moa* with nominals, there are one or two occurrences which do suggest a focal role with nominals:

(kaskas) stailim em nabaut lo bus na tok osem, "<u>mi mo, mi mo</u>*." Wanpla taim nau dok i harim stori na i kirap na i tok osem "okei* <u>yu mo,</u> *tasol yu tingting yumi no pefekt, yumi olgeta i no pefekt."*

(the cuscus) groomed himself in the bush and said <u>"I'm the one, I'm the one."</u> Once the dog heard about this and said "okay, <u>you are the one</u>, but remember that we are not perfect, nobody's perfect." [New Ireland, M, 12]

Bipo okei pait ia em kamap wes tru long ol ailans na <u>ol ples blo mi stret</u>*.*

Before the fight became worse in the islands and <u>our own villages.</u> [Madang, M, 17]

yu no stap wantem ol papa mama o <u>ol perents blo yu stret</u>

you don't live with <u>your own parents</u>. [Eastern Highlands, M, 16]

The use of *stret* and *moa* above appears very similar to the use of *yet*, and could be a generalization from one intensifier to another.

The particle *ia (ya)* has a number of functions, notably in relative clause bracketing and anaphoric reference, as discussed above, but also has a role in emphasis. Mühlhäusler (1985h:344) gives an example which is remarkably like a cleft in this translation:

Em ya i bagarapim meri bilong mi

It is he who assaulted my wife

However, there are other possible explanations, such as interpreting *ya (ia)* as an emphatic particle similar to those in some Austronesian languages. A number of examples where a cleft appears to be introduced by *ia* can be found in the corpus:

(pisin) tokim ol olgeta olsem, "usait toknogutim mi?" Na ol i kirap na ol i tok, "em ia, man ia."

(the bird) said to them "who said those bad things to me?" And they said "It was him, that man." [East New Britain, M, 12]

Em kirap, em askim pa bl' em, "man, papa yu ia yu mekim gut lo, wonem, hap brata blo mi lo (w)onem? Em i go lo taun na em i go mekim nambaut ...?

He asked his father "father, you, why did you help my, what, my half brother? He just goes and wastes his time in town…" [East New Britain, M, 12]

In summary, then, in spite of confirmation of many of Sankoff's findings, some differences remain. The particle *yet* is still widely used as a 'negative polarity item' and is used in a focal role with nouns as well as pronouns. The phrase *long wanem* appears to be used far less frequently to mean 'why?' than in Sankoff's data, and its meaning is usually restricted to the conjunction 'because'. Other intensifiers such as *moa* and *stret* are no longer confined to qualifying adverbials, but occasionally appear with some nominals as well. Certain English terms are appearing, such as the words *oun* 'own' and *stil* 'still' to supplement other Tok Pisin items.

7

Discourse processes

The term 'discourse' has gained considerable currency in recent years, in post-modernist as well as linguistic theory, and it is used in a number of different senses, which are often rather confusing or "incommensurable" (Pennycook 1994). The critical discourse analysis of Fairclough (1995) and others relates language to power and ideology, and shows, for example, how social and political artefacts are constructed through language to create or maintain inequality. This fascinating field clearly has considerable relevance to language use in Papua New Guinea, but is not the focus of this study. In this section, the term 'discourse' is employed in the traditional sense of linguistic discourse analysis as used, for example, in Brown & Yule's standard text (1983). Discourse here indicates the study of those grammatical features that govern the production of extended texts, spoken or written.

Many traditional grammars analyze language at the level of the sentence; criteria for grammaticality, for example, tend to concentrate on this unit. For an investigation of spoken language, this type of analysis is less than ideal, as most speakers do not normally communicate in well-formed sentences. Instead, a stream of discourse emerges, which is governed not only by the constraints of grammaticality but also the physical and social context of the utterance and the pragmatic concerns of the speakers. The functional grammar of Halliday (1978) and others has focused attention on this in recent decades.

The problem has also been recognized recently by a number of creolists. For example, Escure, discussing Creoles in general, states:

> Utterances appear to be arranged according to a hierarchical organization which maximizes clarity and expressiveness in the processing of information. Thus the paragraph or some other discourse-based (as opposed to sentence-based) semantic unit provides better insight into the structural patterns of creole syntax. (Escure 1991:180)

Although the area has been neglected in the past, a number of studies of discourse processes in Creoles have recently appeared, for example, Andersen (1990), Escure (1991, 1993), Masuda (1995) and Spears (1993). Tok Pisin discourse structure has not received much attention; it is hardly even mentioned, for example, in Wurm & Mühlhäusler's monumental *Handbook* (1985). One or two studies, however, have appeared. As discussed in § 6.6.3, Sankoff & Brown (1976) looked at the discourse structure of Tok Pisin and related it to the grammaticalization of particles such as *ia*. Lomax (1983), in an unpublished paper not widely available, discusses cohesion and discourse structure as exemplified by letters and traditional stories in *Wantok Niuspepa* in the second half of 1982. This will be discussed in more detail below.

Much of the field of discourse analysis is concerned with the social use of language, for example, investigating conversational conventions such as turn-taking, and the pragmatics of everyday communication. Pragmatics in Tok Pisin does not appear to have received any attention at all, which is a serious gap in our understanding of the language. A pragmatic study of the language of first language speakers in a naturalistic setting would make an important and worthwhile study. However, the present corpus, consisting as it does mainly of monologue, sheds little light on pragmatics. The texts (i.e. the transcripts of the speech) are mainly narratives of events which happened in the recent past or re-telling of traditional stories, and it is this type of discourse which forms the basis of the analysis presented here.

The aim of this chapter is to give an account of the way the textual structure, or "texture" of Tok Pisin narrative discourse is constructed by first language speakers. Firstly, a consideration of cohesion shows how shorter chunks of text are held together (§ 7.1). The framework of Halliday & Hasan (1976), whose comprehensive account of cohesion in English is still the standard, is used where appropriate, but areas where this is unsuitable for the analysis of oral Tok Pisin texts are discussed. Then the maintenance of coherence in longer segments of text is discussed (§ 7.2), looking at narrative conventions, the description of sequential events and the reporting of speech.

7.1 Cohesion

Cohesion refers to mechanisms for holding together text, which are partly syntactic and partly lexical. The best known work on cohesion in English is Halliday & Hasan (1976), who describe cohesive mechanisms including reference, substitution, ellipsis, conjunction and lexical cohesion. Most of reference can be subsumed under the heading 'deixis', which may refer to people, for example pronouns; places, for example, 'here' and 'there'; or time, for example, 'now' and 'then'. Reference may be endophoric, referring to things present in the text, or exophoric, where the context provides the point of reference. Endophoric reference may refer back (anaphoric) or forward (cataphoric). Another account of cohesion is Beaugrande & Dressler (1981), whose terminology is somewhat different. According to their constructs, pro-forms are semantically empty words standing in place of various referents in the text. These include pronouns as well as pro-verbs and pro-modifiers. Junctive or joining mechanisms include conjunction, disjunction, contrajunction and subordination as well as the cohesive effects of time relations and modality. Beaugrande & Dressler's account also stresses pragmatic factors in the production of cohesive text.

The most comprehensive account of cohesion in *Tok Pisin* appears to be the unpublished dissertation by Lomax (1983). In it he follows Halliday & Hasan's model and applies it to cohesive devices in *Tok Pisin* as shown in two written genres: letters to the editor and traditional folk stories in the weekly Tok Pisin-medium *Wantok Niuspepa*. These genres were selected as being likely to be free from the influence of translated and Anglicized forms. *Wantok Niuspepa*, however, follows Kristen Press's stylesheet, based on the standard established by *Nupela Testamen* and followed by Mihalic (1982), and it is not clear how far the writing has been edited in the production process. In the following sections, an account of cohesive devices in the present corpus will make reference to the above models and to Lomax's findings.

7.1.1 Reference

The fabric of a spoken text is held together to a considerable extent by co-reference to other features either within the text or in the context of its utterance. The meaning of many items cannot be determined except in terms of these referents. Personal deixis is the use of personal pronouns in place of people as referents. This will be discussed in the following section, including possessive and demonstrative uses. Reference to the deixis of place will also be investigated, especially in reference to Lomax's claim that there is "no evidence in Tok Pisin of specific spatial reference deixis" (1983:12). Temporal deixis, using such adverbial expressions as *nau* and *bipo*, is also discussed.

Personal deixis: pronominal reference

The pronoun paradigm of Tok Pisin was extensively discussed in Chapter 5. As was seen, the paradigm is quite variable, for example in the extent of dual and trial forms and the referents of the 'inclusive' and 'exclusive' first person plural forms. Data from the corpus suggest that a number of forms may be becoming obsolete, such as trial forms and *emtupela*. A number of aberrant forms such as *mipela ol* and *empela* (Romaine 1992b:5) and *yumipela* were seen to occur occasionally. Lomax (1983:2) even claims to have found "a 'we' form which could be used to exclude the person speaking", but unfortunately provides no further details of this intriguing prospect. Relative pronouns were discussed in § 6.6. Discussion in this section will be confined to the cohesive role of pronominal reference and how possible ambiguity is avoided.

As noted in Chapter 5, *em* is unmarked for case or gender and is thus potentially ambiguous, especially as *em* is sometimes used to refer to plural referents, as described by Mühlhäusler (1985h:344), and as an introduction to relative clauses. One means of avoiding ambiguity is the use of alternatives to recurring use of *em*, such as full nouns plus the anaphoric marker *ia*. This is especially common with the words *man* and *meri* in narratives where the identity of referents could become confused. In the following extract, for example, it can be seen how the referents are kept distinct by the appropriate use of pronouns or full nouns accompanied by *ia*:

> man ia em kira(p) na em sigaut. Em sigaut na meri ia tanim na em lukim, em lukim man ia na em kira nau em tok ose lo meri ia, em tok ...
>
> the man got up and he called out. He called out and the woman turned and she looked, she saw the man and he got up now, he said to the woman, he said [Morobe, F, 11]

Tupela can occur quite frequently, involving a good deal of redundancy, as this short extract from a 13-year-old boy in Rabaul shows:

> *Tupla go lo nambis nau, tupla kisim kanu blo tupla okei tupla puli(m) kanu blo tupla go daun lo nambis na tupla sidaun na tupla wok lo huk. Huk i go na tupla i no bin hukim wanpla pis na tupla i bin belhat stret.*

> The two went to the beach and they got their canoe. Then they pulled their canoe down the beach and they sat and they fished. They fished but didn't catch anything and they got angry [East New Britain, M, 13]

The referents of *tupela* only become problematic if two pairs are involved:

> *... tupela pikinini wantaim papa i stap i go, na papa kisim narapela meri. Na disla meri em i no save laikim tupla pikinini ia na wanpla taim tupla laik trikim pikinini na tupla karim tupla mangki i go antap long bikpla bus tru...*

> The two children stayed with their father and the father married another woman. And this woman did not like the two children and one time the two (parents) wanted to trick the child(ren), and the two carried the two children into the forest [Western Highlands, M, 15]

It should be noted that the potential for confusion of the reference is also increased as some speakers always use *tupela* to refer to two people, while with other speakers, the use of *ol* may alternate with *tupela*:

> *Em nau tupla bin go nau disla tupla mama tupla bin ronowe go lo peles blo ol*

> So the two went, these two mothers ran away to their village [East New Britain, F, 13]

> *Na disla tupla pikinini meri tupla bin kamap wantaim na tupla bin stap wante papa blo ol. Ol lukautim papa blo ol i go inap em go lapun*

> Now these two girls grew up together and the two stayed with their father. They looked after their father until he was old [Madang, M, 16]

The third person plural pronoun *ol* takes the same form as the plural marker, which could possibly lead to ambiguity, especially when the predicate marker is omitted. In addition, the referent of *ol* can be difficult to determine in such phrases as *ol i wokim pati* 'there was a party on'. In fact there may be no intended referent, and this 'impersonal' use of *ol* is frequently used in the media to translate passive constructions in English, where no agent is specified. An example from the somewhat unnatural style of an NBC news broadcast illustrates the various uses of *ol*, first as an impersonal pronoun equivalent to a passive, secondly as a plural marker and thirdly as a third person plural pronoun:

> *tupela raunwara nau i nogat Salvinia longen, bihain long ol i bin putim ol binatang long ol.*

> the two lagoons now have no Salvinia on them after they introduced the insects to them.

Examples from the corpus of the 'impersonal' use of *ol* include some 30 tokens in the expression *ol i kolim (long) X*, equivalent to 'is called X':

> *em lo hau wanpla ailan long Sipik yet ol i kolim long Walis Ailan, hau na i gat man lo displa ailan.*

> It's about how an island in Sepik called Walis Island, how there came to be people on this island. [East New Britain, M, 18]

> *Olsem long klaimim kokonat o samting, ol diwai ol i kolim long 'kalapim' long hia na long Madang ol i kolim olsem bai i 'go antap long diwai'.*

> Like for climbing a coconut or something, trees, they say 'kalapim' here, and in Madang they say 'go antap'. [New Ireland, M, 16]

In other cases, agents whose identities are only vaguely known may be referred to, for example when reporting crimes or unexplained occurrences. In many cases, *ol* could be translated as an impersonal 'they', or as a passive, as with most of the translations below. In the following extract, the father has seen an unexplained phenomenon (an aeroplane), but no plural referent has been mentioned previously:

> *em i pored, na papa bilongen i bin tokim em olsem "Yu no ken poret, ol no inap mekim wanpla samting long yumi."*

> He was afraid and his father said "don't be afraid, nothing can harm us" [Manus, F, 14]

Other examples include the following:

> *Em stopim kar tasol em go daun, em laik go lukim man ia <u>ol i kilim em pinis</u>*
>
> He stopped the car and went down to see the man <u>who had been killed</u>. [East New Britain, F, 15]

> *wanpla samting sed tu hepen, em papa blo mipla, <u>ol i bin saspektim em nating</u>.*
>
> Something sad happened too, my father <u>was wrongly suspected</u>. [Eastern Highlands, M, 16]

> *i kam lo prifeks em <u>ol i bin votim mi</u> olsem skul vais kepten*
>
> it came to prefects and <u>I was voted</u> school vice captain. [Eastern Highlands, M, 17]

> *wanpla yangpla meri em bin go daun lo wara na displa wara <u>ol i bin bilivim</u> olsem em peles blo masalai*
>
> a young girl went down to the river, and this river <u>was believed to be</u> a spirit's place [East New Britain, M, 16]

Ambiguity can also arise in the case of ***mipela*** 'we exclusive'. Although the addressee is specifically excluded, it may not be obvious exactly which of the remaining possible referents are included in the term. It is quite common for further information to be supplied to identify the referents, as the following examples demonstrate:

> *hetmasta <u>blo mipela</u> tokim <u>mipela olgeta stiudent</u> mas tek pat long dispela kalshoral sho tasol <u>sampela mipela</u> sampela nogat ol kostiums nambaut*
>
> <u>our</u> headmaster told <u>all of us students</u> that we must take part in this cultural show, but <u>some of us</u> did not have costumes. [Western Highlands, F, 16]

> *"mi pudaunim medjik na ad lo <u>mipla</u> swim go insait, <u>mipla enimols</u>" em tok osem.*
>
> "I left my magic powers and it's hard for <u>us</u> to swim inside, <u>us animals</u>" he said. [Morobe, F, 11]

> *Lo grediueishen l' aste em <u>mipla ol pikinini</u> kam lo skul lo eit ouklok.*
>
> At graduation yesterday, <u>we children</u> came to school at eight o'clock [Southern Highlands, F, 14]

> *So <u>mipla sikspla bois</u> <u>mipla</u> go inseit, <u>mipla</u> go inseit na <u>mipla</u> stap*
>
> So <u>we six boys</u>, <u>we</u> went inside, <u>we</u> went inside and <u>we</u> stayed there [Simbu, M, 16]

> *<u>mipla</u> go autsait. <u>Mipla</u> plei plei go nau <u>mipla</u>, <u>mipla fopla meri mipla</u> plei hopskot na ol sampla meri ol go plei basketbol wante ol bois.*
>
> <u>We</u> went outside. <u>We</u> played and played and then <u>we four girls</u> played hopscotch and some girls went and played basketball with the boys. [Morobe, F, 11]

It is common for an apparently redundant pronoun to be inserted or repeated after a subject. This 'resumptive' use of pronouns recalls Keesing's (1988) analysis of the pronoun paradigm in Melanesian Pidgins discussed above. Some examples of the repeated use of pronouns after subjects follow:

> *ol sampla meri <u>ol</u> go plei basketbol*
>
> Some of the girls went to play basketball [Morobe F,12]

> *na desla meri <u>em</u> i no save laikim tupla pikinini*
>
> This woman did not like the two children [Western Highlands, M, 15]

> *Man ia <u>em</u> kirap nau em i go*
>
> The man got up and left [Western Highlands, M, 16]

> *Mi na ol poroman bilong mi <u>mipla</u> wokabaut i go …*
>
> My friends and I walked on [Western Highlands, M, 17]

> *… tasol taim ol diwai <u>ol</u> sa go insait …*
>
> but when the logs went inside [East New Britain, M,13]

The third person singular pronoun is usually glossed as 'he', 'she' or 'it', but in this corpus the use of *em* as 'it' is very infrequent and the referents are almost always human. Non-human referents are usually indicated by the full noun, followed by *ia* where appropriate.

Possessive pronouns

The possessive expression ***bilong*** + pronoun is normally used adjectivally directly following a noun:

> *mama blong em bin dai pinis, na nogat man lo lukautim em osem na, ol ankols blong em bin lukautim em*
>
> his mother had died and there was nobody to look after him, so his uncles looked after him [Southern Highlands, F, 15]

In a few cases, the ***bilong*** + pronoun construction is used without a preceding noun as a possessive pronoun.

> *na em i tokim displa man long tupla i go lo peles blongen, na sla man tokim em tok "mitla go lo blo mi pastaim, blo mi em klostu."*
>
> and he told this man that two of them should go to his village, and this man said to him "let's go to mine, mine is close." [Manus, M, 14]

This was very uncommon in the corpus; in the overwhelming majority of cases, possessives were used with nominals. The sum of the occurrences of what appear to be possessive pronouns are presented in the following examples:

> *Na ol i kam daun nau ol i sherim i go na ol wok lo tok, "em blo yu em blo mi, em blo yu em blo mi."*
>
> And they came down and shared them out and they were saying "that's yours, that's mine, that's yours, that's mine." [New Ireland, M, 12]

> *"tasol yupela no ken go long liklik hap kona long hap em blo mi."*
>
> "but you can't go to that little place over there, that's mine". [Manus, M, 13]

> *em putim lo gel ia em tok "yu kaikai," gel ia krai tsol. N' em karim blongen na em wokobaut i go em tok osem "yu les lo mi oke mi go."*
>
> He presented it to the girl and said "eat this," and the girl only cried. And he carried his (things) and he left, saying "you don't want me, all right, I'm going." [Southern Highlands, F, 15]

> *Ol kilim ol Siapan ia na ol holim wanpla tasol na ol pasim em lo rop na ol tok, 'em blong ol'.*
>
> They killed the Japanese and kept only one and they tied him up and they said "he is theirs." [East New Britain, M, 17]

The phrase *bilong em yet* appears to have the idiomatic meaning of 'by himself' or 'by herself', especially when following *stap*, similar to the examples discussed in § 6.8.

> *tupla i bin bruk long marit na papa i go long stap blong em yet na mama i go stap blong em yet*
>
> the two had divorced and father went to stay by himself and mother went to stay by herself. [East Sepik, M, 16]

Four such examples can be found in the corpus.

Demonstrative pronouns

The normal demonstrative adjective or pronoun is ***dispela*** 'this' or ***ol dispela*** 'these'. The word **datpela* is not recorded, although *datfala* is reported to occur in Solomon Islands Pijin. Like possessives, most demonstratives are used adjectivally with nouns, but in a few cases ***dispela*** can stand alone as a pronoun:

> *ol lain blong Los Nigros i karim ol hap palang, botol, spia na ol kainkain samting manggoru na ol i kam lo pait wantem ol Lele. Taim mi lukim dispela mi poret turu na mi ronowe i go long haus*
>
> the Los Negros villagers were carrying bits of wood, bottles, spears and things, mangrove sticks, and they came to fight with the Lele villagers. When I saw this I was very frightened and ran away to the house. [Manus, M, 13]

> *mipla go olgeta long rif na mipla bin kalap go insait lo solwara na mipla i waswas na pilai. Bihain long <u>displa</u> mipla bin go bek long dom*
>
> we went right to the reef and we jumped into the water and washed and played. After <u>this</u>, we went back to the dormitory [New Ireland, M, 16]

Some other examples of demonstrative pronouns from the corpus are:

> *em i la silip, si sa buruk na wokim planti nois na disla pisin em i wok long belhat lo <u>disla</u> na em i wok lo tok nogut lo disla si i go*
>
> he wanted to sleep, the sea broke and made a lot of noise and this bird was angry about <u>this</u> and he talked abusively to this sea [East Sepik, M, 15]

> *ol sa tingim wantok bl' ol yet na <u>displa</u>, na mi no ting <u>disla</u> i gutpla tumas*
>
> They think about their own relatives and <u>this</u>, I don't think <u>this</u> is very good [Manus, F, 14]

> *nogat planti ol stiudents bin pas na go lo osem ba go lo kolidjes na go l' ol neshnol ai ol aia institiushen ol belhat lo <u>displa</u>*
>
> there were not many students who passed and could go to college and go to national high school, higher institutions and they were angry about <u>that</u>. [Southern Highlands, F, 15]

The plural form *ol dispela* is occasionally encountered, three times in the Manus sample, and once in the East New Britain sample:

> *So em had lo mipla lo painim kaikai na <u>ol disla</u>.*
>
> So it was hard for us to find food and <u>these</u> (things). [Manus, F, 16]

> *Na tai(m) ol ami go ba ol kam arasait na bai ol polis i askim ol kwesten na <u>ol disla</u>.*
>
> And when the soldiers went they came outside and the police would ask them questions and <u>things</u>. [Manus, M, 14]

The following extract contains examples of both possessive and demonstrative pronouns:

> *Tok pinis nau em tring (= dring) <u>blo em</u>, tring <u>blo em</u> pinis nau, <u>disla</u> blo Ostrelia em kirap nau, em hapim <u>blo em</u>, em tring nau, em tok osem "cheer up the mother queen of England"*
>
> After talking, he drank <u>his</u>, when he had drunk <u>his</u>, <u>this one</u> from Australia got up, he raised <u>his</u>, he drank he said "cheer up the mother queen of England" [East Sepik, M, 17]

The use of the particle *ia* with nouns, whose role in anaphoric reference is described below, can also have demonstrative force:

> *(em) tok "na yupla ting se mi giamanim yupla, em <u>man ia</u> i no man blo wokim puripuri, em mi mi man tru."*
>
> (he) said "so you think I am lying to you, it's <u>that man</u> who is not a sorcerer, me I'm a real man." [New Ireland, M, 12]

> *pikinini blo man ia i kirap tok sem "yu lukim em i no meri tru blo yu. Em <u>meri ia</u> em i go na daunim ston ia."*
>
> the man's son said "look, it's not your real wife. <u>That's</u> your wife throwing down the stones." [East New Britain, M, 12]

Anaphoric reference with **ia**

The use of *ia* as a clause bracketing device was discussed in § 6.6.3. However, as noted, the particle has other functions too. In addition to general emphasis, acting as a kind of verbal exclamation mark, *ia* is also used extensively as an anaphoric marker. Anaphoric use of *ia* seems to have been observed only relatively recently. Lomax (1983) describes this function in some detail, but Mühlhäusler does not mention anaphora in the 1985 *Handbook*. He refers only to *ia's* clause bracketing function and its use as an emphatic device or general deictic, although Siegel in the same volume (1985a:532; also 1981) does mention the use of *ia* in the media Tok Pisin to refer back to things already mentioned. As seen in the previous chapter, anaphoric use of *ia* is very common in the narratives in this corpus.

Spatial deixis

Lomax (1983:12) makes the strong claim that in Tok Pisin there is no spatial deixis, i.e. specific reference to place with respect to the position of the speaker. This does not accord with other writers, e.g. Dutton, who notes (1973) the use of ***long hap i kam*** and ***hap i go*** to distinguish position relative to the speaker. Lomax notes examples of ***hap*** in reference to previously mentioned places or positions, but distinguishes these from spatial deixis in that they rely on textual antecedents for their interpretation rather than position relative to the speaker.

Lomax's claim cannot be supported by the present corpus. While it is true that most occurrences of ***hap*** or ***long hap*** relied on textual elements for interpretation, in other cases, and especially with the use of ***hia***, reference was clearly in relation to the speakers or the immediate context. In the following, ***hia*** has no textual antecedent, and refers to the place where the people are sitting talking at that moment:

> *mipla i lusim peles long a siks ouklok na mipla kamap <u>lo hia</u> long nain ouklok so em i longpla wokobaut i kam.*
>
> We left the village at six o'clock and came <u>here</u> at nine o'clock, so it's a long journey. [North Solomons, M, 19]

In the following, the referents of ***lo hia*** and ***disla hap*** (parts of the body) must be extracted from extra-linguistic cues provided by the speaker, such as pointing to the relevant area:

> *tsol wanbla boi mitla sa skul wantem, ol kilim em, ol sutim em <u>lo hia</u> na kamautim <u>disla hap</u> blogen aut.*
>
> But one boy we went to school with, they killed him, shot him <u>here</u> and blew away <u>this part</u> of his body. [Eastern Highlands, M, 18]

In the following, ***lo hia*** 'here' contrasts with ***lo hap*** 'there', the speaker's former place of residence.

> <u>*Lo hia*</u> *em stiudents ol ekt imatiua, <u>lo hap</u> em ol stiudents sa rigadim ol gels sem ikwal a, ol no sa koros.*
>
> <u>Here</u>, the students act immature, <u>there</u> the students regard girls as equals, they don't get angry. [East New Britain, F, 18]

Spatial textual reference in the corpus is almost always anaphoric in nature, but very occasionally, cataphoric reference is used. For example, in the following (somewhat unlikely) sequence of events, the speaker uses ***lo hap*** 'this place' cataphorically before the identity of the conduit is revealed:

> *na man ia i tokim ol tok "sawos (= sapos) yupla paini(m) i nogat rot yupla kam go insait <u>lo hap</u>." Em tok osem nau, em bend daun na opim has bl' em na ol meri ia ol painim i nogat rot nau okei, ol kam go insait lo as blo man ia.*
>
> And the man said to them "if you find there is no road, you can go inside <u>here</u>." He said this and bent down and opened his anus, and the women found there was no road so they went inside the man's anus. [Eastern Highlands, M, 17]

Temporal deixis

The use of temporal sequencing as a means of organizing discourse is discussed more fully in § 7.2.2 below. This section is confined to a discussion of the terms available for referring to time, with particular emphasis on the increasing number of borrowed items appearing in this role. Time sequence markers seem to be particularly prone to influence by English expressions, as also noted by Mühlhäusler (1985n:261):

> *"nau,* **in the end now**, *ol ape i kontrolim ol man*
>
> <u>In the end</u> the apes controlled the people

This is also the case in anglicized varieties such as parliamentary speeches:

> **at the moment** *mi ken tok olsem ...*
>
> <u>at the moment</u> I can say that... [Paias Wingti opening parliament, 1977]

Such borrowing could in many cases be due to the greater specificity of the expressions involved, as clock and calendar time have not been prominent features of traditional discourse patterns. However, stylistic considerations must also be taken into account. The following examples illustrate some typical uses of time and sequence markers. The borrowed expressions are written here as code switches, but this is by no means clear-cut in all cases.

> *Nau long <u>last two weeks</u> ol dozas blo <u>Works Department</u> ol rausim olgeta kokonas nau*
>
> In the <u>last two weeks</u> the <u>Works Department</u> bulldozers have cleared all the coconuts   [New Ireland, F, 19]
>
> *Nau <u>for a while</u>, mi no sawe we... - wara karim mi go daun.*
>
> Now, <u>for a while</u>, I didn't know where, - the river carried me down. [Simbu, M, 19]
>
> *Teistim teistim biain <u>finally</u> em kaikai bol bilong man ia*
>
> He tasted them and <u>finally</u> ate the man's testicles   [Eastern Highlands, M, 16]
>
> *na <u>these times</u> sapos ol man laik go lo bus...*
>
> <u>These days</u>, if people want to go to the bush ...   [East New Britain, F, 15]
>
> *orait <u>then</u> long riten em bai givim yu tupela*
>
> <u>then</u> in return he will give you two   [Western Highlands, M, 14]
>
> *taim blo <u>during Christmas holidays</u> mi bin go lo Not Solomons*
>
> <u>during the Christmas holidays</u> I went to North Solomons   [East New Britain, F, 16]
>
> *Mipla stap go <u>about ten minutes later</u> mipla kam daun.*
>
> We stayed there and <u>about ten minutes later</u> we came down. [Manus, F, 16]
>
> *<u>Firstly</u> taim mi bin - bipo lo mi woki(m) greid wan ...*
>
> <u>Firstly</u> when I was - before I did grade one ...   [East New Britain, M, 17]
>
> *So taim em katim osem nau <u>by that time</u> ia meri ia gat wanpla pikinini pinis*
>
> So when she had cut it, <u>by that time</u> the woman had already given birth to a child.   [Eastern Highlands, F, 17]

The juxtaposition of the introduced European time and calendar system and more traditional descriptions of time can lead to rather unwieldy phrases. In the following, a specific clock time reference is combined rather awkwardly with a more general description of the extremely early hour:

> *Ol i kirap lo <u>traipla hafpastu moning</u>*
>
> they got up <u>very big half past two morning</u>   [Manus, M, 19]

Similarly, the following are somewhat awkwardly integrated:

> *Okei long naintin eiti fo krismas - a i no krismas, <u>between nineteen eighty four</u> lo <u>middle of the hia</u> twin brada blo mi ...*
>
> So at Christmas 1984, no not Christmas, <u>between 1984 in the middle of the year</u>, my twin brother ...   [Eastern Highlands, F, 16]
>
> *na kastom blo mipla ol hailans osem <u>as, like</u> am <u>for the first time</u> gels mipla hevim <u>menstruation that's the time</u> ol wokim pati blo mipla*
>
> And our custom in the Highlands is <u>like</u>, <u>the first time</u> girls have their <u>menstruation</u>, <u>that's the time</u> they have a ceremony for us. [Eastern Highlands, F, 17]
>
> *<u>After four</u> fri taim <u>until six during</u> am lo disla fri taim am mipla i sa hevim shauas*
>
> <u>After four</u>, free time <u>until six during</u>, um in this free time we have our showers. [New Ireland, F, 15]

Further comment on some of these examples appears in the discussion of code switching in Chapter 8.

7.1.2 Substitution and ellipsis

Substitution

Substitution involves replacing one term with another, usually for stylistic reasons. Unlike reference, it is basically a relation in the wording, rather than the meaning (Halliday & Hasan 1976:88), although the distinction between reference and substitution can be blurred. For example, in the English sentence 'I have a boat. Jack has one too', the word 'one' is substituted for 'boat' to avoid repetition of the term. The identity of the two boats is not the same. Words in English which can be substituted in this way include 'one', 'ones' and 'the same', while the main verbal pro-form is 'do' as in 'he keeps pheasants; we do too'. Adverbial expressions which can be substituted for preceding actions include 'thus' and 'likewise'.

In Tok Pisin, words which can be substituted for preceding phrases include *wanpla* and *sampla* to refer to nominals, *wokim* and *mekim* to refer to verbs and *wankain* and *olsem* to refer to the manner of doing something. Lomax (1983:27) gives a number of instances of *wankain* and *olsem*. Some examples from the corpus illustrate the use of these and other substitutions.

The use of *wanpela* or *sampela* can substitute almost any specified antecedent:

mipla olim tripla botol, mi olim <u>wanpla</u>, sista blo anti bl' mipla olim <u>wanpla</u> na anti blo mipla olim <u>wanpla</u>.

We were holding three bottles, I held <u>one</u>, my aunt's sister held <u>one</u> and my aunt held <u>one</u>. [Morobe, F, 11]

Nau em kirap go kisim kanda, i sigirapim paia i lait nau i kukim <u>sampla pis</u> nau wantem sista bl' em, tupla kaikai na gim <u>sampla</u> lo sista bl' em. Biain tupla karamapim <u>sampla</u> lo lip, tupla wokobaut i go.

Now he got some cane, rubbed it to make fire, and cooked <u>some fish</u> with his sister, the two ate and gave <u>some</u> to his sister. Then the two wrapped <u>some</u> in a leaf and left. [East New Britain, M, 12]

em sa baim kaikai na <u>sampla</u> bai em gi(vim) lo meri ia na <u>sampla</u> bai em kisim blong em yet.

She would buy food and <u>some</u> she gave to this woman and <u>some</u> she kept for herself. [Morobe, F, 12]

<u>*Wanpla* neim bloen Asa na <u>*wanpla*</u> neim bloen Elu</u>

<u>One</u> (of the women previously referred to) was called Asa and <u>one</u> was called Elu [East New Britain, F, 16]

The use of *-wan* in compounds, common for example in Bislama, was only represented by a single attestation in the corpus:

Nau mi kirap na to sem, "o nogat yu swingim em isi isi tumas, mi ba wokim <u>fast wan</u> ia, mi fit lo kalap."

Now I said "no, you are swinging it too slowly. I will do a <u>fast one</u>, I can jump on it." [Eastern Highlands, F, 16]

Verbal substitution with *wokim* and *mekim* are illustrated by the following:

em i go na askim ol disla ol manggi ken na ol trikim em olsem, ol i no bin <u>wokim</u>.

He went and asked the boys again and they tricked him that they didn't <u>do it</u> (laugh at him). [East Sepik, M, 16]

lapun meri ia tok "putim disla kokonas baksait long kanu blo yu na yu pul go bek gen long viledj." Na em i <u>wokim olsem</u>

the old woman said "put these coconuts in the back of your canoe and paddle back to the village." And he <u>did this</u> [Manus, M, 13.]

wanpla man ia em no sa hukim fish taim em kisim net bl' em go lo bich. <u>Mekim mekim</u> i go nau, wanpla taim ia em kisim aidia

one man never caught any fish when he took his net to the beach. <u>He carried on doing this</u>, then one day he had an idea. [Morobe, F, 13]

> *Em rausim long narapla ai, ai blong em i orait nau, i op, biain gen, em traim gen long narapla ai. <u>Mekim pinis</u> nau, tupla ai blong em go orait nau*
>
> He took it off one eye, and his eye was all right, open, then he tried the other eye. <u>He did this</u>, and both eyes were all right again. [Manus, F, 11]

The term *olsem* can be used to refer to a manner of doing something previously described:

> *lo ap blo mipla, mipla sa rispektim ol stret na mipla no sawe sa(po)s mipla go lo ap blo ol bai ol rispektim mipla o nogat, <u>kain olsem</u>.*
>
> In our place, we really respect them and we don't know if we go to their place whether they will respect us or not, <u>that sort of thing</u>. [Eastern Highlands, F, 16]

Cataphoric use of *olsem* is one way of beginning narratives, as described below in § 7.2.1:

> *Stori bilong mi em i go <u>olsem</u>.*
>
> My story goes <u>like this</u> [Simbu, F, 13]

The word *wankain* 'the same' may be used in substitution to avoid repetition of a similar object or event:

> *Em nau man ia traim gen. Em wokobaut go tasol <u>wankain samting</u> go kamap.*
>
> So the man tried again. He walked along, but the <u>same thing</u> happened. [West Sepik, M, 16]

However, the borrowing *seim* 'the same' is now much more frequent in all regions, with 101 tokens compared to only 7 for *wankain*:

> *em paitim het blongen na em dai. Na taim bikpla brata go, (di)sla masalai i <u>mekim seim</u> longen.*
>
> He hit his head and he died. And when the elder brother went, this spirit <u>did the same thing</u> to him. [Manus, M, 13]

> *na taim tumbuna blo tupla i dai, tupla i <u>wokim seim</u> olsem em bin tok.*
>
> And when their grandfather died, they <u>did the same as</u> he said. [West Sepik, M, 16]

> *Em i go (ta)sol, em i no stap, na <u>seim, seim samting</u> ia hepen ken na lapun meri i kam.*
>
> He went and he was not there, and the <u>same, same thing</u> happened again and the old woman came. [Simbu, M, 17]

This borrowing appears common in all areas, as the figures from the regional sub-corpora show:

Seim/sem *(meaning 'the same') by region*

Momase	Highlands	Islands
33	28	22

Ellipsis

Ellipsis is described by Halliday & Hasan (1976:142) as a special kind of substitution, a substitution by zero. Ellipsis can involve nominal or verbal elements or whole clauses. Lomax (1983:29) found ellipsis to be widespread in his *Wantok* samples, including ellipsis of the object, subject, subject plus *i*, subject plus auxiliary verb, subject plus verb, verb, past tense markers and *em* as subject of an impersonal verb. Lomax's findings were confirmed in the present corpus, where ellipsis was found regularly in the above categories. Some examples are given below. The missing items are indicated in the English translation:

> <u>*Nau bai stori*</u> *long wanpla femili*
>
> <u>Now (I) will tell you</u> about one family [Western Highlands, F, 16]

> *mi bin lukim <u>na fes taim</u> blo mi blo lukim disla*
>
> I saw (the Malanggan show) <u>and (it was) my first time</u> to see this [New Ireland, F, 16]

> *Em nem blo tupla em, bikpla brata <u>bl' em</u> Koaku na liklik brata <u>bl' em</u> Airina*
>
> Their names were, the big brother's (name) was Koaku and the little brother's (name) was Airina [Eastern Highlands, M, 14]

Mipla wachim <u>taim kamap</u> lo Kieta wof ol manggi biarei bin sut long em.

we watched (them) <u>when (they) arrived</u> at Kieta wharf, the BRA (Bougainville Revolutionary Army) boys shot at them. [Manus, M, 17]

The amount of ellipsis in an utterance appears to be pragmatically determined by the need for both stylistic acceptability and comprehensibility, what Beaugrande & Dressler (1981:64) refer to as the trade-off between compactness and clarity.

7.1.3 Lexical cohesion

Lexical cohesion adds to the coherence of a text by the selection of vocabulary, usually by the use of a super-ordinate noun to refer anaphorically to a more specific item. In English, for example, specific reference to 'an escaped tiger' might be followed by reference to 'the beast', a more general term. Synonyms rather than super-ordinates may also be used in this way, and the term 'lexical cohesion' may also be used in a more general way to indicate the cohesive effect of regular collocations. Lexical cohesion is thus very similar to substitution, except that in the latter case, the substituted words only have meaning in reference to the item substituted.

Since *Tok Pisin* is a Pidgin, albeit an expanded one, it is likely to be somewhat poorer in synonyms and superordinates than some other languages with a longer history, and this would not seem to be a promising area to look for cohesion. However, some examples can readily be produced. Lomax (1983:32) notes the use of such superordinates as **samting, pasin, wok, lain, hap, toktok** and **hevi** in producing lexical cohesion. Some examples from the corpus include replacement by synonyms and by superordinates, including some of the above described by Lomax. In the following, for example, the superordinate term **pasin** 'behaviour, way of doing something' (< *fashion*) stands in place of more specific procedures or behaviour:

Boilim lo sospen tasol, gi(vi)m ol, ol ba kaikai stap. Bat <u>disla pasin</u> ia em ba osem ol ba mekim osem go wan manth o samting olsem

(they) boiled it in a pan, gave it to them and they would eat it. But <u>this procedure</u> they would just do for one month or something like that [Eastern Highlands, M, 17]

man ia laik tingting long kilim disla bik boi na em laik kaikaim disla mangki tasol hat long em na em laik traim long kilim disla mangki. Na tupela mangki na meri ia lukim <u>disla pasin ankol blo em wokim</u> tupela lukim na tupela ronowe i go

the man thought about killing the big boy and eating him, but it was hard to try to kill him. And the brother and sister saw <u>what their uncle was doing</u> and they ran away [Western Highlands, M, 17]

ol i bin sut lo gan nambaut lo - am - taun. Osem i deinjeres stret. Ol bin meikim <u>sampla pasin osem</u> i no stret.

They shot with guns around the - um - town. So it was really dangerous. They did <u>some things like that</u> that weren't right. [Manus, F, 17]

... mi paitim em. Paitim em nau ol saspendim mi, wanpla wik lo aus. Taim mi kam lo haus em ol perents blo mi hatim mi gut tru ia. Em nau disla <u>pasin</u> mi lusim go na pinis.

... I hit him. After I hit him they suspended me, one week at home. When I went home, my parents really told me off. Now I have completely given up this <u>behaviour</u>. [Manus, M, 14]

Ol bin koros lo wanpla kasin brata blo mi na narapla meri. Tupla bin laik kamap frens na maret tasol ol no bin laik. Ol lain blo meri bin agenstim disla <u>pasin</u>.

They were angry with my cousin and another girl. The two wanted to be friends and get married, but they didn't approve. The girl's family were against this <u>behaviour</u>. [East New Britain, F, 16]

In addition to *pasin*, other examples of this type show the use of the superordinates *hap* 'place', *wok* 'work', *samting* 'thing' and *lain* 'group of people' in place of more specific referents:

Em ka(m) lo aus nau bifo haus blo tupla sista bl' em. Em slip <u>lo hap</u> pinis na em lukim ia banana ia no gro gud

he came to the house which his sisters used to stay in. He slept <u>in this place</u> and he saw that the bananas were not growing well. [Eastern Highlands, F, 15]

> *tupla sa go wasim ol kloudhz bl' (d)isla tupla brada na kukim kaikai blo tupla, lusim na tupla sa go antap bek lo shel blo tupla na, taim tupla brada kam - kam bek lo aus (di)sa tupla sa tok ose(m) "usat woki(m) <u>disla wok</u> ia?"*

> the two would wash the clothes of the two brothers and cook their food, leave and go back to their shell, and when the brothers came back to the house they said "who did <u>this work</u>?" [Eastern Highlands, F, 13]

> *"... man blo mi em, wonem ia, dai pinis na mi no nap stap wante yupla, mi bai was lo disla, disla plent," nau em go. Meri ia i go nau em go nau em stap lo disla. Em sa woterim disla <u>samting</u>, plent i go nau <u>samting</u> ia, em go bikpla.*

> "... my husband is dead and I can't stay with you, I'll look after this plant," and she went. The woman went, and stayed with it. She watered this <u>thing</u>, this plant, the <u>thing</u> grew big. [Eastern Highlands, F, 17]

> *man ia rolim em lo mat nau em go singautim ol brada ia kam nau. Em go singautim ol i kam nau, ol <u>lain</u> ia tok ...*

> the man rolled her in the mat and called his brother to come. He called them to come, the <u>group</u> said... [Morobe, F, 11]

The term *samting* is a general word for any object, and is also used as a euphemism for sexually taboo terms. It may also be used cohesively to refer back to more specific referents:

> *ol tumbuna sawe yusim wanpla bembu ia - sampla bembu na - na wok lo pulmapim wara na dring, osem konteina bl' ol. Na baga ia kisim <u>(di)sla samting</u> ia na, koki ia kisim na em lak go.*

> The ancestors used a bamboo and filled it with water and drank, like a container. So the fellow got <u>this thing</u> and the cockatoo got it and was about to go. [Simbu, M, 14]

> *Nau sista bl' em tok "em guria ia, yu mas kilim." So neks dei em go bek ken em kilim <u>disla samting</u>.*

> His sister said "it's a crowned pigeon, you must kill it." So the next day he went back again, he killed <u>this thing</u>. [West Sepik, F, 15]

The use of *hevi* as a super-ordinate noted by Lomax was not found in the corpus. This is no doubt due to the nature of the genres involved; the *Wantok* letters to the editor analyzed by Lomax were frequently concerned with perceived problems that motivated the writers to voice their concerns. Indeed, several similar words in a cohesive chain cited by Lomax - *tingting* 'thought', *askim* 'request', *krai* 'plea', *belhevi* 'concern' and *wari* 'worry'- show the preoccupation with problems in letters to the editor (Lomax 1983:32). Other super-ordinate terms involved in lexical cohesion in the corpus included more recent additions to the lexicon such as *problem*:

> *yangpla manggi lo ia P. vilidj yet em bin mederim wanpla man blo Sepik na <u>displa problem</u> i bin on na ol no bin painim naif we ol i bin mederim em longen*

> a young boy from here, P. village had murdered a man from Sepik, and <u>this problem</u> was continuing and they hadn't found the knife he was murdered with. [Manus, F, 16]

Replacement by synonyms is less common, perhaps because of the limited number of choices available, and it generally appears to be limited to new items which are likely to be misunderstood. Mühlhäusler (1985g) notes the role of synonymy in introducing novel terms, especially in media reports. Again, this corpus would not be expected to reflect this use of synonyms as much as other genres concerned with communicating new ideas, but some examples of this type of explanatory synonymy can be found where alternatives are provided for clarity:

> *Na em sa laikim olgeta meri, na ol meri ol i gat <u>wari o problem</u> nabaut, ol sa go lo disla save meri.*

> And she liked all the women, and if women had a <u>worry or problem</u>, they would go to this wise woman. [Simbu, F, 14]

> *ol man sa bleimim ol sampla ol lapun man meri olsem ol bin <u>sanggumaim o kilim</u> (di)sla man.*

> they blamed some old people saying they <u>poisoned or killed</u> this man. [Simbu, F, 16]

ol gutpla ol samting i kam insait, osem long sait bilong <u>sech, o lotu</u> em i kam insait

good things are coming in (to the village) like to the people of the <u>church or service</u> they are coming in [Madang, M, 19]

ol kukim ain nabaut na, ain ot stap tsol nau ol putim lo skin blo meri ia lo tokaut osem - tokaut lo <u>sangguma, o sosora,</u> (di)sla.

They heated bits of iron, the iron was hot and they put it on the woman's body to make her confess that she was a <u>witch or sorcerer</u>, this thing. [Simbu, M, 17]

yu no stap wantem ol <u>papamama o ol perents</u> blo yu stret olsem na nau em bai mi kisim neim blo yu

you don't stay with your <u>mother and father or parents</u> so I will take your name. [Eastern Highlands, M, 16]

Na tupla bin ... - ol fit man lo go <u>huk o fishing</u>.

And the two were good at <u>fishing</u> [East Sepik, M, 11]

olgeta taim nait em sa silip, masalai sa kisim <u>imidj o pes</u> blo man blongen

Every night when he was asleep, the spirit would take the <u>image or face</u> of her husband. [East New Britain, M, 16]

Lomax notes the cohesive effect of the use of *narapela* (1983:18), which can be used in one of two ways. A single *narapela* depends for its reference on some specific antecedent from which it is distinguished:

Go na em wok lo kaikaim ol planti planti man lo wanpla ailan go, na ol lusi(m) disla ailan nau ol go lo <u>narapla ples</u>.

Still it ate a lot of people who lived on an island, and they left this island and they went to <u>another place</u>. [West Sepik, F, 13]

A reciprocal pair, on the other hand, is used to represent the English sequence of 'one ... another':

disla tupla kiau buruk na <u>narapla</u> go taranggau na <u>narapla</u> go snek na tupla sa stap.

The two eggs broke and <u>one</u> turned into an eagle and <u>the other</u> turned into a snake. [Morobe, F, 11]

Two reciprocal pairs may be involved, apparently without any ambiguity:

tupla lukim draipla ston na tupla go hait. Na <u>narapla brata go hait long narapla sait, na narapla go hait long narapla sait</u>.

The two saw the huge stone and they went to hide. And <u>one brother went and hid on one side and the other went and hid on the other side</u>. [Morobe, F, 14]

Reduplicated *narapela* usually refers to a variety of different places or things:

Na ol man wok lo stat lo ronowe nabaut go lo <u>narapla narapla</u> ples.

And the men started to run away to <u>different</u> villages. [East Sepik, M, 16]

7.1.4 Conjunction

Hall (1943:34) describes *na* as the only "true conjunction" in Tok Pisin, while conjunctional phrases are "rare and illusory in nature". Mühlhäusler (1985h:398) comments on conjunctive relations, describing the use of *na*, *o* and *tasol*, but noting also that *nau* may be the only conjunction used by some older speakers. Romaine (1988a) deals with the conjunctive use of *orait* in her account of expanded Pidgins. According to Halliday & Hasan's classification, conjunctive relations can be additive, adversative, temporal or causal. Examples of *Tok Pisin* conjunctions according to this paradigm would be:

additive	*na, wantaim,*
adversative	*tasol, bat*
temporal	*nau, bihain, long disla taim*
causative	*long wanem, olsem na*

In Beaugrande & Dressler's terminology (1981:71), these would correspond to conjunctive, disjunctive, contrajunctive, subordinating or temporal expressions. Considering the paucity of conjunctions described in earlier times, conjunction seems to be one area where considerable expansion has taken place in recent years, as the examples in the following sections indicate:

Additive conjunctions

The most common additive conjunction is *na*, which can conjoin strings of nominal elements in a clause or strings of clauses. It should be noted, however, that the latter use is overwhelmingly more common than the former. Strings of nominals joined by *na* such as the following in fact look distinctly unusual:

> Ol mango na ol kokonas blong em, kaukau em sa kaikai nating, boinim tasol lo paia na kaikai.

> Mangoes and coconuts, sweet potato he ate as they were, just heated them on the fire and ate them [East New Britain, M, 12]

When the meaning is 'and, together with', the use of *wantaim* is more usual:

> tumbuna blo mi em gat wanpla sista *na* wanpla avinun sista blong em *wantaim* ol fren bl' em la go brukim faiawut.

> My grandfather has a sister and one afternoon his sister and her friends were about to go and collect firewood. [West Sepik, F, 17]

This is the standard pattern in all regions:

Additive use of **wantaim** *by region*

Highlands	Islands	Momase
89	79	78

Linking clauses is by far the most frequent functions of the remainder of the 20,720 occurrences of the conjunction *na*, and lengthy stretches of discourse may be loosely linked as a series of clauses or sentences with *na* in initial position:

> Na em i save olsem dispela em i masalai meri. Na taim long - taim tupela i go stap long haus dispela masalai meri i haskim dispela man, "yu laik long mi kisim sampela kulau blong yu?" Na dispela masalai - a dispela man i tok "yes". Na dispela masalai meri go antap longen.

> And he knew that this was a spirit woman. And when they went to the house this spirit woman asked this man "would you like me to get you some drinking coconuts?" And this spirit, um this man said "yes". And the spirit woman went up. [Manus, M, 13]

Verhaar (1991a) has pointed out that *na* does not always merely conjoin strings of clauses, but has a "serial" use in a variety of syntactic constructions, as exemplified previously in § 6.4. There is also some confusion over the identity of *na* and *nau*. Although these are usually glossed separately as 'and' and 'now', it appears that the two are not distinguished by some speakers. Even the local Papua New Guinea television station EMTV showed this confusion in a recent (1993) advertisement for Heinz baked beans:

> ... wantaim kakaruk *nau* tinpis!

> ... with chicken and tinned fish!

Sequences of clauses are often punctuated by the use of both *na* and *nau*:

> tupla brata i wok lo go kisim kukamba i kam *na* wanpla man i kam *nau* em i pasim ol *nau* i tokim tupla i stap lo haus *nau* tupla i wok lo kaikai.

> The two brothers were bringing the cucumber and a man came and detained them and told them to stay in the house and they were eating. [West New Britain, F, 10]

The use of *nau* in discourse is further discussed in § 7.2.2.

Na may also be used to mark the ending of dependent clauses, as in the following example:

> Taim ol sa stap, na i gat wanpla lapun man sa stap antap long wara

> When they lived there, there was an old man who lived up the river [Eastern Highlands M, 14]

As noted previously in § 5.4.2, an additional additive use of *tupela* is sometimes found, as in *man tupela meri bilongen* (a man and/together with his wife). This does not always involve two people only, as the following example shows :

> ... *tupla save stap <u>tupla mama</u>, na papa blong tupla indai pinis...*
>
> the two of them stayed <u>with their mother,</u> and their father had died. [Western Highlands, M, 15]

Although this use is described in some accounts (e.g. Mihalic 1971:199), this was the only example found in the corpus, and it is thus possible that *tupela* as a conjunction may be falling out of use in the spoken language in favour of *wantaim*. However, a contracted form *mitla* with the apparently novel meaning 'I together with ...' was attested from some young informants in Lae:

> *Mipla stap, <u>mitla sista blo mi</u> kam lo sto. Mitla kam baim pikei na mitla kaikai*
>
> We stayed, <u>I and my sister</u> came to the store. We came and bought PK (chewing gum) and we chewed. [Morobe, F, 10]

> *nau yumi hari(m) sta(p), nogat, <u>mitla M.</u> sidaun lo desk ia, nogat, desk ia tanim na <u>mitla M.</u> brukim baksait blo mitla na mitla onem, M. laf nogut tru.*
>
> Now we listened then <u>M. and I</u> sat in the desk, then the desk tipped and <u>M. and I</u> bent our backs and we two, what, M. laughed and laughed. [Morobe, F, 11]

Adversative relations

The word *tasol* is a very common item in the corpus, with over 2500 tokens. Phonological variants include *tsol, sol* and *chol*, as shown below:

> <u>*wanpla boi na wanpla gel sol*</u> *tupla galap go antap lo kokonat.*
>
> <u>Only one boy and one girl</u> climbed the coconut tree. [Simbu, F, 15]

> *na disla moran ia, em sa givim <u>eg na milk chol</u> l' em.*
>
> and this python, he gave it <u>only egg and milk</u> [Enga, F, 13]

Tasol in clause-initial position indicates its use as a conjunction for adversative relations ('but'):

> *wanbla bishop la go stopim ol <u>tasol ol no arim</u> toktok na ol la go fait. <u>Tasol ol stap</u> i go na ol tingting olsem wonem na ol go be(k) gen lo aus nambaut.*
>
> A bishop wanted to stop them <u>but they didn't listen</u> and they were about to go and fight. <u>But they waited</u> and they wondered why and they went back to their houses. [West Sepik, F, 14]

In other positions, *tasol* usually means 'just' or 'only':

> *em bin kilim disla susa na kaikai na <u>liklik brata tasol</u> i bin stap.*
>
> He killed the sister and ate her, and <u>only the small brother</u> remained [East Sepik, M, 15]

The different uses are exemplified in the following:

> <u>*Tsol las tem tsol*</u> *mi bin rait go na mi tokim em osem ...*
>
> <u>But only last term</u> I wrote and told him that ... [Manus, M, 16]

In the corpus, the use of *bat* in a way apparently identical to that of *tasol* was frequently attested, with 59 tokens:

> *mi raun gut <u>bat</u> meinli ol Musau ol i pulap tru long ap*
>
> I enjoyed myself, <u>but</u> the place was full of Mussau Islanders [New Ireland, M, 12]

> *mipla trevel lo Makam Bridj, mipla ksim a tedi min... - ose i no tedi minit <u>bat osem</u> fotin minits samting.*
>
> We travelled to the Markham Bridge, we took thirty min... - like it wasn't thirty minutes <u>but</u> about fourteen minutes. [Enga, M, 12]

> *Skul laif em gutpla <u>bat tu</u> em skin i dai tumas.*
>
> School life is good, <u>but</u> it's also boring. [Eastern Highlands, F, 15]

No other adversative conjunctions were found.

Causative relations

Standard terms to indicate causative relations include *bilong wanem*? 'why?', *long wanem* 'because' and *olsem na* 'so, as a result'. The form *bilong wanem* is also sometimes used to mean 'because'. This is discussed more fully above in § 6.8.3. The term *bikos* has been co-existing with *long wanem* for some time, and is a common item in the corpus, particularly from the New Guinea Islands provinces. There are some 200 tokens in all:

> Ye <u>bikos</u> em i laikim <u>bikos</u> i gat - am mipla i stap klostu lo solwara
>
> Yes, <u>because</u> he likes it <u>because</u> there are - um we stay close to the sea [New Ireland, F, 14]

> ol no laikim osem bai difens fos i go aut lo Manus <u>bikos</u> em bin givim planti halvim lo ol pipol.
>
> They don't want the Defence Force to leave Manus, <u>because</u> it has given a lot of help to the people. [Manus, F, 17]

> ol bin kros lo naratla brada na ol bin rausim em <u>bikos</u> em sa kabubu tumas lo aus.
>
> They were angry with the other brother and threw him out <u>because</u> he farted too much in the house. [Southern Highlands, M, 18]

A regional breakdown shows the greater frequency in the New Guinea Islands sub-corpus:

Bikos by region

Highlands	Islands	Momase
18	72	24

An interesting development is the introduction of *bikos long*, a prepositional phrase analogous to (and possibly calqued on) the English expression 'because of'. There were three tokens in the corpus.

> Wanpla problem mi wok long feisim nau <u>bikos long kraisis</u> long provins blong mi, long Not Solomons, ol bin stopim olgeta postel sevises long hap
>
> one problem I am facing now <u>because of the crisis</u> in my province, North Solomons, they have stopped all postal services there. [East New Britain, M, 19]

> ol rausim pa(p)a blo mipla, i no rausim em bat osem <u>bikos lo trabol</u> na ol rausim em.
>
> they sent my father away, they didn't sack him, but <u>because of the trouble</u> they sent him away. [Eastern Highlands, M, 18]

The replacement of *olsem na* by *so* seems to be quite recent, as it has not been reported in standard accounts of Tok Pisin. It is quite a common feature in the corpus with some 400 tokens:

> na em i silip <u>so</u> man ia i go bek
>
> and he went to sleep <u>so</u> the man went back [East New Britain, F, 15]

> nogat planti deveropment go ro disla hap <u>so</u> - wat - em wokim - em i kam lo Kainantu
>
> not much development came to this place <u>so</u> he did - he came to Kainantu [Eastern Highlands, M, 15]

The phonological resemblance between *so* and reduced forms of *olsem* may be a factor in its ready acceptance by first language Tok Pisin speakers, and it now looks very much like a standard item.

Other conjunctions: **nogat** *and* **yes**

Nogat

The normal gloss for the word *nogat* is 'no', and this is the way in which the word is most frequently used:

> ...lilik boi ia kirap na tok osem "<u>nogat</u>, yu yet sa rong...
>
> ... the small boy said "<u>no</u>, you are wrong... [Eastern Highlands, F, 11]

In addition to straightforward denial or indicating a negative response, *nogat* is also referred to by Lomax (1983:37) in his analysis of letters to editor of *Wantok* newspaper as a recapitulation marker, serving to emphasize a point:

> *mipela ... i harim dispela toktok na i no gutpela tru. <u>Nogat stret</u>!*
>
> We ... heard this talk and it is not good. <u>No indeed</u>!

The use of *nogat* in recapitulation seems to be associated with the rhetoric of persuasion, as in the following extract from a parliamentary speech by Matiabe Yuwi, former member for Southern Highlands, in 1977:

> *i no olgeta Hailan long Papua Niugini i pait wantaim na olgeta de wik yar yar man indai. <u>Nogat</u>! Em i sampela hap tasol.*
>
> It is not all the Highlanders in Papua New Guinea who fight with each other and every day, week, year people die. <u>Certainly not</u>! It's only in some places.

Nogat also has a well-known role in marking unsuccessful action (Dutton 1973:248, Mihalic 1971:31). This use, too, is well attested in the corpus:

> *em go painim ol pisin lo bus nabaut nau <u>nogat</u>*
>
> he went to look for birds in the bush <u>without success</u> [Eastern Highlands, F, 12]

> *Na lapun <u>painim, nogat</u>. Na em go bek <u>painim nogat</u> nau em askim gen ...*
>
> and the old man <u>looked but couldn't find it</u>. And he went back and <u>looked again without success</u> and he asked again ... [(M, 16, Goroka)]

In some cases, the role of *nogat* appears more like a conjunction, as in the following:

> *Nau sinek ia tok "sapos em, okei em ba stap na ba mitla keikei wantem. Sapos sla fes bon na seken bon, tokim ol go <u>nogat</u> mi keikeim ol."*
>
> Now the snake said "if it's him, he can stay and we will eat together. If it's the first born and second born, tell them to go, <u>otherwise</u> I'll eat them." [Western Highlands, M, 16]

This would appear to have arisen through contraction of *sapos nogat* 'if not' or a negative conditional clause.

However, many puzzling occurrences of *nogat* were found which did not fit any of these descriptions. For example, in the following, the story tells of a boy hiding and waiting to catch sight of some cassowaries:

> *Em was i stap ia, <u>nogat</u> em luki(m) ol muruk*
>
> He stayed watching, <u>(?)</u> he saw the cassowaries [Eastern Highlands F, 12]

Here, the action cannot be described as unsuccessful. On the contrary, the boy had just achieved precisely what he set out to do. Moreover, the word is separated from the preceding verb by a pause, suggesting that it belongs with the following clause or in the role of a conjunction. The exact function of *nogat* in such constructions became clearer by examining a number of occurrences, and it appeared that in every case what does occur is a sudden change of state or perception. In an unchanging field or environment where nothing significant is happening, an object, person or event unexpectedly or abruptly appears on the scene. In these and many other cases, the role of *nogat* would appear to be best interpreted as a conjunction meaning something like 'when all of a sudden', indicating the unexpected onset of an event. In the following examples, all taken from a 12-year old girl in Lae, this interpretation would appear to be the best one:

> *Lo(ng) aste ia mi sta(p) lo(ng) (h)aus, <u>noga(t)</u> wanpla meri ka(m) na to(k) (ol)sem ...*
>
> yesterday I was in the house <u>when (unexpectedly)</u> a woman came and said ...

> *mipla plei go ia <u>nogat</u> ol ringim bel*
>
> we were playing <u>when all of a sudden</u> the bell rang

> *mi wokabaut kam ia <u>nogat</u> wanpla lilik manggi sin(g)aut ose "hoi"*
>
> I was coming along <u>when suddenly</u> a small boy shouted "hoi"

> *Mipla sidaun na stori stap ia <u>nogat</u> diwai kam.*
>
> We were sitting telling stories <u>when (without warning)</u> the branch broke off.
>
> *Mipla stap ia <u>noga(t)</u> ol meri kira(p) to(k), "ol man fait ia yumipla go lukim"*
>
> We were there <u>when suddenly</u> the women announced "the men are fighting. Let's go and see what's happening". [Morobe, F, 12]

In most of the above cases, *nogat* follows *ia*, which may act as an additional signal for imminent change of state. Although this use of *nogat* was most prominent among young people in Lae, it was also attested in other provinces:

> *Nau mi stap yet na mi laik kam autsaid, <u>nogat</u> narapla ken i pairap nau mi siksti kam ia, nogat olgeta man wok (l)o ran i go lo disla, ranawe lo disla hap.*
>
> I was still there and was about to come outside <u>when</u> another one (gun) went off. I came very quickly but everybody was running to this place [Eastern Highlands, M, 18]
>
> *wanpla taim ia wanpla pis na wanpla pisin sa stap. Tupla sa stap ia <u>nogat</u> wanpla taim tupla bin go digim ol yam*
>
> once there was a fish and a bird. The two stayed (without anything happening) <u>when one day</u> they went to dig yams [Enga, F, 13]
>
> *em lak go kisim <u>nogat</u> em lukim lapun man ia has nating*
>
> He was about to go and get it <u>when</u> he saw the old man completely naked [Madang, M, 11]

Whether or not there is substrate motivation for this change is not yet known. It appears more likely to be another case of incipient grammaticalization through common words in discourse being reanalyzed in other roles, with or without substrate reinforcement.

Yes

Lomax (1983: 41) notes that *yes* is a common rhetorical feature of *Wantok* letters, and appears to be best translated as 'well then' or a similar phrase :

> *Mi gat bikpela kros long ol plisman. <u>Yes</u>, ol plisman ...*
>
> I am very angry with the police. <u>Well then</u>, you policemen

This was not at all common in the spoken narratives in this corpus, and it may be a more typical rhetorical device for written opinions. However, one or two tokens could be found:

> *Okei em i go na lapun meri ia i askim em, "<u>yes, yangpla</u> yu laikim wonem?"*
>
> So he went and the old woman asked him "<u>well, young man</u>, what do you want?" [East New Britain, M, 12]

There were also one or two instances where *yes* was used to introduce a topic:

> *<u>Yes,</u> aste long grediueishen em, ol planti lain i kam tasol bikpla ren*
>
> <u>Well</u>, yesterday at graduation, a lot of people came but it rained hard [Southern Highlands, M, 15]
>
> *<u>Yes,</u> stori blong mi go osem, a long naintin eiti nain*
>
> <u>Well</u>, my story goes like this, in 1989... [West Sepik, M, 16]

Most of the remainder of the 60 or so occurrences of *yes* were used simply for affirmation of a fact.

> *bikbos blo peles ia nau i kirap i askim, "yu onem kain man, yu wanpla medjik man, yu wanpla man blo wokim puripuri a?" Na man ia kirap na i tok, "<u>yes</u> mi man blo wokim puripuri".*
>
> The big boss of the village asked him "what kind of man are you, are you a magician, a sorcerer?" And the man said "<u>yes</u>, I'm a sorcerer." [New Ireland, M, 12]

7.2 Maintaining coherence in spoken discourse

As noted above, the texts which constitute this corpus of spoken language are of a somewhat restricted genre. Respondents were mainly involved in telling a story under rather formal conditions, aware that the speech was being recorded on tape by an expatriate visitor of uncertain status. The speech was generally in the form of an unscripted monologue, without interruptions, although one or two friends present occasionally provided some feedback in the form of laughter or other non-verbal responses. It is therefore important to note that generalizations made about this genre are not necessarily applicable to other situations. In particular, phenomena such as turn-taking, which can be observed in natural conversations involving two or more participants, do not apply here. Nevertheless, many respondents produced fluent and copious responses as though a larger audience were present, and, within the limitations outlined above, some conventions of narrative organization can be discussed. These are narrative openings, temporal sequencing and the introduction of quoted or reported speech.

7.2.1 Beginning a narrative

As seen in Slone (2001), traditional narratives have certain discourse conventions. Here also, most narratives, both traditional and contemporary, began with certain conventional features. Stories generally opened with a general or specific time setting, and were often introduced by stating the intention to speak or tell a story, and whether the story was true or not. Traditional stories may, in addition, have started with a formulaic phrase. Some specific time settings can be seen in the following openings:

> *Long last holidei, mi wantem sampla poro - poro, ol manggi blo mi, mipla go raun long wanpla wara, mipla go painim pis.*
>
> Last holiday, I and some friends, my mates, we went to a river, we went to catch fish [East Sepik, M, 15]
>
> *A long naintin eiti tu mi bin, am lo krismas papa blo mi go bringim mi long Motlok na mi wokim greid wan blo mi.*
>
> In 1982 I, um at Christmas my father brought me to Mortlock Islands and I did grade one. [East New Britain, M, 15]

More indefinite time reference, equivalent to 'once upon a time' is usually expressed by *wanpela taim*:

> *Wanla taim i bin i gat wanpla man wanla meri na pikinini blong ol. Ol i bin i stap na wanla taim papa laik go lo wanbla hap*
>
> Once upon a time there was a man his wife and his child. One time the father wanted to go to another place... [Southern Highlands, M, 15]
>
> *Wanpla taim tupla brata tupla stap na bikpla brata i go kalapim galip*
>
> Once there were two brothers and the elder brother went to climb a galip nut tree. [West New Britain, M, 11]

An indication of a greater time depth, putting the story firmly into the realm of the traditional, is usually indicated by **bifo tru** (70 tokens) or an intensified version such as **bifo bifo tru** (53 tokens). **Bifo yet** was rarely encountered, with only three tokens.

> *Long bifo bifo tru long ples blo papa blo mi, ol - bifo tumbuna - ol i no sawe pekpek long as, ol sa pekpek lo maus tasol.*
>
> Long, long ago in my father's village, the ancestors didn't use to defecate through their anus, they would just defecate through their mouths. [West Sepik, F, 13]
>
> *Yes, bifo bifo tru a tupla papa na pikinini meri i stap long wanpla maunten, na wanpla taim ...*
>
> So, a long time ago, a father and his daughter lived on a mountain, and one day, [Eastern Highlands, M, 18]

Otherwise, narratives usually opened with a general statement of the intention to tell a story, where it came from or generally what it was about:

> *Stori bai mi stori len em wanpla stori we i bin kamap taim, mi bin kam lo Kevieng niupla. Taim mi kamap lo Kevieng niupla*
>
> The story I'll tell is about what happened when I first came to Kavieng. When I first came to Kavieng ... [New Ireland, F, 15]

> *Stori blo mi go olsem. <u>Em stori blo wanpla sneik we i bin stap lo Bali bifo</u> lo - em sneik blo klen blo mipla tasol nau em i no mo stap wantem mipla na stori blo mi go olsem. Bifo tru i gat wanpla sneik i stap lo ples blo mipla*
>
> <u>My story goes like this. It is a story about a snake which lived in Bali before</u> - it's my clan's snake, but now it doesn't live with us, and my story goes like this. Long ago there lived a snake in our village [West New Britain, F, 15]

> *<u>Mi gat wanla stori em kam long Chimbu Provins</u>. Disla stori em kam long Chimbu Provins na <u>em wanla trupela stori</u>. Am, i bin gatim tupela - wanla - tupla barata na susa.*
>
> <u>I've got a story from Chimbu Province</u>.[38] This story comes from Chimbu Province and <u>it's a true story</u>. Um, there was once two - one - a brother and sister. [Western Highlands, M, 17]

> *<u>Stori blo mi em olsem</u>. Em olsem <u>wanbla taim</u> mipla bin stap go raun lo Rabaul*
>
> <u>My story goes like this</u>. <u>One time</u> we went around in Rabaul [Manus, M, 17]

The formulaic phrase *stori stori* 'the story tells…' was sometimes adopted for beginnings, but only in the Manus samples, where all 12 tokens were found:

> *<u>Stori stori lo wanpla stori kam long am Sentrol Provins</u>. <u>Stori stori</u> wanpla - wanpla taim lo Rigo, na i no bin gat paia lo Rigo lo bifo.*
>
> <u>The story tells of a story from Central Province</u>. <u>The story says</u>, once upon a time in Rigo, there was once no fire in Rigo. [Manus, F, 14]

> *<u>Stori stori</u>, mi laik stori long tupla sista sta lo peles. Wanpla taim…*
>
> <u>The story goes</u>, I want to tell about two sisters in the village. One time … [Manus, F, 13]

> *Stori blo mi go osem. <u>Stori stori</u> i gat tupla brata.*
>
> <u>My story goes like this</u>. <u>The story</u> tells of two brothers. [Manus, M, 13]

The formula was also occasionally used to finish up:

> *nau ol Kupiano man ol save lukim olsem sinek i nogat lek na em i save wokobaut tasol lo bel blong em. <u>Stori stori i pinis</u>.*
>
> Now Kupiano people see that the snake has no legs and just crawls on its belly. <u>That's the end of the story</u>. [Manus, F, 15]

Rhetorical recapitulation was also sometimes included in the introduction to narratives, repeating the intention to tell a story about a certain topic:

> *Mi laik stori long ol poroman blo mi na mipla bin go painim masrum, <u>longen mi laik stori</u>.*
>
> I want to tell you about my friends and I going to look for mushrooms. <u>That's what I want to talk about</u>. [Western Highlands, M, 16]

7.2.2 Temporal sequence

Time relations may be indicated morphologically by means of tense markers, or by adverbial or conjunctive elements giving information about time of occurrence or stages in a temporal sequence. As discussed more fully above, inflectional tense morphology has not developed in Tok Pisin, although particles such as *bai, bin* and *pinis* can express tense and aspectual distinctions, and a number of time adverbials are used, some of which appear to have developed into aspect particles (*bai*) or conjunctions (*afta long, bihain long*). In narrative sequencing, the expressions *na* and *nau* are widely used, and as noted previously, there is some confusion between the use of the two terms. The phrases *em nau* or *orait* are frequently used to mark the completion of one stage and the beginning of the next.

One of the best-known ways of sequencing discourse is that described by Mihalic (1971:48). He notes the use in narration of *orait* accompanied by repetition of the main verb of the preceding sentence, usually accompanied by *pinis*, as discussed in § 6.3.5. In spite of its frequent use in written Tok Pisin, the 'classic' pattern verb-*pinis-orait*, is very uncommon in the corpus, with only five examples found:

---

[38] Chimbu is a variant pronunciation of Simbu (Province).

em tokim ol na tok "yupla wokim hul l(ong) (di)sla ap" n' ol <u>wokim hul pinis, orait</u> em kilim pik.

He told them "make a hole in this place" and <u>when they had dug the hole</u> he killed the pig. [Simbu, M, 17]

yumi <u>mekim pikinik pinis, orait</u> pa(p)a blo em tokim yumi long kam.

We <u>had our picnic, then</u> his father told us to come. [West Sepik, M, 15]

Okei manggi ia i harim tok tasol i go kisim i kam, <u>putim pinis orait</u> biain nau em i wasim disla lapun meri ia

Then the boy heard but went to get it. <u>After putting it,</u> then he watched the old woman. [East New Britain, M, 12]

Although this *orait-pinis* construction does evidently have a role in sequencing discourse, more common is the use of *orait* alone as a stage marker or with *sapos* in 'if-then' constructions. In the following extended section of narrative, note the frequent use of *orait* separating the stages in a sequence of events:

Em tok, "nogat." <u>Orait</u> taim em i kalapim kokonas i go, em i les wantem, i kalapim kokonas na i tromoi tasol kokonas i kam daun. <u>Orait</u> biain i tok lo pulumapim wara, em i karim baket i go na i pulumapim hap, liklik hap wara tasol na i karim i kam antap. <u>Orait</u> em i tok lo wasim meri ia, lapun meri ia em i no wasim em gut, em i tromoi wara tasol antap lo em. <u>Okei</u> biain nau lapun meri tok, "<u>orait</u> yangpla yu mas go nau, i no ken stap wantaim mi lo hia." <u>Orait</u> taim em i go sidaun lo kanu, em i tok, "bai mi putim disla kokonas biain lo yu na yu no ken lukluk kam biain." Na taim em i laik pul i go nau em i stat lukluk baksait na seim taim disla kokonas i wok lo go drai. <u>Orait</u> biain em i pul i go longwe nau i harim wanpla vois i kam biain na em i tanim, em i ting osem wanpla nais meri - wanpla naispla meri nogat em lukim hap krokodail i silip i stap.

She said "no". <u>So</u> when he climbed the coconut he was lazy, just climbed the coconut and threw the coconuts down. <u>Then</u> later she told him to fetch some water, he carried the bucket and just brought a little bit of water and brought it back. <u>Then</u> she told him to wash the woman, the old woman, he didn't wash her well, he just threw water over her. <u>Then</u> the old woman said "all right, young man, you must go now, you can't stay here with me." <u>Then</u>, when he went to sit down in the canoe, she said "I will put these coconuts behind you and you mustn't look behind." And when he was about to paddle, he looked back, and at the same time the coconuts started to turn dry. <u>Then</u> he paddled a long way and he heard a voice behind him and he turned round, thinking it was a beautiful girl, but it was a crocodile lying there. [East New Britain, M, 12]

Romaine has discussed the use of *okei* as an alternative to *orait* (1992a), noting that it is increasingly used, especially by younger speakers. As discussed in Chapter 3, this is confirmed in the present corpus, where *okei* (including its variants *oke* and *kei*) was considerably more often used, with 940 tokens of *okei* compared with only 149 of *orait*. A differentiation of meaning also appears to be emerging. The use of *orait* is frequently reserved for the alternative meanings of 'all right, in good condition' or 'allowed, permissible':

Biain anti blo mi bin go kisim ol sampla ol diwai lo bus na kam gim em na em <u>orait</u> gen.

Afterwards my aunt went and collected some leaves from the bush and gave them to him and he is <u>all right</u> again. [East New Britain, F, 16]

long mi yet mi ting Manus em <u>orait</u> bikos nogat planti trabel olsem lo hia.

As for me, I think Manus is <u>all right</u> because there is not a lot of trouble like here. [East New Britain, M, 19]

mipla no sa gat dens olgeta taim na, ol komplen lo dens nau, etmasta <u>tok orait</u> l' ol nau, ol putim dens

we never had dances and they complained about the lack of dances, the headmaster <u>agreed</u> and they put on a dance. [West Sepik, F, 17]

The use of *okei*, on the other hand, is not used in the corpus to mean 'all right' in the sense of in good condition. There is the single word expression indicating agreement:

Em tok sem "sa(po)s yu lukim wanpla bikpla fish o liklik fish yu mas sutim tasol." Na papa bl' em tok "<u>okei</u>."

He said "if you see a big fish or a small fish, just shoot it" And his father said "<u>OK</u>." [Morobe, F, 11]

Otherwise, *okei* is exclusively reserved for time sequencing:

> *Em kam, okei em pusi(m) go lo osem baret nau, okei anti blo mi ol kam nau ba ol lak tanim go lo namel gen.*
>
> He came, <u>then</u> he pushed it into the drain, <u>then</u> my aunt came and she wanted to put it back in the middle again. [West Sepik, F, 15]

> *yu no ken lukluk baksait inap yu harim traipla pairap okei bai yu tanim na bai yu lukluk.*
>
> You mustn't look back until you hear a big noise, <u>then</u> you turn round and look. [East New Britain, F, 14]

In many instances, however, recapitulation of the verb may not be accompanied by either *orait, okei* or *pinis*.

> *em i kisim teil blong dok ia na em i <u>kukim</u>. <u>Kukim</u> na em <u>kaikai</u>. <u>Kaikai</u> na em wokim paia na i stap klostu long em i go inap tulait moning nau, em i ron i <u>kam</u> lo peles. <u>Kam</u> na askim mama blong em "a yu lukim dok tu?"*
>
> he took the dog's tail and <u>cooked it</u>. <u>Cooked it</u> and <u>ate it</u>. <u>Ate it</u> and he made a fire and stayed beside it until morning, he <u>ran back</u> to the village. <u>Ran back</u> and asked his mother "have you seen the dog?" [Madang, M, 19]

Recapitulation of items other than the final verb such as the object nominal is also possible, as in the following:

> *em i katim yau blo em nau <u>em pilim pen</u>. <u>Pen nogut tru</u>, kam luki(m) dog ia na dog ia tok ...*
>
> he cut his ear and <u>felt pain</u>. <u>Big pain</u>, he came to see the dog and the dog said ... [East Sepik, M, 15]

More common in such 'head-tail' linkages, however, is the use of *nau* with the repetition of the preceding verb.

> *ol stap antap long hap nau <u>ol sut</u>. <u>Ol sut</u> nau, ol dedi blo mi ... ol i harim*
>
> they were above us and <u>they were shooting</u>. <u>They were</u> shooting and our fathers heard it. [Western Highlands, M, 15]

> *tupla go na manggi ia kirap <u>em go</u>. <u>Em go nau</u> na tupla meri ia tupla pulmapim wara pinis nau tupla go lo aus*
>
> the two went and the boy too <u>went</u>. <u>He went now</u> and the two women got water and went to the house [Madang, M, 12]

Although usually glossed as 'now', *nau* in these cases does not usually indicate that something is happening at the present moment, but orders separate events into a time sequence relative to one another. The frequent use of *nau* in delimiting sequential stages can be seen in the following extended narrative:

> *em no lukim sneik ia n' em kam daun bek. <u>Nau</u> bikpla brata blen go antap. Em go ia em go luki(m) sneik stap antap lo brensh blo diwai <u>nau</u>, em poret <u>nau</u>, em la kalap kam daun ia nogat, sneik ia tok osem "mi man ia, karim mi go daun." <u>Nau</u> em karim em go daun <u>nau</u>, em karim em go daun lo graun <u>nau</u>, liglig brata blen ia em luki(m) sneik ia, em lak ranawei ia*
>
> he didn't see the snake and he came back down. <u>Now</u> his big brother went up. He went and he saw the snake on the branch <u>and</u> he was afraid, he wanted to jump down but the snake said "I am a man, take me down." <u>So</u> he took him down, he took him down to the ground, his little brother saw the snake and wanted to run away. [Goroka, F, 12]

Expression of time sequence within a narrative using *nau* may also rely very heavily on distinctive intonational patterns to indicate separate stages in a sequence. In the following extract, each *nau* is delivered with a characteristic high tone, while the concluding word has a low tone indicating completion. This pattern seems to be more typical of younger speakers :

> *Em nau, tupla <u>sutim nau</u>, tupla karim long, wanem ia, <u>pasim wanpla diwai nau</u>, na tupla pasim rop wantaim <u>leg blong em nau</u> na tupla <u>taitim nau</u> na tupla wokabaut i kam daun.*
>
> They <u>shot it</u>, carried it - <u>tied it to a pole</u> - tied <u>up its legs</u> and came back down. [East New Britain, M, 13]

A distinctive pattern of linking clauses in the Islands sample was first noticed when studying concordance figures of certain collocations (Smith 1996). The following conspicuous differences are found when looking at the co-occurrence of *i* following *na* and *nau*:

Na i and nau i

	na i	nau i
Islands	315	168
Momase	99	13
Highlands	32	13

In the Islands sample, these combinations frequently serve to link clauses in temporal sequence, as the following examples illustrate:

> *em wok lo pul pul i go lukim shedo blong em <u>na i lukim</u> osem meri bl' em, blad.*
>
> He paddled and saw his reflection <u>and it looked</u> like his wife, blood. [East New Britain, M, 12]

> *em kam <u>nau i</u> lukim tupla nau, em sore lo disa (s)amting bloen*
>
> he came <u>now, and</u> saw the two of them, he was sorry for this thing [New Ireland, F, 13]

This process was far less frequent in the other regional samples, where a subject pronoun rather than *i* tends to be used.

7.2.3 Reporting speech

As noted by Mühlhäusler (1985h:413), both direct and indirect quotations can be produced. This is shown by the following examples from the corpus:

> *tupla lukim ol popo wantaim ol pis na tupla <u>tok olsem</u> "mi laik kaikai pis ia."*
>
> The two saw the pawpaw and the fish and they <u>said "I want to eat</u> fish." [East New Britain, M, 11]

> *Tasol nau ol i senisim toktok gen na <u>ol i tok olsem ol i laik</u> buruk lusim Papua Niugini.*
>
> But now they have changed their minds again and they <u>say they want to</u> secede from Papua New Guinea. [East New Britain, M, 19]

The above examples are introduced by *olsem*, (discussed in § 6.7.1), but this is sometimes omitted in both direct and indirect quotations:

> *Fait i go tsol nau, bikman lo ples <u>tok</u> "em inap nau."*
>
> The fight continued, the chief of the village <u>said</u> "that's enough." [East Sepik, M, 16]

> *Em go singaut nau, <u>em tok em go waswas</u> nau, mipla kam ausait*
>
> He called out and <u>said he was going to wash</u>, and we came outside [Morobe, F, 12]

In many cases direct quotations can be distinguished from indirect quotations by the pronoun used, but in the case of a first person narrator reporting his or her own speech, it may not be clear. The following, for example, could be interpreted as either a direct or indirect quotation:

> *Mi tok (")mi no lukim ples na mi mas i go stap pastaim(").*
>
> I said "I haven't seen the place and I must go", or I said that I hadn't seen the place and must go. [Eastern Highlands, M, 16]

Intonation may be the only distinguishing feature. The verb *tok* may be repeated when introducing quotations, as in the following:

> *Sista Magret bin kam na em i <u>tokim em tok</u> "sapos yu gat wone(m) kain tingting lo toktok yu no ken kam totok lo ol ticha blo mi, yu mas kam pastem lo mi na toktok."*
>
> Sister Margaret came and <u>said to him</u> "if you have something to say, don't come and talk to my teachers, you must come and talk to me first." [Manus, F, 15]

This construction looks as though it might be a syntactic means of distinguishing direct quotations from indirect, but this does not always appear to be the case, as it is also used with indirect quotations:

> *ol ami ia bin kisim gan na ol bin putim lo nek blong Komending Ofisa na ol <u>tokim em tok</u> em mas go bek lo Lombrum, ol laik kam distroyim taun.*
>
> The soldiers held a gun to the neck of the Commanding Officer and they <u>told him</u> he must go back to Lombrum, they were coming to destroy the town. [Manus, F, 15]

The phrase *tok i spik* occurs in Mihalic (1971) and is commonly found in various religious materials. It is also reported by Mühlhäusler (1985h:413) as a marker of direct speech, but was not found at all in the corpus. In spite of its institutionalization in biblical texts, it sounds very much like an archaic feature. It was also seen that the expression *tok se* is restricted to samples from New Guinea Islands provinces except where *se* is clearly a reduction of *olsem* in rapid speech.

A distinctive pattern is found in the speech of some speakers in Highlands provinces where *em tok olsem* 'he/she said' always appears after the quotation, as well as or instead of before it:

> *tupla go l' papa bl' em na <u>em to sem</u> "mi laik - mi laikim sla boi" <u>em tog osem</u>. Nau em gi(vi)m dsla boi lo gel ia, "tupla bai marit," <u>em to sem</u>*
>
> the two went to his father and <u>she said</u> "I would like this boy" <u>she said</u>. Now he gave this boy to the girl, "the two will be married" <u>he said</u>. [Simbu, F, 14]

> *<u>em to se</u> "skin blo mi we?" <u>em tok osem</u> ia noga(t), ol kirap na <u>to ose</u> "mipla i no save" <u>ol tok osem</u> nau*
>
> <u>she said</u> "Where is my skin?" <u>she said</u>, but they got up and <u>said</u> "we don't know," <u>they said</u>. [Eastern Highlands, F, 12]

> *em <u>tok osem</u> "yu pulapim na kam biein" na <u>em tok</u> "mi go pas" <u>em tok ose</u>.*
>
> <u>He said</u> "fill it up and then come" and <u>he said</u> "I'll go first," <u>he said</u>. [Simbu, M, 15]

The use of the expression *o* before quotations is reasonably common with 105 tokens, and does not appear to have been commented on before. The expression could often be interpreted as an exclamation:

> *em krai n' <u>em tok</u> "o gutla tru yu kam" em to sem.*
>
> She cried and <u>said "oh!</u> it's good that you have come." [Simbu, M, 15]

However, there are examples where an exclamation does not seem to be an appropriate interpretation, such as the following reported message, where *o* appears to serve as an introduction to what was said:

> *Okei neks dei nau ol sali(m) tok kam tok "<u>o papa go pinis</u> lo Wiwek."*
>
> So the next day they sent word saying "<u>your father has gone</u> to Wewak." [East Sepik, F, 15]

Here it is not clear if quotation marks should be used, as the pronoun qualifying 'father' has been left out. It does appear, however, that among some individuals *o* is becoming re-interpreted as a marker indicating the onset of reported speech:

> *na em kirap n' <u>em tok</u> "o mi ga(t) wei, bai yupla rausim wan wan fedhes bl' yupla na putim lo han blo mi."*
>
> and he <u>said</u> "I have a way, you should pull out some of your feathers and put them into my hand." [West Sepik, F, 12]

> *nau tupla lugim tupla yet na tupla ting <u>mas</u> "o em mitla brada susa tasol" em to(k).*
>
> now the two looked at themselves and <u>thought</u> "we must be brother and sister" he said. [Simbu, M, 15]

> *mi lukim ol lain sidaun lo kar nau <u>mi tok</u> "o em mas kar blo papa blo mi," man mi sore nogut tru.*
>
> I saw the groups sitting in the car and <u>I said</u> "it must be my father's car," and I was very sad. [West Sepik, F, 15]

In some cases the locutionary verb is even omitted before the quotation, adding support to the interpretation of *o* as a marker of the onset of reported speech:

> *em lugim na <u>em</u> "<u>o</u> em mas meri blo mi" em ting osem.*

> He saw it and <u>he (said)</u> "it must be my wife" he thought. [Simbu, F, 14]

In a similar way, the use of *nau* appears in some cases to be used to mark the end of a quotation. In the following, for example, the quotation appears to end in *nau*, with an upward intonation, similar to sequence marking, but it is clear that *nau* is not part of the actual speech, and it indicates that the quoted passage has come to an end:

> *Na em tok "o disla em mas ... disla manggi ia em tok em gat string lo leg ia - ol pasim leg blo em <u>lo string</u>," <u>nau</u>, em go.*

> And she said "o this must be ... this boy who said he had string on his leg - who was tied up <u>with string</u>," and she went [West Sepik, F, 15]

8
Discussion of findings

This chapter rounds off the investigation by looking at its implications for some issues in the study of Tok Pisin and creolistics in general, and drawing some conclusions. The findings impinge on a number of theoretical areas, which were identified in Chapter 2. Firstly, the question of the influence of superstrate, substrate and universals in development will be dealt with (§ 8.1). The findings of the present research are examined to see if any further light is thrown on their relative importance. This is followed by an examination of the relationship between Tok Pisin and English (§ 8.2). One striking finding of the present study is that there is an increasingly close relationship between the lexical inventory of the two languages as a growing number of young people acquire varying degrees of bilingualism as they grow up with Papua New Guinea's English-based education system. At the same time, Tok Pisin is developing in other directions as the influence of local varieties is felt and its own idiomatic patterns become established. This situation will first be discussed with reference to Thomason & Kaufman's model of language contact, to attempt to anticipate possible future trends. Then the question of borrowing, code-mixing and code-switching will be discussed with reference to the present data. Finally, the question of whether "decreolization" is leading to a post-Pidgin or post-Creole continuum is considered. In the conclusion, some recommendations for further research and action are made in relation to the study's limitations and to Papua New Guinea's education and language planning needs (§ 8.3).

8.1 Superstrate, substrate and universals

As noted in Chapter 2, much of the debate surrounding the question of substrate, superstrate and universal influence has been concerned with genesis. The present research does not shed any light on the early periods of Tok Pisin's history, but, as Mühlhäusler is fond of reminding us, Tok Pisin is not an unchanging static entity but an abstraction for a complex of varied and ever-changing ideolects subjected to an equally complex constellation of influences through time. It is thus assumed that the question of substrate, superstrate and universals may still be relevant to the language of young first language speakers of what is now a stabilized and nativized language. A review of the influence of these factors follows.

8.1.1 Superstrate influence

To describe English as the "superstrate" of Tok Pisin could imply that English was a prestigious target language in the early stages of development, or merely that English has supplied the bulk of the lexicon. While the notion of target can be disputed (Baker 1990b), English has clearly contributed the majority of the lexicon to Tok Pisin, and as the vocabulary expands, this contribution appears to be continuing or even growing. However, to refer to English as the superstrate in the later stages of Tok Pisin's development is somewhat unusual, and it is in the area of superstrate influence that there is perhaps the best case for limiting discussion to the origin stage.

As a result, it is considered that the term is not appropriate in a discussion of current developments. As Mühlhäusler notes (1981:58), there is now a fundamentally different process at work from that which obtained during the early formation of the language. Tok Pisin is not a temporary interlanguage on the way to full competence in English, however much early administrators such as Sir Hubert Murray would have liked to believe that such a scenario could exist. What essentially characterizes the present situation is the co-existence of two developed systems in contact. So although the influence of English on Tok Pisin is great, it would be better considered from the point of view of contact-induced change rather than superstrate influence, and further discussion is reserved for § 8.2.

8.1.2 Substrate influences on Tok Pisin

Again, the question of origins will be ignored here, except to note that some of the earlier work on the assumed "substrate" languages of Tok Pisin left something to be desired. Nevertheless, studies such as Keesing (1988) and Crowley (1990a) have greatly advanced our knowledge of the early stages of Melanesian Pidgin. The discussion here is confined to the effects of other languages in current use on the structure and development of contemporary Tok Pisin. Even though there is now a sizeable and growing population of first language speakers, the majority of those who speak Tok Pisin do so as a second language. It is thus to be expected that there would be considerable influence on their speech patterns from other languages spoken. Since the subjects of this study are first-language speakers, substrate influence will be felt only indirectly, as a result of their interaction with second-language speakers in restricted geographical areas. However, as Faraclas has shown (1989), substrate influence may still be influential in the speech of first language users.

That one's first language influences the production of second language forms is uncontroversial, and is the basis of much of the current discussion in language pedagogy, second language acquisition, interlanguage studies and so on. The link to second language acquisition is reasonably obvious, and this was recognized quite early in Pidgin and Creole studies. For example, part of the 1979 Linguistic Society of America conference was devoted to the relationship between second language acquisition and pidginization (Andersen 1983), and it seemed at the time as though this was going to set the agenda for Pidgin and Creole studies in the coming decades. However, the momentum produced by the conference and publication appeared to have been lost until the subject was revived by Mufwene (1990c) and Siegel (1997b, 1999).

Mufwene's paper reviews the substrate hypothesis and some of its shortcomings, and looks at some mutually beneficial ways that it could interact with second language acquisition studies. In particular, the notion of transfer is explored. Siegel (1997b, 1999) takes this further and looks in detail at the way various features from substrate languages could have been incorporated into Melanesian Pidgin. The challenge by Bickerton, Mufwene and others to provide exact details of the processes by which substrate influence is felt is taken up and dealt with head-on. In particular, the two stage process by which features are transferred to the linguistic repertoire of individuals, and the subsequent adoption of some of these by communities (Siegel 1999), is a useful way of explaining this influence.

Prior to the appearance of these articles, the most detailed and convincing demonstration of the relationship between grammatical features in second language Tok Pisin varieties and other languages spoken by the same speaker was Reesink (1990). Particularly useful in this paper is the statistical treatment of the occurrence of various Tok Pisin forms and their homologues in the first language. Speakers of typologically unrelated languages, Usan, Mangap-Mbula and Polopa were recorded in Tok Pisin and their native language, and discourse features such as head-tail linkage, switch reference and clausal conjunctions were examined. He concludes that the results "suggest a high degree of substratum influence on Tok Pisin" (1990:303).

Although the ultimate origins of Tok Pisin lie somewhat earlier in Australia (Baker 1993), substrate influences continued to be felt from Austronesian languages of the Central Pacific during the middle decades of the 19th century, (Keesing 1988) and from New Britain and New Ireland from around the end of the 19th Century (Ross 1992). As Tok Pisin's range spreads further into areas where the typologically unrelated Papuan languages are spoken, considerable interference is likely to be felt. Without a detailed knowledge of all the language spoken in the area, it is difficult to confirm this, but there are a number of indications that substrate forces are at work. Dutton & Bourke (1990) show that the unusual clause-final use of *taim* 'when' in Southern Highlands has direct parallels in the local languages. Similarly, Franklin (1980) relates differentiation of discourse structure using *na* or *i* in the Tok Pisin spoken in Southern Highlands to patterns in the Kewa language spoken in the area.

It is suspected that many of the features found only in certain regions or provinces are due to the indirect influence of substrate grammars. For example, as pointed out by Lynch (p c), the relative frequency of the verb *stap* found in some of the Highlands samples may be related to the large variety of existential verbs which have been described in languages of the Highlands region (Piau 1981). The most obvious case of probable substrate influence is perhaps the regional variation in the presence of the predicate marker *i*. As has already been suggested (Reesink 1990) the absence of the marker in most Papuan languages and its presence in many Austronesian languages goes a long way towards explaining the disparity between the use of the particle in the Islands Region, where Austronesian languages are common, and the other regions, where Papuan languages predominate. Also strongly suspected of substrate influence are the pattern of relative clause marking with *longen*, distinctive patterns of speech quotation in the Highlands, and the much greater use of past marking with *bin* in the Islands. However, this remains to be confirmed by further investigation. Phonological features in Tok Pisin can in some cases be directly linked to substrate phonology, such as the lack of p/f distinction in parts of Bougainville and the Highlands (see also Laycock 1985).

There is some evidence, then, of influence from other languages, but many potential substrate patterns may go unrecognized because of lack of knowledge of the appropriate features in languages of the area (Reesink 1990:303). A word of caution is in order when making synchronic comparisons of forms from different languages. As Mühlhäusler has shown (1986a), such comparisons can be highly misleading without taking into account the historical development of the languages in question. Thus while in many cases substrate influence is suspected, it cannot be conclusively demonstrated without a more in-depth comparison with other languages in contact. It is to be hoped that other scholars with more intimate knowledge of Papua New Guinean languages may be in a position both to recognize relationships to substrate languages in the Tok Pisin described in this study, and to uncover further examples of such influence in due course. Studies by Papua New Guinean scholars would be particularly valuable here.

8.1.3 Evidence for universals in Tok Pisin's development

Bickerton (1981) has stressed the role of universals in the development of so-called abrupt Creoles, where it is assumed that the quality of linguistic input was inadequate for normal modelling, and innate universals in the child brain took over the process. The debate over this alleged bioprogram has tended to obscure the role of universals in later stages of development, but as Mühlhäusler (1985m:456) has noted, universals may still have a significant role during these stages. He has postulated a number of implicational universals during the process of expansion, for example the order of establishment of plural marking in different syntactic positions and degrees of animacy.

Other studies have shown a continual development of new roles arising out of the use of certain items in discourse. The best known is perhaps Sankoff & Brown's (1976) study of the development of Tok Pisin relatives in discourse. One problem always present is unravelling the individual influences and assigning a cause to one or another process. Reesink (1990:297), for example, has shown that there is an alternative substrate explanation for *ia*-bracketed relatives, as deictics can be observed to act as relativizers in a number of Papuan languages. He also points out the obvious but often overlooked fact that universals, being 'universal', are, *ipso facto*, likely to be present in substrate languages (1990:303). Nonetheless, discourse is a promising area to search for universal processes of grammaticalization, in particular those changes arising as a result of frequent, fluent and fast exchanges between peers.

One of the most obvious features of the present corpus is the phonological streamlining which characterizes so much first language speech discussed in § 3.4. Similar changes occur in widely separated parts of the country, and it appears that universal tendencies are operating here, such as assimilation and the loss of final consonants and unstressed syllables, although again the influence of substrate phonology may also be a factor.

Another interesting process is that of functional shift, where the semantic content of a word becomes "bleached" as it takes on a functional role. Numerous cases can be observed in the early stages of Pidgin or Creole formation, for example, the reinterpretation of 'him' as a transitive suffix, but it is less common in the later stages of development. However, a number of possible examples can be seen from the corpus. The apparent change in role of **nogat** 'no, not' from adverbial to conjunction is one example. Others include the occasional use of the serial verb **winim** 'to win' to indicate 'more than', similar to the pattern described for Bislama; the reinterpretation of **longen** 'in it' as a delimiter of relative clauses; the semantic bleaching of **nabaut** 'around' in the Highlands samples, the re-interpretation of **bek**, and the use serial use of **kirap** with verbs of locution to indicate the initiation of a conversation turn.

It appears, then, that substrate languages are still a major influence on first language Tok Pisin, and that universal processes of phonological change and grammaticalization are also operating. Assigning primacy to one process or another may be difficult, and perhaps even unnecessary. As Mufwene points out in the title of his 1986 paper, "the universalist and substrate hypotheses complement one another." Baker too (1994, 1995b) offers an alternative to the substrate-universalist debate in the form of a "creativist" hypothesis, where the utilization of the available resources is stressed. This is a refreshing change of approach, viewing language development, especially genesis, as a creative process in contrast to those models which stress deficiency. Aitchison (1989) has also suggested that the influence of substrates and universal processes may be inextricably linked, as features present in substrate languages are channelled along 'preferred pathways'. Alongside the continued effects of these processes is the phenomenon of English contact-induced change, which is the topic of the following section.

8.2 The relationship between Tok Pisin and English

Notwithstanding the continuing influence of substrate patterns and universal processes of development, it is evident that one of the biggest influences on Tok Pisin as currently spoken by first language speakers in this corpus is English. It is true that most of the informants were enrolled at English-medium educational institutions, and the continual use of English as a medium of instruction would naturally have an effect on the Tok Pisin used, for example, in discussing school-related activities. But even those who had not spent a long time in English-medium education showed a good deal of influence from English, as the following extracts from the speech of a grade 2 student in Morobe show:

> mipla go lo <u>bas stop</u> ... mipla baim <u>presen</u> blo sista blo P. pinis ... mipla kam gim <u>kasin</u> blo P. nau em kisim ... nau mipla wokim <u>fani</u> na mipla plei ... ol i go lo bas na <u>bas muf muf</u> nau ... em laik karim <u>beibi</u> nau ... Pikinini bl' em ia em <u>fat</u> na hevi.

> We went to the <u>bus stop</u> ... we bought a <u>present</u> for P's sister... we gave it to P's <u>cousin</u> and she took it ... we <u>made fun</u> and played ... they went into the bus and the bus <u>moved about</u> ... she was about to give birth to a <u>baby</u> ... the child was <u>fat</u> and heavy [Morobe, F, 10]

The role of English in Papua New Guinea has become firmly established in recent years, as a number of studies have shown (Barron 1986, Romaine 1989, 1991, A-M Smith 1988, Yarupawa 1986). The fates of Tok Pisin and English now seem irrevocably intertwined as the relationship becomes more and more intimate. In present-day Papua New Guinea, the two languages are in frequent and sustained contact in a number of domains. The current amount of borrowing from English would appear to be great in terms of the history of Tok Pisin, with extensive borrowing of vocabulary apparent in certain areas such as Manus (Smith 1994a, 1998b). However, on the scale established by Thomason & Kaufman to describe such situations it would be characterized as one of 'slight to moderate borrowing' (1988:74), which is appropriate in terms of the spectrum of language contact outcomes they describe, including extreme situations where complete systems are taken over wholesale.

One of the major points stressed by Thomason & Kaufman is that the critical factors determining the direction and extent of contact-induced language change are not linguistic but social. If this is true, the fates of Tok Pisin and English are likely to depend on the relative prestige of the two languages, domains of use, the degree of bilingualism and other such variables. Future outcomes may therefore be determined by a number of factors which are unknown at present, and will depend on future policy decisions taken with reference to the language of education, administration, etc.

Thomason & Kaufman draw a clear distinction between borrowing and interference through shift. The current situation in Papua New Guinea involves extensive borrowing from English into Tok Pisin. There is no evidence of interference through shift, as there is no widespread move to abandon Tok Pisin in favour of English or vice versa, although such a scenario cannot be ruled out in the future. Mühlhäusler (1979) drew attention to the varied and sophisticated ways that new lexicon was emerging from the internal resources of the language. Although such processes are still in evidence, one surprising finding of the present study was the relative neglect of such word-formation processes in favour of wholesale borrowing from English, and this demands some explanation. In the following section, the relationship between the two languages will be examined more closely, taking into account recent work in the areas of borrowing and code-switching, and the question of the possible development of a post-Creole continuum.

8.2.1 Borrowing and code-switching

Where Tok Pisin begins and ends

When dealing with a corpus such as this, there may be considerable difficulty in assigning an unequivocal language identity to certain parts of utterances. Leaving aside for the moment the philosophical question of whether such entities as 'languages' actually exist, and hence whether the problem is worth pursuing (Mühlhäusler 1996:7), it can be seen that the language of most of the corpus is undoubtedly Tok Pisin, while there is the occasional insertion of what stands out as an English phrase or expression. Between the two poles lies a grey area where it may be difficult to say exactly what language certain forms belong to.

This is perhaps best illustrated by looking at some concrete examples. In the following, the whole utterance is quite evidently Tok Pisin apart from a sudden switch to an English phrase:

> *mipla sa kolim mipla yet - mipla ol stap we - <u>we live where PNG begins and ends.</u>*
>
> we call ourselves, we live where - <u>we live where PNG begins and ends.</u> *[*West Sepik, M, 16*]*

A look at a somewhat larger sample of the same text shows that there were a number of such changes, usually referred to as code switches, towards the end of the story:

> *Na antap ples ol i kolim Pamheu lo bikpla brata, <u>after big brother</u>, na tamblo ol i kolim Chau <u>after small brother</u>, so ples antap nau i gat big... - <u>more population than</u> ples tamblo. Na ol ples antap ol i stap klostu long boda mak blong Indonesia na Piendji, so mipla sa kolim mipla yet - mipla ol stap we - <u>we live where PNG begins and ends.</u>*
>
> And they called the upper village Pamheu from the big brother, (switch Eng) <u>after big brother</u>, (switch TP) and below they called Chau (switch Eng) <u>after the small brother</u>, (switch TP) so the village above has a big, (switch Eng) <u>more population than</u> (switch TP) the village below. And the villages above are close to the border mark between Indonesia and PNG, so we call ourselves - we live where - (switch Eng) <u>we live where PNG begins and ends.</u> [West Sepik, M, 16]

A number of observations relate to the switching activity in this extract. It should be noted that although this extract contains a number of code switches, this frequency was not reflected in the story as a whole, which contained only two other switches in a 650 word sequence. In one or two cases there was a definite break in the discourse, represented, for example, by repetition of the phrase *lo bikpela brata* by its translation 'after big brother' or a by a sudden break in the middle of a phrase *mipla stap we* ... before the item in the new code begins. In other words, there is a discontinuity. It appears that the English expression 'we live where PNG begins and ends' is something of a catch-phrase in this area, no doubt frequently heard in English, and this may have influenced the story teller to insert other English phrases near it. It could be that this story is frequently heard in English, and that these are key phrases in the narrative. It sounds, in fact, as though bits of translation are inserted.

A somewhat shorter borrowed fragment appears in the next extract, parallel but slightly more specific than the Tok Pisin equivalent, and again it appears to be a kind of translation to provide extra information:

> *em ... kisim (di)sla meri ia nau katim em go liklik nau, go <u>into pieces</u> nau,*
>
> he got this woman and cut her up small, <u>into pieces</u> [Enga, F, 12]

In the following extract, on the other hand, there is no discontinuity. An English phrase has been incorporated, but it is continuous with the rest of the utterance. English phonology and morphology are retained, for example, there is no *-im* on *ekscheinj*, and the non-standard phonemes /ch/ and /j/ are used, but the phrase could be credibly represented as either English or Tok Pisin:

> *seim taim ol polis i <u>ekscheinj faia</u> (<u>exchange fire</u>) long ol na mipla i silip ananit lo kar.*
>
> at the same time, the police <u>exchanged fire</u> with them and we lay down under the car. [East New Britain, M, 14]

Cases similar to the above in that English phonology is retained, but where morphological adaptation is made, include the following:

> *Na biain mipla bin sa <u>chalenjim</u> ol - ol narapla skul lo plei soka na mi sa - mi sa putim planti gol*
>
> And afterwards we <u>challenged</u> other schools to play soccer and I scored many goals. [East New Britain, M, 13]

> *ol kisim sampla lain l' ap wantem n' ol go putim ol lo djeil na ol <u>kweschenim</u> ol*
>
> they took some people from over there with them and put them in jail and they <u>questioned</u> them. [Simbu, F, 12]

The next extracts are similar, but the phonology has also been adapted to fit standard Tok Pisin patterns. Thus the borrowed items, while not standard in Tok Pisin, fits seamlessly into the phonology, morphology and syntax of the language:

> *Ol <u>militen</u> kam stap long hap na - i no <u>militen</u> bat em mas ol raskol nambaut o ol laik <u>tretenim</u> ol wonem ia nambaut.*
>
> The <u>militants</u> came and stayed there - they weren't <u>militants</u> but they must have just been criminals or they wanted to <u>threaten</u> the what's its. [Eastern Highlands, M, 16]

> *mi paitim em. Paitim em nau ol <u>saspendim</u> mi, wanpla wik lo aus.*
>
> I hit him. Hit him so they <u>suspended</u> me, one week at home.   [Manus, M, 14]

In many other cases like this, because of a basic phonological similarity between the English and Tok Pisin form, little or no adaptation is necessary to incorporate a non-standard item:

> *Ol edmasta <u>invaitim</u> planti ol manmeri nambaut.*
>
> The headmaster <u>invited</u> a lot of people.   [Southern Highlands, F, 14]

> *mi <u>komperim</u> wantem skul we mi bin <u>atendim</u> bifo mi kam ose, i no gutpla*
>
> I compared it with the school I attended before I came, like it wasn't good.   [East New Britain, F, 18]

In the following, a standard item from the Tok Pisin lexicon is used, but the semantics belong to English:

> *na mi stap go na ... mi <u>pasim</u> greid siks mi kam lo aiskul.*
>
> I stayed there and passed my grade six (exam) and went to high school   [Manus, M, 14]

As the above cline of examples illustrates, the exact boundary mark where Tok Pisin 'begins and ends' is by no means clear-cut.

Matrix and embedded languages

The phenomenon of code-switching has received considerable discussion in recent years, with works such Myers-Scotton (1992, 1993a, b, c, 1995) and Poplack (1980, 1987, 1988, 1993) helping to dispel many misconceptions about the subject. Myers-Scotton's work in Africa is concerned both with linguistic constraints on code-switching, such as where in a sentence switches may occur (1993b), and with the social functions of code switches, such as the expression of membership of certain groups (1993c). In the latter work, code-switching is seen as a means of negotiating status rights and obligations, and is explained in terms of a theory of markedness.

A major theoretical advance came with the Matrix Language Frame model, set out in Myers-Scotton (1993b). According to this model one and only one language constitutes the matrix, which sets the grammatical frame of the utterance, i.e. it determines morpheme order and provides the 'system morphemes', while 'content morphemes' can come from either the matrix or the embedded language. Items from the embedded language may be morphologically integrated as 'mixed constituents', or consist of embedded 'islands' which retain the grammatical structure of the embedded language. Using this terminology, the matrix language of the present corpus can be clearly identified as Tok Pisin. The examples cited in the section above included both embedded islands and mixed constituents with content morphemes from English supplemented with inflections from Tok Pisin. Poplack's work is mainly concerned with constraints on code-switching. It has been shown that intra-sentential switching is more likely to occur at certain positions in the utterance known as 'equivalence sites', defined as sites around which constituent order in the two languages is homologous.

A number of observations pertaining to the present corpus can be made. Firstly, 'classic' code-switching as defined by Myers-Scotton is extremely uncommon, with a little over 100 switches occurring in the whole corpus (see § 8.2.1). Again it may be the nature of the genre - unscripted monologue - which determines this, and code-switching may be more common in naturalistic social settings and in certain genres such as parliamentary debates (Nekitel 1990). Secondly, there was little evidence of code-switching to achieve social goals such as prestige or demonstration of group identity. Most switches appeared to be motivated by referential requirements. Thirdly, what constitutes a code-switch is in many cases problematic. In particular, the adoption of non-standard lexical items deserves a closer examination.

According to Myers-Scotton's analysis, items such as ***reprodiusim***, ***chalenjim*** and ***othoraizim*** are code-switches consisting of mixed constituents, as they take their root form from one language and inflection from another. The crucial question is where to draw the line between what is incorporated as a regular item in Tok Pisin's lexicon, and what is a foreign form. Myers-Scotton does consider this issue (1993b:163) and concludes that there is basically no difference in the process by which code-switching and borrowed forms are produced. However, the lexical entries of borrowed forms become part of the mental lexicon, whereas in code-switching this is not the case. It should be remembered that Myers-Scotton's theory was developed with African languages which were typologically quite different from one another. Its applicability to Pidgins such as Tok Pisin, where the lexis is mainly drawn from English anyway, is more open to question. Moreover, checking out the inventory of the 'mental lexicon' is by no means a straightforward task. There seems no *a priori* reason to assume that the process by which the 'new' words above enter the language is any different from the one whereby old established items such as ***putim*** 'put' or ***kilim*** 'kill' became established.

Romaine (1992a:232) has also addressed the problem of nonce borrowing of non-standard items adopted on an ad hoc basis to cope with specific referential or other needs. Her criterion is that single occurrences should count as nonce borrowing. In a relatively small corpus such as the present one, however, this produces some problematic results. For example there are several occurrences of the word ***mapo*** 'mythical little person', as it is a central feature of one of the stories, although the word is clearly a borrowed item, and surely unknown to the great majority of Tok Pisin speakers. Less culturally specific items which look very close to standard English such as ***ankonshes*** 'unconscious', ***baptais*** 'baptise' and ***distebim*** 'disturb' are also attested several times. On the other hand, the common and well-known word ***malolo*** occurs only once in the Highlands and Momase samples and not at all in the Islands sample. It is evident that much larger corpora would be needed to give a realistic picture of such frequencies. What criterion, then, is appropriate to determine whether a recently derived English item occurring in the present corpus should be regarded as a regular part of the Tok Pisin lexicon?

Morphological integration could be considered as one criterion. Poplack & Meechan (1995:223) have used a 'variationist' method to show that borrowed items tend to be structured differently from those in multi-word fragments or monolingual discourse. However, many morphologically integrated items are nevertheless designated as 'mixed constituents' in Myers-Scotton's schema, and there seems to be some confusion over what constitutes an established item. It appears that the best criterion to use to distinguish regular items from nonce borrowing or code-switching is simply frequency of production, as also suggested by Myers-Scotton (1993b:163). Poplack & Meechan (1995:200) also give diffusion into the monolingual community as a criterion for inclusion as a loan word. Analysis of the present corpus cannot offer definitive judgments on this problem, and a more intensive survey of the use of items in question among various populations of Tok Pisin speakers would be needed to determine what should be included in the regular Tok Pisin lexicon. Monolingual Tok Pisin speakers, however, are likely to be increasingly difficult to find. The task may be better left to the next generation of dictionary makers.

Language mixing

These problems also lead to the old question of whether 'mixed languages' exist. Such phenomena have been described, and a number of languages such as Michif, Ma'a and Media Lengua seem to be serious contenders for mixed language status (Bakker & Mous 1994). With regard to code-switching, Gardner-Chloros (1995) has suggested that the languages involved may be less discrete than many propose, and that "code-switching should instead be considered as a much broader, blanket term for a range of interlingual phenomena within which strict alternation between two discrete systems is the exception rather than the rule" (1995:68). Myers-Scotton has also had to look more closely at mixed codes in recent versions of her Matrix Language Frame model. In what appears to some to be a rearguard action to salvage a flawed theory (Picone 1997), she has introduced the concept of the 'composite matrix' to accommodate situations such as that where complex lexical structure is derived from two or more different languages. Is it possible that a mixed Tok Pisin-English code could emerge?

In the present corpus, there is considerable evidence that the Tok Pisin lexicon is getting closer to English as more English words are borrowed. However, one piece of evidence that speakers are continually aware of the distinctiveness of the two languages comes from occasional instances of self-correction or 'self-repair' of forms which do not fit easily into the 'matrix' grammar. Switches from a more standard Tok Pisin form to a more recently introduced item, or vice versa, show a certain tension between alternative choices predicated on an awareness of language identity:

> ***Woki(m) osem tsol go nau, tenpla rat pas long, disla trep blo <u>lapun - e wich</u> ia nau, wich ia ka(m) antap nau, em lukim ol.***
>
> They carried on doing this and ten rats were stuck in this trap made by the <u>old woman - erm the witch</u>. The witch came in and saw them. [West Sepik, F, 15]

As previously noted, phonological repairs also take place:

> *Mipla wetim bas go go go, nogat afta... - abinun nau, mi belat nogut tru.*
>
> We waited and waited for the bus, it didn't come until the afternoon, I was really angry [Simbu, F, 18]
>
> *koki ia em tok osem, "yu wok lo fai... - paitim mi, nau - nau bai mi go ..."*
>
> the cockatoo said "you hit me, so I will go ... " [Simbu, M, 14]

Some other examples were reported in Chapter 3. There may be an apparent awareness by the speaker that some words are borrowed and as a result out of place or less appropriate than standard alternatives. This may be manifested as hesitation, awkward phrasing or switching to a safer alternative. In the following example, the speaker begins to use the word *tritim* 'to treat' as in the phrase 'treated us well', but hesitated and switched to *wokim gutpela pasin*, 'behave well', a more usual Tok Pisin expression:

> *taim papa blo mi kam anta(p) lo kisim (mi)pla go bek mipla no bin, laik lo go bek bikos, em ba - em no trit... - a wokim) gutpela pasin lo m(i)pla*
>
> when my father came up to get us to go back, we didn't want to go, because he would - he didn't treat - er behave well to us. [West Sepik, M, 15]

Other examples of this kind are as follows:

> *wanpla manggi ron go insait long ro- ron in front of -in frant long wanem ia bas na bas ia kilim em*
>
> a boy ran into the roa... - ran in front of - in front of a bus and the bus killed him. [Enga, M, 12]
>
> *na ol tok "tapos yupla no rete... - a - kisi' gan ka(m) lo mipla, em ba mipla kam bek gen lo narapla taim gen na kukim haus bl' yupla wantem," ol to se*
>
> and they said "if you don't return - er - give back the gun to us, we'll come back another time and then we'll burn your houses," they said [Simbu, F, 12]

Expressions for ages, times and dates in particular often appear to be compromise forms between the two languages with an uneasy syntactic fit. They often show evidence of borrowing of whole chunks or fixed phrases, with unknown long-term consequences for the morphology and syntax of bilingual speakers:

> *Mi stat lo Komini Skul blo mi taim mi eitpla yias old*
>
> I started community school when I was 8 years old [West Sepik, M, 15]
>
> *Am, afta, befo Niu Yia, em abaut tri oklok mipla bin baim sampla rais, na sampla tin fish*
>
> Um after, before New Year, about three o'clock we bought some rice and some tinned fish [Simbu, M, 16]
>
> *Na mipla ba gat presenteshen b' mipla long, am Disemba twentififth.*
>
> And we will have out presentation on um December the twenty fifth [East Sepik, F, 16]
>
> *Evri moning mipla kechim bas abaut siks ouklok. Dropim mipla lo jankshen, okobaut kam lo skul. I teikim mipla abaut teti minits tsol l' wokobaut lo jankshen kam lo skul.*
>
> Every morning we catch the bus about six o'clock. Drop us at the junction, walk to school. It only takes us about thirty minutes to walk from the junction to the school. [Manus, M, 14]

A number of instances can be found where the close relationship between English and Tok Pisin leads to what could be considered intermediate varieties, but it should be noted that only ten or so of the informants produced language of the kind illustrated below. One such passage is the following, where it is frequently difficult to determine the boundaries of what is English and what is Tok Pisin:

> *Long Bougenvil ia mi gat dedi blong mi we - em stap long Bougenvil na, mipla misim em stret. So last - a tem tu holide tsol, mipla no sa kisim eni nius o eni toktok lo ol osem em orait o em osem em gat samthing rong long em, osem tasol, ... tem tu em - mipla ... bin risiv wanpla leta. Na mi bin wanda osem usat stret raitim disa leta bikos mi ken telim osem em raiting bilong dedi bilong mi.*
>
> In Bougainville I have my Dad who - he stays in Bougainville and we really miss him. So last - er term two holiday, we didn't get any news or any information about them like he's all right or

there's <u>something wrong</u> with him, so ... in term two he - we ... <u>received</u> a letter. And I <u>wondered</u> who had written this letter, because I could <u>tell</u> it was my Dad's <u>writing</u>. [Manus, F, 16]

The competing influence of English and Tok Pisin in lexis, semantics and syntax is evident. There are a number of English borrowings, as well as new semantic properties of existing words such as ***telim*** and ***misim*** which have adopted the semantics of their English equivalents. Influence on the syntax is seen in such expressions as ***tem tu olidei*** 'term two holiday', ***samthing rong*** 'something wrong' and *i no ... eni* 'not any', while the transitive verb ***risiv*** is unmarked by *-im*. A similar situation can be seen in the case of the following passage:

> mi raun go daun lo aus na mi toki(m) dedi long <u>onim tivi</u>, <u>bat</u> dedi tok osem mipla - mi mas wetim na <u>teknishen</u> go na - go l' aus na go <u>opereitim</u> gut tivi. So mipla bin weit i go i bin <u>teikem longpla taim</u> liklik, taim teknishen go daun lo aus em go stretim tivi nau, dedi bin <u>putim on</u>, <u>bat stil</u> i no klia gut, <u>so</u> <u>teknishen</u> kam antap ken na em kam traim long painimaut - painim - putim gut am <u>setalait</u> - <u>dis</u> <u>so det</u> i ken ksim gut am satelait, so mipla bin traim ken, na i bin kamap gut, so mipla - mipla gat disla am <u>privilij</u> lo <u>evim tivi</u> long Manus Ai Skul, bikos em <u>da</u> - em em fest lo - fest skul long Manus long gat tivi na mipla amamas <u>det</u> mipla ken <u>koup</u> - osem mipla ken <u>aptudet wantaim ol nius</u> na ol narapla samting we i kamap l' ol narapla <u>pats long disla weld</u>.

> I went down to the house and I told Dad to <u>turn on</u> the TV, <u>but</u> Dad said we must wait for the <u>technician</u> to go to the house and <u>operate</u> it properly. So we waited, it <u>took quite a long time</u>, when the technician went down to the house and fixed the TV, Dad <u>put it on</u>, <u>but it was still</u> not clear, <u>so</u> the technician came up again and tried to find out - fix the <u>satellite dish</u> properly <u>so that</u> it could pick up the satellite, so we tried again, and it came up good, so we have the <u>privilege</u> of <u>having TV</u> in Manus High School because its <u>the</u> - it's the first school in Manus to have TV and we are happy <u>that</u> we can cope - that we can <u>be up to date</u> <u>with the news</u> and the other things happening in the other <u>parts of this world</u> [Manus, F, 16]

There are a number of interesting observations here. The first is the free borrowing of terms from English for modern concepts, such as ***tivi*** 'TV', ***teknishen*** 'technician' and ***satelait*** 'satellite'. Anglicized words such as ***(h)evim*** 'have' and ***teikim*** 'take' are preferred to standard alternatives such as ***gat*** and ***kisim***. English idiomatic expressions are calqued, for example, ***aptudet wantaim*** 'up to date with' and ***teikim longpela taim*** 'take a long time'. Other borrowings include connectors such as ***bat stil*** 'but still' and ***so det*** 'so that'; and ***det*** 'that' is used as a complementizer.

The case of ***(h)evim*** 'have' (35 tokens, nearly half from the Islands sample) is an interesting one. There is an adequate referential alternative in the common word ***gat***, but as Romaine has commented (1992a:149), substituting lexis may involve more than merely filling referential slots with a different token and affect the semantic and syntactic properties of the language. The use of ***hevim*** illustrates this, as it is usually used with calques of English idiomatic expressions using the verb 'to have' where the possessive meaning is not primary. Thus the resulting expression may be affected in the direction of English semantics and argument structure.

> *lo disla fri taim - am - mipla i sa <u>hevim shauas</u>, shaua blo mipla, dres ap na kam daun long mes long siks ouklok.*

> in this free time - um - we <u>have our shower</u> dress up and come down to the mess at six o'clock. [New Ireland, F, 15]

> *Wanpla taim, disla chif, em laik hevim wan... - em lak ga... - <u>hevim wanpla miting</u> na, em kolim olgeta dog bl' em kam*

> Once this chief wanted to <u>have a meeting</u> and he called all his dogs to come. [Simbu, F, 16]

> *mi bin go lo Not Solomons na mi - mi - <u>mi bin go hevim holideis blo mi</u> lo hap*

> I went to North Solomons and <u>I had my holidays</u> there [East New Britain, F, 16]

The following extract from the Eastern Highlands shows a variety of switches between Tok Pisin and English rather than intermediate forms:

> *Na taim ol sin(g)sin(g) go <u>that night</u> na osem go <u>debrek</u> okei lo twelf ouklok disla hap ol wokim ol mumu na kastom blo mipla ol hailans osem <u>as like um for the first time</u> gels mipla hevim <u>menstruation that's the time</u> ol wokim pati blo mipla lo osem mipla <u>big girls</u>.*

> And when they sing, <u>that night</u> until <u>daybreak</u> then at twelve o'clock they make an earth oven at this place, and our Highlands custom is that <u>as like um for the first time</u> girls, we have our <u>menstruation, that's the time</u> they make a celebration for us like we are <u>big girls</u>. [Eastern Highlands, F, 17]

In some cases, the switch to an English phrase such as 'that's the time' is clear-cut, while other items such as **debrek** 'daybreak' could equally well be considered Tok Pisin as English. Nevertheless, in all the above three cases of 'mixing', the language used over all is much more satisfactorily described as Anglicized Tok Pisin than "Tok Pisinized" English.

To put these samples in perspective in terms of the corpus as a whole, it is worth looking in some detail at the kind of switches which were made and by whom. The transcripts of a total of 80 of the 536 informants indicated the presence of some kind of switch to English. Some of these were excluded from consideration, as they involved a story, usually humorous, which featured a switch to another language as an intrinsic part of the story, as in the following example:

em i no bin go lo skul na i bin kirap na i bin ridim dis... - sain ia i bin tok olsem <u>be aware of crocodiles - be aware crocodiles are here</u>.

he hadn't gone to school and he got up and read this - the sign said "be aware of crocodiles - be aware crocodiles are here." [East New Britain, F, 18]

This left 54 informants who made a total of 116 switches. Of these, 31 informants produced only one and 10 produced only two switches, leaving only 13 informants, or 2.4% of the total, who used three or more switches in their speech samples. Of the single switches, these often involved the verbal habit "I mean" (13 cases).

wanpla keiv sa kilim ol man, em lo ples blo mama blo mi lo Morobe lo Siboma, <u>I mean</u> Salamoa.

One cave can kill people, it's in my mother's village in Morobe at Siboma, I mean Salamoa. [West Sepik, F, 15]

Others were explanations of referents which were better known by English names, including borrowed acronyms:

bat em osem maks blo mi sapos alauim bai mi go, nogat em osem mi laik go kamap osem <u>heavy diesel fitter</u> o samting osem long taim mi finishim greid ten

but it's like if my marks allow it, I'll go (to university), if not I'll go and be a <u>heavy diesel fitter</u> or something like that when I finish grade ten. [Mendi, M, 15]

Em nau ol bin faiarim kar blo ol pipisi - <u>Provincial Police Commander</u>. Ol bin spoilim kar blo em nogut stret.

So they set fire to the car belonging to the PPC - <u>Provincial Police Commander</u>. They totally spoiled his car. [Manus, F, 15]

Not all of these were rendered accurately:

Mipla sta sta go mipla plei - mipla plei <u>who's get the ball</u> go nau nogat mama blong em ia ol stori stap.

We stayed there and played "<u>who's got the ball</u>" and his mother was telling stories. [Morobe, F, 11]

Of the remainder, most (32 switches) were related to the description of time.

Okei lo Mande moning <u>the following day</u> mipela i go lo gaden. Mipela go lo ples blo papa lo gaden.

OK, on Monday morning, <u>the following day</u> we went to the garden. We went to the village of the owner of the garden. [Western Highlands, M, 15]

taim tumbuna bl' ol dai ol wokim pinis, <u>some weeks later</u> ston i bin kamap, (dis)pla ston bin kerap lo si, na ol i givim neim olsem tumbuna blo ol iet

when their grandfather died they had made it, <u>some weeks later</u> the stone appeared, the stone appeared in the sea, and they gave it their own grandfather's name. [West Sepik, M, 16]

This could no doubt be due to the fact that many such precise time measures were introduced through the medium of English and have no direct parallel in traditional life.

From the above discussion it is seen that code-switches occur rather infrequently in this corpus, and tend to be motivated by referential rather than social considerations. Even in the case of extensive borrowing of new lexis, the borrowed items are generally integrated into the Tok Pisin matrix, and the number of occurrences of "embedded islands" of English is small. The question of what can be considered an established item in Tok Pisin and what should be labelled an *ad hoc* or irregular borrowing is a difficult one which requires further consideration. There are some samples of discourse which appear to involve a certain amount of mixing between the two languages. If this process were to become more pervasive, the question then arises whether Tok Pisin and English could merge into one another, with a continuum of intermediate varieties. This is considered in more detail in the following section.

8.2.2 The post-Creole continuum

Hall's life cycle model (1966) represented a considerable advance in the theoretical basis of Pidgin and Creole studies, and led to a stimulating re-evaluation of many language contact situations. Most significantly, the dynamic nature of these languages became a central feature, and discussion of the processes involved tended to highlight inadequacies in static models of language which had long been prevalent. However, this does not mean that all contact languages necessarily follow the prescribed stages of an ideal cycle. In particular, the later stages encompassing "decreolization" and the immersion of the Creole in a post-Creole continuum have generated a good deal of discussion.

According to Hall's model, renewed contact between a Creole and the original lexifier language is likely to lead to a process of "decreolization". This label implies an opposite process to that of creolization. Put simply, instead of the replacement of superstrate features with substrate patterns, the superstrate patterns are gradually re-imposed and Creole features lost. A number of situations characterised as post-Creole continua have been described in the Caribbean, the most well-known probably being in Jamaica (DeCamp 1971). Such continua have also been described in Guyana (Bickerton 1975b), and in Belize (Escure 1993), and the concept has become firmly established in writing on Creoles and their lexifiers. A typical continuum is usually described in terms of a number of vertically stratified "lects", ranging from an "acrolect" at the top which approximates the standard lexifier language, to a "basilect", which exhibits the most Creole features. In between are a number of "mesolects". Typically, individual speakers have a repertoire covering a range within the continuum, and various lects will be selected according to social and other factors.

The question of whether such continua constitute a single system for which a single all-embracing grammar can be written is still the subject of debate. Nor is there general agreement about how these continua came into being. The position of various researchers is summarized in Mufwene (1997). Those such as Alleyne (1971) and Le Page (1960) maintain that continua developed from what was already a stratified situation in the early years of development, and the present-day continuum reflects that initial social variation. Others such as Rickford (1987) attribute the range of varieties to differential decreolization under the influence of the lexifier. Mufwene (1997:181) supports the multiple origins model, but considers that the variation may be due to divergence from a basilect rather than social stratification.

Winford (1997) sums up the present position in a recent examination of the status of some alleged post-Creole continua. He also opts firmly for the multiple origins model, suggesting at the same time that attempts to find a single grammar are inappropriate:

> I argue for a co-existent systems approach to these situations, which sees the continuum as a sociolinguistic construct, the result of interaction between relatively stable grammars in contact, producing complex patterns of variation conditioned by social and situational factors and constrained by the degrees of overlap or mismatch between these grammars. This kind of intersystemic variation is not a candidate for inclusion in a single grammar, though it lends itself to analysis in terms of systematic principles of contact-induced change and variation. [Winford 1997:274]

Perhaps because of the existence of these detailed descriptions of post-Creole continua in the Caribbean, observers of Tok Pisin have tended to assume that this is a logical outcome in Papua New Guinea also. The ingredients all seem to be there: an English lexifier Pidgin in renewed intense contact with its lexifier, accompanied by a situation of modernization and increased social mobility. Because Tok Pisin is an expanded Pidgin for much of the population, an alternative term "post-Pidgin continuum" is sometimes used, and such continua have been described in some parts of West Africa (Todd 1982). As mentioned briefly in chapter two, a number of comments to the effect that a continuum is emerging in Papua New Guinea have been made. These, however, have generally been comments incidental to the main focus of the study in question, and not based on an intensive study of all the factors involved. In Solomon Islands Jourdan (1989) did carry out a thorough analysis of the relationship between Pijin and English, but describes the situation there as one of code-switching rather than restructuring along a continuum.

Other studies in Papua New Guinea have strongly suggested that a continuum is at least in the process of developing. Bickerton (1975a) and Sankoff (1976) both considered some two decades ago that this is the likely outcome of contact between Tok Pisin and English. Aitchison (1981) and Kale (1990) see the situation they describe as one of an incipient continuum. Other writers also consider that a form of continuum may already be emerging (O'Donnell & Todd 1980, Romaine 1992a).

A look at the present corpus suggests that, at least on the basis of the present data, the current situation cannot be characterized as a continuum. While the influence of English on contemporary Tok Pisin is undeniable, there does not appear to be the overlapping range of forms described, for example, for the Caribbean continua that would justify such a term. There is definite discontinuity between Tok Pisin and English in the huge majority of cases. Siegel (1997c), in the most detailed study to date, comes to a similar conclusion for all of Melanesia. He looks at Pijin in the Solomon Islands and Bislama in Vanuatu as well as Tok Pisin in Papua New Guinea and similarly shows the discontinuity which exists between these varieties and the local varieties of English.

The data in this corpus, especially from areas such as Manus and New Ireland, indicate that lexical borrowing from English has led to a certain amount of phonological and semantic convergence, but the adopted lexical items are generally fully integrated into the Tok Pisin "matrix". Although some English phonemes may be adopted unchanged, they appear to be optional allophones, and examples of minimal pairs involving introduced English phonemes were hard to demonstrate. Syntactic patterns generally conformed to those of standard Tok Pisin. A few cases of awkward accommodation did occur but these were uncommon and idiosyncratic. However, there were some morphosyntactic developments in the direction of English. Plural marking with -s appears to be increasingly redundant and approaching obligatory status for some items. Verbal phrase structure tended in some cases to follow more typically English patterns, and English words or phrases tended to be used as cohesive devices in longer pieces of discourse. However, it was nearly always clear that the language being spoken was Tok Pisin, and obvious switching involving extensive 'embedded language islands' did not appear to be taking place regularly.

Such convergence as is demonstrated here would not appear to justify the term post-Creole continuum, as there is still a very clear discontinuity between the two systems (c.f. Platt 1990). Although studies by Yarupawa (1986), Barron (1986) and A-M Smith (1978, 1988) have shown that some expressions used in Papua New Guinea English have their origin in Tok Pisin, there is no evidence to show that PNG English is being radically restructured in the direction of Tok Pisin. That there are some unique syntactic patterns in Papua New Guinea English influenced by Tok Pisin as well as vernacular languages has been known for some time (A-M Smith 1978), but this does not mean that the two languages are converging to the extent that easily identifiable intermediate varieties exist. There is a stronger case for considering Papua New Guinea English as an interlanguage form on the way to the development of standard English. If a continuum of any sort currently exists, it seems more likely to be between the Papua New Guinea variety of English and Standard English (Smith 1978, 1988), where something more closely approaching an overlapping continuum of forms appears to be developing.

Anglicization of Tok Pisin has frequently been expressed in terms of a rural-urban dichotomy (e.g. Romaine 1989:20), and this may indeed have been an important factor as Papua New Guinea's urban areas developed. However, a close examination of the present corpus shows that in many cases the distinction between rural and urban does not appear to be very clear-cut here. Some of the most Anglicized forms were found in Manus and New Ireland, but the urban areas in these provinces are not extensive. A detailed discussion of the situation in Manus appearing in an earlier paper (Smith 1994a) illustrates this point. What might be considered Manus's "urban" area, the township of Lorengau, is very limited, consisting of a few stores, a couple of hotels and some government facilities and housing areas. The population is estimated at "nearly 3,000" (Schooling & Schooling 1980:3). However, there is a good deal of movement between traditional settlements and the town, by sea in motorized canoes, or up and down the main highway in motor vehicles. Thus the exact resident population is difficult to determine, and many people from out-of-town areas visit temporarily to go to the market, the hospital or for other specific purposes. Delineation of distinct "urban" and "rural" cultures in this tightly knit community would appear to be an over-simplification. Tok Pisin is almost universally understood, and spoken in a wide range of domains in all parts of the province. This is not unique to Manus, and it may be that the urban/rural distinction is not so relevant to current linguistic change in parts of Papua New Guinea as it may have been in other regions in earlier decades.

A more critical factor in Manus, as well as in some other provinces such as New Ireland, appears to be the combination of the widespread primary use of Tok Pisin and the high degree of English-medium education, whether in an "urban" or "rural" context. Among such a population, familiarity with institutions, procedures and fine distinctions of meaning appears to be leading to a shared common knowledge which is the pre-requisite for large-scale adoption of new lexis from English. Among language planners, such adoptions tend to be rather frowned upon, and the use of the internal resources of the language are preferred as a source of innovation (Lynch 1975a, Mühlhäusler 1979:423, 1985f), although this is perhaps paradoxical considering the history of Tok Pisin. However, it seems that in the absence of vigorous official language planning initiatives, the trend of wholesale borrowing is likely to continue. Balanced against these innovative trends are conservative factors, such as the need to communicate with other second language Tok Pisin speakers, especially those not fluent in English.

In the future, lexical, phonological and semantic convergence could lead to a position where morphosyntactic mixing is facilitated and becomes more extreme. If a post-Pidgin or post-Creole continuum is going to emerge, I would suggest that the most promising place to look is not necessarily in urban settlements but in provinces such as Manus and New Ireland where there are large proportions of the population fluent in Tok Pisin and well-educated through the medium of English. Careful documentation of the incipient changes currently occurring in such a bilingual population could provide interesting comparative data on how the contact situation develops.

8.3 Conclusion and recommendations

In this final section, the place of first language Tok Pisin in the varied array of language styles and competencies existing in the country today is reviewed. Firstly the balance between the forces for maintaining uniformity and those for promoting variation is discussed. Then a number of recommendations for further study are made, suggesting areas where follow-up studies could usefully be made. These include studies investigating a more comprehensive array of varieties, and those directed towards the provision of data for educational and language planning needs.

8.3.1 Uniformity and variation

As can be seen from the preceding sections, there is a certain amount of variation along regional lines, but also an underlying uniformity, especially in the lexical frequencies of commoner items. However, such differences as exist do not appear to present any serious impediment to comprehension or communication. As discussed in Smith (1990a), there appear to be forces promoting the differentiation of regional or provincial variation counter-balanced by other forces towards national uniformity. It is the interplay of these factors which is likely to determine the extent of differentiation of regional accents, dialects and varieties in the coming decades. In the following sections, these processes will be looked at in more detail.

Factors promoting uniformity

The development of Tok Pisin was predicated on a need for communication among those without a common language. Thus during Tok Pisin's history, there have been severe constraints on the amount of variation possible if this role as a lingua franca were to be retained. This is still the case today, and for much of Papua New Guinea's population, Tok Pisin's main use is as a second language to communicate across language boundaries. This is the over-riding factor promoting uniformity. The situation is somewhat different for first language speakers, but the normative pressure from second language speakers is likely to mean that the more radical changes do not become community norms. As Mühlhäusler puts it (1977b:574):

> The use of Tok Pisin as a *lingua franca* is operative in filtering out drastic changes such as may have occurred during the creolization of other varieties in other social contexts.

Unlike the allegedly unrestrained bioprogram-induced blossoming of the early stages of abrupt Creoles, in current Tok Pisin, innovations do not appear to be primarily motivated by creolization. As Sankoff & Laberge note in an often quoted passage (1973:45):

> ... native speakers appear to be carrying further tendencies which were already present in the language. We are not arguing that the presence of native speakers creates sudden and dramatic changes in a language, but rather that their presence may be one factor in influencing directions in language change.

Wurm (1986), quoted in Romaine (1992a:341) considers that differences in Tok Pisin are disappearing, and there are other factors suggesting that this may be the case. Communications within the country have improved markedly in the past few decades, and many rural villages now have access to radio broadcasts in Tok Pisin. Government literature in Tok Pisin is also disseminated, although the effectiveness of the messages is often open to question (Franklin 1990). Self-help publications in Tok Pisin such as Bergmann (1982) are available to a variety of rural institutions. Most significant, perhaps, the weekly newspaper *Wantok Niuspepa* is reaching increasing numbers of people, and again this will tend to have a standardizing effect, although it is possible that separate written and spoken styles will become differentiated (Romaine 1988b, Siegel 1983, 1985).

Nor should the influence of religious materials be under-emphasized. In addition to biblical texts, there is a large variety of booklets available on various aspects of health, agriculture, education and other topics produced by a number of missions. Texts such as *Nupela Testamen* have an aura of respectability about them such that the linguistic forms they contain are given a certain legitimacy. However, this may again mean that a certain "religious register" is recognized, rather than the texts directly influencing the way people speak. The structure *tok i spik* to introduce quotations, for example, appears to be obsolete in the spoken language in spite of its frequent use in *Nupela Testamen*. Popular culture such as rock music and films also have a unifying effect, giving wide currency to fashionable catch phrases and expressions. For example, the use of **bras** for 'brother', formerly heard almost exclusively in Bougainville, became popular in mainland tertiary institutions in the 1980s following the release of the film *Tukana*.

An important factor promoting uniformity is the amount of population movement currently taking place. In the course of the current investigation, very many of the informants described extensive movement of residence due to parents' work or visits to relatives, and motivation is high to experience life in other parts of the country. Some areas are also designated primarily as inter-ethnic settlement areas, such as the oil palm schemes of Oro and West New Britain provinces, and large mining operations also tend to have a work force of very varied origin. The unifying influence of the four National High Schools has also been considerable, and many students in these institutions expressed pride in having many friends from different parts of the country.

Related to this large-scale mixing of people is widespread intermarriage, not only between different language groups within a province, but between provinces and regions as well. While national identity is no doubt another unifying factor, the effect of standards arising from language planning initiatives appears to have been small. The use of Tok Pisin in education, as we have seen, is increasing, and sooner or later this must force educators and administrators to confront the question of standardization of the variety used in instruction, especially if Tok Pisin itself is to become a school subject. A final factor is the self-consciousness about stigmatized regional varieties mentioned above. A great deal of humour relies on making fun of strange ways of expressing ideas and what is satirized as bucolic pronunciation, and this could induce self-censorship of deviant forms.

Factors promoting variation

As seen above, the role of Tok Pisin as a lingua franca tends to buffer more drastic changes which may result from individual divergence. However, the situation is changing somewhat as the number of native speakers increases and the use of Tok Pisin spreads to more and more domains of life. This is true not only of urban areas but also those rural areas characterized by severe linguistic fragmentation and a long history of Tok Pisin use. Studies such as Kulick & Stroud (1990), Smith (1992a) and Yarupawa (1996) also show that in some rural areas, Tok Pisin is the language of choice among young people with apparently adequate vernacular alternatives. In such situations, the constraints of second-language norms may not apply to the same extent.

It is well known that young people in various parts of the world are often motivated to define their own youth culture through linguistic means. Although there is no current evidence for the emergence of a street argot associated with youth culture in Papua New Guinea, generational differences could easily lead to such differentiation. Some of the expressions used by the young people in the present corpus might well sound strange or even incomprehensible to an older generation. To begin with, some of the extreme reductions, coupled with a daunting speed of delivery, may be difficult for second language speakers to understand:

> ***I stap ol i lukim nau, tevel kam pai(t) wantem tupla go nau, kilim tul antaim (=tupela wantaim).***
>
> They saw now the spirit came and fought with the two, killed them both. [West Sepik, M, 14]

mipla stap nau sista bl' mi ka(m) n(a) tok "m(ipe)la ba(i) go lotu nau"

We stayed and my sister came and said "we're going to church." [Morobe, F, 11]

In addition, some of the vocabulary and expressions used may have emerged from youthful play groups:

em la kam anta(p) lo (h)aus t(a)sol, tupla bainad blo papa na mama bilong em stap na katim em na em <u>dis nating</u>

he wanted to go up to the house but his parents' two bayonets were there and cut him and he <u>disappeared</u>. [Madang, F, 12]

Similarly, catch phrases such as *em bai hat* 'your proposition is unsuccessful' or calques of English idioms such as *fulim raun* 'to fool around' may be inaccessible to speakers of standard rural Tok Pisin.

Due to the influence of substrate factors, second language speakers have no doubt always shown a fair amount of variability, but with increased mobility and communications it would be expected that this would decrease. However, as seen in the previous section, evidence from the present corpus indicates that the indirect influence of substrate phonology, syntax and discourse processes is still present.

Mention was made in the previous section of the possible unifying effect of nationalism. On the other hand, within Papua New Guinea there are also political tensions promoting regionalism over nationalism. The New Guinea Islands region, for example, has been the home of a number of movements aiming for regional autonomy or even secession. In such a climate, differences rather than similarities in language are more likely to be emphasized. Regional second language varieties of English, for example in Milne Bay (Yarupawa 1986), could also influence emerging varieties of Tok Pisin.

In conclusion, a variety of factors appears to exist promoting both uniformity and variation. The impression from the present study is that regional differences are relatively small and declining in certain areas such as the lexical inventory, but differentiation of idiom and syntax is also evident, and more studies are needed to find out more about the full extent of regional variation. In particular, a much larger database would be desirable before further standardization initiatives are undertaken. The language appears to be becoming more like English in certain respects as large numbers of lexical items are borrowed, while in other respects it continues to develop along its own independent line as new idioms emerge and existing structures become modified to conform to new discursive needs or under the influence of the other languages spoken in the area.

8.3.2 Suggestions for further research.

The findings of the present investigation suggest a number of areas where follow-up studies are indicated. The limitations of the corpus and data collection methods prevent more wide-ranging conclusions from being drawn, and further studies with more varied genres or among more carefully controlled populations would be useful. The findings also have a number of implications for education and language planning, and further work in these areas is recommended.

Firstly, there is still much to be known about geographical variation in Tok Pisin use. The present study did not touch on the Southern (Papuan) Region or the National Capital District, and the use of Tok Pisin in these areas would make a fruitful field of investigation. Samples from various provinces within the range of the present study were also rather small, for example, North Solomons, West New Britain and Enga provinces, and further work in these and other locations, including more rigidly controlled investigations of rural and urban environments would be useful.

Although the focus of this study is on the language of adolescents, the younger children were excluded from the corpus to minimise the effect of age-related factors, and much more could be found out about developmental features, including controlled acquisition studies. No longitudinal studies of the acquisition of Tok Pisin appear to have been made, and this is another gap which needs to be filled. Romaine (1992a) has shown that age is an important variable in the acquisition of certain features, and follow-up studies related to this are needed.

The genre of the speech samples collected is also somewhat restricted, and a more thorough investigation of language in more naturalistic settings would help to answer some of the questions about code-switching, language attitudes, post Creole continua and so on. The ideal investigators here would be Papua New Guinean researchers with access to a variety of social situations and native speaker insights into Tok Pisin and other languages spoken. Participant observation studies, especially those leading to the production of corpora of speech, would be most valuable, including investigations of men's and women's activities and children's play groups.

The question of gender differentiation has not been addressed by the present study. There are indications that gender does not have a significant effect on the variables examined in Romaine's corpus (1992a:232), but Faraclas (1989) shows that some gender differences are apparent in his study of intonation patterns in East Sepik. A fuller analysis of the language of male and female informants would thus be of interest. Gender studies from a more critical perspective, and critical discourse analysis in general would also be illuminating. Another surprising omission from the literature is a virtual absence of anything about pragmatics in Tok Pisin, and surely a study of pragmatic features must be a high priority for future research.

The remaining gaps would be easier to fill with more and larger corpora from a wider range of sources. Written corpora would be useful too, and the written materials collected by Romaine (1992a) and Verhaar (1996) are a useful start in this respect. Printed material such as *Wantok Niuspepa* articles and stories are already prepared in electronic format, and collecting such a corpus would be much more straightforward than recording and transcribing speech. It is to be hoped that the archives of *Wantok* will be available to researchers in future. It would also be helpful if other corpora were made more generally available to researchers. It is the intention of the present investigator that the corpus assembled here be made available in due course, and hopefully other researchers will also make materials more widely available for further analysis.

The findings of the present study relating to the intimate relationship between Tok Pisin and English have obvious relevance to education policy. The almost exclusive use of English in education from the earliest primary grade to the tertiary level is a feature of the Papua New Guinea education system. Although a number of voices have been raised against this policy (Dutton 1976, Lynch 1979b, McDonald 1976) it is only recently that the primacy of English has been seriously challenged. The government's education sector review (Papua New Guinea Department of Education 1991) acknowledged the importance of English while stressing the need for the preservation of Papua New Guinean values, including a greater role for vernacular education, especially at pre-primary level. However, implementation of the recommendations could be far from straightforward, as discussed by Oladejo (1992).

The role of Tok Pisin is somewhat more problematic, as it falls between the stools of indigenous culture and international modernization. There are still negative attitudes to the language held by many, including speakers themselves. However, Siegel's work on Tok Pisin in education (1985b, 1992a, 1997d) has provided some much-needed evidence to refute the commonly held belief that education in a Pidgin inhibits linguistic and intellectual development. The documented success of Tok Pisin-medium "prep" schools in the Sepik area, together with the *de facto* use of a good deal of Tok Pisin in primary schools has probably set the scene for greater involvement in the education system in the future.

The present study has shown that Tok Pisin is not being abandoned by those in English-medium education, confirming Swan & Lewis' (1990) findings that the language is still popular and widely used. Buschenhofen (1997) has shown that English, too, continues to be held in high esteem, and it appears as though the two languages are both valued, and destined to co-exist among young educated Papua New Guineans for some time. Evidence from this study supports the view that there is an important role for Tok Pisin in the education system, having demonstrated the facility with which young people can switch from one language to the other, and transfer concepts via borrowed lexis. This suggests that, especially in the early stages of education, instruction through Tok Pisin, a language with which many beginning students are familiar, would be a superior vehicle for the teaching of both literacy and content subjects.

The findings are also relevant to the issue of language planning. The question of standardization will need to be addressed sooner or later if Tok Pisin is to have a greater formal role in education and development. The authors of the major standards that have been adopted, such as those of religious publications, have done a careful and conscientious job with planning and standardization, but not all widely disseminated information in Tok Pisin has been so successful or well thought out (Franklin 1990). A major shortcoming affecting even the better publications is a lack of knowledge about the acceptability of the various linguistic choices to Tok Pisin speakers in different regional locations, and this, too, needs further investigation.

In conclusion, research into the use of contemporary Tok Pisin in various regions and contexts is still minimal, and it is recommended that more large scale studies of the use of Tok Pisin in different areas be carried out. In particular, large-scale corpora of spoken language and more comprehensive corpora of the language spoken in all provinces would be useful to assess the use of various forms. More research is also needed into attitudes to and the acceptability of variants, and testing the comprehensibility and adequacy of written standards. Until more information is available, it is suggested that no major language planning policy initiatives should be undertaken.

It is to be hoped that Papua New Guinean researchers, especially those who are themselves first language or fluent second language speakers of Tok Pisin, will be at the forefront of future developments. They would be ideally placed to gain access to spontaneous speech in many situations that expatriate researches find it difficult to access, and would be able to interpret findings with the insight of native-like competence and immersion in the culture. The work of Dicks Thomas (1990a/b, 1996) is a promising beginning in this respect, and continued institutional support of such work is needed.

Manus dancers

Saveman (expert) placing a magic spell on a *marila* (love charm) at Lae (Morobe)

Appendix

Samples of speech from different regions

The following are somewhat more extended selections illustrating speech from informants in each of the different regions. A number of footnotes are appended to highlight items which have been referred to in the main text or are otherwise of interest.

1. Momase

The following story was told by A, aged 16 at Aitape, West Sepik Province on 1st September 1992. Her father is from Aitape and her mother from East Sepik. She had lived all her life in the West Sepik Province, from where this origin story comes.

[1] *Displa stori em kam long ples blo mama blo mi.* [2] *Mama blo mi yet i stori long mi.*
[3] *Long wanpla taim, lo wanpla ples, i gat ol sampla lain i stap, na wanpla taim wanpla man i tokim meri blong em osem "mipla nogat kaikai lo aus na mi ba go was long abus long bus."* [4] *Orait abinun i kam na em i wokobaut i go wantem ol spia bino - - na banara bilong em.* [5] *Taim em i go daun long bus em i no painim wanpela abus.*[1]
[6] *Orait long neks dei ken em i go na katim wanpela saksak i go daun klostu long wanpla raunwara na saksak i stap na i sting*[2] *liklik na long nait em i go bek long was.* [7] *Na em i kilim wanpela pik i kam na i kaikai binatang blong saksak.* [8] *Taim em i kilim na em i katim i stap na tudak i kam, n' em i wokim wanpela haus arere long dispela raunwara na i simukim ol abus bilong em.* [9] *N' em i slip long nait i stap.* [10] *Em i putim bilum bilong em andanit long sanggana*[3] *bilong em na em i slip.*
[11] *Na long nait wanpela bikpela sneik i stap insait long wara i smelim ol smel bilong abus na i kam antap.* [12] *N' em i kaikaim*[4] *olgeta abus bilong man na i daunim man tu na, go daun gen long wara.* [13] *Man i silip i go na em i laik tanim na em i pilim osem, em i pas,*[5] *na em i tra - - em i laik opim ai na em i lukim olsem olgeta hap i tutak.* [14] *Na em pusim han i go insait long bilum bilong em na em i kisim wanpela sel kina.*[6] *na em i katim bel bilong sneik na em i kam autsaid.*
[15] *Pinis em i kilim sneik na em i kisim go lo ples bilong em.* [16] *Na em i stori l' ol lain long ples, na ol i katim sneik na kukim na ol i kaikai.* [17] *Taim ol i kaikai pinis, olgeta i kamap osem ston na ol i sta lo maunten lo ples blo mama blo mi.* [18] *Em tasol stori blong mi.*

[1] This story comes from my mother's village. [2] My mother told it to me herself.
[3] Once in a certain place some people lived and one day a man said to his wife "we haven't got any food in the house, I'm going to find some game in the bush." [4] Afternoon came and he went off with his spears and bow. [5] When he went to the forest he didn't find any game.
[6] The next day he went and cut a sago tree down close to a lagoon, and the sago was left and was going rotten and in the night he came back and lay in wait. [7] And he killed a pig that came to eat the sago grubs. [8] When he killed it and cut it up it got dark, and he made a shelter bedside the lagoon and smoked all his meat. [9] Then he went to sleep for the night. [10] He put his string bag under his arm and slept.
[11] And in the night, a big snake which was in the water smelled the meat and came out. [12] And he ate all the man's meat and swallowed the man too and went back into the water. [13] The man kept on sleeping and he wanted to turn over and felt that he was stuck and he wanted to open his eyes and he saw that everything was dark. [14] And he pushed his hand into his string bag and got a kina shell and cut open the snake's belly and came outside.
[15] In the end he killed the snake and brought it to his village. [16] And he told everyone in the village about it and they cut up the snake and cooked it and ate it. [17] When they had eaten it they all turned into stone and they are on a mountain near my mother's village. [18] That's all of my story.

---

[1] The word *abus* refers to animal food from the bush.
[2] The word *sting* can mean both stink and be rotten.
[3] This refers to the armpit.
[4] Eating flesh by non-human agents often has the *-im* suffix.
[5] *Pas* = 'stuck' from the English word *fast*.
[6] Although *kina* is the name of the PNG currency, it originally refers to pearl oyster shells, often cut into strips or crescents for body ornamentation.

2. Highlands

This is a transcript of the speech of P aged 10, recorded at Goroka, 7th December 1990. His parents are both from the Watabung area, but he says that he does not know their language and always uses Tok Pisin at home. He has lived all his life in and around Goroka. Perhaps because of he is quite young, some aspects of the story appear a bit confusing, for example, sometimes the identity of referents of pronouns such as *em* are not immediately apparent.

[1] *Wanpla taim tupla pikinini - tupla - wanpla bikpla gel na wanpla liklik boi, tupla sa stap wantem lapun bubu blo tupla na mapapa blo tupla dai pinis na, tupla stap wantem lapun bubu blo tupla na tupla[7] tok - disla lapun bubu blo tupla tok "yu mas - onem ia[8] - yutla stap l' em mi bai go daun lo gaden na - wonem ia kisim sampla kaikai na kam antap."*
[2] *Em tokim tupla osem nau, em digim hol andanit[9] lo post nau, em putim tupla andnit nau, em putim sampla kaikai go insait na em karapim - ol putim lif banana antap na em karap sampla giraun antap nau, em tok "yutla stap andanit bai mi go lo gaden na kam." *[3]* Em tok osem nau, em larim tupla nau em go ia nogat, tupla stap nau pa - sla lapun pa[10] blo tupla raun lo bus blo tu... - em kam bek nau em tok - em painim go nau, ol tok, tupla liklik boi na gel ia tupla sta andanit lo graun nau tupla tok "yes" nau, em rausim graun nau, em rausim tupla kam ausait nau, em askim tupla "lapun ma blo yutupla go we?" *[4]* Nau em tok osem nau, tupla tok "em go lo gaden."*
[5] *Nau, lapun pa blo tupla beinim lapun ma blo tupla go lo gaden nau,* [6] *dsla tupla liklik boi na gel ia tupla stap go go na, avinun nau, tupla wet longpla taim nau, avin... - tupla tok "mitla biainim ol go."*
[7] *Nau, tupla go ia nogat, tupla paul lo rot nau, tupla go lo narapla hap nau, tupla go insait lo bus nau, disla masalai paulim et blo tupla nau kisim tupla go ogeta nau, disla tupla liklik boi ia tupla wonem ia nau, tupla go lo aus blo wanpla lapun meri, disla masalai paulim tupla logen[11] ia.*
[8] *Nau disla tupla go insait nau, tupla go insait lo sla haus ia nogat, disla lapun meri ia i stap nau, em tok "yutpla - yutla[12] kam lo - wonem ia - yutla kam lo wonem nau?" *[9]* Em tok - tupla tok "mitla laik go lo - go l' lapun bubu blo mitupla na mipla kam lo rot ??ia tasol mitla paul na mitupla[13] kam." *[10]* Nau, desa liklik - wonem ia - brata blogen ia em pulapim em insait lo wanpla liklik sel ia, na em na em angap lo nek blongen.* [11] *Nau em tok "putim sel bl' yu wantem onem ia na mitla go lo gaden na wok nau." *[12]* Em trik em nau, liklik gel ia wantem em ?? putim sel bloen antap lo - wonem ia nau, kabot nau tupla go daun lo gaden.* [13] *Tupla go nau, disla lapun meri ia, em stap tamblo nau, disla tupla wok pinis tupla kam antap nau, nait nau, tupla silip.[14]* [14] *Tupla wokim paia nau, liklik gel ia slip indai[15] nau, disla lapun meri ia, em sekim lo sel ia nogat,[16] liklik boi ia stap nau, em kisim em n' em daunim em pinis nau.*
[15] *Disla liklik gel ia, lo moning nau liklik gel ia kirap nau, em tok - em laik kisim sampla kaikai na trome go insait lo disla sel ia liklik brata blogen ba kaikai.* [16] *Em to sem em kisim wonem ia nau em lak kisim go sel ia nogat, lapun meri ia tok "mi ..." - em - sla lapun meri ia tok "em no stap." *[17]* Em tok osem nau, disla liklik gel ia lulug insait lo wonem ia sel ia nogat em no stap nau, disla liglig[17] gel ia karai karai stap nau, em karai karai longpla taim nau, uset ia, em kirap nau em tok "okei" nau lapun meri ia go lo gaden.* [18] *Nau liglig gel ia stap nau, em kisim paia lait pinis nau em katim ogeta sla retpla kon ia nau em putim antap lo haus ia.* [19] *Nau em kisim wonem ia paia nau em kukim nau, em tok "mi go lo maunten,* [20] *win, win mas blou ia na mi go lo maunten.* [21] *Faia okei yu mas faia." *[22]* Em tok osem nau, em go lo maunten, win nau, win wok lo blouim faia ia, nau em - em go lo maunten, faia nau wonem ia disla haus ia paia.[18]*
[23] *Nau em kukim ogeta wonem ia samting blo lapun meri ia na ogeta - wonem ia - poisin[19] blongen ia nau, disla liglig gel ia go - go nau em go stap wantem wanpla anti blongen nau, disa tup... - tupla sa stap nau, sla liglig gel ia tok "mi bai - wonem ia - i go na painim kaikai lo bus i kam." *[24]* Na em tok osem nau,*

---

[7] There is considerable redundant use of the dual.
[8] Fillers such as *wanem ia* or variants are very common when searching for the right word.
[9] The usual form is *ananit*.
[10] Reduced form of *papa*.
[11] A phonological variant of *longen*, found especially in Eastern Highlands.
[12] The forms *yutupela* and *yutla* are seen to be interchangeable here.
[13] *Mitupla* and *mitla* are also used interchangeably.
[14] Note the use of *nau* in sequencing events.
[15] An idiom, literally "sleep die" meaning to be fast asleep
[16] *Nogat* as a conjunction appears to relate to events contrary to expectations.
[17] Velar fricatives are frequently voiced, a typical Highlands feature.
[18] Interchangeable *faia* and *paia*.
[19] *Poisin* here probably refers to objects for sorcery.

em kam ia nogat, disla liglig brata blongen ia, em tanim pisin na em kam sanap lo diwai nau, em wok lo sigaut sigaut i stap nau, lig sista blongen luglug go antap ia nogat em lukim pisin ia nau, em tok, disla pisin ia tok "yu go ..." - em wokim sampla sain n' em tok "yu go hariap ol - sla lapun meri ia em kam ia em - em wok lo painim yu painim yu yet ia na em laik kilim yu ia na yu mas go hariap." [25] Nau, em kam ia - nogat em no harim tok blo pisin ia nau em kam kam ia, nogat em kam lo are[20] lo wanpla wara. [26] Nau lapun meri ia ron...- smelim em smelim em kam nau em kam klostu lo gel ia nau, pisin ia kisim wanpla diwai pinis nau em trome go lo wara nau abrusim wara na go lo hap blo gel ia nau, gel ia go antap lo diwai ia nau em wokobaut kam kam lo arere lo wara ia. [27] Nau, sla pisin wantem ia tupla go na, sla meri ia kam ia nogat em wok lo wel wel lo diwai ia nau pudaun go daun lo wara ia nau, wara karim em go.

[1] Once upon a time, two children, one big girl and one small boy stayed with their grandfather and their parents had died and they lived with their grandfather and they said - their grandfather said "you two stay here, I will go to the garden and get some food and come back."
[2] He told them this and dug a hole underneath the house post and put the two underneath and put some food inside and covered them up - they put banana leaves over and he put some earth on top and said "you two stay under there, I'll go to the garden and come back." [3] He said this and left the two there and went away, the two stayed there, their grandfather went round in the bush ... he came back and said - he was looking for them, they said, the little boy and girl who were under the ground said "yes," he cleared away the ground, he took the two outside, he asked them "where did your grandmother go?" [4] He said this and the two said "she went to the garden."
[5] Now the grandfather followed the grandmother to the garden. [6] The little boy and girl stayed there until afternoon, the two waited for a long time and they said "let's follow them."
[7] Now the two went but they went the wrong way, they went to another place, they went into the bush, this bush spirit confused their thoughts and took them completely, these two went to the house of an old woman, this bush spirit who had confused them.
[8] The two went inside, they went inside this house, the old woman was there, she said "what are you two doing here?" [9] The two said "we were about to go to our grandmother but we got lost and we came here." [10] Now this little, what, her brother, she put him inside a little shell and hung it round her neck. [11] Now she said "put your shell with the what's it? and we'll go to the garden and work." [12] She tricked her and the little girl put the shell with him on top of the what's it, cupboard, and the two went down to the garden. [13] The two went, this old woman stayed down below, the two did it and cambe back up, it was night so they went to sleep. [14] They made a fire and the girl was fast asleep, this old woman checked the shell and sure enough the boy was in there she got him and swallowed him.
[15] The small girl, in the morning she got up, she said - she was about to get some food and throw it inside the shell for her little brother to eat. [16] She said she got, what - she was about to put in in the shell and the old woman said "I..." - she, the old woman said "he's not there." [17] She said this, the small girl looked inside the what, the shell, and he wasn't there, the little girl cried and cried, she cried for a long time and who? she got up and said "OK" and the old woman went to the garden. [18] The little girl stayed, she got a fire brand and cut all the red corn and put it on top of the house. [19] Now she got the fire and burned it, she said "I'm going to the mountain. [20] The wind must blow and I'm going to the mountain. [21] Fire, you must flare up". [22] She said this, she went to the mountain, the wind, the wind fanned the flame, she went to the mountain, the fire, what, the house caught fire.
[23] Now it burned all the old woman's things and all her poison, this little girl went - went and stayed with an auntie, the two lived there and the small girl said "I'm going to bring some food from the bush." [24] She said this and came, but her little brother had turned into a bird and came and perched on a tree, he was singing and singing, his little sister looked up and saw the bird, she said - the bird said "you go..." - it made some signs to say "you go quickly, they - this old woman is coming, she's looking everywhere for you and she wants to kill you and you must go quickly." [25] Now she came, she didn't listen to what the bird said, she came to the bank of a river. [26] Now the old woman ran - smelled her and came close to the girl, the bird got a piece of wood and threw it into the river and crossed the river to where the girl was, the girl went on to the piece of wood and walked to the river bank. [27] Now she and the bird went off, the woman came but she was slipping on the wood and she fell down into the water and the river carried her away.

---

[20] Shortened form of *arere* meaning side.

3. Islands

This sample was recorded at Kavieng, New Ireland Province on 31st July 1990 when D was 14. Her father is from Mortlock Islands, North Solomons and her mother is from Lihir Island, New Ireland. She had lived in Kavieng for most of her life.

[1] *Wanpla taim wanpla man nem bloen Yakop.* [2] *Em bin go nau i go lo - i go huk.* [3] *I[21] go huk nau na wanpla klaud ia i bin kam nau karamapim ap ia em bin huk nau i go nau i wok lo olsem tutak nau[22].* [4] *Em kirap nau i go arasait nau i pul nau.* [5] *I sta(t) lo pul pul pul pul pul pul nau go nau i tok se[23] bai kamap lo wanpla ailan bai i go tasol.* [6] *Kirap nau i go lo wanpla ailan nau.* [7] *I wok lo pul i go nau go painim wanpla ailan.*

[8] *Lo disla ailan i gat wanpla haus tasol.* [9] *Na em i go nau go lukim disla haus nau i nogat man insait.* [10] *Okei kirap na i tok osem bai go na bai wokobaut raunim disla ailan[24].* [11] *Wokobaut i go raunim disla ailan nau go nau i go bungim wanpla lapun meri.* [12] *Disla lapun meri ia em em gat wanpla haus tasol na nogat narapla nau.* [13] *Em tasol sa silip lo disla ailan.* [14] *I go nau go painim lapun meri ia nau lapun meri bin karim paiawut.* [15] *Na i go nau i tok osem, "inap mi alpim yu?"* [16] *Nau lapun - lapun meri kirap tok "okei."* [17] *Nau i karim paiawut nau go bringim em lo haus nau lapun meri ia i gim em kaikai i salim em na i tok go kalapim[25] kulau[26].* [18] *Go nau i tok i tokim em tok, "go kalapim disla kulau mi toki yu kulau i no orait."* [19] *Okei go kalapim kulau nau kisim nau go nau tokim em, "yu putim baksait lo kanu blo yu na yu go sapos yu go na sapos yu harim wanpla pairap baksait yu lukluk kam baksait.* [20] *Sas[27] yu lukluk kam baksait bai yu lukim wanpla samting."* [21] *Nau em putim nau i pul nau.*

[22] *I pul pul pul pul pul pul pul pul[28] nau go nau i harim wanpla samting i pairap nau baksait lo kanu.* [23] *Laik lukluk go baksait nau wanpla stailpla[29] meri stret i sindaun baksait.* [24] *Kirap em tok, "ai yu kam painim wonem, yu kam ose 'nem na yu kam lo mi."* [25] *Na em kirap tok sem "na bai mitupla maret nau."* [26] *Nau kisim em nau tupla go.*

[27] *Tupla go lo ailan blong em nau ol man i lukim em na ol tok, "ai yu kisim meri ia we?"* [28] *Em tok, "nogat mi go kamap lo wanpla ailan na wanpla lapun meri mi halpim em lo kisim ol samting nau kirap nau i tokim mi lo kalapim kulau na mi putim baksait lo kanu blo mi nau na i pairap nau em nau meri ia kamap."* [29] *Na ol i kirap tok, "man stailpla meri stret."* [30] *Ol i djeles nau lo em nau.*

[31] *Kirap nau kasen barata blo manggi ia nau i go na i tok se bai go na bai go kisim wanpla meri.* [32] *I go nau i go na i no tingim wonem samting barata bl' em i bin tokim em bai mas wokim.* [33] *Okei em i go i go lo disla ailan ia lapun meri stap longen nau i go na i go na lapun meri ia bin wokobaut ken wantem paiawut i kam ken.* [34] *Na em i go na i no halpim[30] meri ia.* [35] *I go tasol i go na i tok osem, "ai mi laikim wanpla kulau ia, mi laikim meri mi laikim meri."* [36] *I go nau lapun meri kirap tok, "na yu wet pastem mitupla go lo haus."* [37] *Tupla go lo haus nau tupla go nau kaikai nau.* [38] *Lapun meri ia gim em kaikai.* [39] *Em kirap tok, "yu gim mi hariap kulau mi laik go nau lo ailan blo mi ia, i tutak nau."* [40] *Man ia - man ia kirap, a meri ia kirap na i tok osem tok, "bai mi gim yu lo wonem yu no halpim mi."* [41] *Okei man ia kirap tok, "nogat yu gim mi hariap. Sas nogat bai mi paitim yu."* [42] *Kirap nau lapun meri kirap salim em go kisim narapla kulau.*

[43] *I go nau na i no kisim kulau kisim tarai.* [44] *Salim em lo go kisim na i no tokim em lo wonem kain tarai bai kisim.* [45] *Kirap nau kisim tarai nau i go na disla tarai ia i gat krokodail insait.* [46] *I go kisim nau kam putim baksait loen nau na i tokim em, "yu go yu putim baksait lo yu, sas yu harim pairap yu lukluk kam baksait."*

[47] *Okei em i go nau i pul pul pul pul pul i go i harim samting pairap nau i lukluk nau krokodail.* [48] *Krokodail i stap baksait longen.* [49] *Em kirap tasol i tok, "ei man mi ting se meri na nogat krokodail ia."* [50] *Kirap tasol kisim pul ia paitim hed blo krokodail ia pul i buruk.* [51] *Em kirap tasol i pul tasol lo han i*

---

[21] Note the copious use of the particle *i* throughout this passage, in contrast to the other samples.
[22] Note too the frequent use of *nau* in discourse.
[23] The complementiser *se* does not seem to be a contraction of *olsem* here, unlike in most other areas.
[24] Note there is no overt subject in many sentences, when it is clear who is being talked about.
[25] *kalapim* is literally to jump
[26] A *kulau* is a green coconut for drinking while a dry one is known as *tarai*
[27] Reduced form of *sapos*
[28] Continuing action is frequently indicated by this kind of iteration.
[29] Stail was originally a noun, which led to the compound *stailmeri*. Now used here as an adjective.
[30] The usual word for help is *halivim*

go go nau krokodail i - i swim i go bek nau i go nau i go lo ailan blo em wantem lapun meri ia na man nau ia i drai nau i go bek lo ailan nau go i stap nau na ol man i lap long em. [52] *Em tasol.*[31]

[1] Once upon a time there was a man called Yakop. [2] He went to - he went fishing. [3] He went fishing and a cloud came and covered up the place he was fishing, and so it went on until it was dark. [4] He got up and went outside and paddled. [5] He started to paddle and paddled and paddled and decided he would go to an island. [6] He started to go to the island. [7] He was busy paddling, looking for the island. He kept on paddling and came to the island.

[8] On this island there was a house. [9] And he went and looked at the house and there was no-one inside. [11] So he decided to walk around the island. He walked around the island and met an old woman. [12] Only this woman had a house - there was nobody else. [13] Only she slept on this island. [14] So he found the old woman and she was carrying firewood. [15] And he went and said "can I help you?" [16] And the old woman said "OK." [17] So he carried the firewood and brought it to the house and the old woman gave him food and sent him to climb a coconut tree. [18] She told him "go and climb this coconut tree, the coconuts are not all right." [19] So he climbed the tree, got them and she said "put them in the back of your canoe, and if as you go you hear a noise behind you, look back. [20] If you look behind you, you'll see something." [21] He put them in and paddled.

[22] He kept on paddling and heard a noise in the back of the canoe. [23] He looked behind him and a really nice-looking girl was sitting at the back. [24] He said "what are you looking for and how come you have come to me?" [25] And she said "we're going to be married." [26] He got her now and they went.

[27] They went to his island and everyone saw him and said "where did you get this girl?" [28] He said "Oh, I went to an island and an old woman I helped to get some things told me to climb a coconut and I put them in the back of the canoe and there was a noise and the girl appeared." [29] And they said "oh boy! She's really smart." [30] They were jealous of him now.

[31] The boy's cousin said that he was going to go and get a girl. [32] He went and he didn't think of the things his cousin told him he should do. [33] So he went to the island where the old woman lived and again the old woman came walking with firewood. [34] And he didn't go and help the woman. [35] He just went and said "I want a green coconut, I want a girl, I want a girl." [36] The old woman said "wait and we'll go to the house." [37] The two went to the house and ate. [38] The old woman gave him food. [39] He said "hurry up and give me the coconut, I want to go back to my island, it's getting dark." [40] The woman said "why should I give you one, you didn't help me." [41] The man said "no, give me one at once. If you don't, I'll beat you." [42] So the old woman sent him to get another green coconut.

[43] He went and he didn't get a green coconut, he got a dry one. [44] She sent him to pick one but didn't tell him what kind to get. [45] So he took the dry coconut and this one had a crocodile inside. [46] She went and got it and put it in the back of the canoe and said "put it behind you. If you hear a noise, look round."

[47] So he paddled off and he heard a noise and he looked behind and he saw a crocodile. [48] The crocodile was behind him. [49] He said "Oh, no, I thought it would be a girl but it's a crocodile." [50] He got his paddle and hit the crocodile on the head but the paddle broke. [51] So he paddled with his hands and the crocodile swam back to its island with the old woman and the man was empty-handed and went back to the island and everybody laughed at him. [52] That's all.

---

[31] This is a very familiar story with many variants. Usually the ending is somewhat more sinister, with the jealous brother killing the hero, taking his wife and living happily ever after.

Tubuan ancestor figures in the Siassi islands

References

Adone, Dany & Plag, Ingo (eds) 1994 *Creolization and language change.* Tübingen: Niemeyer.
Ahai, Naihuwo 1987 Husat i save tok Tok Pisin, wantaim husat, na long wanem taim? Paper to Papua New Guinea Linguistic Society, Lae.
—— 1989 Language choice and information flow in education. Thirlwall & Hughes (eds), 50-56.
Aitchison, Jean 1981 *Language change: progress or decay?* London: Fontana.
—— 1989 Spaghetti junctions and recurrent routes: Some preferred pathways in language evolution. *Lingua* 77:151-71.
Alleyne, Mervyn 1971 Acculturation and the cultural matrix of creolization. Hymes (ed.), 169-86.
Andersen, Roger W 1983 *Pidginization and creolization as language acquisition.* Rowley, MA: Newbury House.
—— 1990 Papiamentu tense-aspect, with special attention to discourse. Singler (ed.), 59-96.
Arends, J, Muysken, P, & Smith, N (eds). 1995 *Pidgins and Creoles: An introduction.* Amsterdam: Benjamins.
Bailey, Charles-James N & Maroldt, K 1977 The French lineage of English. Meisel (ed.), 21-53.
Bailey, Richard W & Görlach, Manfred (eds) 1982 *English as a world language.* Ann Arbor: University of Michigan Press.
Baker, Philip 1987 Historical developments in Chinese Pidgin English and the nature of the relationship between various Pidgin Englishes of the Pacific region. *Journal of Pidgin and Creole Languages,* 2:163-207.
—— 1990b Off target? *Journal of Pidgin and Creole Linguistics,* 5:107-19.
—— 1993 Australian influence on Melanesian Pidgin English. *Te Reo,* 36:3-67.
—— 1994 Creativity in creole genesis. Adone & Plag (eds), 65-84.
—— (ed.) 1995a. *From contact to Creole and beyond.* London: University of Westminster Press.
—— 1995b Motivation in Creole genesis. Baker (ed.), 3-15.
Baker, Philip & Corne, Chris 1986 Universals, substrata and the Indian Ocean Creoles. Muysken & Smith (eds), 163-83.
Bakker, Peter 1989 A Basque-Amerindian pidgin in use between Europeans and Native Americans in North America c 1540-1640. *Anthropological Linguistics,* 31:117-47.
Bakker, Peter & Mous, Maarten (eds) 1994 *Mixed Languages: 15 case studies in language intertwining.* Amsterdam: IFOTT.
Baldauf, R jr & Luke, A (eds). 1990). *Language Planning and Education in Australasia and the South Pacific.* Clevedon: Multilingual Matters.
Bálint, András 1969 *English-Pidgin-French phrase book and sports dictionary.* Port Moresby: Author.
—— 1973 Towards an encyclopaedic dictionary of Niuginian (Melanesian Pidgin). *Kivung,* 6(1):2-3.
Barron, Colin. 1986 Lexical nativisation in Papua New Guinean English. *Department of Language and Communication Studies report no 7.* Lae: University of Technology.
Beaugrande, Robert de & Dressler, W U 1981 *Introduction to Text Linguistics.* London: Longman.
Bee, Darlene 1971 Phonological interference between Usarufa and Pidgin English. *Kivung,* 5(2):69-95.
Bell, H L 1971 Language and the army of Papua New Guinea. *Army Journal,* 264:31-42.
Bellwood, P S, Fox, J J & Tryon, D (eds) 1995 *The Austronesians: Historical and comparative perspectives, 2nd Ed.* Canberra: Department of Anthropology, Australian National University.
Bergmann, Ulrich (ed.) 1982 *Save na Mekim: Buk bilong kain kain wok na kain kain samting bilong helpim sindaun bilong yumi.* Lae: Liklik Buk Information Centre.
Bible Society 1966 *Nupela Testamen.* Port Moresby.
Bickerton, Derek 1974 Creolization, linguistic universals, natural semantax and the brain. *University of Hawaii Working Papers in Linguistics,* 6(3):125-41.
—— 1975a Can English and Pidgin be kept apart? McElhanon (ed.) 21-27.
—— 1975b *Dynamics of a Creole System.* Cambridge: Cambridge University Press.

―――― 1979 The status of *bin* in the Atlantic creoles. Hancock (ed.), 309-14.

―――― 1980 Creolization, linguistic universals, natural semantax and the brain. Day (ed.), 1-18.

―――― 1981 *Roots of Language*. Ann Arbor: Karoma.

―――― 1984 The language bioprogram hypothesis. *Behavioral and Brain Sciences*, 7:173-221.

―――― 1986 Creoles and West African languages: A case of mistaken identity? Muysken & Smith (eds), 25-40.

―――― 1993 Subject focus and pronouns. Byrne & Winford, (eds), 189-212.

Blount, B & Sanches, M (eds) 1977 *Sociocultural Dimensions of Language Change*. New York: Academic Press.

Blust, Robert (ed.) 1991 *Currents in Pacific Linguistics: Papers on Austronesian languages and ethnolinguistics in honour of George W. Grace*. Canberra: Australian National University (*Pacific Linguistics*, C-117).

Bradshaw, Joel 1982 Word order change in Papua New Guinea Austronesian languages. PhD thesis, University of Hawaii.

Brash, Elton 1971 Tok pilai, tok piksa na tok bokis: Imaginative dimensions in Melanesian Pidgin. *Kivung*, 4(1):12-20.

―――― 1975 Tok Pisin! *Meanjin Quarterly*, 34(3):320-27.

Brown, Gillian & Yule, George 1983 *Discourse Analysis*. Cambridge: Cambridge University Press.

Burton, Frank 1978 *The Politics of Legitimacy: Struggles in a Belfast community*. London: Routledge and Kegan Paul.

Buschenhofen, Paul F 1997 Language attitudes of final year high school and first year university students in Papua New Guinea. Paper to SEAMO Regional Seminar, RELC, Singapore, April 1997.

Bybee, Joan 1985 *Morphology: A study of the relation between meaning and form*. Amsterdam: Benjamins.

Bybee, Joan & Fleischman, Suzanne (eds) 1995 *Modality in Grammar and Discourse*. Amsterdam: Benjamins.

Byrne, Francis 1991 Approaches to 'missing' internal (and external) arguments in serial structure: Some presumed difficulties. Byrne & Huebner (eds), 207-22.

Byrne, Francis & Holm, John (eds) 1993 *Atlantic meets Pacific: A global view of pidginization and creolization*. Amsterdam: Benjamins.

Byrne, Francis & Huebner, Thom (eds) 1991 *Development and Structures of Creole Languages: Essays in honor of Derek Bickerton*. Amsterdam: Benjamins.

Byrne, Francis & Winford, Donald (eds) 1993 *Focus and Grammatical Relations in Creole Languages*. Amsterdam: Benjamins.

Camden, Bill 1977 *A Descriptive Dictionary: Bislama to English*. Vila: Maropa.

Capell, A 1969 *A Survey of New Guinea Languages*. Sydney: Sydney University Press.

Carle, Rainer et al (ed.) 1982 *Gava`: Studies in Austronesian languages and cultures*. Berlin: Reimer.

Cassidy, F G 1971 Tracing the pidgin element in Jamaican Creole (with notes on method and the nature of pidgin vocabularies). Hymes (ed.), 203-21.

Chandler, Brian 1989 *Longman Mini-concordancer, version 1.01*. London: Longman.

Charpentier, Jean-Michel 1979 Le Pidgin Bislama(n) et le multilinguisme aux Nouvelles-Hébrides. *Langues et Civilizations à Tradition Orale*, 35. Paris: SELAF

Cheshire, Jenny 1982 *Variation in an English dialect: A sociolinguistic study*. Cambridge : Cambridge University Press.

―――― (ed.) 1991 *English Around the World: Sociolinguistic perspectives*. Cambridge: Cambridge University Press.

Chomsky, Noam 1968 *Language and Mind*. New York: Harcourt, Brace & World.

Chowning, Ann 1983 Interaction between Pidgin and three West New Britain languages. *Papers in Pidgin and Creole Linguistics* 3:191-206. Canberra: Australian National University (*Pacific Linguistics* A-65).

―――― 1986 Refugees, traders and other wanderers: The linguistic effects of population mixing in Melanesia, 407-434. Canberra: Australian National University (*Pacific Linguistics* C-94).

Clark, Ross 1979 In Search of Beach-la-mar: towards a history of Pacific Pidgin English. *Te Reo*, 22/23:3-66.

Cogen, Cathy et al. (eds.) 1975 *Proceedings of the First Annual Meeting of the Berkeley Linguistics Society*. Berkeley: Linguistics Society.

Comrie, Bernard 1976 *Aspect: An introduction to the study of verbal aspect and related problems*. Cambridge: Cambridge University Press.

—— 1981 *Language Universals and Linguistic Typology: Syntax and morphology*. Chicago: University of Chicago Press.

—— 1985 *Tense*. Cambridge: Cambridge University Press.

Comrie, B, Matthews, S & Polinsky, M, (eds) 1996 *The Atlas of Languages*. New York: Facts On File.

Conrad, Bob 1990 Problems in translating from Tok Pisin to Mufian. Verhaar (ed.), 307-22.

Coulmas, Florian (ed.) 1997 *The Handbook of Sociolinguistics*. Oxford: Blackwell.

Crowley, Terry 1987a Serial verbs in Paamese. *Studies in Language*, 11:35-84.

—— 1987b Serial verbs, prepositions and complementation in Bislama. Paper to International Conference of Tok Pisin, Madang, 1987.

—— 1988 Referential and expressive expansion in Bislama. Ms.

—— 1989a English in Vanuatu. *World Englishes*, 8(1):37-46.

—— 1989b Review article: Sources and structures in Melanesian Pidgin. *Journal of Cross-Cultural and Interlanguage Communication*, 8(4):397-409.

—— 1989c Say, C'est, and subordinate constructions in Melanesian Pidgin. *Journal of Pidgin and Creole Languages*, 4(2):185-210.

—— 1990a *From Beach-la-mar to Bislama: The Emergence of a national language in Vanuatu*. Oxford: Clarendon Press.

—— 1990b Serial verbs and prepositions in Bislama. Verhaar (ed.), 57-89).

—— 1990c The Position of Melanesian Pidgin in Vanuatu and Papua New Guinea. Verhaar (ed.), 1-18.

—— 1991 Genesis of a preposition system in Bislama. Harlow (ed.), 389-415.

—— 1994 Melanesian languages: do they have a future? Paper to Linguistic Society of PNG Conference, Lae, June 1994.

Crowley, T, Lynch, J, Siegel, J, & Piau, J 1995 *The Design of Language: An introduction to descriptive linguistics*. Auckland: Longman Paul.

Day, Richard, R (ed.) 1980 *Issues in English Creoles: Papers from the 1975 Hawaii Conference*. Heidelberg: Groos.

DeCamp, David 1971 Towards a generative analysis of a post-creole continuum. Hymes (ed.), 349-70.

DeGraff, M F 1993 Is Haitian Creole a pro-drop language? Byrne & Holm (eds), 71-90.

Dillard, J L 1970 Principles in the history of American English - Paradox, Virginity and Cafeteria, *Florida FL Reporter*, Spring/Fall 1970.

Dutton, Thomas Edward 1973 *Conversational New Guinea Pidgin*. Canberra: Australian National University (*Pacific Linguistics* D-12.).

—— 1976 Language and national development - long wanem rot? Inaugural Lecture, University of Papua New Guinea.

—— 1980 *Queensland Canefield English of the Late Nineteenth Century*. Canberra: Australian National University (*Pacific Linguistics* D-29).

—— 1983a Birds of a feather: A pair of rare pidgins from the Gulf of Papua. Woolford & Washabaugh (eds), 77-105.

—— 1983b The origin and spread of aboriginal pidgin English in Queensland. *Aboriginal History*, 7:90-122.

—— 1985 *Police Motu: Iena sivarai (its story)*. Port Moresby: University of Papua New Guinea Press.

—— (ed.) 1992 *Culture Change, Language Change: Case studies from Melanesia*. Canberra: Australian National University (*Pacific Linguistics* C-120).

—— 1994 Intercultural contact and communication in south-east Papua New Guinea. Pütz (ed.), 223-37.

Dutton, Tom & Bourke, Michael 1990 *Taim* in Tok Pisin: an interesting variation in use from the Southern Highlands of Papua New Guinea. Verhaar (ed.), 252-62.

Dutton, Tom & Kakare, Iru 1977 *The hiri Trading Language of Central Papua: A first survey*. Port Moresby: University of Papua New Guinea.

Dutton, Tom & Mühlhäusler, Peter 1979 Papuan Pidgin English and Hiri Motu. Wurm (ed.), 225-42.

—— & —— 1984 Queensland Kanaka English. *English World Wide*, 4(2):231-63.

Dutton, Tom & Thomas, Dicks 1985 *A new course in Tok Pisin*. Canberra: Australian National University (*Pacific Linguistics* D-67).

Dutton, T, Ross, M & Tryon, D (eds) 1992 *The Language Game: Papers in memory of Donald C Laycock*. Canberra: Australian National University (*Pacific Linguistics* C-110).

Edmondson, J A, Feagin, C & Mühlhäusler, P (eds) 1990 *Development and Diversity: Language variation across time and space. A festschrift for Charles-James N. Bailey*. Arlington, Texas: SIL.

Escure, Geneviève 1991 Serialization in creole oral discourse. Byrne & Huebner (eds), 179-92.

—— 1993 Focus, topic particles and discourse markers in the Belizean creole continuum. Byrne & Winford (eds), 233-47.

Fairclough, Norman 1995 *Critical Discourse Analysis: The critical study of language*. London: Longman.

Faraclas, Nicholas 1989 Prosody and creolization in Tok Pisin. *Journal of Pidgin and Creole Languages*, 4:132-39.

—— 1990 From Old Guinea to Papua New Guinea: a comparative study of Nigerian Pidgin and Tok Pisin. Verhaar (ed.), 91-169).

Foley, William A 1986 *The Papuan Languages of New Guinea*. Cambridge: Cambridge University Press

—— 1988 Language birth: the processes of pidginization and creolization. Newmeyer (ed.), 162-83.

Franklin, Karl J (ed.) 1973 *The Linguistic Situation in the Gulf District and Adjacent Areas, Papua New Guinea*. Canberra: Australian National University (*Pacific Linguistics* C-26).

—— 1975 Vernaculars as bridges to cross-cultural understanding. McElhanon (ed.), 138-49.

—— 1980 The particles *i* and *na* in Tok Pisin. *Kivung*, 12(2):134-44

—— 1990 On the translation of official notices into Tok Pisin. Verhaar (ed.), 323-44.

Gardner-Chloros, Penelope 1995 Code-switching in community, regional and national repertoires: the myth of the discreteness of linguistic systems. Milroy & Muysken (eds), 68-89.

Givón, T 1979 Prolegomena to any sane creology. Hancock (ed.), 3-35.

—— 1990 Verb serialization in Tok Pisin and Kalam: a comparative study of temporal packing. Verhaar (ed.), 19-55.

Goodman, Maurice 1994 Pidgin Hawaiian. Letter to the editor, *Journal of Pidgin and Creole Languages*, 9:215-16.

Goulden, Rick J 1989 The source of Tok Pisin structures. *World Englishes*, 8(2):147-156.

—— 1990a Language, identity and change in West New Britain. Unpublished Ms.

—— 1990b *The Melanesian Content in Tok Pisin*. Canberra: Australian National University (*Pacific Linguistics* B-104.).

Greenberg, Joseph H (ed.) 1963 *Universals of Language*. Cambridge (Mass.): MIT Press.

Grimes, Barbara (ed.) 1992 *Ethnologue: Languages of the world, 12th edition*. Dallas, Texas: Summer Institute of Linguistics.

Hall, J H, Doane, N, & Ringler, D (eds) 1992 *Old English and New: Studies in language and linguistics in honor of Frederic G Cassidy*. New York: Garland.

Hall, Robert A 1943 *Melanesian Pidgin English: Grammar texts and vocabulary*. Baltimore: Linguistics Society of America.

—— 1955 *Hands off Pidgin English!* Sydney: Pacific Publications.

—— 1966 *Pidgin and Creole Languages*. Ithaca: Cornell University Press.

Halliday, M A K 1978 *Language as Social Semiotic*. London: Edward Arnold

Halliday, M A K & Hasan, R 1976 *Cohesion in English*. London: Longman.

Halliday, M A K, Gibbons, J & Nicholas, H (eds) 1990 *Learning, Keeping and Using Language, Vol. II: Selected papers from the 8th World Congress of Applied Linguists, Sydney, Australia, 16-21 August 1987*. Philadelphia: Benjamins.

Hancock, Ian F 1977 Recovering creole genesis: approaches and problems. Valdman (ed.), 277-94.

—— (ed.) 1979 *Readings in Creole Studies*. Ghent: Story-Scientia.

—— (ed.) 1985 *Diversity and Development in English-related Creoles*. Ann Arbor, Karoma.

Harding, T G 1967 *Voyagers of the Vitiaz Strait*. Seattle: University of Washington Press.

Harlow (ed.) 1991 *VICAL2 Western Austronesian and Contact Languages: Papers from the Fifth International Conference on Austronesian Linguistics*. Auckland: Linguistic Society of New Zealand.

Harris, John W 1991 Kriol: The creation of a new language. Romaine (ed.), 195-212.

Healey, L R 1975 When is a word not a pidgin word? McElhanon (ed.), 36-42.

Heller, M (ed.) 1988 *Codeswitching: anthropological and sociolinguistic perspectives*. Berlin: Mouton de Gruyter.

Holm, John A 1988 *Pidgins and Creoles Volume 1: Theory and structure*. Cambridge: Cambridge University Press.

—— 1989 *Pidgins and Creoles Volume 2: Reference survey*. Cambridge: Cambridge University Press.

—— 1992 Tracking creole etymologies: The case for cross-lexical-base comparison. Hall et al (eds), 229-37.

Holm, John A & Kepiou, Christopher 1993 Tok Pisin i kamap pisin gen? Is Tok Pisin repidginizing? Byrne & Holm (eds), 341-53.

Hooley, Bruce A 1962 Transformations in Neomelanesian. *Oceania*, 33:116-27.

Hymes, Dell (ed.) 1971 *Pidginization and Creolisation of Languages*. Cambridge: Cambridge University Press.

Independent Television Network 1990 *ITN Factbook*. London: Guild.

Jourdan, Christine 1985a Creolisation, nativisation or substrate influence. What is happening to *bae* in Solomon Islands Pijin. *Papers in Pidgin and Creole Linguistics*, 4:67-96. Canberra: Australian National University.

—— 1985b *Sapos iumi mitim iumi:* Urbanization and creolization in the Solomon Islands. PhD thesis, Australian National University.

—— 1989 Nativization and anglicization in Solomon Islands Pijin. *World Englishes*, 8(1):25-35.

—— 1990 Solomons Pijin: An unrecognized national language. Baldauf & Luke (eds), 166-81.

Kale, Joan 1990 Language planning and the language of education in Papua New Guinea. Baldauf & Luke (eds), 182-96.

Keesing, Roger M 1988 *Melanesian Pidgin and the Oceanic substrate*. Stanford: University Press.

Knowles, G, Williams, B & Taylor, L. 1996 *A corpus of formal British English speech. The Lancaster/IBM spoken English corpus*. London: Longman.

Koefoed, Geert 1979 Some remarks on the baby talk theory and the relexification theory. Hancock (ed.), 37-54.

Kulick, Don. 1992 *Language shift and cultural reproduction: socialization, self and syncretism in a Papua New Guinea village*. Cambridge: Cambridge University Press.

Kulick, Don & Stroud, Christopher 1990 Code-switching in Gapun: Social and linguistic aspects of language use in a language-shifting community. Verhaar (ed.), 205-34.

Labov, William 1972a *Language in the Inner City*. Philadelphia: University of Pennsylvania Press.

—— 1972b *Socilinguistic Patterns*. Philadelphia: University of Pennsylvania Press.

—— 1990 On the adequacy of natural languages - 1. The development of tense. Singler (ed.), 1-58.

Landtmann, Gunnar. 1927 *The Kiwai Papuans of British New Guinea*. London: Macmillan.

Laycock, Donald C 1970 *Materials in New Guinea Pidgin (Coastal and Lowlands)*. Canberra: Australian National University (*Pacific Linguistics* D-5).

—— 1979 Multilingualism, linguistic boundaries and unsolved problems in Papua New Guinea. Wurm (ed.), 81-99.

—— 1982 Linguistic diversity in Melanesia: a tentative explanation. Carle et al (eds), 31-37.

—— 1985 Phonology: Substratum elements in Tok Pisin phonology. Wurm & Mühlhäusler (eds), 295-307.

Laycock, Donald C & Winter, W (eds) 1987 *A World of Language: Papers presented to Professor S A Wurm on his 65th birthday*. Canberra: Australian National University (*Pacific Linguistics* C-100).

Le Page, Robert 1960 *Jamaican Creole*. London: Macmillan.

Lee, Ernie 1995 Unexpected shared features in Melanesian Pidgins/Creoles. Is Broken a Melanesian Pidgin/Creole? Paper presented to Second International Conference on Oceanic Linguistics, Suva, Fiji, July 1995.

Lefebvre, Claire (ed.) 1991 *Serial Verbs: Grammatical, comparative and cognitive approaches*. Amsterdam: Benjamins.

Lefebvre, Claire & Ritter, Elizabeth 1993 Two types of predicate doubling adverbs in Haitian Creole. Byrne & Winford (eds), 65-91.

Lichtenberk, Frantisek 1980 A grammar of Manam. PhD thesis, University of Hawaii.

—— 1995 Apprehensional epistemics. Bybee & Fleischmann (eds), 293-327.

Litteral, Robert 1969 *A Programmed Course in New Guinea Pidgin*. Milton, Qld.: Jacaranda.

—— 1970 The phonemes of New Guinea Pidgin. Ukarumpa, Summer Institute of Linguistics. Ms.

—— 1975 A proposal for the use of Pidgin in Papua New Guinea's education system. McElhanon (ed.), 155-65.

—— 1990 Tok Pisin: the language of modernization. Verhaar (ed.), 375-85.

Lomax, R W 1983 Aspects of cohesion and discourse structure in Tok Pisin (Melanesian Pidgin). MA thesis, University of Leeds.

Lumsden, John 1990 The bi-clausal structure of Haitian clefts. Seuren & Mufwene (eds), 741-59.

Lynch, John 1975a Expanding Tok Pisin vocabulary. Lynch (ed.), 21-26.

—— (ed.) 1975b Pidgins and Tok Pisin. *Department of Language Occasional Paper no. 1*. Port Moresby: University of Papua New Guinea.

—— 1979a Changes in Tok Pisin morphology. Paper presented at 13th PNG Linguistic Society Congress, Port Moresby.

—— 1979b Church, state and language in Melanesia. Inaugural lecture, UPNG, May 1979.

—— 1990 The future of Tok Pisin: Social, political and educational dimensions. Verhaar (ed.), 387-97.

—— 1993 On the origin of Tok Pisin *na*. *Language and Linguistics in Melanesia*, 24(2):95-97.

Masuda, Hirokuni 1995 TSR formation as a discourse substratum in Hawaii Creole English. *Journal of Pidgin and Creole Languages*, 10:253-88.

Matthews, Stephen & Yip, Virginia 1994 *Cantonese: a comprehensive grammar*. London: Routledge.

McDonald, B (ed.) 1976 Language and National Development: The public debate 1976. *Department of Language Occasional paper no. 11*. Waigani: University of Papua New Guinea.

McElhanon, K A 1978 On the origin of body image idioms in Tok Pisin. *Kivung*, 11(1):3-25.

—— (ed.) 1975 *Tok Pisin i go we?* Port Moresby: Linguistic Society of PNG (*Kivung* special publication 1).

Meisel, Jürgen M (ed.) 1977 *Langues en contact - Pidgins - Creoles - Languages in contact*. Tübingen: Gunter Narr.

Mihalic, Frank 1957 *Grammar and Dictionary of Neo-Melanesian*. Westmead, NSW: Mission Press.

—— 1971 *The Jacaranda dictionary and grammar of Melanesian Pidgin*. Milton, Queensland: Jacaranda.

—— 1977 Interpretation problems from the point of view of a newspaper editor. Wurm (ed.) 1117-26).

—— 1982 *Stail Buk bilong Wantok Niuspepa*. Port Moresby: Word Publishing.

—— 1986 *Konstitusen bilong Independen Kantri Papua Niugini*. Boroko: Word Publishing.

—— 1990 Obsolescence in the Tok Pisin vocabulary. Verhaar (ed.), 263-73.

Milroy, Lesley 1980 *Language and social networks*. Oxford: Blackwell.

―― 1987 *Observing and analysing natural language: A critical account of sociolinguistic method.* Oxford: Blackwell.
Milroy, L & Muysken, P (eds) 1995 *One speaker, two languages: cross-disciplinary perspectives on code-switching*. Cambridge: Cambridge University Press.
Moody, James 1992 Towards a language policy for education in Papua New Guinea. Paper presented to 13th Extraordinary Meeting of Faculty of Education. Port Moresby: UPNG.
Mosel, Ulrike 1979 Early language contact between Tolai, Pidgin and English in the light of its sociolinguistic background (1875-1914). *Papers in Pidgin and Creole Linguistics*, 2:163-81. Canberra: Australian National University.
―― 1980 *Tolai and Tok Pisin: the influence of the substratum on the development of New Guinea Pidgin*. Canberra: Australian National University (*Pacific Linguistics* B-73).
Mufwene, Salikoko, S 1986 The universalist and substrate hypotheses complement one another. Muysken & Smith (eds), 129-62.
―― 1988 English pidgins: Form and function. *World Englishes*, 7(3):255-67.
―― 1990a Creoles and universal grammar. Seuren & Mufwene (eds), 783-807.
―― 1990b Time reference in Kikongo-Kituba. Singler (ed.), 97-117.
―― 1990c Transfer and the substrate hypothesis in creolistics. *Studies in Second Language Acquisition*, 12:1-23.
―― 1997 Introduction: Understanding speech continua. *World Englishes*, 16(2):181-84.
Mühlhäusler, Peter 1975 Sociolects in New Guinea Pidgin. McElhanon (ed.), 59-75.
―― 1976 Samoan Plantation Pidgin English and the origins of New Guinea Pidgin: An introduction. *Journal of Pacific History*, 11(2):122-25.
―― 1977a Creolisation of New Guinea Pidgin. Wurm (ed.), 567-76.
―― 1977b On regional dialects in New Guinea Pidgin. Wurm (ed.), 522-37.
―― 1978a Papuan Pidgin English rediscovered. Wurm & Carrington (eds), 1377-446.
―― 1978b Samoan Plantation Pidgin and the origin of New Guinea Pidgin. *Papers in Pidgin and Creole Linguistics*, 1:7-119. Canberra: Australian National University.
―― 1979 *Growth and Structure of the Lexicon of New Guinea Pidgin*. Canberra: Australian National University (*Pacific Linguistics* C-52).
―― 1980 Structural expansion and the process of creolization. Valdman & Highfield (eds), 19-55.
―― 1981 The development of the category of number in Tok Pisin. Muysken (ed.), 35-84.
―― 1985a Etymologising and Tok Pisin. Wurm & Mühlhäusler (eds), 177-219.
―― 1985b Good and bad pidgin: nogut yu toktok kranki. Wurm & Mühlhäusler (eds), 275-91.
―― 1985c History of the study of Tok Pisin. Wurm & Mühlhäusler (eds), 15-33.
―― 1985d Inflectional morphology of Tok Pisin. Wurm & Mühlhäusler (eds), 335-40.
―― 1985e Internal development of Tok Pisin. Wurm & Mühlhäusler (eds), 75-166.
―― 1985f Language planning and the Tok Pisin lexicon. Wurm & Mühlhäusler (eds), 595-664.
―― 1985g Synonymy and communication across lectal boundaries in Tok Pisin. Hancock (ed.), 134-68.
―― 1985h Syntax of Tok Pisin. Wurm & Mühlhäusler (eds), 341-421.
―― 1985i The external history of Tok Pisin. Wurm & Mühlhäusler (eds), 35-64.
―― 1985j The lexical system of Tok Pisin. Wurm & Mühlhäusler (eds), 423-40.
―― 1985k The number of Pidgin Englishes in the Pacific. *Papers in Pidgin and Creole Linguistics*, 4:25-51. Canberra: Australian National University.
―― 1985l The scientific study of Tok Pisin: Language planning and the Tok Pisin lexicon. Wurm & Mühlhäusler (eds), 595-664.
―― 1985m Tok Pisin and its relevance to theoretical issues in creolistics and general linguistics. Wurm & Mühlhäusler (eds), 443-83.
―― 1985n Variation in Tok Pisin. Wurm & Mühlhäusler (eds), 233-73.
―― 1986a Bonnet blanc and blanc bonnet: Adjective-noun order, substratum and language universals. Muysken & Smith (eds), 41-55.
―― 1986b *Pidgin and Creole Linguistics*. Oxford: Blackwell.
―― 1987 Tracing the predicate marker in the Pacific. *English Worldwide*, 8:97-121.

―― 1990a On the origins of the predicate marker in Tok Pisin. Verhaar (ed.), 235-49.

―― 1990b Review of Roger M Keesing, *Melanesian Pidgin and the Oceanic Substrate*. *Pacific Studies*, 14(1):147-51.

―― 1990c Tok Pisin: Model or special case. Verhaar (ed.), 171-85.

―― 1991a Queensland Kanaka English. Romaine (ed.), 174-79.

―― 1991b Watching girls pass by in Tok Pisin. Cheshire (ed.), 637-46.

―― 1996 *Linguistic ecology: language change and linguistic imperialism in the Pacific region*. London: Routledge.

Müller-Gotama, Franz 1996 Topic and focus in Sundanese. *Anthropological Linguistics*, 38:117-32.

Mundhenk, Norm 1990 Linguistic decisions in the 1987 Tok Pisin bible. Verhaar (ed.), 345-73.

Murphy, J J [1943] 1966 *The Book of Pidgin English*. Brisbane: Smith & Paterson.

Muysken, Pieter (ed.) 1981 *Generative Studies on Creole Languages*. Dordrecht: Foris.

―― 1995 Code-switching and grammatical theory. Milroy & Muysken (eds), 177-98.

Muysken, Pieter & Smith, Norval (eds) 1986 *Substrata Versus Universals in Creole Genesis: Papers from the Amsterdam creole workshop, April 1985*. Amsterdam: Benjamins.

Muysken, Pieter & Veenstra, Tonjes 1995 Serial verbs. Arends et al (eds), 289-301.

Myers-Scotton, Carol 1992 Comparing code-switching and borrowing. Eastman (ed.), 19-39.

―― 1993a Common and uncommon ground: Social and structural factors in codeswitching. *Language in Society*, 22:475-503.

―― 1993b *Duelling languages: grammatical structure in codeswitching*. Oxford: Oxford University Press.

―― 1993c *Social motivations for code-switching: Evidence from Africa*. Oxford: Clarendon.

―― 1995 A lexically based model of code-switching. Milroy & Muysken (eds), 233-56.

―― 1997 Code-switching. Coulmas (ed.), 217-37.

Naro, A J 1978 A study on the origins of pidginization. *Language*, 54:314-49.

Nekitel, Otto M 1984 Language planning in Papua New Guinea: A nationalist viewpoint. *Yaglambu*, 11(1):1-24.

―― 1990 The role and use of language in Papua New Guinea's trilingual parliament: A synopsis of success and constraints. University of Papua New Guinea: Department of Language and Literature. Ms.

―― 1994 Review of *Atlantic Meets Pacific: A global view of pidginization and creolization*, Francis Byrne & John Holm. *Language and Linguistics in Melanesia*, 25(2):194-96.

Newmeyer, Frederick J (ed.) 1988 *Linguistics: The Cambridge survey, Volume IV, Language: The sociocultural context*. Cambridge: Cambridge University Press.

O'Barr, W & O'Barr, J (eds). 1976 *Language and Politics*. The Hague: Mouton.

O'Donnell, W R & Todd, Loreto 1980 *Variety in Contemporary English*. London: Allen & Unwin.

Oladejo, James 1992 A critical appraisal of the education sector review and its implications for language education in Papua New Guinea. Paper to seminar on applied educational research, Goroka, Sept 1992.

Olewale, Ebia 1977 General thoughts on teaching in pidgin. Wurm (ed.), 639-42.

Papua New Guinea Department of Education 1991 *Education Sector Review: Deliberations and findings*. Port Moresby.

Pawley, Andrew K 1975 On epenthetic vowels in New Guinea Pidgin. McElhanon (ed.), 215-28.

―― 1993 A language which defies description by ordinary means. Foley (ed.), 87-129.

Pennycook, Alastair 1994a Incommensurable discourses? *Applied Linguistics*, 15(2):115-38.

Piau, Julie Ann 1981 Kuman classificatory verbs. *Language and Linguistics in Melanesia*, 13(1-2):3-31.

Picone, Michael 1997 L2 and pidginization - reply. Internet posting to CreoLIST discussion forum, 16th May 1997.

Platt, John 1990 Indigenized Englishes and post-creole continua: Similarities and differences. Halliday et al (eds), 189-95.

Polinsky, Maria & Smith, Geoff P 1996 Pacific. Comrie, Matthews & Polinsky, (eds), 90-109.

Poplack, Shana 1980 'Sometimes I'll start a sentence in Spanish y termino en Espanol': Toward a typology of code-switching. *Linguistics*, 18:581-618.

―― 1988 Contrasting patterns of codeswitching in two communities. Heller, M (ed.), 215-44.

―― 1993 Variation theory and language contact. Preston, D (ed.), 251-86.

Poplack, Shana & Meechan, Marjory 1995 Patterns of language mixture: nominal structure in Wolof-French and Fongbe-French bilingual discourse. Milroy & Muysken (eds), 199-232.

Preston, Dennis R (ed.) 1993 *American Dialect Research: an anthology celebrating the 100th anniversary of the America Dialect Society*. Amsterdam: Benjamins.

Pütz, Martin (ed.) 1994 *Language contact and language conflict*. Amsterdam: Benjamins.

Reesink, Ger 1990 Mother tongue and Tok Pisin. Verhaar (ed.), 289-306.

Renck, G L 1977a Mission lingue franche: Kâte. Wurm (ed.), 839-46.

―― 1977b Mission lingue franche: Yabêm. Wurm (ed.), 847-53.

Rickford, John 1987 *Dimensions of a Creole continuum: history, texts and linguistic analysis of Guyanese Creole*. Stanford: Stanford University Press.

Roberts, Julian M 1995 Pidgin Hawaiian: A sociohistorical study. *Journal of Pidgin and Creole Languages*, 10:1-56.

Robertson, Ian E 1990 The tense-mood-aspect system of Berbice Dutch. Singler (ed.), 169-84.

Romaine, Suzanne 1985 Relative clauses in child language, pidgins and creoles. *Papers in Pidgin and Creole Linguistics*, 4:1-23. Canberra: Australian National University.

―― 1988a *Pidgin and Creole Languages*. London: Longman.

―― 1988b Some differences between spoken and written Tok Pisin. *English World-wide* 9:243-69.

―― 1989 English and Tok Pisin (New Guinea Pidgin English) in Papua New Guinea. *World Englishes. Special issue on English in the South Pacific*, 8:5-23.

―― 1990 Variability and Anglicization in the distinction between p/f in young children's Tok Pisin. Edmonson, Feagin & Mühlhäusler (eds), 173-85.

―― 1991 The Pacific. Cheshire (ed.), 619-36.

―― (ed.) 1991 *Language in Australia*. Cambridge: Cambridge University Press.

―― 1992a *Language, Education and Development: Urban and rural Tok Pisin in Papua New Guinea*. Oxford: Oxford University Press.

―― 1992b The inclusive/exclusive distinction in Tok Pisin. *Language and Linguistics in Melanesia*, 23(1):1-11.

―― 1993 The decline of predicate marking in Tok Pisin . Byrne & Holm (eds), 251-60.

―― 1995a "Lice he no good". On [r] and [l] in Tok Pisin. Werner, Givón & Thompson (eds), 309-18.

―― 1995b The grammaticalization of irrealis in Tok Pisin. Bybee & Fleischmann, (eds), 389-427.

Romaine, Suzanne & Wright, Fiona 1986 A sociolinguistic study of child language acquisition, creolization and language change in Tok Pisin in Papua New Guinea. Report to Unitech/Max-Planck-Institut fur Psycholinguistik, Nijmegen.

―― & ―― 1987 Short forms in Tok Pisin. *Journal of Pidgin and Creole Languages*, 2:63-67.

Ross, Malcolm 1985 Effects of Tok Pisin on some vernacular languages. Wurm & Mühlhäusler (eds), 539-56.

―― 1991 The sources of Austronesian lexical items in Tok Pisin. Paper to PNG Linguistic Society, June 1991.

―― 1992 Sources of Austronesian lexical items in Tok Pisin. Dutton, Ross & Tryon (eds), 361-84.

Sadler, Wesley 1973 *Untangled New Guinea Pidgin*. Madang: Kristen Press.

Salisbury, R F 1967 Pidgin's respectable past. *New Guinea*, 2(2):44-48.

Sankoff, Gillian 1968 The social aspects of multi-lingualism in New Guinea. PhD thesis, McGill University.

―― 1976 Political power and linguistic inequality in PNG. O'Barr & O'Barr (eds), 283-310.

―― 1977a Creolization and syntactic change in New Guinea Tok Pisin. Blount & Sanches (eds), 131-59.

―― 1977b Multilingualism in PNG. Wurm (ed.), 265-307.

—— 1977c Variability and explanation in language and culture: Cliticization in New Guinea Tok Pisin. Saville-Troike (ed.), 59-73.

—— 1984 Substrate and universals in the Tok Pisin verb phrase. Schiffrin (ed.), 104-19.

—— (ed.) 1986 *The Social Life of Language*. Pittsburgh: University of Pennsylvania Press.

—— 1991 Using the future to explain the past. Byrne & Huebner (eds), 61-74.

—— 1993 Focus in Tok Pisin. Byrne & Winford (eds), 117-40.

—— 1994 An historical and evolutionary approach to variation in the Tok Pisin verb phrase. Beals et al. (eds), 293-320.

Sankoff, Gillian & Brown, Penelope 1976 On the origins of syntax in discourse: a case study of Tok Pisin relatives. *Language*, 52(3):631-666.

—— & —— 1986 On the origins of syntax in discourse: a case study of Tok Pisin relatives. (*Language* article reprinted with minor revisions). Sankoff (ed.), 211-55.

Sankoff, Gillian & Laberge, Suzanne 1973 On the acquisition of native speakers by a language. *Kivung*, 6(1):32-47.

Sankoff, Gillian & Mazzie, Claudia 1991 Determining noun phrases in Tok Pisin. *Journal of Pidgin and Creole Linguistics*, 6:1-24.

Saville-Troike, Muriel (ed.) 1977 *Linguistics and anthropology*. Washington: Georgetown University Press.

Schiffrin, Deborah (ed.) 1984 *Meaning, Form and use in context: linguistic applications*. Washington DC: Georgetown University Press.

Schiller, Eric 1993 Why serial verb constructions? Neither bioprogram nor substrate! Byrne & Holm (eds), 175-82.

Schooling, S & J 1980 A preliminary sociolinguistic and linguistic survey of Manus Province, Papua New Guinea. Summer Institute of Linguistics: Ms.

Scorza, David & K J Franklin 1989 *An Advanced Course in Tok Pisin*. Ukarumpa: Summer Institute of Linguistics.

Scott, Mike & Johns, Tim 1993 *MicroConcord*. Oxford: Oxford University Press.

Sebas, Willie 1993 *Sagothorns: i gat kik (audio cassette)*. Rabaul: Pacific Gold Studios.

Sebba, Mark 1987 *The Syntax of Serial Verbs: An investigation into serialization in Sranan and other languages*. Amsterdam: Benjamins.

Seiler, Walter 1985 The Malay language in New Guinea. *Papers in Pidgin and Creole Linguistics*, 4:143-53. Canberra: Australian National University.

Senft, Gunter 1986 *Kilivila: The language of the Trobriand Islanders*. Berlin: Mouton.

Seuren, Pieter 1991 The definition of serial verbs. Byrne & Huebner (eds), 193-205.

—— 1993 The question of predicate clefting in the Indian Ocean creoles. Byrne & Winford (eds), 53-64.

Seuren, Pieter & Mufwene, Salikoko (eds) 1990 *Issues in Creole Linguistics. Linguistics*, 28(4):641-903.

Shnukal, Anna 1988 *Broken: An introduction to the creole of Torres Strait*. Canberra: Australian National University.

—— 1991 Torres Strait Creole. Romaine (ed.), 180-94.

Siegel, Jeff 1981 Developments in written Tok Pisin. *Anthropological Linguistics*, 23(1):20-35.

—— 1983 Media Tok Pisin. *Papers in Pidgin and Creole Linguistics*, 3:81-92. Canberra: Australian National University.

—— 1984 Introduction to the Labu language. *Papers in New Guinea Linguistics* 23:83-157. Canberra: Australian National University (*Pacific Linguistics* A-69).

—— 1985a Current use and expansion of Tok Pisin: Tok Pisin in the mass media. Wurm & Mühlhäusler (eds), 517-33.

—— 1985b Tok Pisin in formal education in Papua New Guinea. *The Carrier Pidgin*, 18(3):8-9.

—— 1987a *Language Contact in a Plantation environment: A sociolinguistic history of Fiji*. Cambridge: Cambridge University Press.

—— 1987b Spreading the word: Fijian missionaries in the New Guinea Islands. Laycock & Winter (eds), 613-21.

—— 1990 Review of Roger M Keesing, Melanesian Pidgin and the Oceanic Substrate. *Pacific Studies*, 14(1):109-27.

—— 1992a Teaching initial literacy in a pidgin language: A preliminary investigation. Siegel (ed.), 53-65.

—— 1992b The future of Tok Pisin: Another look. Dutton, Ross & Tryon (eds), 405-08.

—— (ed.). 1992 *Pidgins, Creoles and Non-standard Dialects in Education. Occasional Paper no. 12.* Melbourne: Applied Linguistics Association of Australia.

—— 1993 Pidgins and creoles in education in Australia and the southwest Pacific. Byrne & Holm (eds), 299-308.

—— 1996 *Vernacular Education in the South pacific: A report to AusAID*. Armidale: University of New England.

—— 1997a Dialect differences and substrate reinforcement in Melanesian Pidgin. Paper to Second International Conference on Oceanic Linguistics, Univ. Waikato, New Zealand, January 1997.

—— 1997b Mixing, Levelling and pidgin/creole development. Spears & Winford (eds), 111-49.

—— 1997c Pidgin and English in Melanesia: Is there a continuum? *World Englishes,* 16(2):185-204.

—— 1997d Using a pidgin language in formal education: Help or hindrance? *Applied Linguistics*, 18(1):86-100.

—— 1998 Review of Verhaar, J W M, Towards a reference grammar of Tok Pisin: An experiment in corpus linguistics. *Journal of Pidgin and Creole Languages*, 13:172-80.

—— 1999 Transfer constraints and substrate influence in Melanesian Pidgin. *Journal of Pidgin and Creole Languages* 14:1-44.

Sinclair, John 1987 *Collins COBUILD English Language Dictionary*. London and Glasgow: Collins.

Singler, John V 1990a Introduction: Pidgins and creoles and tense-mood-aspect. Singler (ed.), vii-xvi.

—— (ed.) 1990b *Pidgin and Creole Tense-mood-aspect Systems*. Amsterdam: Benjamins.

Slone, Thomas H (translator and ed.) 2001 *One thousand one Papua New Guinean nights. Folktales from* **Wantok** *newspaper.* PNG: Masalai Press, 2 vols.

Smeall, Christopher 1975 A quantitative analysis of variation: *i* in Tok Pisin. Cogen, Cathy et al (eds), 403-09.

Smith, Anne-Marie 1978 The Papua New Guinea Dialect of English. *ERU Research Report* 25. Port Moresby: UPNG.

—— 1984 Inflection in educated Papua New Guinean English verb phrases. Paper to Papua New Guinea Linguistic Society conference, 1984.

—— 1987 The use of aspect in Papua New Guinea English. Paper to AILA conference, Sydney, August 1987.

—— 1988 English in Papua New Guinea. *World Englishes,* 7(3):299-308.

Smith, Geoff P 1986a A preliminary investigation of the spoken Tok Pisin of some urban children in Lae and Goroka. *Language Departmental Report no 10.* Lae: University of Technology.

—— 1986b *Traim Paspas : a stage play in Tok Pisin*. Lae: Department of Language and Communication Studies, Unitech.

—— 1987 *Iko : a stage play in Tok Pisin*. Lae: Department of Language and Communication Studies, Unitech.

—— 1988 Insights into Tok Pisin vocabulary: Three classes of words which can cause avoidable problems. Paper presented to Peace Corps Language Workshop, Goroka, December, 1988.

—— 1989 *A Crash Course in Tok Pisin for Newcomers to Papua New Guinea.* Lae: Department of Language and Communication Studies, Unitech.

—— 1990a Creolized Tok Pisin: Uniformity and variation. Baldauf & Luke (eds), 197-209.

—— 1990b Idiomatic Tok Pisin and referential adequacy. Verhaar (ed.), 275-87.

—— 1991 Cohesion in contemporary Tok Pisin. Paper presented to 6th International Conference on Austronesian Linguistics, Hawaii, May 1991.

—— 1992a Language obsolescence in Morobe Province, Papua New Guinea: Two contrasting case studies. Dutton (ed.), 115-21.

—— 1992b Survival and Susuami: A ten year perspective. *Language and Linguistics in Melanesia*, 23:51-56

—— 1994a Husat i bin othoraizim? New verbs in Manus Tok Pisin. Paper presented to Seventh International Conference of the Society for Pidgin and Creole Linguistics, Georgetown, Guyana, August 1994.

—— 1994b Tok Pisin and Cantonese: Why the similarity? Paper presented to Papua New Guinea Linguistic Society Conference, Lae, July 1994.

—— 1995a Language choice in an acutely multilingual society: Communication and development in Papua New Guinea. Paper to Second International Conference on Oceanic Linguistics, Bali, April 1995.

—— 1995b Word frequency and regional language varieties in Tok Pisin. Paper presented to Second International Conference on Oceanic Linguistics, Suva, Fiji, July 1995.

—— 1997a Focus and topicalization in first language Tok Pisin. Paper to Second International Conference on Oceanic Linguistics, Univ. Waikato, New Zealand, January 1997.

—— 1997b *Yet* in Tok Pisin: Its current roles and competitors. Paper to Australian Linguistic Society conference, University of New England, September 1997.

—— 1998a Concordance studies of the language of adolescent first language Tok Pisin speakers. Tent, Jan & Mugler, France (eds), S*ICOL: Proceedings of the Second International Conference on Oceanic Linguistics*, vol. 1, *Language Contact*, 135-46. Canberra: Australian National University (*Pacific Linguistics* C-141).

—— 1998b English and Melanesian Pidgin in the Admiralty Islands. *Links and Letters*, 5:107-123.

—— 2000 Tok Pisin and English: the current relationship. Siegel, J (ed.), *The processes of language contact. Case studies from Australia and the Pacific.* Montreal: Éditions Fides, 271-91.

Smith, Geoff P & Matthews, S 1996 Pidgins and Creoles. Comrie, Matthews & Polinsky, (eds), 144-61.

Spears, Arthur K 1990 Tense, mood and aspect in the Haitian creole preverbal marker system. Singler (ed.), 119-42.

—— 1993 Foregrounding and backgrounding in Haitian Creole discourse. Byrne & Winford (eds), 249-65.

Spears, Arthur K & Winford, D (eds). *The Structure and Status of Pidgins and Creoles.* Amsterdam: Benjamins.

Steinbauer, Friedric 1969 *Concise dictionary of New Guinea Pidgin (Neo-Melanesian) with translations in English and German.* Madang: Kristen Press.

Stewart, John M 1963 Some restrictions on objects in Twi. *Journal of African Languages*, 2:145-49.

Sumbuk, Kenneth M 1987 Preliminary report on the level of comprehension in Tok Pisin based on the mini survey conducted in the University of Papua New Guinea. Paper to Papua New Guinea Linguistic Society conference, July 1987.

—— 1993 Is Tok Pisin a threat to Sare? Byrne & Holm (eds), 309-17.

Swan, J & Lewis, D J 1990 Tok Pisin at university: An educational and language planning dilemma in Papua New Guinea. Baldauf & Luke (eds), 210-33.

—— & —— 1987 'There's a lot of it about': self-estimates of their use of Tok Pisin by students of the Papua New Guinea University of Technology. Laycock & Winter (eds), 649-63.

Taylor, Andrew 1978 Evidence of a pidgin Motu in the earliest written Motu materials. Wurm & Carrington (eds), 1325-50.

Taylor, Douglas R 1961 New languages for old in the West Indies. *Comparative Studies in Society and History*, 3:277-88.

Thirlwall, C & Hughes P J (eds) *The Ethics of Development: Language, Communica-tion and Power.* Vol. 6 of papers presented to 17th Waigani Seminar. Port Moresby: University of Papua New Guinea.

Thomas, Dicks 1990a A course in practical Tok Pisin. Verhaar (ed.), 399-409.

—— 1990b *Diksinare bilong* Tok Pisin. Paper to international conference on Tok Pisin, Madang, July 1987.

—— 1996 Sotpela grama bilong Tokpisin. MA thesis, University of Papua New Guinea.

Thomason, Sarah G 1983 Chinook jargon in areal and historical context. *Language*, 59:820-71.

Thomason, Sarah G & Kaufman, Terrence 1988 *Language Contact, Creolization and Genetic Linguistics.* Berkeley: University of California Press.

Todd, Loreto 1978 *Pidgins and Creoles.* London: Routledge & Kegan Paul.

—— 1982 The English Language in West Africa. Bailey & Görlach (eds), 281-305.

—— 1984 *Modern Englishes: Pidgins and creoles.* Oxford: Blackwell.

—— 1985 Lexical patterning in Cameroon pidgin and Tok Pisin. Hancock (ed.), 116-33.

—— 1990 *Pidgins and Creoles.* London: Routledge & Kegan Paul, 2nd edition.

Todd, Loreto & Mühlhäusler, Peter 1978 Idiomatic expressions in Cameroon Pidgin and Tok Pisin. *Papers in Pidgin and Creole Linguistics,* 1:1-35. Canberra: Australian National University.

Troy, Jakelin 1990 *Australian Aboriginal Contact with the English Language in New South Wales, 1788 to 1845.* Canberra: Australian National University (*Pacific Linguistics* B-103).

—— 1994 Melaleuka: A history and description of New South Wales Pidgin. PhD thesis, Australian National University.

Tryon, Darrell 1987 *Bislama: An introduction to the national language of Vanuatu.* Canberra: Australian National University (*Pacific Linguistics* D-72).

—— 1991 Wanem Bislama? Blust (ed.), 509-19.

Turner, L D 1974 *Africanisms in the Gullah dialect.* Chicago: Chicago University Press

Valdman, Albert (ed.) 1977 *Pidgin and Creole Linguistics.* Bloomington: Indiana University Press.

—— 1991 Decreolization or dialect contact in Haiti? Byrne & Huebner (eds), 75-88.

Valdman, A & Highfield, A (eds). 1980 *Theoretical Orientations in Creole Studies.* New York: Academic Press.

Verhaar, John W M (ed.) 1990 *Melanesian Pidgin and Tok Pisin. Studies in Language Companion Series vol. 20.* Amsterdam: Benjamins.

—— 1991a Questions and answers in Tok Pisin. Blust (ed.), 521-34.

—— 1991b 'Serial' *na* in Tok Pisin. *Language and Linguistics in Melanesia,* 22:127-141.

—— 1991c The function of *i* in Tok Pisin. *Journal of Pidgin and Creole Languages,* 6:231-66.

—— 1996 *Towards a Reference Grammar of Tok Pisin: An experiment in corpus linguistics. Oceanic Linguistics Special Publications, Vol. 26.* Honolulu: University of Hawaii Press.

Walsh, D S 1978 Tok Pisin Syntax and the Eastern Austronesian factor. *Papers in Pidgin and Creole Linguistics* 1:185-197. Canberra: Australian National University.

Washabaugh, Bill 1975 On the development of complementizers in creolization. *Working Papers on Language Universals,* 17:109-40.

Werner, A, Givón, T & Thompson, S A (eds) 1995 *Discourse Grammar and Typology: Papers in honor of John W.M. Verhaar.* Amsterdam: Benjamins.

Whinnom, Keith 1977a Lingua Franca: Historical problems. Valdman (ed.), 295-310.

—— 1977b The context and origins of Lingua Franca. Meisel (ed.), 3-18.

Williams, Jeffrey P 1993 Documenting the Papuan-based pidgins of insular New Guinea. Byrne & Holm (eds), 355-67.

Winford, Donald 1993 *Predication in Caribbean creoles.* Amsterdam: Benjamins.

—— 1996 Common ground and TMA. *Journal of Pidgin and Creole Languages,* 11:71-84.

—— 1997 Re-examining Caribbean English creole continua. *World Englishes,* 16(2):233-79.

Wolfers, Edward 1971 A Report on Neo-Melanesian. Hymes (ed.), 413-19.

Woolford, Ellen 1979a *Aspects of Tok Pisin Grammar.* Canberra: Australian National University (*Pacific Linguistics* B-66). (Revised version of 1977 PhD thesis, Duke University, North Carolina.)

—— 1979b Variation and change in the *i* 'predicate marker' of New Guinea Tok Pisin. *Papers in Pidgin and Creole Linguistics,* 2:37-49. Canberra: Australian National University.

—— 1981 The developing complementizer system in Tok Pisin. Muysken (ed.), 125-39.

Woolford, Ellen & Washabaugh, William (eds) 1983 *The Social Context of Creolization.* Ann Arbor: Karoma.

Wurm, Stephen A 1971 *New Guinea Highlands Pidgin: Course materials.* Canberra: Australian National University (*Pacific Linguistics* D-3).

—— 1973 The Kiwaian language family. Franklin (ed.), 219-60.

—— (ed.) 1977 *New Guinea Area Languages and Language Study*, Vol. 3: *Language, culture, society, and the modern world*. Canberra: Australian National University (*Pacific Linguistics* C-40).

—— 1979 *New Guinea and Neighbouring Areas: A sociolinguistic laboratory*. The Hague: Mouton.

—— 1982 *Papuan Language of Oceania*. Tübingen: Gunter Narr.

—— 1985a Phonology: Intonation in Tok Pisin. Wurm & Mühlhäusler (eds), 309-34.

—— 1985b The status of Tok Pisin and attitudes towards it. Wurm & Mühlhäusler (eds), 65-74.

—— 1986 Promotion of national languages and development of a lingua franca in the Pacific Islands: Problems and perspectives. Wurm (ed.), 55-81.

Wurm, Stephen A (ed.) 1986 *Language: Identity and communication*. Paris: UNESCO.

Wurm, Stephen A & Carrington, Lois (eds) 1978 *Second International Conference on Austronesian Linguistics: Proceedings*. Canberra: Australian National University (*Pacific Linguistics* C-61).

Wurm, S A, Laycock, D & Mühlhäusler, P 1984 Notes on attitudes to pronunciation in the New Guinea area. *International Journal of the Sociology of Language*, 50:123-46.

Wurm, S A & Mühlhäusler, P (eds). 1985 *Handbook of Tok Pisin (New Guinea Pidgin)*. Canberra: Australian National University (*Pacific Linguistics*, C-70).

Yarupawa, Shem 1986 Milne Bay informal variety of English. *Department of Language and Communication Studies Research Report no 9*. Lae: University of Technology.

—— 1996 Domain dependent code choices: Musom language. *Language and Linguistics in Melanesia*, 27(1):83-100.

Mount Hagen show

Watching the Mendi show for free (II)

A Lae-based drama group performing a dance from Kiwai (Western Province)

Two members of the above drama group

Index
and abbreviations

A

Aboriginals 14, 16
acquisition 19-20, 200, 213
acronyms 113
Adzera 44
Africa(n) 4, 204
African languages 4, 19, 24
Ahai, Naihuwo 6, 21, 28, 223
Aitape 30-31, 217
Aitchison, Jean 5, 7, 27, 151, 154, 201, 210, 223
Alleyne, Mervyn 209, 223
America(n) 3, 6
Amerindian 4
anaphoric reference 178
Andersen, Roger 20, 173, 200, 223
Aramot viii, x
Arawa 30, 33
Arends, Jacques 3, 223
Atlantic Creoles 3, 24, 27, 142
Australia(n) 7-8, 12, 14-19, 200
Australian National University 5
Australian Pidgin English 25, 96
Austronesian 8-11, 15, 18, 25, 115, 118, 147, 161-162, 171, 200

B

"baby talk" 24
Bahasa Indonesia 12
bai 20, 59, 125-128, 140-141
Bailey, Charles-James 150, 223
Baker, Philip ii, vii, 4, 13-14, 25-26, 60, 62, 96, 125, 199-201, 223
Bakker, Peter 4, 205, 223
Bálint, András 6, 223
Baluan 114
Barron, Colin 6, 202, 210, 223
Basque 4
Beaugrande, Robert 173, 183, 186, 213
Bee, Darlene 6, 25, 43, 223
bek 139-140, 201
Belize 27, 209
Bell, H L 5, 223
Bellwood, P 8, 223
Bergmann, Ulrich 6, 212, 223
Bible Society 5-6, 116, 223
Bickerton, Derek 4, 6, 20, 23-27, 124-125, 129, 142, 147, 162-163, 200, 209-210, 223-224
bifo tru 191
bikos 188
bilingualism 27, 75, 87, 202
bilong 59, 82-83, 177
bilong wanem 164-165
bin 102, 129-130, 140-141
bioprogram 20, 26, 124, 211

Bislama 6, 14-16, 19, 21, 27, 109, 116, 119, 134, 142, 145-147, 153, 159, 181, 210
Bismarck Archipelago 9, 12, 16-18
Black English 24
Bligh, William 13
Bolgy, Rose vii
borrowing 95-100, 111-112, 202-09
Bougainville (island) 12, 31, 40, 43, 132, 201, 212
Bougainville, Louis 14
Bourke, Michael 25, 200, 226
BRA = Bougainville Revolutionary Army
Bradshaw, Joel 142, 224
Brash, Elton 6, 21, 224
British New Guinea 12
broadcasting 212
Broken, see Torres Strait Broken
Brown, Gillian 6, 150, 155, 173, 224
Brown, Penelope 173, 201, 232
Buang xi, 20, 166
Buka 30-31
Buka Passage 33
Buriat 136
Burrage, Ken ii, vii
Burton, Frank 36, 224
bus(h) 46
Buschenhofen, Paul 214, 224
Bush Pidgin 21, 36, 43
Bybee, Joan 126, 135-136, 224
Byrne, Francis 4, 142, 162, 224

C

cafeteria principle 24
calques 111-112, 169, 207, 213
Camden, William 15, 224
Cantonese 59, 62, 161
Capell, A 8, 224
Caribbean 3, 209
Caribbean Creoles 162, 210
Carrier Pidgin 3
Cassidy, Frederic 3, 224
Catholic 31-32
Central Pacific 65, 76, 200
Central (Province) 10, 28, 244
Chandler, Brian 100, 224
Charpentier, Jean-Michel 15, 224
Cheshire, Jenny 36, 224
Chinese 19, 59, 62, 161
Chinook Jargon 3
Chomsky, Noam 25-26, 224
Chowning, Ann 5, 25, 224
Clark, Ross 4, 13, 17, 225
clefting 162-163, 166
cliticization 84-87
code-switching 6, 27, 44, 47, 89, 94-95, 202-09
coherence 190-197
colonial history 12,

complementation 158-161
compounding 105-106
Comrie, Bernard 25, 124, 225
conjunction 185-190
connectors 96
Conrad, Bob 5, 225
contact situations 10
continuum 20, 27-28, 202, 209-11
convergence 210
Cook, James 13
Cooper, Br. Bernard vii
copra 14
corpus 39-41
Corne, Chris 4, 223
cotton 14
CreoLIST 3
Creole(s) 3-4, 6, 17, 19, 24-26, 28, 115, 124-125, 129, 136, 142, 162-163, 173, 200-01, 209, 211
creolization 6, 19-20, 22, 66, 211
Crowley, Terry vii, 4, 6, 13-15, 17, 21-22, 25, 62, 65, 109, 119, 134, 142, 145-146, 153, 159, 200, 225

D

Daru ii
Daru Kiwai 11
data collection and analysis 35-38
DeCamp, David 27, 209, 225
"decreolization" 209
DeGraff, Michel 3, 225
deixis 179-180
demonstrative pronouns 177-178
D'Entrecasteaux 14
Dillard, J 24, 225
discourse 173-197, 201
dispela 149-150
Dobu 11
Duke of York Islands 18, 93
Dressler, W U 174, 183, 186, 213
Dutch 12-13, 24
Dutch New Guinea 12
Dutton, Tom 4-5, 8, 11, 13, 16, 21-22, 25, 60, 82, 116, 125, 128-129, 137, 154, 156, 162, 164, 166, 179, 189, 200, 214, 225

E

East Africa 94
Eastern Highlands 10, 28, 32, 34, 40, 45-46, 50, 52-54, 57, 60-62, 69-70, 77-78, 81, 86, 89-90, 92, 98, 104-105, 107, 115, 119-120, 122-123, 129-131, 135, 137-138, 144, 148, 150, 152-154, 157, 160, 163-165, 168-169, 171, 176, 179-181, 183-184, 191, 195-196, 203, 207, 218
East New Britain 10, 28, 31, 33-34, 38, 40, 57, 61, 66-69, 75, 79, 81, 89-91, 93, 97, 105-106, 108, 119, 122-123, 129, 131-137, 139-143,

239

145, 147, 150, 152-153, 155, 157-160, 164-172, 174, 176-181, 183, 185-186, 188, 190-191, 193-195, 203-204, 207-208
East Sepik xi, 10, 22, 28, 31, 34, 40, 51, 54, 57, 60-61, 67, 69-70, 75, 78, 80, 91, 95, 106, 119, 122-123, 127, 130, 135-137, 139, 141, 143-149, 153, 160, 163, 166, 168-170, 177-178, 181, 185, 187, 191, 194-196, 206, 214, 217
-ed (suffix) 89-90
education 21, 27, 202, 211-212, 214
Eleman 11
ellipsis 182-183
em 82-83, 156, 166-167
emphasis 115, 161-172
en 82-83, 102, 156
Enga 8, 10, 28, 32-34, 40, 50-52, 57, 60-61, 63-65, 79, 86, 89, 91, 97-98, 100, 119-120, 123, 128, 132, 147, 149, 153, 155-156, 160, 165, 168, 187, 190, 203, 206, 213
English 1, 4, 6, 12-14, 16-21, 23-24, 27, 31, 35-36, 38-39, 44-45, 48, 54, 56, 64-66, 71-72, 74-76, 81, 87-100, 103-107, 115, 121, 125, 131, 133, 137-139, 144, 146, 150-151, 154, 159, 161-163, 167-169, 179, 181, 183, 199, 202-211, 214
Erub 16
Escure, Geneviève 27, 142, 173, 209, 226
European 7, 11, 13-14, 16-17, 24, 180
expansion 19

F

Fairclough, Norman 173, 226
Faraclas, Nicholas 6, 53, 162, 200, 214, 226
Fenton, Jack vii
Fiji(an) 7-8, 14, 17, 19
First World War 18
fis(h) 46-47
Fleischmann, Suzanne 135-136, 224
focus 161-172
Foley, William 8-11, 77-78, 226
Ford, Kevin vii
foreigner talk 13, 24
France 12
Franklin, Karl 5, 116, 200, 212, 214, 226, 232
French 3, 7, 13, 24, 150, 159

G

Gapun 6, 22
Gardner-Chloros, Penelope 205, 226
Gazelle Peninsula 5, 18
gender (of informants) 214
genesis 24-25, 27
German 5, 15-18, 71, 93, 113
Germany 12, 18
Givón, T 142, 144, 226
go 134-135, 143
Gogodala 11
Goodman, Morris 26, 226

Goroka vii, 28, 30-32, 45, 189, 194, 218
Goulden, Rick 4, 18-19, 25, 226
grammaticalization 147-148, 173, 201
Greenberg, Joseph 62, 115, 226
Grimes, Barbara 8, 21, 226
Gulf (Province) 10, 28
Guyana 27, 209

H

Hall, Robert 4, 24, 27, 71, 162, 185, 209, 226
Halliday, M A K 161, 173-174, 181-182, 185, 227
Hamau, John vii
Hancock, Ian 4, 227
hap 183
Harding, T 11, 227
Harris, John 16, 227
Hasan, R 173-174, 181-182, 185, 227
Hawaiian Creole English 4, 26
Hawaiian Pidgin English 6, 26
Healey, L R 6, 94, 227
Henganofi 30, 32, 40, 60
Highlands region 5, 19, 25, 28, 31-33, 34, 40, 43, 47, 50-52, 56-57, 61-63, 74, 78, 85, 87, 96, 101-103, 116-117, 119-121, 123, 127, 130-134, 151, 154, 156-160, 182, 186, 188, 195, 200-01, 205, 217
Hiri Motu 11, 16, 19, 21, 28, 100
Holm, John 3, 5, 19, 224, 227
Holzknecht, Suzanne vii, 77
homonyms 52-53
Hooley, Bruce 5, 227
Huon 11, 14
Huon Peninsula 12
husat 150-153
Hymes, Dell 3, 6, 227

I

i ("predicate marker") 115-124
ia 154-156, 178
Iha, Patricia vii
-im (transitive marker) 59-62, 94, 106
inap 121, 137
Indagen 44
Indian Ocean 4
Indian Ocean Creoles 162
idiomatic language 108-114
Indonesia(n) 7, 12, 16
Independent Television Network 8, 227
informants 29-34
-ing 87-89
interference 27
interlanguage 21
Irian Jaya 7-8, 12
Islands region 28, 33-34, 40, 47, 56-57, 61, 63, 74, 78, 82, 85, 87, 101-103, 117-119, 123, 127, 130-131, 133-134, 141, 151, 154, 156-157, 159-160, 182, 186, 188, 194-196, 200, 205, 207, 213, 220, 222

ITN = Independent Television Network

J

Jamaica 27, 209
Johns, Tim 100, 232
Jourdan, Christine 6, 20, 27, 29, 31, 125, 209, 227
Journal of Pidgin and Creole Studies 3

K

Kaack, Jill vii, 37
Kabiufa 32
Kainantu 30, 32
Kairiru 31
Kakare, Iru 11, 226
Kalam 144
Kale, Joan 6, 27, 210, 227
kam 134-135, 143
kamap 143
Kâte 11-12
Kaufman, Terrence 3, 11, 26, 44, 75, 199, 202
Kavieng 30, 33, 37, 220
Keesing, Roger 4, 13-15, 17, 25, 59, 62, 65, 76, 115, 162, 176, 200, 227
Kehatsin, Justin vii
ken 137, 140
Kepiou, Christopher 5, 19, 227
Keravat 30, 33
Kewa 200
Kila, Ana vii
Kilivila 162
Kim, Jeehoon ii, vii
Kimbe 30-31, 33
kinship terms 96
kirap 86, 102, 138-139, 143, 201
Kiwai 11, 16, 238
Knowles, G 23, 227
Koeford, Geert 24, 227
Kokopo 34
Kondiu 30, 32
Kokopo 33-34
Kriol (of Australia's Northern Territory) 15-16
Kristen Press 174
Kuanua 11
Kulick, Don 6, 22, 27, 212, 227
Kundiawa 30-31

L

Label 106
Laberge, Suzanne 20, 54, 125, 211, 232
labour trade 16-18
Labov, William 6, 35-36, 227
Lae xi, 5, 28, 30-31, 109, 113, 120, 151, 154, 187, 189-190, 216, 238, 244
laik 59, 85-86, 128-129, 140
lain 184
Landtmann, Gunnar 16, 227
Language Bioprogram Hypothesis 4
language planning 21
La Perouse 14

Latin 100
Laycock, Donald 5, 8, 18, 20-21, 25, 43-44, 48, 56, 93, 201, 227-228, 236
Lee, Ernie 16, 228
Lefebvre, Claire 142, 162, 228
Le Page, R B 209, 228
lexical cohesion 183-185
lexicon 18, 93-104, 199, 204-05
Lewis, D J 6, 21, 214, 234
Lichtenberk, Frantisek 136, 162, 228
"life cycle" 23, 27, 209
Lihir Island 220
Lingua Franca 12
lingua franca 10-12, 16-17, 19, 28, 211-212
Litteral, Robert 5, 43, 228
Lomax, R W 6, 155, 173-174, 178-179, 181-185, 189-190, 228
long 59, 82-83, 156-158, 201
long wanem 164, 172
Lorengau 30, 33, 36, 210
Lou 114
Lumsden, John 162, 228
Lynch, John vii, 6, 21, 54, 59, 71, 74, 76-77, 84-85, 116, 127, 129, 131, 200, 211, 214, 225, 228

M

Ma'a 205
Macassa(n) 16
Madagascar 8
Madang ii, 5, 10, 20, 25, 28, 30-31, 34-35, 40, 43, 57, 61, 63, 66, 69, 71, 79, 81, 83, 85, 90, 106, 108, 116, 118-119, 123, 125, 128, 130, 144, 146, 148-150, 152, 160, 163, 166, 168-169, 171, 175, 185, 190, 194, 213
Maisin 8
Malabang 20, 66, 68
Malabunga 33
Malay 12, 19
Manam 162
Mangap-Mbula 200
Manus 10, 20, 27-28, 31, 33-34, 40, 44, 46-47, 50-51, 54-56, 59-61, 63-64, 66, 70, 72, 74-75, 77, 80, 84-86, 88-89, 91-92, 94, 98, 100, 104, 119 107-108, 114, 118, 123, 126-127, 129, 131, 133, 137-139, 143, 146, 148-149, 152-154, 157-160, 164-166-168, 170, 175, 177-178, 180-181-184, 186-188, 192-193, 195-196, 202, 204, 206-08, 210-11, 216
Maroldt, K 150, 223
mas 136-137, 140
Masuda, Hirokuni 173, 228
Matthews, Stephen vii, 6, 59, 225, 228, 234
Mauritius 4
Mazzie, Claudia 147-148, 232
McDonald, B 6, 21, 214, 228
McElhanon, K 5, 21, 228
Media Lingua 205
Mediterranean 13
Meechan, Marjory 94, 205, 231

Melanesia(n) 7-8, 10, 13-14, 16-18, 25, 27, 63, 93
Melanesian Pidgin English 3-4, 6, 13-18, 59, 76, 96, 115, 125, 130, 162, 176, 200, 210
Melpa 100
Mendaña 13
Mendi xi, 30, 32, 36, 113, 208
Michif 205
Middle English 150
Mihalic, Francis vii, 4-6, 18, 41, 43-44, 48-49, 60, 62, 82, 93, 95-96, 100, 104, 106, 116, 125, 129, 131, 144, 150, 154, 159, 162, 174, 187, 189, 192, 228
Milne Bay Province 10, 28, 213
Milroy, Lesley 35-36, 94, 228-229
Mioko 18
mipela 176
mission(arie)s 4, 10-12, 18
mixed languages 205
moa 171
modals 135-137
Momase 28, 31-32, 34, 40, 47, 56-57, 61-62-63, 74, 78, 82, 85, 87, 96, 101-103, 117-119, 123, 127, 130-131, 133-134, 151, 154, 156-160, 182, 186, 188, 195, 205
monogenesis 13
Moody, Jim vii
Morobe ii, viii, x-xi, 5, 10, 12, 20-21, 28, 31-32, 34-35, 40, 43, 47, 51, 57, 61, 64, 67, 71, 75, 80-81, 83, 85-86, 97, 102, 105, 107, 116, 119-120, 123, 125, 128-129, 131, 133-137, 139, 141, 146, 148-149, 155, 160, 170, 174, 176, 181, 184-185, 187, 190, 193, 195, 202, 208, 213, 216
morphology 59-92
Mortlock Islands 220
Mosel, Ulrike 4, 18, 25, 63, 70, 229
Motu 11
Mount Hagen 30, 32, 237
Mous, Maarten 205, 223
MPE = Melanesian Pidgin English
Mufwene, Salikoko 4, 26, 200-01, 209, 229, 232
Mühlhäusler, Peter vii, 3-7, 12-13, 15-25, 36-37, 43, 56, 59-60, 62-68, 70-71, 75, 78, 80-83, 87, 103, 105-108, 113, 115-116, 121, 129-130, 147, 150-151, 158, 162, 169, 171, 173-174, 178-179, 184-185, 195-196, 199, 201-202, 211, 226, 229-230, 236
Müller-Gotama, Franz 162, 230
multifunctionality 105
multilingualism 10, 17, 25
Mundhenk, Norm 116, 129, 157, 230
Murphy, J 5, 230
Murray, Sir Hubert 199
Muysken, Pieter 3-4, 23, 94, 223, 229-230
Myers-Scotton, Carol 27, 94, 204-205, 230

N

na 186, 195, 200
nabaut 102, 201

narapela 185
Naro, Anthony 24, 230
Nataleo, Maran vii
National (newspaper) 113
National Broadcasting Corporation 155, 175
National Capital District 10, 28, 213
nativization 1, 22
nau 186, 194-195, 197
nautical jargon 14
Near East 13
NBC = National Broadcasting Corporation
Nekitel, Otto 6, 117, 204, 230
Nembi Plateau 25
Netherlands 12
New Britain 4-5, 11-12, 17-18, 43
New Caledonia 7-9, 12
New Guinea(n) 9-12, 15-20, 115, 142
New Hanover 95, 104
New Hebrides, see Vanuatu
New Ireland ii, 10, 12, 18, 28, 31, 33-34, 40, 43-44, 57, 61, 68-70, 72, 75, 79, 83, 89-91, 100, 108, 117-119, 122-124, 133, 138-141, 144, 146, 150, 156, 159-160, 164-169, 171, 175, 177-178, 180, 187-188, 190-191, 195, 207, 210-211, 217
New South Wales 14, 16-17
New South Wales Pidgin English 59, 62
New World 4
nogat 188-190, 201
Northern (Province) 10
Northern Territory (Australia) 16
North Solomons 9-10, 28, 31, 33-34, 40, 47, 57-58, 61, 90, 92, 106, 119, 123, 129-130, 134, 140, 148, 159-160, 179, 213, 220
Northwest Pacific 4
Norway 3
noun phrase 147-150
NSW(PE) = New South Wales (Pidgin English)
Nupela Testamen 36, 116, 157, 174, 212

O

Oceanic 15, 25, 77
O'Donnell, W R 27, 210, 230
okei 193-194
ol (plural marker) 65-71, 175-176
Oladejo, James 214, 230
Old English 150
Olewale, Ebia 6, 230
olsem 158-159, 182, 188, 195-196
olsem wanem 164
onomatopoeia 113
orait 192-194
Oro Province xi, 10, 28, 212 (also called Northern Province)

P

Pacific 3-4, 7-8, 12-18, 24-25, 65, 142
Pacific Gold Studios 113

Pacific Pidgin English 12, 14, 25, 76, 125
Pahoturi River ix
Pak 114
Papitalai 33
Papua(n) viii-ix, 8, 11-12, 16, 19, 21, 25, 28, 77, 115, 200-201, 213
Papua New Guinea Department of Education 214, 230
Papua New Guinea University of Technology vii, 28, 35
Papuan Pidgin English 15-16
pasin 183
Pawley, Andrew 48, 230
PE = Pidgin English
-pela 59, 62-65
Pennycook, Alastair 173, 230
phonology 43-58, 93, 200-01, 203
phrasal verb elements 90
Piau, Julie 200, 225, 230
pichin 47
Picone, Michael 205, 230
Pidgin(s) 3-4, 6, 10-11, 13-14, 17, 19-20, 25-28, 59, 65-66, 94, 124, 142, 183, 200-01, 205, 209
Pidgin Portuguese 13, 24
pinis 130-131, 140, 192-194
pis(h) 46-47
pisin 47
plantations 14-15, 17
Platt, John 210, 230
plural marking 65-76
PNG = Papua New Guinea
Pokris, James vii
Police Motu 11
Polinsky, Maria 7, 22, 225, 230
Polopa 200
Polynesia(n) 8, 16, 95, 104
Pombrut 33
Poplack, Shana 27, 94, 204-205, 231
Popondetta xi
Port Moresby 4, 11, 28, 244
Portuguese 3, 13, 19, 24
possessive pronouns 177
pragmatics 173-174
pronouns 76-87
psycholinguistic(s) 20

Q

Queensland 4, 14-16, 96
Queensland Canefield English 16
Queensland Kanaka English, see Queensland Canefield English

R

Rabaul 5, 18, 30-31, 33, 129
Ramoaaina 18, 93
Ramu 9
redundancy 66
reduplication 68-69, 105
Reesink, Ger 6, 25, 200-201, 231
reference 174-180
relativization 150-158
Renaissance 13
Renck, G 11, 231

reported speech 195-197
"resumptive" pronouns 176
Reunion 4
Rickford, John 209, 231
Ritter, Elizabeth 162, 228
Roberts, Julian 26, 231
Robertson, Ian 3, 231
Romaine, Suzanne vii, 3, 5, 13, 20, 22, 27, 35, 37, 39, 43-44, 51, 54, 59, 70-72, 74, 81-83, 94, 96, 102, 115-117, 120, 125-126, 150-151, 162, 174, 185, 193, 202, 205, 207, 210, 212-214, 231
Ross, Malcolm vii, 4, 18, 93, 95, 162, 200, 226, 231
Rotokas 9
Russenorsk 3
Russia 3

S

-s (pluralizer) 59, 71-76
Sadler, Wesley 5, 231
Salisbury, R F 5, 18, 231
Samoa(n) 14-17
Samoan Plantation Pidgin 16
sampela 147-148
Sanches, M 224
samting 184
sandalwood 14
Sankoff, Gillian 6, 10, 19-20, 27, 37, 54, 104, 116, 120, 125-127, 129, 140-141, 147-148, 150, 155, 162-163-168, 170-173, 201, 210-211, 231-232
Sare 22
save 59, 85-86, 132, 140
Schiller, Eric 142, 232
Schooling, S & J 210, 232
Scorza, David 5, 232
Scott, Mike 100, 232
se 159-160
Sebas, Willie 113, 232
Sebba, Mark 142, 232
second language acquisition 200
Second World War 16, 18
Seiler, Walter 12, 232
seim 182
semantic changes 103, 207
Senft, Gunter 162, 232
Sepik 5, 9, 11, 22, 25, 28, 62, 113, 214 (see also East Sepik and West Sepik)
serialization 134-136, 142-147
Seuren, Pieter 142, 232
shift 26-27
Shnukal, Anna 6, 16, 162, 232
Siassi viii, x, 11, 222
Siegel, Jeff vii, 4, 5-6, 13-15, 21, 25, 27, 142, 145, 150-151, 155, 178, 200, 210, 212, 214, 225, 232-233
Simbu 10, 28, 32, 34, 38, 40, 50-51, 55-57, 60-61, 63, 65, 67, 69-70, 75, 79, 81, 83-84, 95, 97, 100, 107-108, 119-120, 122-123, 126, 128, 132-134, 137, 139, 143-144, 146, 149, 156, 158, 160, 163-168, 176, 180, 182, 184-185, 187, 193, 196-197, 203, 206-207

Sinasina 55
Sinclair, John 39, 233
Singler, John 4, 124, 233
Slone, Thomas 6, 191, 233
Smeall, Christopher 6, 116, 233
Smith, Anne-Marie 6, 202, 210, 233
Smith, Geoff ii, 6-7, 20-22, 27-28, 41, 98, 100, 103, 109-112, 116-117, 138, 144, 194, 202, 210-212, 230, 233-234
Smith, Norval 3, 223, 230
so 188
Solomon Island(er)s 7-9, 12-13, 16, 27, 209
Solomons Pijin 6, 14-16, 20, 27, 29, 116, 125, 153, 162, 209-10
Southeast Asia 8
Southern Highlands xi, 10, 19, 25, 28, 32, 34, 40, 51, 57, 61, 83, 89, 92, 113, 119, 123, 130-131, 137, 146, 152, 157-158, 160, 168--169, 176-178, 187, 189-191, 200, 204
Southern region 28, 213
South Sea islanders 16
Spanish 3, 12-13, 19, 24
Spears, Arthur 3, 173, 234
stablization 19
standardization 213
stap 134, 140, 200
Steinbauer, Friedric 5, 234
Stewart, William 142, 234
stret 171
Stroud, Christopher 6, 22, 212, 227
Suau 11
substrate 24-27, 54, 104, 115-116, 118, 142, 147, 199-201, 213
substitution 181-182
sugar 14
Sulawesi 16
Sumbuk, Kenneth 6, 22, 234
Summer Institute of Linguistics 5, 8
Sundanese 162
superstrate 24, 26, 199
Swan, J 6, 21, 214, 234
synonyms 184-185
syntax 115-172

T

taim 25, 200
Taiwan 8
Taraka 120
tasol 171, 187
Taylor, Andrew vii, 11, 234
Taylor, Douglas 24, 234
Taylor, L 23, 227
Thomas, Dicks 5-6, 162, 215, 226, 234
Thomason, Sarah 3-4, 11, 26, 44, 75, 199, 202, 235
Thursday Island 16
tich(a)(s) 47
tis(a)(s) 47
TMA (tense, modality, and aspect marking) 124-142
To'aba'ita 136
Todd, Loreto 3, 6, 21, 27, 209-210, 230, 235
Tok Masta 21

Tolai 4, 18-19, 25, 63, 70, 95-97, 100, 106, 163, 167
topicalization 161-172
Torres Strait Broken 6, 15-16, 162
Torres Strait Creole, see Torres Strait Broken
Torres Strait Island(er)s 8, 14
Torricelli 9
trade languages 10-11, 14
transfer 200
Trans-New Guinea 9
trepang 14
Troy, Jakelin 4, 13-14, 16, 235
Tryon, Darryl 6, 15, 223, 226, 235
tru 171
tubuan 222
Tuno, Jill vii
Turner, Lorenzo 24, 235

U

UG = universal grammar
uniformity 211-213
Unitech = Papua New Guinea University of Technology
universal grammar 26
universals 7, 25-26, 70, 115, 199, 201
University of Papua New Guinea 43
University of Technology (Unitech) 109
Usan 200
Usurufa 25, 43
Utu 33

V

Valdman, Albert 3, 235
van Dieman 14
Vanimo 1, 30-31, 46
Vanuatu 7-9, 12, 14-16, 27, 142, 210
variation 20, 24, 29, 211-213
Verhaar, John 5-6, 23, 145, 158, 186, 214, 235
Vunakanau 33

W

Wabag 30, 32
Waia Ahnon 33
Walsh, D S 4, 235
Wampit 32
wankain 182
wanpela 147-148, 191
wantaim 186
Wantok Niuspepa 4, 6, 21, 36, 43, 155, 173-174, 184, 189, 212, 214
Watabung 218
watpo 164
Waritsian 44
wasmara 164
we 150-151, 153-154, 161, 164
West Africa(n) 3, 27, 142, 209
West African Pidgin English 3
westap 164
Western Highlands 10, 28, 32, 34, 40, 44, 46, 50, 54, 56-57, 60-61, 63, 70, 75, 81, 84-85, 89, 92, 94-95, 100, 102, 105, 107, 117, 119, 122-123, 130, 138, 142-144, 150, 153, 156-157, 160, 167, 175-176, 180, 182-183, 187, 189, 192, 194, 208, 237
Western Province ix, 10, 28, 238
West New Britain ii, 10, 25, 28-29, 33-34, 40, 57, 61, 119, 123, 139, 142, 144, 146, 159-160, 167, 186, 191-192, 212-213, 244
West Sepik 1, 10, 28, 31, 34, 40, 44, 46-47, 50-52, 55-57, 61-62, 64-65, 67-71, 75-77, 79-80, 82-86, 90-92, 96, 98, 100, 104, 106-108, 119, 123, 127-128, 131-133, 135-138, 140-141, 143-146, 149, 152, 154, 158, 160, 165, 167-171, 182, 184-185, 186-187, 190-191, 193-194, 196-197, 203, 205-06, 208, 213, 217
Wewak 30-31
WH = Western Highlands
whaling 14
Whinnom, Keith 13, 235
wh-questions 163-166
Williams, B 23, 227
Williams, Jeffrey 11, 235
Winford, Donald 4, 125, 136, 142, 162, 209, 224, 234-235
Wingti, Paias 179
wok 184
wok long 86-87, 133-134, 140
Wolfers, Edward 5, 235
Woolford, Ellen 5, 116-117, 120, 158, 163, 235
word frequency 100-103
word order 115, 163
Wright, Fiona 35, 54, 231
Wurm, Stephen 5, 9, 11, 20, 37, 53-54, 56, 116, 150, 173, 212, 235-236

Y

Yabêm 11
Yarupawa, Shem vii, 6, 22, 202, 210, 212-213, 236
yes 190
yet 104, 167-171
Yimas 11
Yip, Virginia 59, 228
Yule, George 173, 224
Yuwi, Matiabe 189

Faces of singsing dancers from Central Province performing at Port Moresby

Tree dancers from West New Britain performing at Lae